On Directing

Harold Clurman

On Directing

COLLIER BOOKS

A Division of Macmillan Publishing Co., Inc.

NEW YORK

COLLIER MACMILLAN PUBLISHERS

LONDON

Macmillan Publishing Co., Inc.
866 Third Avenue, New York, N.Y. 10022
Collier-Macmillan Canada Ltd.

Library of Congress Catalog Card Number: 72-77648

First Collier Books Edition 1974

On Directing is also published in a hardcover
edition by Macmillan Publishing Co., Inc.

Printed in the United States of America

To Robert Whitehead

"In the theatre, the work of the author does not exist any longer."

—Luigi Pirandello

"The theatre is a body politic and the art of it a single art, though the contributors to each display of it must be many."

—Harley Granville-Barker

"Artists build theories on what they would like to do, but do what they can."

—André Malraux

Contents

PART III

PART IV

Introduction

THERE ARE several reasons for the presumptuous title of this book. I do not call it "The Art of Directing" because, to begin with, such a title might be taken to mean that there is only one art of directing, one method, one correct way.

The slightest experience in the theatre teaches us that this is not so. Many English and several American directors, for example, require actors to commit their lines to memory before rehearsals have begun. To other directors such a practice is sinful! Many directors see little value in having the cast sit together for more than one or two sessions reading the play. They wish to have the cast on its feet—in movement—from the very first day of rehearsal. So distinguished a director as the late Jean Vilar, for many years the head of the state-subsidized Théâtre National Populaire of France, writes that the cast should spend one-third of the rehearsal time "script in hand with buttocks on the chair." This particular injunction may be ascribed to the fact that, in general, the French theatrical tradition places so much emphasis on the written and spoken word.

Every director makes his own "law," depending not only on his own temperament or artistic inclination, but on the circumstances of production. Since this is so, I cannot in good conscience write a "how to" book. This book is not intended to teach anyone how to direct a play. Though there are several manuals of stage direction that are said to have proved useful to students, I doubt that any director of distinction has learned his job through such reading. And very few people have learned to direct by constantly reading and seeing plays. (Peter Brook asserts that this was his chief source of instruction.)

Most directors acquire their technique by having first worked in the theatre as actor, stage manager, scene designer, producer or playwright. The great Russian director Vakhtangov, according to his pupil Nikolai Gorchakov, "believed that directors should be trained at a theatre, learning as they went along. He affirmed that a director-to-be should accumulate experience at every rehearsal and work out his own laws of directing."

What I propose is to set down my thoughts on the theatre in general as they have formed themselves through my own work as a director. This, then, is the statement of a person who has occupied a central position in the *making* of theatre. It is addressed not simply to the prospective director, the student or the already practicing theatre worker with that profession in mind, but perhaps even more to enthusiastic playgoers, to the important audience whose interest in the theatre is something more than casual.

I shall be dogmatic only to the extent of my own convictions; and not even all of these, I trust, are altogether and permanently established with me. James Gelb, a stage manager who has often worked with me, tells a story about how he came to choose the theatre as a career. He had wandered into an open discussion of stage problems in which a large number of professionals were engaged. One person after another rose to hold forth and each one prefaced his remarks with the phrase "In my opinion—." "Ah," Gelb thought, "if this business is only a matter of opinion, it's just the thing for me!"

Still, I do not wish my readers to suppose that the open-mindedness or subjectivity of my approach to the matters to be dealt with means that I take them to be mere matters of opinion. There is such a thing as knowledge. Ignorance of craft—not at all uncommon in the profession—is what I hope this book will in some measure serve to reduce. If there are principles, or, at any rate, guidelines, it behooves us for the better conduct, proficiency and enjoyment of the work to seek them out and to enunciate them as clearly as possible. Common sense, which entails a grain of humorous skepticism, should not be excluded from the quest.

The direction this book deals with assumes the existence of a written text, a drama, what most stage folk call a "script." For the past ten years or more, however, productions have come into being in which, to begin with, little or no script existed. Plays are based on a theme or a rough scenario on which the actors, guided by a director, improvise movement, gesture and visual and auditory effects together with occasional spoken lines. The verbal text is shaped in its final form by the director in frequent collaboration with the author of the scenario. Speech, the use of words (*literature*), is employed as a prop to the overall theatrical concept and structure, the enacted play.

This tendency, much in vogue today, is often dubbed "new theatre." Actually, it marks a return to the theatre's origins. Words did not constitute the core of the rituals and tribal celebrations of primitive communities. Even in the classic Japanese theatre the dramatist or "playwright" was considered a minor figure. The acting or performance was the crucial factor.

Theatre precedes drama. This historical fact has immense

aesthetic impòrtance. But in our traditional modern theatre we reverse the process: we convert or "translate" drama into theatre. This creates a confusion from which theatre criticism and theatre practice have both suffered. To quote Ellen Terry, "The Drama is the child of the theatre. It goes to my heart that the child should be brought up to despise its parent." Subsequent chapters (especially the one on "The Audience") may help resolve the apparent conflict.

There are two reasons for bringing this matter up here. Since this book deals largely with my own experience and beliefs, stage direction is discussed in a manner more or less typical of the contemporary theatre. I do not preclude the possibility of a book on a technique of direction for the "new theatre"—some have already been attempted—but that is not the objective of this one.

I do not, however, mean that what I have to say here applies to only one type of production. New principles of direction are rare; they are usually only variations on the old. Though Peter Brook, for example, has learned much from the exponents of the "new theatre," his productions of *King Lear* and *A Midsummer Night's Dream* follow the "rules of the game" observed by directors for at least the past hundred years. What is new in the Brook productions (Grotowski's may be another matter) is the idiom of action, the unusually free approach to texts which were formerly interpreted in an entirely different vein. The difference is mainly one of feeling, content, style. But these are different with every director of stature: each has his own artistic bent.

Part I

Part I

CHAPTER 1

"The Director's Theatre"

IT HAS BEEN a commonplace (I first heard the formulation some years ago from Peter Ustinov) that while the French is a playwright's theatre, the English an actor's theatre, the American is a director's theatre.

This contains as much truth as most such dicta do. Considered aesthetically, it is a total falsehood. The theatre cannot live through any single organ of its being. The theatre as an art is indivisible. The finest text is often seriously damaged or destroyed by an inadequate cast or improper direction, occasionally by inept physical (scenic) treatment or even by the wrong playhouse.

Excellent acting has been known to compensate, that is, to lend value and meaning to wretched literary material. But the ablest direction will sometimes fail with the best of actors when the dramatist's contribution is basically empty or dull.

On the other hand, we have all seen brilliant performances —viewed as independent factors—rob meritorious dramas of their significance *as theatre.*

Anouilh's *The Waltz of the Toreadors*—one of his most scintillating plays—failed in Paris because, as Anouilh once admitted, he chose to direct it himself. With better casts and two different directors the play was successful in both London and New York.

Before proceeding any further a decisive distinction, crucial to my "argument," must be made. There is a certain ambiguity in theatrical terminology which ultimately leads to critical confusion. We speak of "the play," by which we mean the written text (or script). The play signifies *drama,* a form of literature. On stage it becomes a production. The play does not exist in the theatre as a written text; it has been absorbed in the process of production. Drama is "translated" or transformed into the person of the actor—"the body of the art of the theatre," as Stark Young put it. But the actor does not exist in isolation on the stage. His physical being—appearance, voice, movement, manner of address—is seen in a specific environment. Architectural and scenic elements mediate through color, illumination, costume, music, etc. All these materially alter or enhance the quality of the original script. This new phenomenon born from the fact of production is the Play.

That is what Pirandello meant when he said, "In the theatre the work of the author does not exist any longer," and what Stark Young with less precision suggested when he wrote, "Drama is not literature but literature in terms of the theatre." Granville-Barker put it another way. "The playwright," he said, "is essentially a collaborator, even though he be the creative beginning of the collaboration."

All these apothegms need further explanation and qualification, to which we shall repeatedly return. To begin with, I shall simply assert that the theatre is not an art of separate elements arithmetically cumulative but an art which might be seen to form a single organism. One or several members of this organism may make the whole function, that is, come to life. To make an analogy from another art we might say that while a painting may be discussed in terms of color, drawing and composition, it is a *picture* that we look at. The "heart" of the theatre is not situated in one of its organs, though certain of these may nourish and quicken the others.

The director is important certainly, but he is not all-important. Though without the actor the theatre is almost inconceivable, not even he contains the art. This may be said also of the playwright himself. No part is the whole!

Certain actors have infused life into texts held to be faulty or threadbare. Shaw, in an essay which is one of the masterpieces of theatre criticism, speaks of Duse's artistic superiority to Sudermann, the author of "Magda" (*Heimat*). *La Dame aux Camélias* may be said to have endured by virtue of extraordinary embodiments of the title role. But perhaps there is more to *La Dame* than we commonly suppose. The great Russian director Meyerhold thought so.

It is also true that gifted directors with the collaboration of responsive casts have occasionally made lively theatre out of feeble scripts. Some texts, on the other hand, are themselves so vital that they have sustained our interest in rather indifferent performances. We can all remember the painful occasions when Shakespeare on the stage has not only been rendered dull but nearly unintelligible through productions in which the flaw was not merely a matter of muffled, incorrect or inaudible speech.

The question of the director's importance is not as simple as it might appear because, to begin with, due to the theatre's nature, it is not the director alone who gives the play its direction. This is something which the neophyte director, for his own efficiency and well-being, should constantly bear in mind. The director has an independent function but, like everyone in the theatre, he must depend on his collaborators.

The direction of a play is to a certain extent implicit in its script. The playwright as playwright is in part a director. If he is truly a man of the theatre (some playwrights only suffer the theatre but do not feel they belong to it) the playwright "sees" the play on the stage as he writes. His dialogue as well as his notations of stage behavior suggest movement and part of the total physical life that the script is to acquire when it is produced.

If this thought should depress a would-be director he may rejoice in the correlated axiom that the director, as we shall discover, contributes in more ways than one to the making of the play.

In passing we may recall Gordon Craig's injunction to the dramatist that he refrain from setting down any remarks at all about the direction or performance of his text. But Craig always went too far, in the manner of the poet he was, to emphasize a new and extremely valuable way of thinking about the theatre.

Actors also contribute to and partially shape direction. I am not referring to the actor's possible insistence on having his own way in interpreting a role—and hence the play. This is a hazard that we shall discuss in a later chapter. The actor willy-nilly contributes to the direction of a play through his natural temperament, intuition, imagination and skill. Indeed, the good director will stimulate the actor to make such a contribution. Too great a dependence on the director is unhealthy for both actor and play.

I saw an interesting production of Tennessee Williams' *The Glass Menagerie* in Paris in which the very meaning of the play was considerably altered because the actress playing Amanda had very little of the substance of Laurette Taylor's genius. This may have been due to miscasting (a directorial blemish) or possibly to a misinterpretation or even to the director's having a different interpretation from the one I supposed was justified.

This is a subtle matter, involving both critical judgment and, if you will, theatre aesthetics. It must be broached at another point. Let us remind ourselves at this juncture that one of the agonies and wonders of the theatre is that the play is always a *new* thing with each production, indeed with almost every performance. This thought so distressed Craig that he went so far as to maintain with his usual bent toward paradox that acting was no art at all. Still, at another time he devoted a whole volume to extolling the art of Henry Irving!

Significant bits of byplay ("business" in stage parlance) are often introduced by actors through spontaneous invention. Only an obtuse director refuses to take advantage of such enrichment of the play's fabric. Still, he has the right and duty to veto what he considers inappropriate or misleading. The director may therefore be forgiven when he takes credit for some of the actors' improvisations and accepts compliments for them!

The play's scenic arrangement (the floor plan, architectural form, visual style, etc.), for which the director is responsible even when he has had little to do with their actual design, is another contribution to the shaping of a play's meaning. Boris Aronson's sets added special lustre to such musicals as *Cabaret, Company* and *Follies,* but by his own admission his setting of Odets' *Paradise Lost* (which I directed) detracted from what he had felt about the play when he saw it acted on the bare stage. But in such cases, as we have already implied, the director rather than the designer must be held to account.

Even the audience may affect the direction of a play. An extreme instance of this was *Arsenic and Old Lace,* which legend has it was directed as a thriller but which, because of the opening-night audience's reaction, was transformed into an uproariously approved farce. It was played as such from that moment to the end of its long run.

In what sense then can the term "the director's theatre" be justified? The director, as we think of him today, is a recent phenomenon in theatre history. In my early days as a playgoer —in the "teens"—hardly any director except David Belasco enjoyed program credit. This does not mean that the play had not been directed in one fashion or another.

The director has to some degree always been present. The

playwright sometimes served in that capacity. Aeschylus is said to have directed his plays, as we know Molière did his. The *Choregus* (leader of the Chorus) in the Greek theatre was in effect a director. In other instances, the director was the producer, the leading actor or the actor manager. Even if it is conceivable for a theatrical performance to be produced without anyone officially in charge, it is clear that someone, through force of nerve, prestige, talent or power, will give the performance some sort of coherence.

The director as we know him today is a product of the nineteenth-century theatre. For convenience' sake (I will not dispute the accuracy of this statement with scholar or historian), let us say that modern direction began in 1866 with the Duke of Saxe-Meiningen, who was chiefly a painter and a stage designer. The actual staging of his productions was done by Ludwig Kronek but the Duke himself was the founder and moving force of the Meiningen Players. It is also worth noting that Otto Brahm, the creator in 1889 of the famous German Free Theatre who introduced Gerhardt Hauptmann and other of the new realists to the playgoing public, was first a critic and never actually staged his productions. But like the Duke of Meiningen, Brahm set the tone and the style, and placed the stamp of his personality on his company.

What Meiningen did was to establish the idea of *ensemble* playing, the coordination of the various components of an acting company so that a unified impression might be created —the total performance summing up to a Play. This coordination included not only the main actors, but bit players and the so-called extras or supernumeraries as well. Meiningen, moreover, was much concerned with historical authenticity in costuming, furnishings and all those objects used on the stage which come under the heading of "props" (or "properties"). Beyond their historicity he wished them to be tasteful and set in a theatrically helpful arrangement.

The Meiningen Players influenced not only Stanislavsky, the famous Russian director (in discussing them the famous Russian director emphasizes Kronek rather than the Duke), but also André Antoine, who *circa* 1887 introduced naturalism to French theatregoers. Henry Irving, too, fell under the Meiningen spell.

What crystallized the concept of stage direction as we understand it today may be gathered from the writings, beginning in 1905, of Gordon Craig. The mainspring of the Craig doctrine is his insistence on unity. A Play, Craig insisted, is not a text on which actors, setting, music, etc., are superimposed, but a single body of which all the separate elements are parts. This precept, from which I derive my own "credo," has manifold consequences.

In the early nineteenth century in England—to go no further back and to confine ourselves to theatre of our own language—the texts of plays were hardly respected and perhaps as a result were barely respectable. What was then called Shakespeare on the stage was nothing Shakespeare would have acknowledged or even recognized. Shakespeare and most other dramatists were treated as mere scenarists. Their characters and plots were employed as vehicles for the exhibition of actors' talents.

Costumes and props were not only a matter of the actor's (or theatre lessee's) choice, but were generally what the theatre had in stock and were rarely relevant to a particular period or a definite style. "Scenery" was conventionalized without regard to period, place, mood or specific use. The companies were composed of stars—some of them magnificent actors—supported by routine players who often were accorded no more than two or three rehearsals with the guest star. The star dictated stage positions (he himself usually occupied stage center), movement and business, to which the other actors had to accommodate themselves. That was the "staging." People came to see the great man do his stuff.

There could be very little differentiation in lighting except between the bright and the dark. Means of illumination were primitive and not readily controllable. Interpretation was implicit chiefly in the star's performance.

With the renewal of interest in the literary or artistic aspects of a play and the increased technical methods for the projection of a play's significance on the stage a leader became a necessity. If all the elements of production were to be made into one theatre work—a true Play—then there had to be some-one to conduct them to that end. Hence the emergence of the contemporary stage director.

In America today the author is contractually the pivot of the organized production. His consent must be obtained as to choice of cast, director and general interpretation. But, to quote Boris Aronson, "The theatre is a collective art in which the strongest man rules."

The playwright very rarely exercises his legal right either because he is timid or more frequently because he is intelligent enough to realize his incapacity. Beyond his own writing he is seldom a practiced theatre craftsman. He is usually un-certain as to the means which most suitably serve to embody his text. There are playwrights who are effective directors of their own and sometimes other people's scripts, but the talent for writing and the talent for directing are infrequently to be found in the same person. So at this point we need not dwell on the playwright, who only partially understands the sig-nificance of what he has written or appreciates the theatrical potentialities of his script.

The actor is (hopefully) a creator. Samuel Johnson said that the actor only *recites:* but no living playwright is happy if his actors do no more than that. As a creator the actor has an artis-tic weight of his own—not to speak of the other kinds of influ-ence he may unadvisedly exert. How the actor is to be dealt with so that he not only will be "effective" for himself and his admirers but also for the entire "team" responsible for the play is one of the chief problems of direction.

We are now better prepared to understand why the term "the director's theatre" has come into use. That fine American actor Louis Calhern once declared, "The reason why the di-rector has become so powerful is that there are no more great actors." If we pursue this line of argument we might conclude that the reason why the director up until very recently has been less important in England than in America is that there are still so many splendid actors or, at any rate, stars there. It is a fact that on the whole English actors of note prefer directors who "interfere" as little as possible, though there has been a change in this regard in the past twenty-five years.

Such actors wish the director to be utterly precise in "blocking" (or staging) a play—that is, in assigning the placement of actors on the boards and indicating crosses from one position to another—but they are wary about being *directed*—that is, helped in the creation of their parts. The assumption is that there must be a conflict between director and actor or that where the actor is a truly creative person (and what star thinks of himself as anything less?) he needs little or no "outside" assistance.

The assumption is mistaken. It is based on the practice of the two artistically least organized theatres of the Western world: the English and the American. Even the value of ensemble playing was regarded with skepticism by the playwright-critic St. John Ervine on the grounds that actors of eminent stature through personal artistic bias must of necessity rebel against the "totalitarianism" of the ensemble idea. Even the Meiningen Players, where the director, Kronek, according to Stanislavsky, was very much the dictator, numbered among their members such a fine artist as Albert Basserman who throughout his career worked with directors of first-rate calibre: Otto Brahm and Max Reinhardt.

Reinhardt's various companies were always composed of magnificent actors. The original Moscow Art Theatre, the prime example in the early twentieth century of the ensemble ideal, boasted a company in which at least six members possessed star radiance. Though contrary evidence may be adduced from the examples of such productions as Peter Brook's *Marat/Sade* or Tyrone Guthrie's *The House of Atreus* (cast with good companies without "star names"), I should like to make it axiomatic that the finer an acting company is, the greater the need for a masterly director. This may ensure that what is presented are plays rather than exhibitions.

Meyerhold's theatre in the Soviet Union (till his career was stamped out by state interdiction and the ukase on "socialist realism") and Brecht's Berliner Ensemble—perhaps, too, Joan Littlewood's first company at Stratford East in London— might be dubbed "director's theatres." These theatres, and others like them (Grotowski's Laboratory Theatre, for example), are theatres in which the director is a true leader, that is, an educator, a person with a special aesthetic and technique who trains his company accordingly. Still, even Meyerhold leaned heavily on two or three brilliant actors, just as Brecht's Berliner Ensemble profited greatly by the presence of Weigel, Schall and Ernst Busch.

Toward the end of his career Max Reinhardt was inclined to believe that our industrial age of mass production was not conducive to the formation of outstanding actors. (He might perhaps have cited our American theatre as an example.)

There is something in this. The disarray of the American theatre economy at present makes the development of major actors extremely difficult. There is not sufficiently sustained employment. Of gifted young people there are enough to establish as many permanent troupes as there are anywhere else. But even the so-called successful actor in America is usually confined to a limited range of parts. He seeks a fat role in a hit show, lest he diminish his market value. He fears for his status as a desirable performer. A good many very able actors in America today are more often active in scene classes (or "studios") than on the stage. They supplement these "workouts" with appearances in summer stock and guest performances in regional theatres, films and on television. The young actor perforce remains an amateur.

One of the worst effects of this situation is the actor's loss of confidence in his profession and in himself. Psychologically the American actor under fifty is nearly always a "beginner." By the time he is fifty he is either out of the theatre or a warped person.

Who can encourage, inspire, renew the faith of the actor in

this condition? Why, the new medicine man, the well-known, the much-touted director! A superstition surrounds this character. (Superstition, even if only in the form of publicity, is always a sign of a sick state of affairs. Where nothing is secure, magic must work its wonders.) The director, the actor trusts and prays, will sustain him, make him a star. The director as fetish is a symptom; "the director's theatre" is very often little better than a commercial tag.

Capable direction is no doubt a vital factor in the making of a sound production. There is certainly a distinction to be made between the abilities of one director and those of another. But if we list the plays which have been highly successful on Broadway we may well arrive at the conclusion that any number of efficient directors might have returned box-office hits from their scripts. The quality of each production would have been different with each director, but it is rarely the quality of direction which is perceived by the audience, whose spokesman is the run-of-the-mill critic, but rather the degree of monetary success the production may achieve. No matter: When a director has turned out two or three hits, supernatural powers are attributed to him; he is regarded as a "genius," the cause of everyone's prosperity and joy.

Signs of this peculiar syndrome may be observed at early rehearsals of a new Broadway show. Except where a star actor is involved (in which case he has been consulted as to the desirability of a particular director or is aware of the director's prestige) many actors—especially the younger ones—sit in a state of quasi-cataleptic expectancy. They are waiting to be electrified, exalted, transfigured. They seem to have converted themselves into so many vessels into which they hope the director will pour the elixir of his greatness.

At one time I might have agreed with Granville-Barker who said, "The art of the theatre is the art of acting or it is nothing." But this is only a partial truth, though it is always worth keeping in mind. Later I arrived at what I believed was a happy formulation: "The director is the author of the stage play," a generalization of which I am now somewhat skeptical. It is deceptive; a good measure of conceit is concealed in it. It may lead to disappointment and trouble for all concerned. The art of the theatre is contained in the entity of production in which the director may play a crucial role.

Direction is a job, a craft, a profession, and at best, an art. The director must be an organizer, a teacher, a politician, a psychic detective, a lay analyst, a technician, a creative being. Ideally, he should know literature (drama), acting, the psychology of the actor, the visual arts, music, history, and above all, he must understand people. He must inspire confidence. All of which means he must be a "great lover."

CHAPTER 2

Choosing the Script

IF WE THINK of a director in terms of Broadway only, there is little to say about the choice of a script. The director chooses what he can find. In "dry" seasons when, as is quite common at present, there is a dearth of new script material, a director may feel as Joshua Logan did when he said, "If I discover a script I can finish reading, I'll do it."

Joshua Logan is an eminently successful director. Why should he have any difficulty choosing a script? The answer is that with the latter-day shrinkage of production (a condition which dates back to the depression of the thirties) and the consequent lack of theatrically competent writing the competition for scripts has become hectic.

There are perhaps no more than a half-dozen "hot" directors on Broadway; every producer and playwright has his own favorite. If Tennessee Williams, Arthur Miller, Edward Al-

bee or Neil Simon (or their agents) prefer one particular director, the others will not even be offered the opportunity to
read the new play. The pattern remains the same with inexperienced producers and playwrights: they habitually turn to
the "surefire," the "hit directors."

Every season brings forth one or two "geniuses" among
directors. This means that when a young director not yet
tagged as one of the "top" men is fortunate enough to have
staged a "smash," he will immediately be showered with offers. One might say that this should be regarded as altogether
normal. True—if producers and playwrights judged the newly
acclaimed director solely on his merits as a director. But very
few producers or playwrights are capable of judging a director's intrinsic abilities. The box office is their barometer. That
is why so often after his initial success the director's subsequent failure usually meets with sharp disfavor as ignorant as
the praise previously accorded him. This is the law of the
jungle—I mean the Broadway theatre.

The European director is not in the same case. (Nor possibly is the director of a regional theatre in the United States.)
When an English director finds himself without a new script
he will choose to direct a play by Shakespeare or Ibsen or
Shaw or Congreve. Tyrone Guthrie directed very few new
plays—and most of them were in America. A German director is not only in a position to choose among the classics or
among plays of the contemporary continental and American
output, but very often he will seek to do a play produced in
one of the theatres in Berlin, or Munich, or Vienna, or in another of the fine theatres in such cities as Cologne, Hamburg,
Frankfurt, *et al.* His production will be entirely his own, not
a replica of the original one. This is true in the Soviet Union
and other of the East European countries as well. When I
visited Moscow in 1934 I saw two utterly dissimilar productions of Gorky's *Yegor Bulitchev* during the same week—one
at the Moscow Art and the other at the Vakhtangov Theatre.

The American director is limited in his choice of scripts

not only by the economic straits in which the Broadway theatre is bound, but also by our lack of repertory companies
(which rarely undertake to produce new scripts) and by the
commercial inadvisability of reviving old plays. Off-Broadway has profited by this situation: such plays as Williams'
Summer and Smoke and O'Neill's *The Iceman Cometh* and
Long Day's Journey into Night have had their life renewed
and been "redeemed" off-Broadway.*

Because of the high cost of production (Odets' *Awake and
Sing* in 1935 cost $6,000; it would cost $100,000 today) and
the restricted audiences who can afford the resultant high
price of tickets, Broadway managers must think of the script's
chances of success. This has always been a dominant factor in
the selection of scripts—even though no one has ever been
able to determine exactly what will be "commercial"! One of
my own box-office hits was Carson McCullers' *The Member
of the Wedding*, so commercially dubious that only one theatre owner would consent to house it.

Directors have artistic or temperamental dispositions. To
the degree that they have some freedom of choice they exercise it according to their taste and what they deem to be their
specific talent: what they not only like but feel they can do
best. I myself have hesitated to do certain plays of which I
approved critically but which I judged might be more satisfactorily treated by other directors.

This was perhaps a mistake. The director often extends his
capacities by undertaking assignments which he may at first
consider outside his "line." Typecasting of directors is almost as habitual with producers as it is of actors.

When my direction of *Awake and Sing* met with approval a
great many scripts about depressed middle-class families were
sent to me. When I was complimented for my direction of

* The shortage of new plays has brought about a change: the successful
revivals of *You Can't Take It with You*, *The Show-Off*, *The Front Page*, and
Harvey are beginning to turn producers' thoughts to the prospect of prosperity in such ventures.

Odets' *Golden Boy* I found myself inundated with scripts about toughs of the race track, jazz bands and kindred rackets. (I had never seen a prizefight before the production of *Golden Boy*.) When I did *The Member of the Wedding* I was hailed as a specialist in plays about children! But it is not only the producer or the playwright who may hold a narrow view of a director's gifts but the director himself.

Ask a director what sort of script he would like to stage and he will probably answer, "A good one"—which is no answer at all. When the question was put to me years ago I usually replied, "I prefer a well-written script with a theme of contemporary relevance couched in theatrically poetic terms." To be somewhat more specific about "contemporary relevance" I went on to say that I sought a "realistic" core in every play, a reflection of some immediate issue. I was not referring to *topicality* nor did I care for scripts which might be classified as reportage or stage journalism. By "theatrically poetic" I meant the scripts had to "sing" their themes, to be written in eloquent language, to be possessed of vivid characterization, color, a degree of glamor and intensity.

I was also and still am attracted by scripts which offer "juicy" parts for actors, parts which demand flair and virtuosity. I had decided that I was, among other things, an "actor's director."

Since then I have done plays of a rather different nature than those of the thirties and forties: Giraudoux's *Tiger at the Gates,* Anouilh's *The Waltz of the Toreadors,* O'Neill's *Desire Under the Elms* and *A Touch of the Poet,* Shaw's *Heartbreak House,* Chekhov's *Uncle Vanya,* all of which may be thought of as having broadened the scope and redefined the earlier canon.

None of these examples nor any personal declaration of intention, however, is truly pertinent to the question we have to deal with here. It would still not be to the point if I extended my list to indicate the scripts I would have liked to have done but was not asked to do. What the question, broadly speaking, comes to is this: Is there any criterion, apart from excellence and personal inclination, that may serve to guide a director in his choice of scripts?

A question the director may put to himself is this: To what audience do I hope the projected play will appeal? I am not alluding to "audience appeal" in general, for this is a term which, when employed without regard to specific circumstances, begs the question. Strindberg's *The Ghost Sonata* and *Dream Play** are almost everywhere deemed important as dramatic literature. They have audience appeal in Sweden and in most mid-European theatres. Short of amazing productions I would judge that they would have very little appeal on Broadway. But an excellent production off-Broadway, or in a "club" theatre or at a university theatre of "advanced" tastes might lend these scripts audience appeal.

It was perhaps ill-advised to do Sartre's *No Exit* or Beckett's *Waiting for Godot* on Broadway. But I do not mean that such plays should never be done there: there must always be producers and directors who will engage in enterprises of artistic merit deemed commercially foolhardy. (Producer Robert Whitehead persuaded me to risk *The Member of the Wedding* on Broadway.)

Before 1930 the leading producers presented four plays a season, of which at least two, they surmised, would fail (at no great financial loss), but at present even such a "popular" piece as the Brecht-Weill *Threepenny Opera* would not, I believe, prosper on Broadway any more than it did when it was first presented there in 1933.

If what I am suggesting here seems crassly commercial it is worth noting that Goethe, as theatre director at Weimar, said that he would not produce a play no matter how much he admired it if he were certain that it had no chance of pleasing his audience. Of course he, too, may have been wrong since there can be no certainty in these matters.

* *Dream Play* was a success at the Comédie Française in 1970, but the Comédie Française is a nationally subsidized repertory theatre.

Audiences differ in different places and under different conditions. It is not being "artistic" to be unconcerned about audience reactions. To discount the nature of one's audience is to be anti-theatre. The audience is the theatre's prime factor and chief "actor." In the deepest sense it is the audience —the community or a particular segment of it—which produces the play.

In former times—in ancient Greece, in the Middle Ages, in seventeenth-century France, in other words, in more or less homogeneous societies—the audience's composition was known; it could be taken for granted. The "artists" were very much part of their audience; artists and audience were, to a large degree, one. In heterogeneous societies such as ours, audiences are bewilderingly varied. It is natural to expect a receptive audience for Jack Gelber's *The Connection* or Barbara Garson's *MacBird!* in small Greenwich Village playhouses but it would surely be quixotic to suppose that the same is true at theatres on West Forty-fifth Street.

Ambitious directors from New York appointed to regional theatres often insist on selecting plays they like simply because they believe them to be good ones. This is praiseworthy; it may also prove disastrous. One must know what one's audience is prepared for, what its disposition is. But on the other hand, recent experiences in Washington, San Francisco and Minneapolis indicate that theatres (often subsidized) in such centers attract audiences far more catholic in their tastes than those who attend the Broadway theatre.

It is certainly possible to educate an audience, but can one imagine something like *Who's Afraid of Virginia Woolf?* being produced on Broadway in 1917? The Theatre Guild itself was amazed—as were all the professional wiseacres—when Molnar's *Liliom* and Andreyev's *He Who Gets Slapped* became hits in the early twenties. But the directors of the Theatre Guild were hardly aware of the change which had come about in the New York audience between 1915 and 1920 even though they were themselves representative of that new audience. Even as late as 1928 they thought they were flying in the face of destiny (that is, the theatregoing public) when they produced O'Neill's *Strange Interlude*—one of their greatest box-office successes.

There is an element of hazard (beyond the monetary) in all theatrical production and it is part of the theatre's challenge that it should exist. It is a serious fault to be overfearful of failure. Many an artist has been crippled by it. Still, a director who neglects to consider certain aspects of a script's prospective life in the theatre doesn't know his business. Historical timing itself may be something to consider. The English were said to resent John van Druten's agreeably innocuous comedy *The Voice of the Turtle*—intrinsically unrelated to any war situation—when it was produced in London shortly after the end of hostilities in 1945. The dalliance of an American army man in New York at the time of the blitz in London did not amuse the West End.

Just as a true Theatre, that is, a permanent producing unit, because it looks toward its ideal public, in time develops its loyally attentive audience, so also it fosters its own playwrights. Clifford Odets emerged from the 1931–41 Group Theatre's acting company to be hailed as the dramatic spokesman of the decade. Hauptmann attached himself at first to Otto Brahm's German Free Theatre. Chekhov was encouraged to write all his plays after *Ivanov* and *The Seagull* flopped for the Moscow Art Theatre. Shakespeare wrote for the company of which he was a member, designing parts for particular actors on its roster.

Some directors—rarely in recent times, though as we know from the example of the *commedia dell'arte* not uncommon in the past—begin with a theme, a skeletal plot or a scenic notion and through improvisation develop scripts with the cooperation of a writer. The results are sometimes strikingly pertinent and lively. Recent examples in the American theatre are the productions of Joseph Chaikin and Jean-Claude van Itallie's *America, Hurrah!* and *The Serpent* for the Open Theatre. Their relevance to the theatre in general has already been mentioned in my introduction.

Years ago when I spoke to the governing board of the Theatre Guild about the possibility of developing dramatists for the company which was to become the Group Theatre, I suggested that we make young writers part of the organization —even assign them jobs. The response was something like outrage. "You mean you want dramatists to write with your actors in mind?!" I pointed out that Edmond Rostand had written *Cyrano de Bergerac* for Coquelin with a by no means deplorable outcome. I might have even more pedantically mentioned that Shakespeare and Molière had written certain roles with particular actors of their permanent companies in mind.

This leads to another phase of our topic. I have sometimes undertaken to stage a script about which, solely as a piece of writing, I was rather indifferent when I learned that I could cast a particular actor who I felt would give it special interest, a new dimension. On the other hand, I have admired certain scripts which I hesitated or refused to direct because at the moment I found no actor (or company) available that I believed capable of doing these scripts justice. For, I cannot too often repeat, a script cannot do all the "work" as a play; it does not play itself.

This is not merely a personal view. When some years ago I asked Helene Weigel, then the managing director and leading actress of the Berliner Ensemble, why it had not produced Brecht's *Schweik in the Second World War* which had been done in Paris and many other cities both in Germany and elsewhere, her reply was, "We haven't the right actor for it."

Perhaps a director of a community or university theatre need not be so scrupulous or severe. Still, one has to bear in mind what a particular audience will accept in the way of acting. I have also seen quite respectable companies in community playhouses strain their actors' capacities with results which were entirely unacceptable and unequivocally detrimental to the comprehension of the dramatist's intention.

CHAPTER 3

Reading the Script

THE DIRECTOR has chosen a script with enthusiasm or a considerable degree of trembling. (His trembling diminishes sensibly if the script is one which is well tried and generally admired.) His work is about to begin. It begins by reading the script—in a new way. For now he is no longer thinking of the script's "possibilities": it has become a task, a reality with which he has to contend.

Bernard Shaw in a little essay, "Rules for Directors," has some excellent things to say. The very first is: "The director, having considered the play and decided to undertake the job of directing it, has no further concern with its literary merits or its doctrine (if any)." An extraordinary statement! The script's literary merits will have played some part in the director's choice. He may have been attracted by its writing. But good writing (fine dialogue) in itself is only one facet of a

script's interest. There is also its theme, which must involve
the audience and serve as a tie that binds the stage artisans
(the director, the actors, the designer *et al.*) together.

The director reads the script. He reads it again and again
and again. He need not read it in consecutive daily sessions.
In fact, he would do well, if time permits, to set it aside for
a while after each reading and check on what he remembers
of it. He might even try to forget it. He should let it work on
him before he works on it. First impressions—and he must regard the first two or three preliminary readings as first impressions—are often deceiving, that is, conventional. To begin
with, even experienced directors may see little more in a
script than an intelligent theatregoer would. Like him, the
director will be amused, laugh or cry, shudder or thrill.
These reactions are not without value; they may even prove
important. (Stanislavsky thought them *very* important.) But
they do not suffice as guides to the directorial problem,
which, I repeat, is to translate the script's words into the
language of the stage where men and women of flesh and
blood who move in three dimensions among real objects are
to replace description. The theatre is a new medium. If the
director is not careful he may find to his dismay that the lines
which seemed to soar on the page sound flat and dull when
actors begin to speak them and the audience is called on to
hear and "see" them.

The director will undoubtedly be stimulated by new insights as his acquaintance with the script grows more intimate. He will take note of them in his mind or, better still,
on paper. Among my early notes for a (unsuccessful) play by
Clifford Odets, *Night Music,* I find such things as "there is a
constant sense of *impermanence* and insecurity in the people
and in the town. . . . When Steve [the central character] cries
out for a 'better world' he means a 'secure' world." Another
note further on, without apparent connection with the first:
"Steve's toughness is a kind of lovemaking. If he were soft, he
feels he might be scoffed. Harsh, he always gets a response!"

Or again: "Everyone carries a little suitcase. The characters seem to have no other possessions except those they carry in their little suitcases." I find isolated quotations from the play's dialogue: clues to character or to mood such as "Steve speaks of 'punching around in the dark.'" Still another note reads "All the characters are romantic dreamers."

Such disparate impressions, the images which form themselves higgledy-piggledy in the director's mind, should not be rejected because they appear disorganized or "impractical." They may at first seem "mystical," too imprecise for definite use. When I read Odets' *Awake and Sing* it made me think (perhaps irrelevantly and certainly inaccurately) of the "chaos" in cubist paintings. (Good cubist paintings are not at all chaotic.) And when I read the same author's *Paradise Lost* (his second play) I imagined seeing lights refracted through a multicolored prism. I was not at all certain what these reactions denoted or how they might serve my purpose. Yet they finally did enter into my calculations and produced definite results.

As the readings progress and a great number of "stray" thoughts accumulate, a general production scheme begins to shape itself in the director's mind. After the director has read the play, let us say, a dozen times, he must put some questions to himself to which he must find specific answers.

Before stating the nature of these questions and the kind of answers they require I should make it clear that my reference to a dozen readings is an arbitrary one. I have already said that these readings may occupy a month or more during which the director may allow time for his mind to turn away from the script. During these hiatuses the script will still be exercising a "secret" effect on him.

Meyerhold once said that with the ordinary script he had to deal with—a new Soviet piece, for example—he found six to eight weeks a sufficient time to prepare and rehearse the production. But, he added, he had been thinking about certain plays such as Gogol's *The Inspector General* for years, during which he set down notes, drew sketches, read commentaries and dreamed about the project. The same, he said, was true of his plan to direct *Othello*. (He never did.) The project, he remarked, occupied his thoughts for even a longer time than the Gogol play—for one does not improvise Shakespeare! Not, at any rate, in "respectful" interpretations.

My notes—production ideas, thoughts on the visual aspects of the play, remarks about the characterization of the various roles—are all put down in writing, helter-skelter to begin with, in ever more formal order as rehearsal time approaches. There is nothing obligatory about the *writing* of notes: it is a matter of personal preference. I am not sure I know what I really think until I am able to articulate my intuitions and reflections in this way.

In questioning other directors I have learned that this practice of writing one's general and then one's specific instructions (*to oneself*) is more common than I had supposed. Reinhardt did it brilliantly; Jean Vilar recommended it. Directors developed in the Group Theatre—Elia Kazan, Robert Lewis—also follow this procedure.

Whether or not directors set their thoughts down on paper, the general process I have described goes on in their minds. It is this mental process I would stress rather than the "literary" activity. On the other hand, in *teaching* direction (wherever such a dubious course is hazarded) I suggest that the teachers insist on having the students state in writing all that they propose for themselves and their collaborators—actors, designers, etc.—in the planning of a production. General notions or a nebulous inspiration may delude the student.

Vilar in his essay on direction says, "The work of production should include a written analysis of the play. The director must not despise this thankless job. The drafting of such an analysis compels the director to a clear and exhaustive knowledge of the play."

Such an analysis is more or less what I have been describ-

DATE May 5 19 77

NAME _____

ADDRESS _____

SOLD BY	C. O. D.	CHARGE	ON ACCT.	ACCT. FWD.
1	On Directing			2 75
2				
3	Respect for Acting			8 95
4				
5				
6				
7				
8				
9				
10				
11				
12				

32

SIGNATURE

11 90

V22-3   GRAND & TOY

ing. I say "more or less" because in itself the word "analysis" is ambiguous. Analysis may mean no more than a statement of the play's theme, its "message," its language or literary quality. Analysis is "less" than what I have been discussing, for what the director should be thinking about are the *means* whereby theme, message, etc., are to be *embodied*.

The process is a progression from the general to the particular. After careful perusal of the script the director becomes clear about its theme. But the theme of a play, roughly stated, is not what the director seeks in reading. Any intelligent reader will know that Chekhov's *The Cherry Orchard* dramatizes the decline of the gentry in czarist Russia and the rise of the industrial middle class, and that *Hamlet* is about the dangers of indecision—or similar platitudes. Such knowledge is of little use to the director.

Certain dramatists deny the presence of any "theme" at all in their plays. "I do not write plays with themes," a well-known playwright said to me once. "I write about people." The gentleman had a point but was assigning too narrow a definition to the word "theme."

The theme of a play may consist of a mood, an attitude, a general sentiment—the abstract essence of a play's inspiration. Thus I have heard *Twelfth Night* spoken of as "a game, a toying with life." In the purely intellectual construction of the term, not every play has a theme, but in the broader sense of an overall "feeling," which is present even in the purest form of dance or non-representational painting, every play does possess a theme.

What the director should establish for himself is the script's content in *dramatic* terms. He may begin by asking himself what the audience is to feel and enjoy in seeing the play. Still, even this is not sufficiently basic groundwork. To begin active direction a formulation in the simplest terms must be found to state what general action motivates the play, of what fundamental drama or conflict the script's plot and people are the instruments. What behavioral strug-

gle or effort is being represented? It is best, though perhaps
not altogether essential, that the answer should be expressed
as an *active verb:* for drama (and acting) are based on doing,
on action. (Do not tell the actor "You are in love" but "You
love," that is, "You pay attention to" or "You take care of,"
"You help," etc.)

Richard Boleslavsky, my first formal instructor in theatre
(after Jacques Copeau, who influenced rather than taught
me), called the answer to the questions I have just put the
play's *spine.* It is a term Boleslavsky probably inherited from
his work at the Moscow Art Theatre where he was trained.
(The term must have suggested itself because the body's spine
holds the vertebrae in place, and these might be compared to
all the smaller actions and dramatic divisions in the play.) In
An Actor Prepares Stanislavsky calls the "spine" the play's
main or through action which leads to what he calls the
"super-problem"—the dramatist's basic motivation in writing
the play.

Many things are contained in O'Neill's *Desire Under the
Elms:* passion, Oedipal impulses, confessions of unhappiness
and hate, guilt feelings, paternal harshness, filial vindictiveness, retribution. But what holds all these ingredients together, what makes a complete meaning, a single specific
drama of them all, is the play's spine. As director, I determined that the play's spine, or, if you will, its "main action,"
was a struggle for the Farm, abbreviated into the bare "to
possess the Farm."

With this as both starting point and interpretive goal I
was able to make a dramatic whole from the various strands
in the script. The older brothers, learning that they will
never possess the Farm, give up their share of it, abandon it
to their younger brother and go off to seek material satisfaction in California. The young wife seduces her stepson because she has been promised the Farm if she gives birth to a
boy, and her dreams of bearing a child may be more easily realized through the stepson than through the boy's father,

whom she has married for the sake of goods and security. The young man is attracted to his stepmother, but in taking her yields not only to his desire but to an impulse to avenge himself against his father who dominates him. When the acquisitive drive gives way to desire and becomes transformed into love, the conflict is joined on a higher plane. The play ends with the sheriff coming to arrest the guilty couple for murder of their child; his final words—the last lines of the play—are "It's a jim-dandy farm. . . . Wished I owned it!" In short, even the subsidiary characters of the play must in some way be related to its spine.*

Gordon Craig thought *Hamlet* a quest for Truth which he (Hamlet) discovers by means of the Play wherein he will catch the conscience of the King. The quest for Truth ("to seek the Truth") was the spine, the dramatic seed, main action or super-problem of Craig's *Hamlet*. Hamlet seeks for Truth everywhere—among his friends, his beloved, his mother. Everywhere, with the single exception of Horatio, he finds little but lust, deceit, conventionality, corruption, chicanery, frivolity and foolishness. Everyone is blemished by the kingdom's gilded world, the rotten state of Denmark.

If the reader should find himself protesting that this is too narrow or distorted an interpretation of *Hamlet,* the point to be remembered is not that I consider Craig's interpretation correct but that his direction of the play sprang from the dramatic premise—or spine—I have cited. He drew from it all the consequences of his production: its sets and costumes, his instruction to the actors. To cite only one detail: Everyone was wrapped in gold tissue, except Hamlet, who was clothed in black; Ophelia, too, was contaminated by the court atmosphere.

Hamlet has been interpreted in countless ways. (Often it is not interpreted at all, merely staged.) According to Jan Kott, a Polish production some years ago made *Hamlet* a political

* Further examples of the use of the spine will be found in my **Production Notes**, pp. 179-266.

play in a world of universal suspicion with everyone spying on one another as in Nazi Germany or in Stalin's Russia. What is in question here is not the "true" interpretation but how the interpretation of any script is arrived at and then fulfilled through the stuff of stage life.

The director chooses the spine of the play, the key or springboard of his interpretation, according to his own lights, not to mention the actors he has at his disposal, the audience he wishes to reach and the hoped-for effect on that audience, for he and his audience in a very critical sense are part of the play. It is no accident that the production of *Hamlet* mentioned by Jan Kott was devised in Poland.

But what of the author? Has he no say in the matter? We shall return to this most pertinent query further on. We must continue now with the next step in the director's preparation for the production as he studies the script. Defining the spine, the function of which is intended to *guide himself* in all his other tasks, is the first artistically inescapable step. Where a director has not determined on a spine for his production, it will tend to be formless. Each scene follows the next without necessarily adding up to a total dramatic "statement."

The second step—intimately correlated with the first—is to find the manner in which the spine is to be articulated. It is conceivable that the spine a director has fixed in his mind and *named* might serve any number of different productions with a similar intention. Thus to say that the spine of *Desire Under the Elms* may be summed up as "to possess the Farm" does not necessarily lead to the detailed and practical uses to which it was put. By itself, it presents no "picture." One critic spoke of my production of *Desire* as grandiose, almost operatic. This critic supposed the play's personages to be humbler than the larger-than-life figures I endeavored (and apparently succeeded) to depict. The distinction is not one of "content," in the sense of an intellectual statement or idea, but of *style*—the particular tone, mood, atmosphere, emphasis and "dimension" in which the idea is conveyed.

Style in the abstract may not be difficult to define for literary purposes, although there is something elusive about all aesthetic distinctions. (The reason is that the manner in which something is said is in itself part of its content; indeed one is usually inseparable from the other.) Style is related to the artist's—in this case, the dramatist's—particular way of seeing and feeling things, his spiritual vocabulary, his personal or temperamental stress, his "face" and individuality which make him himself and no one else.

Shaw's *Heartbreak House,* for example, might be described thematically as a picture of the educated middle class in the limbo of their waning power and effectiveness in England. But the same with the exception of locale might be said of *The Cherry Orchard.* My spine for *Heartbreak House,* that which sets all the characters in motion, is the desire, as one character puts it, "to get the hell out of this place"—the place being the condition of a particular social group.

So far, so good! But such a spine might be treated somberly, lyrically, naturalistically, or, as some critics, taking Shaw at what appeared to be his word, in a Chekhovian key. What struck me, however, in reading *Heartbreak House* was its extravagance, a manner very close to comic opera! In intellectual purpose the text is entirely serious but in its body or mode it is akin to what the French call *vaudeville.* As a stage piece it is a lark and almost as remote from Chekhovian realism as Gilbert and Sullivan. Therefore in its stage treatment, I believed, it had to be made as playful and gay as if it were a fashionable bit of camp.

Apart from the parallel with Chekhov which Shaw mentions in his preface to *Heartbreak House,* it may be worth considering how he envisioned his plays on the stage. There is a strong indication in his letters to Granville-Barker, his managerial partner and frequent interpreter as actor-director, that Shaw's theatre taste inclined to the theatrical rather than to any of the modified forms of naturalism which the work of Ibsen, Galsworthy and Granville-Barker himself called for. In a letter to Granville-Barker Shaw wrote, "When will you understand that what has ruined you as a manager is your love for people who are 'a little weak, perhaps, but [have] just the right tone.' The right tone is never a little weak perhaps; it is always devastatingly strong. Keep your worm for your own plays; and leave me the drunken, stagey, brass-bowelled barnstormers my plays are written for. . . ." And again to Barker, "You hate the thing [barnstormers' acting] because it is so blatant and unreal . . . my plays are built to stand that sort of thing."

In one of his little essays Shaw said, "I went back to the classical style and wrote long rhetorical speeches like operatic solos, regarding my plays as musical performances. . . . As a producer [the English theatre word for our director] I went back to the forgotten heroic stage business and the exciting or impressive declamation I had learned from the old-timers."

In the same piece Shaw tells of an actor playing Burgess in Candida "who after rehearsing the first act in a funereal mute, solemnly put up his hand as I vengefully approached him, and said 'Mr. Shaw: I know what you are going to say. But you may depend on me. In the intellectual drama I never clown.' And it was some time before I could persuade him to clown for all he was worth." In my production of *Heartbreak House* there was a considerable amount of "clowning."

Judging from photographs of the original London production under Shaw's supervision I would say there was much less clowning. Was I then falsifying Shaw? I doubt it. I was doing the play—a dismal failure in 1919—for an American audience in 1960. My audience would accept a frolicsome interpretation of the material more readily than the English audience immediately after the First World War, and understand its serious implications.

This is not a defense of my production of *Heartbreak House*—ancient history as such things go in our theatre. I am addressing myself to the problem frequently raised by students as to the director's prerogatives in the treatment of a script—particularly a "classic."

There is perhaps an analogy with performances of music. We do not hear Bach or Mozart precisely as they were rendered in their day. Our audiences would probably not enjoy them if we did. But such an argument would be an evasion: the analogy will not hold. The director discerns a script's style—the production method best suited to convey its quality and meaning—not through the stage directions set down in the script or through discussion with the author himself, but by what the author has actually written: his plot line and his dialogue. The director then translates his understanding of the material into stage language. When Louis Jouvet was told that his Tartuffe was not Molière's, the actor retorted, "Do you have his telephone number?"

I am not suggesting that a director make a play "modern" by indulging in arbitrary tricks with it, though on occasion this may have some interest and value. Generally speaking, I do not approve of fanciful "stylization" as a display of directorial ingenuity. A production should be all of a piece; it should reveal no discrepancy between the text the audience hears and what it sees. It should strike the audience as being in every way self-consistent.

The actor who chose to play Shaw's Burgess solemnly was obtuse because he misread the part, which had little to do with traditional realism, even though Shaw in his early years claimed to be a follower of Ibsen.

Realism, by the way, is itself a style—a comparatively new one in theatre history. And there are various sorts of realism. Hardly any two notable playwrights have exactly the same style; for example, Chekhov's realism is not Ibsen's. All theatre must be real, but not all theatre is "realistic." And "stylization," an extremely vague term which covers a multitude of sins, is in itself no style at all. Those who "stylize" a script through caprice are dilettantes.

Let us be somewhat more exact about our terminology. All plays worthy of the name have a style. "Stylization" has come to designate any style which markedly departs from the "realistic." When actors paint their faces to resemble masks, when furniture and props stand askew on the stage, we speak of "stylization." This is a shorthand indication that conventional realism has been eschewed. But stylization is of many kinds; only a method of presentation particular to each play may be spoken of as a style.

We read of the Greek, the Elizabethan, the Renaissance, the neo-classic styles. Such nomenclature is more historic than aesthetic. It rarely leads the director to a specific solution of his task. Many designers dealing with a text of a by-gone era consult illustrations (plates) from the period for architectural shapes, costumes and stage settings. The results —except when the designer is stimulated to his own concepts through such investigation—are closer to archaeology than to creative activity.

One source of a play's style may be related to its national or racial roots. An American, English or French cast, for example, will not duplicate the exact tone of a Chekhov play. Perhaps it shouldn't try! But within their own limitations every director and his company should study the salient traits of alien behavior patterns, "psychology" and environment which they wish to approximate. They may serve as clues to some aspects of a play's style.

It may be helpful at times to study the actual "soil" from which a dramatist's work has emerged. A trip to our Southland may throw some light in preparation for some of Tennessee Williams' plays. Books relating to costumes, manners, morals and everyday practices, and other literature—verse, novels, chronicles and diaries—as well as the folk music of a particular people and time may also prove invaluable in the quest for a convincing style. My long residence in Paris probably influenced my direction of Anouilh's *Colombe* and *The Waltz of the Toreadors*. In doing *Golden Boy* I received a considerable education through visits to the haunts of the boxing world and through many meetings with its personnel.

It is important to remember that style in the theatre is not chiefly a matter of décor, costumes and the like, but of acting.

The most basic actions—ways of speaking, sitting, walking, smiling, eating, expressing love—are affected. Have you never seen an actress in elaborate court costume of the sixteenth or seventeenth century cross the stage as if she were on her way to a tennis match?

Jules Feiffer's play *Little Murders,* a London success and a failure in its first New York production, offers a striking example of stylistic confusion in the direction of acting. The play was a cartoon of contemporary American mores. Everything said and done was outrageously caricatured. The constant sounds of shooting to kill on an ordinary city street were more or less taken for granted as normal. The effect was properly comic. At the end of the second act the sympathetic ingenue of the play, while talking to her lover in her home, is shot and killed by an unseen triggerman from the street. The production was ruined: the fun was over.

Such a "death scene" might have been rendered as funny as the rest of the play without sacrificing any of its satiric bite. The actress's fall should have been made as hideously grotesque as horrible catastrophes and brutalities are made in movie cartoons.

In one production of *Macbeth* the director's announced intention was to stage the play as a savage epic. Macbeth's first appearance struck the keynote: he looked like a hairy beast. But in the scene in which Lady Macduff teases and fondles her little son what we were shown was a genteel young woman being as charmingly maternal as she might be in a commonplace domestic comedy. If the production had been true to the proposed style, all of the acting would have been physically primitive.

I can make my last assertion clearer by another example in a production of a play about Jacob and Rachel I saw many years ago in Paris. The director conceived the characters as creatures barely past the neolithic stage of civilization. Makeup, clothes and vocal timbres corresponded to this conception. Nothing was so memorable for me as the moment

when Jacob, to flatter his prospective father-in-law took to
tickling Laban's feet, to which the older man reacted with
something like animal "giggles" and movements to show
how much he appreciated the compliment.

What is wrong with most "traditional" productions of
Shakespeare (this usually means nothing but the nineteenth-
century English manner) is that they have little relation to
the nature of Shakespeare's writing. The same is true of
Molière. I once saw a Molière play done by youngsters in
Greenwich Village which a reviewer condemned as a distor-
tion. All he meant was that the play was not being staged as
it was in Paris. But the rowdy Village show was far closer to
Molière's high jinks than the "conservatory" recitation of
Molière so frequently seen at the Comédie Française, the
"House of Molière."

The conflict between director and playwright is a common
subject of controversy. We have all read about Chekhov's
complaint that Stanislavsky had turned his characters into
"crybabies." With authors long dead the issue is certainly a
legitimate aesthetic and literary subject for critical dispute.
But we may arrive at a firmer grasp of this ticklish problem if
we cite instances of our common experience among contemporary playwrights and directors.

Clifford Odets set *Golden Boy* in such places as an Italian
fruit vendor's home, a gymnasium and a prizefighter's dressing room. He set *Rocket to the Moon* in a dentist's office in
mid-Manhattan. Most of the sets I had Mordecai Gorelik design for these plays had very little resemblance to the designated locales. The reason for this is that in reading the two
scripts I did not feel that either of the texts was primarily
concerned with a depiction of the stated environments or
with the business of boxing or dentistry. Audiences accepted the settings—rather free abstractions—as "characteristic," i.e. realistic!

I envisioned one of the characters in *Golden Boy*, Fuselli,
an Italian gangster, as a sort of "Renaissance prince." He

seemed to me to possess a certain elegance, there was something almost "aristocratic" about him. He would be as meticulous about his dress as a courtier; his gait and address would strike the unaware observer as particularly poised and polished. Elia Kazan played the role in accordance with this aim.

When Odets saw a complete run-through of the play during the third week of rehearsal he protested that I had made Fuselli into an utterly unbelievable figure not at all like the New York gangster he had imagined. I knew little about gangsters, and those I had encountered had no similarity to Kazan's Fuselli. But I insisted that the personage that we had set on the stage was the very image of *what Odets had written*; with some vehemence I maintained that I had "invented" nothing. Odets allowed Kazan and me to go ahead with our interpretation as much for the sake of peace as from conviction.

After the play's opening when Thomas Dewey (then New York's District Attorney) and J. Edgar Hoover had, on different occasions, seen the play they complimented Odets for having so keen a perception of the true nature of gangsters. His intuition as a writer was greater than his visual stage sense.

I have often thought that the productions of Edward Albee's plays—particularly *A Delicate Balance* and *Tiny Alice*—might have been rendered truer to his texts and probably more convincing to their audiences if his director, Alan Schneider, had not followed the auctorial instructions so faithfully. The realistic or semi-realistic settings did those plays a disservice.

Jean Vilar, a director who scrupulously adhered to the dramatist's text with a minimum of scenic elaboration or embellishment, asked, "How many playwrights would be capable of giving one a precise analysis of their play or even of their plots!" Chekhov never tried to explain any of his plays to his director or actors—though he would complain when he found something "wrong." Stanislavsky wasn't wearing the right clothes as Trigorin in *The Seagull,* for example. When asked to be more specific Chekhov would only say, "But it's in the play. Read the play." There were no references to the characters' apparel in any part of the text.

This does not mean that the playwright does not "understand" his script. In a very real sense he thinks in another medium than the director: in words—speeches, story line, situations, characters. The director's medium is the behavior of living men and women, physical shapes, lights, color, movement. When a director controverts the playwright he does so only to arrive at a result more congruous with what the playwright has conceived than that which the playwright *believes* he has written.

The director may, of course, be mistaken. The playwright is often converted. The text has been absorbed in the production. The audience or the critic may serve as the final judges. The issue may always hang in the balance, with no final "verdict." That is part of the theatre's incalculability. It explains why there can be so many different productions of the same play. As a critic, I did not altogether approve of the Peter Brook-Paul Scofield *King Lear* but I found it far more interesting than any other production I have seen in which the director assumed the humble position of the dramatist's lackey. Gorky was wise or simply shrewd when he assured both directors of *Yegor Bulitchev*—one at the Moscow Art Theatre, the other at the Vakhtangov Theatre—that each had done the play in exactly the right way, though the two productions were so dissimilar that they looked as if they had been based on two different scripts.

To sum up: A particular rather than a generic style is what the director must achieve for each play. Generic styles only befit academe.

Another way of viewing the moot subject of new productions of revered drama considered to be too "far out" or distortions was astutely put by Grotowski when his treatment of Calderón's *The Constant Prince* was challenged as a desecration.

Grotowski extended the issue beyond the individual case. He was well advised to do so because those who protested could not be sure how much Grotowski's adaptation had retained of the original, for they had no Polish. Nor has it been determined whether those familiar with the language could understand what they heard: Grotowski's company speaks (or shrieks) the lines at an extremely rapid pace.

The Polish director held that every theatre piece represents the thought and feeling of the company which produces it. It is their work as much as the dramatist's. Though Chekhov may have been justified in claiming that the Moscow Art Theatre (or Stanislavsky's) *Cherry Orchard* was not presented as he (Chekhov) had conceived it, the staged play was theirs. If it had substance and valid meaning, then their *Cherry Orchard* was as much a creation as Chekhov's writing. The audience which saw Stanislavsky's *Cherry Orchard*, sprung from Chekhov's text, had been moved, indeed transported, by it.

We never see Shakespeare's *Hamlet* on the stage, only that of Walter Hampden, John Barrymore, John Gielgud, Nicol Williamson and so on and on. Shakespeare's *Hamlet* exists solely in the book. A vast literary fraternity has argued for centuries as to what it connotes.

The issue about which students are constantly questioning their teachers is not resolved by so simple an example as the Stanislavsky-Chekhov "controversy." Grotowski also pointed out that Meyerhold's *The Inspector General* was decidedly the creation of that master director. He had cut the text, rearranged some of the scenes and added new material. Yet many respected Russian critics found Meyerhold's production closer to Gogol's genius than any of the "faithful" productions they had seen.

I have never consciously "tampered" with a masterpiece. My view as a critic, however, is that a director may choose his own interpretation of any text if the result gives pleasure and has creative value. But text and theatrical body must be rendered compatible with each other, and carry conviction as coherent theatre pieces. Dramatists from Shakespeare to Giraudoux have done no less, revising old plays from which they wrought their own original work.

A difficulty arises when a production which takes "liberties" with an honored text is not intelligible or aesthetically satisfying on its own account, that is, when one's enjoyment depends on previous knowledge of the work from which it derives. Richard Schechner's *Dionysus in 69,* part translation of, part improvisation on Euripides' *The Bacchae,* was effective and meaningful, while his *Makbeth* project, which employed no other lines than a portion of Shakespeare's, was not. There was entertainment in Joseph Papp's *Hamlet* experiment but it did not constitute a self-sustaining play. André Gregory's ingenious and well-performed *Alice in Wonderland,* which retained much of the book, also had its bright moments, but it, too, failed to be independently valid.

The director (if permitted) has the right to do what he pleases with a script provided what results is persuasive, enriching and consistently intelligible in itself. My complaint against William Ball's production of *The Three Sisters* was not that he had played fast and loose with Chekhov but that the results were trivial. The same director's *Six Characters in Search of an Author,* in which the acting company of Pirandello's script was presented as juvenilely American, possessed imaginative impact.

My personal preference is for *complete* plays, by which I mean original texts created in view of or as parts of specific productions. The work of Bertolt Brecht provides the best contemporary example. When I asked Brecht if he felt that his plays had to be staged exactly as he had done them, he answered, "Certainly not." Yet I have seen very few productions of his plays produced in a different mode which did not diminish them.

CHAPTER 4

Script Work
with the Playwright

ONLY CRITICS, scholars, students and assiduous playgoers of literary inclination complain about the liberties Tyrone Guthrie, Peter Brook or (in France) Roger Planchon take with the "classics." Shakespeare and Molière have neither immediate heirs nor telephone numbers. But living playwrights are present not only on the telephone but in person. One of the director's duties is to deal with them. With only four exceptions the playwrights whose scripts I have staged were very much alive. I have had very little difficulty with any of them during the time of production; dissatisfaction, if any, came later!

To direct with the playwright attending every rehearsal in the early days of staging may prove as disturbing to a director as having an editor look over his shoulder while he is engaged in writing his first draft would be to a novelist. I must

confess gratitude for a playwright's absence for at least half
the rehearsal period. Many playwrights of their own accord
stay away for this duration, since their continuous presence
may not only bore them but may dim their judgment.

Rehearsals of a play constitute a *creative process* as delicate and arduous as the writing of the script itself. The process is not helped, it is impeded, by nervous impatience or the
insistence on immediately convincing results. These are the
fruits of gestation. While this is going on, what we see is
rarely pleasing as "performance." Only the late stages of rehearsal provide testimony as to the progress made.

Under ordinary circumstances the playwright's script is the
core and basis of the theatrical event. To begin with, the
playwright is the director's closest collaborator. The script,
once chosen, is to be respected as are all the people—actors,
scene designer, costumer, musicians and, ultimately, the audience—who compose the Play.

The playwright confirms or initiates the choice of the
director. He is presumed to have confidence in the person to
whom his script has been entrusted. The director, likewise,
has supposedly elected to stage the script because he admires
it. As with marriage, there is often an element of uncertainty
on both sides. A playwright may have been persuaded to accept a director by the producer or by the star. Directors have
been known to undertake an assignment because they believed the producer even more astute than themselves or because of their esteem for a particular actor or quite simply
because they needed employment.

The playwright may have checked with his professional
friends to ascertain whether the recommended director is
the "right man" for his particular play. "Yes," the writer may
have said, "X did a fine job with that play about those New
York toughs but will he know how to handle my play about
polite society?" or "So-and-so is great with heavy drama, but
my play is a scintillating comedy," etc., etc., *ad nauseum.*

"There is a genuine impulse in this script, and some fine

dialogue," the director may have mused, "but the plot is somewhat predictable, the construction a little feeble. Will the author realize the need for correcting these flaws? And even if he is ready to do so, is he capable of it?"

Under normal conditions—if conditions in our theatre can ever be thought of as normal—mutual regard exists on both sides. Once the director has conveyed his enthusiasm for the script (and he had better do so as playwrights are even more touchy than actors), the playwright is prepared to listen to his opinion and advice on matters of cast, setting, etc.

Ideally the director should have no other function than to direct. It is a great relief to a director, unless he is an inordinate egotist, to come upon a script which requires little or no revision. One occasionally encounters such scripts. Cutting is often necessary, but experienced writers readily concur with suggestions which entail certain minor changes. Eugene O'Neill, extremely attentive to the integrity of his texts, agreed, at his director's suggestion, to extensive cuts in *Strange Interlude*.

Bernard Shaw never permitted his scripts to be cut. Having watched many productions of his plays (I myself have directed three), I venture to believe him to have been mistaken. An early uncut, though excellent, production of *Misalliance* was a failure in New York, while some years later an inferior one with judicious cuts proved far more effective. Europeans, I have observed, tolerate *longueurs* in a play far more patiently than Americans.

Neophyte playwrights frequently offer their scripts to directors with the assurance that "though the script needs further work, I am sure I can do it satisfactorily with your help." This may show a commendable modesty, but it betrays an amateur attitude. Some directors encourage it—it flatters them—and some have been known to profit financially from the practice of contributing to the "rewrite."

This is not to deny that many scripts have been greatly strengthened by the guiding hand of a sympathetic and perceptive director. A knowledge of play structure and dramatic writing, a combination of artistic sensibility and stage acumen, are therefore important, possibly indispensable, qualifications for the direction of a new play. (In Europe—particularly in Germany—the director often performs the auctorial service with the assistance of the theatre's *Dramaturg*, literary manager or "play doctor.") But as Elia Kazan once said, "If you aren't willing to go ahead with the direction of a script in its unrevised and perhaps still imperfect state then you had best not do it at all." This may be overstating the case but it is sufficiently astute to be given serious consideration.

The first order of business, then, in preparing for a production should be a series of director-dramatist consultations. They ought to discuss (and agree on) the operative content of the script. Sometimes the director is sufficiently eloquent and cogent (to the playwright's surprise and delight) to add to or alter the playwright's material. New lines or scenes may be suggested to clarify the script's theme or story points. There may be divergent opinions on any of these matters but the responsibility for any changes ultimately rests with the writer.

Stanislavsky did not direct the Hebrew production of *The Dybbuk* (Vakhtangov did) but it is said that he suggested the symbolic character of the Stranger to the author. In the preliminary outline of Odets' *Golden Boy* Joe Bonaparte's father was a musician. I argued that he should be a much humbler figure. Odets finally made him a fruit vendor.

In an early draft of the same play one of the characters was Joe Bonaparte's older brother, a fellow who sold score cards at the ball park. Though minor, he was a well-drawn figure. Odets' purpose in introducing him was thematically irrelevant. The spine of the play, as I had adduced it, was "to win in the *fight* of life." Odets meant his play to show a person who "fought" the wrong way—one damaging to human personality.

I asked for a "fighter" whose struggle contrasted with that

of the misguided protagonist. Odets then made the older brother a labor organizer—a familiar ("committed") type in the thirties. As this character was usually in the "field" away from home, he could exercise little influence on Joe, but it was clear that he also "fought" and was not doing so for "fame and fortune."

Playwrights have from time to time blamed me (after the fact) for not having insisted on more drastic cutting or for having made suggestions detrimental to the play's effectiveness. After the opening of *Rocket to the Moon* Odets himself decided to eliminate a character and an eight-minute scene which he had come to consider redundant. The Group Theatre, under whose auspices the play was produced, rarely tried out its plays in pre-Broadway tours.

When Arthur Miller's *Death of a Salesman* was being readied for rehearsal, its director, Elia Kazan, made several suggestions meant to clarify the play's plot. Miller complied. When the revised script was read, doubt was expressed as to the efficacy of the changes. Asked his opinion, Walter Fried, the play's co-producer, ventured, "The play is clearer now, but less interesting." The script was put into rehearsal as originally written.

In the controversies over the revision of Tennessee Williams' *Cat on a Hot Tin Roof* the author intimated that he yielded to Kazan's reasoning on the issue. I was not present at the conferences. For purposes of illustration, however, I shall describe ("allegorically") what may have happened. The director voices his criticism of Williams' ending; the playwright demurs. This goes on for hours, perhaps for days. The director becomes ever more convinced that his criticism is sound; the playwright maintains his position with decreasing resolution. The director finally says, "Please try my ending. If it doesn't work during the tryout we will go back to the original version. But I'm sure I'm right artistically. I'm on even surer ground as to the audience reaction. The change may make the difference between a hit and a flop." The playwright yields. The new third act is written and tried. The play is a hit; the director is vindicated.

In the backlash of later criticism from friends and professional commentators the ending urged by the director is denounced as a compromise. The author, it is objected, is bidding for sympathy, he has gone soft, etc., etc. The playwright then ruefully explains that the ending was not altogether his idea. As testimony, he has both endings published.

Whatever our personal judgment in the matter may be, the author evinces bad faith if he defends himself with the excuse of pressure from the director. The director has no jurisdiction over the play's verbal text. The audience judges the Play as a whole—what it sees and hears—and need not concern itself with what role each of the collaborators in its making has performed. That is a special consideration within the province of criticism, though the critic is rare who is able to distinguish between a script and its direction.

The question of assigning blame for failure or credit for success, about which we often hear talk (it is likely to be empty chatter), brings us to another aspect of the dramatist-director relationship in the preliminary phases of production.

During the tryout period of Dorothy Parker and Armand d'Usseau's play *The Ladies of the Corridor* it became evident that a good portion of the audience was upset by a suicide scene near the end of the play. I asked the authors if in view of this reaction they wished to eliminate it. Their answer was an emphatic "no." I did not insist. The play—admired by George Jean Nathan, who also found the scene undesirable—failed. There were no recriminations. But my forbearance, many thought, was a directorial blemish. Perhaps so. The question remains whether it was that scene alone which caused the play's failure.

The atmosphere of the theatre world is predominantly naive. There is always the all-too-human urge to find a "villain," somebody to reprove for every misadventure. Any excuse will do. But even a good reason—such as the one just mentioned—may not be the true one. And why must failure inevitably be deemed shameful or reprehensible?

Many faults were found with my direction of Tennessee Williams' *Orpheus Descending*—nearly all of them after the play's "mixed" reception. In Philadelphia, immediately before the New York opening, the author assured me that none of his previous plays had been so truly interpreted. With the play's failure he exercised the privilege of changing his mind. (I had exactly the same experience with Clifford Odets in the production of his *Night Music*.) I had permitted a leading character in *Orpheus* to be shot in full view of the audience as set down in the script. We had been warned by Gore Vidal that this was a mistake. When the play closed I had some misgivings on this score. But there were other criticisms: the setting was wrong, the casting was misguided, etc.

I had occasion to see the play again in Paris and then in London. In these productions the killing of the woman was not staged with such brutal directness as in mine. There were also quite different sets. The productions were received exactly as mine had been. The play was a success in Moscow where it was "freely" adapted—no doubt to emphasize the barbarous cruelty of American life!

A learned man of the theatre once asserted that Lillian Hellman's *The Autumn Garden* was not as successful as its writing warranted because its setting was too literal. An interesting sidelight on this is the fact that the set had been designed in consultation with the author before I had been engaged as director—a sign of the artistic disorganization and ignorance of the director's function. I myself agree with my colleague's criticism of the set. I would have asked for something quite different, although I am by no means certain that the author would have accepted the style of set I thought suitable. I am convinced, however, that the play—Miss Hellman's best, I believe—would not have been anything more than a *succès d'estime* if the set had been "ideal." It is one of the misfortunes of the American theatre that if a new play is done on Broadway and is not a "smash," it is almost never seen there again.

Let us now return to the initial director-playwright consultations, which, I repeat, should precede the director's notes on the play's theme: spine, style, etc. The director has asked many questions of the playwright. The playwright sometimes proves reticent or less than explicit in reply. On the other hand, he may say things about the origins of the script: how and why he came to write it; he may make allusions to its characters and milieu, or to its ideologic and social background. These remarks may reveal facets of the script the director did not immediately apprehend. He will often learn as much from what he discerns through such personal contact with the playwright's attitudes as he has from the playwright's specific explanations. His observation of the playwright's general cast of thought may possibly become a factor in the eventual treatment of the script.

More useful results will ensue from director-playwright colloquies when they actually get down to cases. This occurs when rewriting is to be done, or during the sessions devoted to the choice of actors and in the joint examination of set and costume designs. Most important will be the playwright's observations and criticisms at rehearsals.

Should the director at the outset be uncertain as to what script revisions are needed he had best leave well enough alone. The rehearsal period itself will prove a most instructive time for both director and playwright. The director can only be persuasive if he is sure of his ground. He must constantly assume when dealing with a practiced dramatist that the latter has given more thought to the writing and construction of his play than anyone else.

Years ago that shrewd showman David Belasco remarked that "plays aren't written, they are made," i.e., revamped. This was generally true on the Broadway of Belasco's time and still holds true of musicals, farces and melodramas. It is far less true of drama today. The theatre now is increasingly devoted to writing which aspires to the status of literature; the good playwright is a literary artist. The director must be aware of what the literary sensibility entails.

I recall my experience with Carson McCullers' *The Member of the Wedding*. A novelist, she had had almost no previous contact with the stage. Someone was chosen to dramatize her book. He tried to make a "regular play" of it. I never read that dramatization but I was informed not only that Mrs. McCullers had rejected it but that it had rendered her seriously ill. She was then persuaded to undertake the dramatization herself.

The first directors who read her dramatization thought it theatrically hopeless. They maintained that it had to be drastically revised for it to be a viable stage piece. When called in to direct it I was asked what revisions I would demand. "None," I replied to the consternation of certain people who had Mrs. McCullers' success very much at heart. What, not to "fix" a script so awkward, repetitious, undramatic!

I did nevertheless suggest a few additional lines to sharpen certain situations and representative ideas. When Mrs. McCullers tried her hand at following my suggestions I realized at once that she was incapable of doing more than she had done to begin with. With all its faults her script was a complete expression of what she had to say. "Fixing" it to satisfy some arbitrary notion of professional dramaturgy would ruin it. (A play's form cannot be imposed by technical rules. A play's form rises out of its own organic nature.) Two scenes were cut at the out-of-town tryout. They had been entertaining and revealing episodes in the novel but destroyed the play's unity on the stage. Some minor cuts were made. The play was presented in New York very much as Mrs. McCullers had written it. It worked.

Another instance of artistic discretion, indeed wisdom, concerns a brief exchange between Lillian Hellman and myself in regard to her play *The Autumn Garden*. During rehearsals Miss Hellman agreed to some suggested cuts. She herself was dissatisfied with the final scene. She rewrote it several times. One day before the rehearsal period had begun she asked me if I had any fundamental criticism of her script. With some diffidence I told her that while the whole tenor of her play was an ironical presentation of its characters, she had not made them as "forgivable" as they might be. I pointed out that though Chekhov's characters were often foolish and feckless, one ended by loving them. "True," was Miss Hellman's immediate response, "but I'm not as good as Chekhov." I had nothing further to say. My criticism had been "just"— and futile.

The director should not be sanguine about the writer's ability to exceed his limitations. Nor, generally speaking, should he be too hopeful of compensating for a script's inherent weaknesses by further writing. If there is to be an extension of the playwright's scope—or an attenuation of his faults —it must be accomplished through direction. I once heard a producer exclaim about a comedy he had bought, "If only the dialogue was as deft as Maugham's!" Understandable as sentiment, it was silly as project. There is a kind of criticism in the theatre which no matter how justified in the absolute is practically speaking not only idle but harmful.

During rehearsals (or sometimes during the lapse of time between the writing of a play and its first rehearsal) playwrights themselves often discover passages, scenes, even whole acts which demand alteration. When I read *Awake and Sing* for the first time I realized that its second act was a brilliant achievement but I was reluctant to accept the play as a whole. I could hardly explain my reservations. I spoke of its "cramped atmosphere." This was not a reference to the environment in which the play's action took place but to something in the writer's outlook. This left Odets thoroughly puzzled. One day, however, he announced that he had cut the script's first twenty pages and after discussion with me had rewritten the last act. I hadn't realized (this was my first independent venture as a director) that the script's major defects could be remedied by protracted study and effort by both dramatist and director.

When I read the first draft of William Inge's *The Dark at the Top of the Stairs* I was uncertain as to what troubled me about it. But its initial deficiency was immediately discerned by Elia Kazan, who directed it. Inge revised it along the lines indicated by that director. Inge, like the early O'Neill, is one of those playwrights whose work acquires a body on the stage not always apparent in the "book."

The theatrical impact of Sidney Kingsley's *Men in White* was barely evident to more than a handful of people before it reached the final moments of production under Lee Strasberg's beautiful direction.

In the long haul of a play's production the writer himself may begin to find fault with his script. A week before the opening of *Golden Boy* Clifford Odets felt certain that its last act did not follow logically from the premise of its second. He was at fault, he admitted, and had to rewrite the entire act. It took all my dialectic powers to prevent his making the change.

I conclude: Most sound craftsmen—directors and dramatists—work well together with little friction. Unpleasantness usually arises when the director makes demands on the playwright without regard to their initial understanding on the script's essential form and meaning. A playwright doesn't want his play "improved" if the improvement leads to making a different play than his own. He wants *his* voice to be heard, unless he thinks of himself as a journeyman prepared to provide a commodity which might somehow prove profitable. But not many playwrights think of themselves in that light.

CHAPTER 5

Settings

THIS BOOK is arranged in segments; production does not advance in such orderly steps. Two, three or more activities are engaged in at almost the same time. The director, playwright and producer—the usual trio of American practice—may have begun casting during discussions of the script. After having decided the nature of the play—its spine and style—the director goes on to a more detailed study which entails the drafting of a scene-by-scene production plan. To be efficient in this he holds advisory consultations with the production designer.

There are variations in this procedure. On and off Broadway, where rehearsal time for a "straight" play, as differentiated from a musical, is three and a half weeks before previews, the designer must undertake his job six weeks, at the very least, before rehearsals commence. While permanent companies abroad and certain of our regional theatres build their sets and sew costumes in addition to fashioning and gathering such accessories as furniture, drapes and hand properties within the theatre's premises, all this preparation in our professional theatre is delegated to separate and independent companies. These are located at some distance from the theatre. At the same time, in the same shops, other productions for different managements are usually being readied to meet other opening-night deadlines. This makes for haste.

In some European theatres—the Berliner Ensemble, for example—the designer attends nearly all the rehearsals to observe the working out of details of movement and the "business" which has been invented by the director and the actors. The designer is therefore not obliged to fix the ground plan— placement of platforms, set pieces, objects of use, etc.—before he has had the opportunity to attend rehearsals. The ground plan is technically the crucial element in setting. The artist's design in these European theatres is "custom tailored." With us, the actors and director are constrained to fit the setting which has been designed and is already being built prior to the first rehearsal. The actors in my productions (and probably in most others) are always shown a quarter- or half-inch model of the setting before they begin the joint reading of the play. The setting itself is rarely placed on stage till very late in the rehearsal period. But seeing the model helps the actors visualize the play's environment.

The tight rehearsal schedule in our theatre has unfortunate consequences. For one thing, it gives designers an undesirable independence. They frequently take to their drawing boards with insufficient knowledge of what actors are to use their settings, what their physical limitations may be and what they are going to be required to do. Much of a play's movement arises from the stimulation of rehearsal. Since the designer cannot anticipate this, the actors' spontaneity in the invention of stage business may be limited by the setting.

Not long ago a designer devised a very fine set for a new

musical. It consisted of a series of scaffolds placed high above the stage floor with winding steps descending to the main playing area. But many members of the cast were of a certain age; they found the descent from the top scaffold to the stage floor perilous. Railings, not previously provided because the set was deemed more attractive without them, had to be supplied during the dress rehearsals, which was both time-consuming and costly. A stage setting should be adjusted to the play's action, and not the reverse.

The choice of a designer is part of the director's function. I have already mentioned an occasion when the producer and playwright engaged a designer before a director had been assigned. On seeing the completed sketch of the set, already under construction, the chosen director realized at once that it would be an impediment rather than an aid to him.

The director does not dictate to the designer.* He serves as the designer's guide, critic and, if possible, inspirer. He communicates his vision of the play to the designer and designates the technical problems he foresees. He does not, for instance, order "a setting in blue" or arbitrarily insist on some special mechanical device such as a revolving or a jack-knife stage, a particular kind of cyclorama, scenic projections, etc.; he describes the role the set should play in the production's desired effect. He writes the "notes" which the designer is to sound. (This is also the key to the actor-director relationship; but of this, later.) The designer's creative contribution is manifested in his solution of the problems posed.

The director speaks of the play's style: its atmosphere, mood, the kind of impact he would have the play produce. He indicates the sort of movement he will call for, the most important acting areas, the position of entrances and exits, the matter of timing between scenes.

---

* There are always exceptions. For my production of Roblès' *Montserrat* at the Habimah Theatre in Israel, the designer, a noted Israeli painter, was an artist whose work I did not know. I therefore instructed him minutely on every aspect of the set and costumes. They were virtually of my design.

A stage setting is not a picture. Nor is it primarily decoration. Audiences understandably tend to applaud sets which are pretty or imposing. Robert Edmond Jones, a pioneer in his day, thought of sets chiefly in terms of mood, the spiritual ambience in which a play was to be immersed. "A stage setting," he said, "is not a background, it is an environment." His was a reaction against both the conventionalized renderings of living rooms, mansions, outdoor scenes, etc., commonly in use in the late nineteenth century, and the more detailed realism for which David Belasco between 1900 and 1920 was much admired and which in many respects still obtains as the Broadway norm.

What matters most in modern stage design is the proper use of space. Designers today attempt first of all to fulfill the various demands of action and movement. Certain designers have termed settings "machines for actors." Atmosphere, suggestions of place and time, along with decorative elements, need not be neglected on that account.

Though Gordon Craig was Robert Edmond Jones' chief influence in the designing of atmospheric settings Craig did not confine himself, in theory at least, to that one element alone. "No scene that I have worked at," Craig said, "was worked at for its own sake. I thought solely of the movement of the Drama . . . of the actors, of dramatic moments. . . . I saw as I progressed that *things can,* therefore should, play their parts as well as people, that they can combine with the actor and plead with the actor to use them."

For the production of Giraudoux's *Tiger at the Gates,* first produced in London, I chose Louden Sainthill as designer. The author's notation as to setting indicated no more than "a terrace [outside a palace] overlooking other terraces." Sainthill was in England, while I was still in New York. I suggested that he begin work alone without specific instructions from me. He was then to send me a sketch of what he proposed.

I received a beautiful picture, lush in color, baroque in

ornament, elaborate in structure. It was something I would have been pleased to hang in my apartment or enter in an exhibit. It was not at all what I had in mind.

I had not then seen Christian Bérard's setting for the original Paris production. After I had directed the play, I did see a photograph of it and I could not help but admire it. But it was not a setting I would have requested for my production. Bérard's set, though there were a few elevations in it, was largely flat: movement had to be confined to the stage floor. This was no doubt suitable for the French production, but not for mine. The script is markedly rhetorical. Reading it, one would suspect that it consisted of nothing but fine speeches.

The French are endlessly pleased by fine language, beautifully spoken. The English, and more especially Americans (and it was chiefly a New York audience I was thinking of), are bored by "talky" shows: they demand overt action. How was I to create this in a play which required first of all that its verbal splendor be thoroughly appreciated?

I asked Sainthill to eliminate most of the purely decorative elements (even color) and to eschew ordinary furnishings: chairs, tabourets, settees and the like. He was to arrange a setting of asymmetrically ordered planes (or platforms) rapidly descending from about ten feet above floor level, at the height of which Michael Redgrave as Hector was to make his first triumphant entrance. On this stage, every step the actors made would cause them to ascend or descend in space. Thus they were always beheld in movement; without the audience being entirely aware of it, the setting "propelled" the actors—up and down.

The actors had to be surefooted: the stage incline was steep. In his London review of the production Kenneth Tynan wrote that the setting appeared to have been designed for mountain goats! I might have countered that the play's legendary characters were not lambs or that the part of Asia Minor where Troy, the play's locale, was presumed to have stood was mountainous and that I was trying to suggest its topography. But none of this would have been relevant. I was concerned only with devising playing areas which would make every figure stand out boldly and, above all, serve as a "podium" for Giraudoux's sumptuous writing while at the same time enforce movement and induce a sense of physical action. Color was supplied by vivid costumes.

Another detail is worth mentioning. Despite himself the designer clung to considerations of realism. He had the platforms painted an indefinite tan because in the open space of a palace courtyard, he pointed out, the sun would have tarnished the "stone." This gave the set an unpleasantly muddy color. I overlooked the blemish in London but had the steps repainted an "impossible" pearl blue in New York.

It is a mistake to think of a setting as a copy of a real place. What matters is the sort of reality the play aims at. And every play has its own reality. Boris Aronson's room for Arthur Miller's *The Price* was ostensibly realistic. But as Aronson composed it, the apparent mess, a deserted room full of stored furniture, became a sculpted form which bespoke the passage of time, the rich substance of a now abandoned family life, the dissolution of former middle-class comfort. "Real life" milieus are nowadays rendered in ever more markedly abstract designs. But abstraction or stylization must communicate something of a play's essence. Still, a design should not be totally declarative: it should not "say everything." A setting must serve as a contributing factor to a play's "message," not be a thing in itself.

It is occasionally asserted that apart from considerations of economy, the theatre might profit if all "scenery" were eliminated. Nonsense! There is always a setting in the theatre. The audience always sees *something* and what it sees inevitably conveys an idea of some sort and should perform a meaningful function. A bare stage, as Aronson once cannily remarked, is more difficult to design than any other.

A number of Brecht's practices have now become routine.

He never availed himself of the traditional curtain, did not conceal the sources of stage illumination, was frugal in the use of furniture. He used white light only. Settings for his productions were usually given a more or less neutral background. He wished his audience to be aware that they were in a theatre, so that there would be no pretense of naturalistic imitation. Above all, he hoped to make the spectator see the play in objective repose instead of being bemused by what he deemed false glamor. His chief aim, in short, was to direct the audience's attention to what the actors were saying and demonstrating.

Yet his settings (actually Teo Otto's) were both handsome and rich in tonal values. A Parisian critic observed that there were several hundred different shades of brown in the settings for *Mother Courage*. The background throughout his *Galileo,* including exteriors, was covered with bronze foil which recalled the sedate opulence we associate with the Italian Renaissance. Mother Courage's medium of livelihood, her wagon, was tooled with meticulous care to indicate the wear and tear of her long peregrinations through Europe and the vehicle's steady decline, symbolic of her own.

I have said that the director should not dictate to the designer. More emphatically: he should stimulate his powers of invention. Ben Edwards' setting for my production of Eugene O'Neill's *A Touch of the Poet* owed nothing to any instruction from me. O'Neill's stage directions and text were his sole guide. But for my production of Arthur Laurents' *The Time of the Cuckoo* I spoke to Edwards about the tremulous shimmer of the Venetian canals which made the adjacent buildings look as if they were veiled in a watery tissue. The effect was overly conspicuous at first but was later modified. For Anouilh's *The Waltz of the Toreadors* I suggested that Edwards seek inspiration in Cézanne's and Vuillard's colors. When in a similar vein I suggested that Aronson make the set for Inge's *Bus Stop* look like an Edward Hopper painting, his rejoinder was, "Why not like an Aronson?"

To Moredecai Gorelik I spoke of the motorcar sleekness of many offices in which wealthy business executives conduct their affairs, apropos of John Howard Lawson's *Success Story* which Lee Strasberg directed in 1932 for the Group Theatre. (On this occasion Strasberg granted me the privilege of serving as scenic adviser.) A few days later Gorelik showed me a reproduction of a cubist painting by Braque: superimposed planes of black and brown. "Is this what you mean?" Gorelik queried. I confess to having been slightly puzzled at the time, but agreed to have him translate this abstraction into a serviceable locus for the play's action. He did so. The result was like no office I had ever before seen but one which was altogether right for the play; furthermore, one that the audience accepted as "real."

From my hypothesis that Odets' *Golden Boy* had little to do with pugilism but had much to do with winning the battle of the ego he shaped the play on the severe nudity of a boxing ring though the script called for no visible match. Properties required by the action were placed on the bare platform. The homey warmth of the Italian father's household was conveyed by the texture of the woodwork in the scenic frame. Though the text contained references to the city, a gray velour cyclorama served as a backdrop throughout. For a scene in Central Park nothing was visible but an isolated bench against a fragment of stone wall. Two nights prior to the play's opening a friendly playwright confided to Odets that he thought the production had ruined the play (oh, these whisperers in the night!) because cops amble through parks, also dogs, and one hears the seductive hiss of passing limousines—and none of these things were present in the production. When I was told about this I blurted out, "Yes, and why doesn't Hamlet carry an umbrella when called to meet the ghost at the approach of the wet Danish dawn?"

As an instructor in scenic design at various colleges, Gorelik formulated his method by saying that all settings should stem from a basic metaphor, a central image inspired by the play or the director's interpretation of it. A valuable insight. In retrospect I think of a very early Aronson setting for a scene in Hell which he inserted inside the outline of a huge human cranium, as later in *Cabin in the Sky* he set the inferno imagined by poor blacks with an immense refrigerator in the background.

As I am dealing with settings as part of the director's craft I omit references to the minutiae of scenic mechanics. While these may be extremely important in the smooth running and ultimate success of a production, they are rarely of the *first* importance. They chiefly concern the designer, the builder and the stage carpenter. These associated craftsmen may, for example, be obliged to make certain adjustments in design and construction in a production which is to troop extensively through the country where transportation by train or truck is involved. I have been told, for instance, that when Maxwell Anderson's *Anne of the Thousand Days* was being tried out in Philadelphia the actors, clothed in voluminous costumes, were hardly able to get through the spaces provided for making their entrances. The entire setting had to be redone for the New York opening.

The likelihood of such accidents is increased in the Broadway theatre because there are no permanent theatre organizations with their own coordinated technical staffs. Playwrights belong to a guild of their own, loosely related to Equity, the actors' union. The stagehands have their own union, with their own separate interests, the scenic artists theirs, the business managers, directors, box-office personnel and ushers likewise.

It is on this account that Boris Aronson has said he would call his book on the theatre "Organized Calamities." It is a miracle that so much good work is done in our theatre, but as Nemirovitch-Danchenko, co-founder and co-director with Stanislavsky of the Moscow Art Theatre, once remarked on learning that a Theatre Guild production he liked had been rehearsed for only four weeks, "It's a miracle and I don't believe in miracles."

The division, or more precisely, the contention, of labor in our theatre begins with real estate. Very few producers or directors nowadays possess their own theatres. They rent them when they have a play to put on, an eventuality ever more infrequent since the thirties. It is not within the province of this book to expatiate the damage to the theatre as an art caused by this circumstance. But the fact that the buildings in use for our productions are all structured in exactly the same way is unquestionably restricting to freedom in scenic design.

There is nothing absolutely wrong with the old "picture frame" arrangement of the stage as a raised platform cut off from the audience by a proscenium arch within which sets are placed. It developed from the needs of a society in which plays were written to its measure. Plays and theatre architecture have almost always been engendered within a single matrix.

The proscenium stage has long served the theatre and will continue to do so for many years to come. Brecht and other non-realists among playwrights have employed it without artistic embarrassment. But it does not facilitate—it impedes —some types of production. For the presentation of new types of plays today and for the new ways we believe they should "happen," the old playhouses are the wrong instruments.

Solutions by way of new edifices proliferate to the point of fetishism. In many cases they are hasty and arbitrary, a matter of guesswork, often products of architectural fantasy or snobbery. (The lobbies and public facilities—coatrooms, bars, lavatories—are always superb.) Theatres in the round do away with the proscenium arch; they by no means constitute a universal panacea. Nor is the arena theatre with a thrust stage always serviceable. I have found that producing Chekhov in such a theatre leads to awkward staging. The lines of sight anywhere apart from the center of the house make for distortion of vision. These bring about falsifications in stage movement which do not exist in the theatres for which Chekhov's plays and many others were written. Architectural "improvements" or experiments abstracted from the total theatre organism disable it.

It is surely desirable to bring the audience and the playing area in closer contact than the old theatres permit. Having actors enter from the rear of the house and pass through the aisles to the stage is occasionally interesting but sometimes ludicrous. I found it so when the Spanish peasants of Lorca's *Yerma* emerged from the special entrance in the middle of the Vivian Beaumont Theatre auditorium and passed onto the stage in front of the fashionably dressed ladies and gentlemen in Row A. Audiences are generally prepared to play the theatre game in any way directors propose. But that does not mean that all methods are sound.

The use of an empty space which may be adapted to any structure including a variable disposition of the audience for particular occasions might prove of inestimable value. When desired, this allows an easy interpenetration or mingling of actors and spectators. But merely to depart from the so-called peep-show or theatre-of-illusion architecture, which some theorists condemn as "archaic," does not prevent aesthetic fraudulence. When Max Reinhardt, many years ago, had actors rise from the audience to heckle the orators in the convention scene of Büchner's *Danton's Death* the device was a thrilling and justified novelty. But since then I have seen more traditionally staged productions of the play which were equally exciting.

Architectural changes in theatre structure are valid only when they are generated by the intrinsic demands of particular kinds of performance. These in turn depend on social, economic, geographical and historical circumstances. Because necessity dictated the use of factories as the site of certain theatre activities during the early years of the Russian

Revolution, a good many settings were made to simulate industrial environments. What is right in theatre architecture as in setting is that which conforms to the artistic purpose of the stage event and the conditions surrounding it.

The varying structural schemes devised by the Grotowski productions correspond to the intimate communion to which his art aspires. It is no whim or personal eccentricity which reduces his theatre to a seating capacity of no more than a hundred. When his company goes abroad he painstakingly seeks a location which approximates his own workshop theatre in Poland.

The very meaning of Ronconi's *Orlando Furioso,* with its mad riot, street-fair hurly-burly and crowd folly, called for an Italian piazza or such a place as Les Halles in Paris.

A theatre's or a setting's very dimensions affect a play's impact. In a relatively intimate house in Rome *Rugantino* was a charming musical gambol. In the vast expanse of New York's Mark Hellinger Theatre it became feebly exotic. *Waiting for Godot* cannot retain either its comedy or its tension in a large auditorium. While Rouben-ter-Arutunian's set for Edward Albee's *All Over* was an interesting and in many respects a fitting one, it rendered the play remote by its inordinate size in a theatre too large for the play's repressed motion.

Theatre discussion which fails to consider all the circumstances attendant on the production of plays in particular times and places tends to produce little but hot air. In the commercial theatre where, I repeat, real estate interests control playhouses, producers are often constrained to contract for theatres which cripple their efforts. The system, the system is to blame!

CHAPTER 6

Casting

"CHOOSE A GOOD SCRIPT," I sometimes advise students, "cast good actors—and you'll all be good directors!" There is more than a little truth in the jest. Casting constitutes the first step in the practical interpretation of a play.

Casting possibilities in small permanent companies are limited. The Group Theatre (1931–41) had only twenty-five actors to choose from. The British National Theatre has about seventy, as does the Royal Shakespeare Company; the Moscow Art Theatre had more than a hundred. The larger companies command a sufficient number of good actors to deal satisfactorily with any play they wish to produce.

With time the permanent company develops a common vocabulary of work, an ease and a bold variety of interplay, and above all, a most helpful rapport between actors and director. The director knows his "instruments," the shortcomings and assets of every member of the company. Everyone is responsive to the others. All function smoothly together as a unit.

Seeing the Royal Shakespeare Company in Brook's *Midsummer Night's Dream,* followed immediately after in a production of Maxim Gorky's *Enemies,* a play of quasi-Chekhovian character, afforded me once again a most impressive example of the range of styles a permanent company may be able to encompass. The actors' capacities are extended through membership in a permanent company. It is not talent alone which has made it possible for Laurence Olivier, Maggie Smith, Albert Finney, Peggy Ashcroft, Robert Stephens and many others to achieve their great scope of characterization. Think of the roles these stars have been called upon to play within a relatively short time. Maggie Smith appeared in *The Beaux' Stratagem* and in *Hedda Gabler* during the same season. Laurence Olivier's repertoire in recent years has included Shakespeare, Sheridan, Farquhar, Chekhov, Osborne and O'Neill. We think of such actors as being "able to play anything." While this is not literally true, it is as much a sign of the advantages of permanent company organizations as of their individual gifts.

Although there have been a few attempts to create them, the American theatre has almost no such companies. We proceed on the basis of "piecework": for every new production an entirely new cast must be found—somehow, somewhere. Casting a play in this fashion is an arduous task.

To begin with, the New York director chooses among the actors he has seen and admired in the course of his playgoing or among those with whom he has previously worked and liked.* If among these two groups he finds actors who are available and interested in the plays and parts for which they are summoned, the job of casting is greatly simplified.

---

* Equity insists that there be a limited number of "open calls" for which any member of the union may apply for a part. I doubt whether many actors have been engaged through this procedure.

We must remember that in casting new plays, the writer, who contractually has the last word in the matter, must sometimes be persuaded that the actor the director wants is the right choice for a particular role. The producer also carries weight in the decision. There are hesitations and debates.

It is customary to seek stars for leading roles. But nowadays stars or "movie actors" no longer assure success. In England a weak play may hold the boards for several months if a cherished actor appears in it. Not only is the public there more loyal to its actors than we are, but there is a more steady stream of playgoers and the economics of the theatre are less stringent. Unless a play in New York is found to possess intrinsic interest (and receives favorable notices), it cannot be "saved" by a star. Our theatregoing public is no longer as interested in its actors as it was before 1929.

The "open market" method of casting in our theatre is further complicated by the fact that comparatively few actors nowadays achieve a shining reputation by work on the stage alone. Many of our most promising actors have abandoned the stage for films. (This trend began in the thirties and has continued until very recently. The gradual decline of Hollywood may reverse the tide. But there is still television.) The actors whom films have made famous exercise extreme caution in venturing onto Broadway's treacherous paths. The people engaged in casting are therefore obliged to seek players free of commitments to films, television and advertisement. The problem of casting often reduces itself not to the question of the best actor for a particular part but of "Who can you get?"

The main business of casting is accomplished by means of auditions or readings. Even well-known actors are frequently asked to read, especially at the insistence of the playwrights. Reading for parts is a species of theatrical shopping, usually distasteful or painful to the actor, unless he has little New York experience and is hoping to "break through."

Apart from those few managements which employ a person

capable of making intelligent recommendations to the ruling triumvirate (director, playwright and producer), scripts are sent to agents who arrange for their actor clients to be interviewed by the crucial Three. Those whose appearance and experience make them likely candidates for a role are given the script to look over a day or two before the readings are held.

I have never charted the statistics but I have the impression that at times hundreds of actors have been interviewed for a play which requires a cast of no more than ten in addition to several understudies. I must have heard at least a dozen readings a day for weeks to choose players even for some of the lesser roles. The number of auditions for musicals is astronomical. Whatever the objections to this procedure, directors and actors are obliged to suffer it. It is unavoidable given the ordinary conditions of production.

There are some directors and producers—fortunately very few—who ask actors to read "cold," that is, without time to look through the entire play and to think about the role for which they are expected to indicate their fitness. The practice is stupid and shameful. To avoid the embarrassment and uncertainty involved in the routine of auditions, I have occasionally suggested that the playwright judge an unknown actor by allowing him to play a scene he has acted with satisfaction to himself and others in a previous engagement. But playwrights almost never concur: they want the lines of *their* plays read. This may be a symptom of a deficiency in their understanding of acting.

The candidate for a role reads part of a scene, a whole scene or, in some instances, several scenes. The partner for these readings is the stage manager, who usually "feeds" the actor his cues in a flat, neutral voice. What does the director gather from such readings? He checks the actor's suitability as a physical type. He may already have considered this at the initial interview, but at the reading, which ordinarily takes place in a theatre, the director is in a better position to determine the effect of the actor's presence, his voice and speech.

The actor may also reveal some aspects of his (or her) dramatic sensibility and intelligence. Still, the results are rarely conclusive. Many good actors read badly. This is sometimes due to resentment at having to read at all and sometimes to a reticence about externalizing emotions without sufficiently genuine inner motivation. There are actors (particularly those with extensive radio experience) who read with remarkable facility. During the rehearsal period they often fail to reveal much more than efficiency in reading. Due to these hazards, actors are sometimes requested to read at three or four different auditions. Some of them refuse.

When a choice has been made—the director's judgment is usually preponderant, though it may prove a mistake to "force" it on the playwright—it is the producer's responsibility to negotiate the terms of the actor's engagement. The transaction (contractual details such as billing, salary, etc.) is almost always conducted for the actor by an agent. It is one of the odd and distressing aspects of the system that actors seem to have become entirely dependent on their agents. Many agents request their actor clients not to contact producer or director without their (the agent's) previous advice and consent. The actor has been reduced to a commodity and gradually comes to regard himself in that light. There are, to be sure, agents helpful to actor and producer, but some are a plague.

Having outlined the mechanics of casting as professionally practiced, we reach the heart or the "art" of the matter. What I have said might lead one to suppose that the actor's physical type is the main consideration. It isn't and shouldn't be. Does the actor "look the part"? It is the simplest question to deal with. The director deludes himself who yields to the temptation to believe that an affirmative answer settles the matter. An actor's looks will impress an audience initially but after his first five minutes on stage it becomes aware of what he or she communicates (or fails to communicate) through *acting*. This is even true of conspicuous good looks. The pretty woman, the handsome man, will naturally please an audience at once. But if either of these creatures proves inept or dull, a damaging "backlash" ensues. As a rough working rule, it may be said that for tiny roles without special dramatic bone the correct physical type is especially desirable.

It is recorded that Edmund Kean, who was of small stature, made a great Macbeth. Still, though actors resent the emphasis on "type," there are parts in which the right physical image (along with ability) is very nearly decisive. The credibility of *Uncle Vanya,* for example, is considerably weakened if the audience does not share in both Astrov's and Voinitsky's intense appreciation of Yelena's magnetic attractiveness. On seeing a production of O'Casey's *Cock-a-Doodle-Dandy* in which feminine allure is repeatedly referred to with a mixture of eager appetite and apprehension, I was put off when the ladies presumed to personify devilish charm in no way corresponded to the description.

Before discussing the less superficial phases of the subject, it should be pointed out that the reason for the stress on physical type is due to the brief rehearsal period in our theatre and the consequent panic pressure of time. Casting for type simplifies the director's task in creating characterizations. With type casting, characterizations come "ready made." Some actors (their number is happily in decline) not only acquiesce to this routine, they promote it by the assurance that they've "played this sort of part many times."

There is more to the notion of "type" than the actor's physical attributes. "Type" may be thought of as the quality of an actor's inner disposition, his true self, which may be belied by his outward appearance. An actor I have directed was very nearly ruined because while he looked like the kind of forthright, ruggedly upstanding, dignified American whose counterpart we sometimes see in the U.S. Senate, he always disappointed the audience in such parts. He was actually a person of introverted nature.

Stanislavsky, a strikingly handsome man, confessed that he

was rarely well suited to roles of romantically successful lovers. He was most effective in "character roles"—roles in which the actor assumes the "mask" of a person markedly different from himself. Though quite personable, Paul Muni was always best in such parts: in fact, he began his career at an early age playing old men. Very few producers believed he could play anything else. To be themselves such actors must transform themselves. Meskin, a veteran of Israel's Habimah Theatre, a splendid actor who has never been known to strike a false note, is virtually incapable of portraying evil: it is a dimension wholly foreign to his nature.

There are beautiful women without sex appeal and plain ones aglow with it. Rare indeed is the actor, no matter how gifted, who can "play anything." That is why Stanislavsky in *My Life in Art* says, "The misunderstanding of one's true ability and calling in art is the strongest obstacle in the further development of an actor. It is a blind alley in which he spends dozens of years until he realizes his mistake."

A part may be viewed in many different lights. Have we not seen Iago played as a fiend, a playboy, a colorlessly blunt military man and as a "Iago from Chicago"? Is Lear a decrepit old fool, a heroic patriarch, a nice old papa cursed with nasty kids or a monster of pristine pride? Many of the so-called interpretations we read about are not interpretations at all, but accidents of talent and personality. Interpretation may be said to exist only where a deliberate choice has been made among the myriad possibilities. The individual role is one part of the entire play; where a sense of the whole play is lacking, the definition of the theatre as "a collective art in which the strongest force wins" is inescapable.

In Odets' *Golden Boy* there was a difficult choice to be made in casting the role of Joe Bonaparte. He is a musically inclined youth who also happens to be endowed with a physique and skill for boxing. He belongs to an Italian immigrant family and has developed the all-American desire to get ahead, to become "somebody." So he chooses the fighting game.

There were three members of the Group Theatre's acting company who were capable of playing the role satisfactorily (eventually all did). Odets preferred young John Garfield. But there was also Elia Kazan, strong and fiery. He had given first-rate performances in two of Odets' earlier plays: *Waiting for Lefty* and *Paradise Lost*. The most experienced actor of the three was Luther Adler, somewhat older than the others and not quite so convincingly "in the pink."

The fact that Bonaparte becomes a champion of the ring mattered less to me than that he was a yearning boy with something in him of the potential artist. There had to be in him that fluidity of emotive faculties and the peculiar vulnerability which frequently accompanies ambivalent impulses. There was an honest simplicity in Garfield that resembled callowness. His Joe Bonaparte would not have been as conscious of himself or as articulate as Odets had made him. There is a mounting hysteria in Joe due to his inability to resolve his inner dilemma, a hysteria which leads to his destruction. With Kazan, I surmised (one cannot be *certain* in these matters), Joe's suffering might reveal itself only after the situation had come to its crisis. The audience, I believed, should perceive the immanence of tragedy before its final crystallization. The boy's fate is contained in his character rather than in the logic of circumstances. Luther Adler's fluent and rich sensibility struck me as the right quality for the role. When cast he was trained to "look it" by a hard and prolonged gymnasium workout. In the same play Kazan was superb as the gangster Fuselli; Garfield unforgettable as Siggie, the lovably vulgar hackie.

A director's choice in casting is delicately nuanced and motivated by a variety of considerations. In reading Williams' *Cat on a Hot Tin Roof* one would suppose that the role of Maggie, the "Cat," demanded a strong-willed and slightly embittered personality. Kazan feared that if these were made the girl's salient characteristics, the role might become unsympathetic and her quandary a matter of indifference to the audience. He therefore chose Barbara Bel Geddes, whose natural charm would emphasize Maggie's normal American womanhood.

Because there is no absolute in these matters, there is an endless fascination in seeing the same role transfigured by different interpretations and personalities. In many of the permanent companies in Europe several actors are chosen to alternate in the same role during the play's life in the theatre's repertoire. Roles and plays are human things, not fixed or static. They must forever remain fresh and new. Above all, they must make sense within a specific context. Complete control on the director's part is impossible—is not, in fact, really desirable.

A prime factor in casting, one too often overlooked, is that the process should not concentrate solely on individual parts but on the nature of the company as a whole. One might cast a play with actors, each one individually "right," yet not acceptable in conjunction with the others. This goes beyond the obvious matching of ages, homogeneity in family relationships, the height or weight of actors who play scenes together. An excellent actor may simply not "mix" with others equally proficient. I do not refer to personal incompatibility and the ensuing temperamental clashes, but to the requirement for unity of texture which a production must possess if it is to signify more than a disparate assemblage of talents.

The unity I speak of has to do with social and cultural background, the ways in which the actors have been trained, their techniques and artistic ideals. Combining actors, even when all are qualified for their particular assignments, without their possessing something in common in all these respects may have the same disquieting effect as a real tree placed on the stage among painted ones: it becomes difficult to ascertain which causes the greater disharmony, the real or the artificial.

To sum up: Any choice in casting becomes pointless unless one has determined how each of the characters is connected with the play's spine and style. To understand that connection better we must return to the study of the script, which has continued from the first day the director has agreed to undertake his assignment.

The Director's
Work Script

HAVING READ the script six or more times and decided what
the play's main action or spine is, the director would then do
well to study the play in still another way. He should read all
the parts separately *as if he himself were going to act each of
them.* This will help him find the *spines or the chief motivat-
ing action for each character.* The character's spine must be
conceived as emerging from the play's main action. Where
such a relation is not evident or non-existent, the character
performs no function in the play. There is no basis for a true
characterization unless the character's prime motivation or
spine is found.

The chief motivation or spine for each character must be
conceived and stated from the character's own viewpoint. The
audience, usually given to moralistic judgments—favorable or
otherwise—will draw its own conclusions. Thus Iago is a vil-

lain, Lady Macbeth a fiend, Gertrude a bitch, Horatio a pure soul, Polonius a fool, James Tyrone in O'Neill's *Long Day's Journey into Night* a bad father. But the actors who play these roles must think of them in positive terms. A director might conceivably tell the actor playing the part that Iago wants "to right an injustice done him by Othello." Didn't Othello neglect to appoint him to the office he deserved! James Tyrone has contributed to the ruin of his wife and sons. He is a "stingy bastard," etc. But the spine I assigned for the actor playing the role was "to maintain the family." The fact that his efforts in this direction result in disaster is the play's drama.

Very few people who behave badly consider themselves "wicked." They justify themselves, and the director who plans their theatrical embodiment must "justify" them too. The actor who plays a villain as such (with negative intent) is usually a bad actor: obvious, stagey and often involuntarily laughable.

In speaking of these hypothetical characters I have repeatedly used the words "doing" and "action." Drama signifies action and the characters in all plays must be viewed chiefly in terms of what the fundamental pattern of their behavior is. Every character has his own spine, his own main action. And this, I repeat, is always to be considered as a function of the play's spine.

No one is constant in the nature of his behavior. The peaceful man may lash out fiercely. The ardent revolutionary will at times act mildly, the kindly teacher may take to the whip. But in every case these changes of behavior must be judged to have their origin in the character's prime motivation. It is a good rule for directors and actors to find those moments in a play where the bad guy behaves like a good guy and the decent fellow turns savage.

Not all people similarly motivated are alike. Not only may the reasons for particular types of action have different causes, but every character is marked by special traits, individual *characteristics.* Thus, two aspects of a role must be jointly considered: the basic character and its external characteristics. The fiery leader may stammer. The stammer may be a symptom of some inner disturbance, the consequence of overzealousness or an attempt at control. Or it may be a strikingly accidental trait, as is sometimes associated with Hotspur in *Henry IV.* The inner and outer characteristics constitute a *characterization.* The two aspects of the characterization, as just noted, are often but not always interrelated. Certain actors stress a character's outer features to the neglect if not altogether to the exclusion of everything else because these are most readily communicated to an audience and therefore most stagily effective. Every theatregoer recalls some performance in which an actor's peculiar accent or an idiosyncrasy of gait, facial expression, voice, costume or makeup rendered it memorable.

A more specific example in the study of character in drama is furnished by references to Odets' *Golden Boy.* The spine chosen for the play was "to win the fight of life." (Naming the spine is a personal aid to the director: in itself it has no other merit. Its importance, I repeat, is that it helps clarify the director's thinking.) The spine of *Golden Boy* is most directly applicable to the central character, Joe Bonaparte. Joe's father enacts the play's spine by encouraging what is best in his family and friends. This may be clarified by defining his spine as "to preserve the integrity of those about him." (As I have lost the original notebook I am no longer certain of how I actually designated the spines of this play.) Joe's brother-in-law Siggie's ego is sustained by the acquisition of that symbol of well-being which for him is a splendid cab of his own. His spine is "to enjoy the attributes of comfort and position due his estate." The gangster Fuselli satisfies his ego by his determination to bend everything to his own will. His spine is "to possess." The character called "Tokyo," Joe's trainer, wants to do his job well, "to work honestly."*

---

* Further examples of spines for other plays will be found in the series of Director's Notes on pp. 179–266.

Joe was outwardly characterized as somewhat adolescent in manner: his "poetic" speeches were not spoken pompously but gropingly like a kid trying to articulate what he feels but does not altogether comprehend. Soft at the core, he is fresh with youthful bluffness. His father was depicted as a lusty, smiling, immovably moral person in love with the world in its humblest aspects. Tokyo spoke softly, an intrepid worker given to few words. Fuselli had the fierce gravity, the muted power and the sleek grace of a master of men. His suave manner boded trouble. There was a faint hint of the homosexual in his masculinity.

Such notations describe the "flesh" overlaying the spines; they are "colors" immanent in what the dramatist has written. The descriptions and explanations for these "colors" in the director's notebook may cover pages. I try to imagine what a character's life story—early environment, childhood experiences, etc.—has been before we encounter him in the play. Joe Bonaparte, Odets tells us, is cross-eyed, a trait to which I paid no attention because besides being precariously "comic," it was something the audience would be unable to see unless made grotesque. But Joe may have suffered being called a "sissy" because as a boy he carried a violin in a neighborhood where other boys sported baseball bats. Fuselli, another "wop," also found the going tough till he learned the trick of terrorizing people.

The more detailed the background the director imagines for the play's characters, the richer the performances become —with good actors! The antecedent life histories are only helpful to the actor if they lead him to kindred material wrought from his own imagination. The director's intentions, howsoever interesting, may leave the actor untouched. In either case, what is imagined should stem from certain elements in the playwright's script. "My" characterizations derive from three sources—the script, the actor's imagination, my own nature.

The characters' spines had best be stated as *active verbs*. The spine is an active response to a wish: the characters *want* something and *do* something to satisfy that wish. They are often impeded in that satisfaction; sometimes they succeed in satisfying it or are deflected from it by either more pressing desires or a realization of the vanity of what they had previously wanted. The simultaneous wishes, aims and actions of all the characters cause the conflicts which create the play's argument.

For a production at one of the Moscow Art Theatre's studios, Michael Chekhov who, if I remember correctly, directed it, chose "to play with life" as the spine for *Twelfth Night*. This also suggests the *style* of that production. The director's next step, in that instance, was to specify in what way each of the play's characters plays with life. It certainly cannot be the same for Malvolio as for Sir Toby.

To repeat an already cited example*: My spine for *Desire Under the Elms* was "to possess the Farm." The "Farm" in that play is the actual object over which the characters struggle, but it is also the symbol of the land, the country. The play's theme might be translated metaphorically as "Who or what force shall possess America?" How and by whom is the struggle waged? Each of the play's characters wants to gain possession of the farm in his or her own way. Those who despair of ever owning it—the two elder brothers—go west to gain a similar benefit: gold.

Not all directors, again I repeat, commit their thoughts to a notebook, or not to the extent that I do or to the much greater extent that Max Reinhardt did. But nearly all directors think and plan in a similar fashion though they may not use the specific terms I employ. Many work largely by "instinct." The *formal structure* which my interpretation of a play takes *is a personal guideline and not something to be spelled out, read to the actors or literally insisted upon at rehearsal.*

The notation of the play's spine and characterizations pre-

---

* Repetitions are unavoidable and necessary in this essay because its various elements overlap, each being integral with the other.

cedes the drawing up of the director's "score." When rehearsals begin, the director has already digested all that he has thought or written about in his preliminary work with the script. He may not even refer to it again, till perhaps after the production has opened. In a state of puzzlement as to the drift of a production, I have at times looked back to my notes to remind myself of my original intention. On reading my published notes for Miller's *Incident at Vichy** after the play had closed, Joseph Wiseman remarked, "You know, Harold, about eighty percent of what you had in mind was actually accomplished." Regardless of whether this estimate was true or not, I was immensely pleased. I am relatively content when only half of my production idea is realized.

From the director's notes to the stage there is a long, long road. The production may prove inferior or superior to that which has been adumbrated beforehand. The plan and the execution are of an altogether different nature. They are in different "languages." The production is composed of real bodies and concrete materials, not of verbal and intellectual imponderables. I cannot too often repeat that the director's work is not a solo performance: it is a graph for and, at best, an inspiration to his collaborators—the acting company and all the other members of the production staff.

Theatre is not an accumulation of ingredients: it is a composite organism greater or lesser than its several components. That is what makes the discernment of how it has been wrought a most difficult if not a wholly impossible undertaking. But in this we approach the area of theatre criticism, about which comment must wait for a later chapter.

The search for and the conclusions as to the nomenclature and composition of the play's various spines, style, theme, "philosophy," relevance, its atmosphere and mood, the social and historical background from which it springs, the imagined biographies of the characters antecedent to the play's

* The *Incident at Vichy* notes will be found on p. 242.

events—all these are still only the first steps toward the director's "score." The foregoing procedures are indispensable;
they are not the thing itself.

The director's working script is his score. It follows the play
scene by scene, line by line. I arrange it in the following way:
I insert a blank sheet of paper facing each of the pages in the
play's text. I divide the clean sheet into three more or less
equal columns.*

The first and most important column notes the particular
action of the moment. It states what each character—in silence
or through speech—is doing, or, more precisely, what he wants
or intends to do. These actions, too, are always designated by
active verbs: to warn, to plead, to threaten, to reprove, to
punish, to heal, to flatter and so on as the case may be.

The prescription to use an active verb for each specific
action may appear arbitrary and didactic. But it is, if not
mandatory, extremely helpful. It avoids such generalizations
as "getting angry," "being modest," "feeling hurt": these
tend to encourage histrionic clichés. Stanislavsky described
the first step in embodying love on the stage as "to pay attention," and at a later point of its emotional development as
"to take care of" or "to care for"—actions. He decried the use
of phrases which describe behavior in terms of abstract sentiment: to love, to hate, to be kind, etc.

When Ophelia, for example, is coarsely teased by Hamlet
at the play which is to catch the conscience of the King, she
is not simply to act "wounded"; rather she protects her dignity, that is, she does something definite, acts in some positive
fashion.

This leads to the second column of the director's notations
in which he sets down the manner in which the basic action
is to be carried out. The first column states what is to be done,
the second how it is to be done. Actors speak of the instructions given in the second column as adjustments. To use the
previous example, we may then say Ophelia "protects her

* Examples of this arrangement of the script are to be found on pp. 269-289.

dignity" with such adjustments as "in a pained voice" or "in sad reproof" or in whatever given manner befits the character and the scene. If Ophelia, as some directors have audaciously conceived her, is not the pure creature we ordinarily take her to be but a girl corrupted by the hypocrisy of the court, her action might be "to counter the thrust" (in the first column) and (in the second column) "provocatively" or "flirtatiously."

Continuing with the same scene, let us suppose the director sees Ophelia slapping Hamlet's possibly searching hand, the slap would be noted in the third column. This is the column in which the director indicates the *overt physical activity* which manifests both Ophelia's action and adjustment. Hamlet's use of his hand in speaking of "country matters" would also be inscribed in the column devoted to activities.

To reiterate in strict order: the three columns are (1) the basic *action,* (2) the attitude or *adjustment* which colors the aforesaid action in the circumstances of the scene and (3) the *overt physical activity* which accompanies the action.

I speak of an activity accompanying an action rather than extending or completing it because there are activities which are not organically related to the action. Thus Bessie (the mother) in *Awake and Sing* while chiding her husband and correcting her children's behavior (actions) is setting the table, which may be said to relate to her spine ("to take care of everything") but not directly to the action of chiding her husband or correcting her children.

In the same play Ralphie, Bessie's son, *sings the praises* of his girl friend's charms ("She's like French words"), which is his action, while at the same time putting on a new pair of trousers. This last is an activity but hardly a direct consequence of his action, though he is preparing to visit the girl. The juxtaposition of the boy's lines and the activity given him are not simultaneous in the script.

When, however, Moe Axelrod in *Awake and Sing,* the petty racketeer who boards with the Bergers, learns that Hennie Berger, with whom he has had an affair, is to marry another man, his casual reply has the action "to hide his feelings," while he bites into a thick slice of cake he has bought for the family. The biting of the cake at that moment is the activity he resorts to to appear casual and to hide his feelings.

There is a scene in Odets' *Paradise Lost* in which a young violinist comes to end his relationship with the girl he had hoped to marry. He must explain that he is too poor for matrimony. As he enters, she waits for him anxiously at the far end of the room. He approaches her hesitantly. The action might simply come under the heading "to greet" with an adjustment of tension. They both wear glasses, a minor touch in their characterizations. When the young man comes face to face with the girl he removes his glasses, she removes hers—and they kiss. These activities (or bits of business) were not part of the original script; they were the director's invention.

Actions are not always obvious in the author's writing. They occasionally seem to contradict the dialogue's surface connotations. In the park scene of *Golden Boy*—often used for film tests and by students for class exercise—many of the lines suggest a tender love scene. But the girl, who has been sent by her lover, the boy's would-be manager, to persuade Joe to take up professional fighting, studies Joe *to discover* how best to carry out her objective. Joe, self-absorbed and dimly aware of her purpose (these are his adjustments), pays little attention at first, then begins *to probe* into her character and attitude toward her lover (this is his action) in an aggressive manner—a further adjustment. The scene as a whole, with short lapses in which Joe muses aloud about what music means to him as well as about the high-powered motor cars (further actions), has something in the nature of a conflict about it. The scene ends with Joe brashly proclaiming (action—to decide or resolve) that he'll enter the fighting game.

It was, I believe, the Russian director Vakhtangov who suggested that every scene be given a name or a descriptive tag to provide keynotes as an aid to director and actors in finding the right actions and adjustments. I have occasionally taken advantage of this "pointer," calling one scene "The Trap," another "The Showdown," still another "Release." This is especially valuable when the descriptive titles do not superficially appear to correspond to the actions indicated by the lines alone but reveal the scene's true character.

A production I directed in 1949 with the Habimah company of Israel, Emmanuel Roblès' *Montserrat* (a translation of the original text, not the Lillian Hellman adaptation), ends with a duologue between two officers of the Spanish army, which has been sent to South America to suppress Bolívar's struggle for independence. One of the officers is an embittered authoritarian, contemptuous of "the people," the other an idealistic humanist. The scene read like a debate. To preserve the intellectual mode of the writing would not only have crippled the play's climax but would have struck the audience as wearisomely wordy. This was the only scene written by Lillian Hellman which I filched from her version (a scene, incidentally, that she cut in her production of the play). In my script I called the scene "The Last Battle" and directed it as if each of its speeches was a fierce blow. It proved a great audience success.

The quizzing of a murder suspect in a film I directed, a whodunit called *Deadline at Dawn* (RKO, 1945), contained little more than a series of questions. I called it "The Seduction," an attempt *to woo* the suspect into an admission of guilt.

A scene running to several pages of text may be comprised of only one or two basic actions. An action doesn't change with every spoken line, although the adjustments may do so, diminishing or gathering intensity as the scene progresses. An action changes when it is fully carried out, in which case another action ensues, or when it is interrupted by the unexpected entrance of another character, the ringing of a telephone or the intrusion of an unexpected event, or simply when a character changes his mind.

In *Death of a Salesman* Willy Loman comes to see his boss

to request a less tiring job. He is hesitant and circuitous in his effort to explain his situation but his action is interrupted by the boss's tactics aimed to deflect Willy from what he guesses is Willy's intention. These tactics are an action. The action continues till Willy's outburst, which then turns into the action "to protest" or "to denounce." The scene would be impossible to play if Willy and his boss were obliged to change their actions with every line they speak. Each of these characters has only two or three actions in this relatively long scene. It should also be noted that every scene or *unit* (sometimes called a "beat") of a scene has its own climax.

The great Russian director Meyerhold had something else in view when he declared "Words in the theatre are only a design on the canvas of motion," but his dictum may be applied here. Writing is not the theatre's last word! Stage business is born of free association on the part of the director and/or actors from the premises of the script's basic actions.

It is certainly no recent discovery that theatre may be expressive without the use of any verbal text, though today some folks talk as if it were. The point impressed me in a special way when Ray Bolger remarked that he didn't dance with his legs and feet alone. The dance he was referring to was the moment in the musical *Where's Charley?* which, he explained, sprang from Charley's dilemma: how to get away from the girls' embraces so that they wouldn't discover his real identity while he was posing as their aunt. The answer led not to words but to twists, leaps and a delightfully complex choreographic routine, in itself a whole scene.

The fanciful antics of Peter Brook's *Midsummer Night's Dream* are suggested by Shakespeare's text, "A man is but an ass, if he go about to expound this dream . . . And those things do best please me that befall preposterously," lines which offer a clue to the extravagance of the whole production. When Brook placed ladders on both sides of the stage on which characters ascend to a rostrum above the stage or descend from it, he was doing what the goblin Puck says of himself, that he is constantly going "Up and down, up and down. I will lead them up and down—."

The third column of my working script, the activities column, is usually left blank before rehearsal. There are, however, certain "high moments" which I do prepare and note in the script in advance of rehearsal. After the production has opened, the stage manager, as my assistant, writes down all the business which the actors and I have devised together. There are directors who invent all or most of the business beforehand. I do the greatest part of this during rehearsals. There is no particular value judgment attached to either practice. It is a question of the director's disposition, the kinds of gifts he has, how he "operates."

The removal of the eyeglasses preceding the kiss in *Paradise Lost* occurred to me in the preparation of my script. When directing the end of the second act of *Uncle Vanya* in which Yelena eagerly anticipates playing the piano, I staged the scene as follows: She sits down at the keyboard, opens the piano; Sonya enters and tells Yelena that her father (Yelena's husband) in the next room objects to her playing. Yelena quietly closes the lid and looks up helplessly at Sonya. This, too, was planned before rehearsal.

Some such notations of business—such details as setting the actors' positions, moments where actors are to cross from one point of the stage to another, where they are to sit or rise, in other words, the whole job of blocking—may be found in my working script, but not many. I find that observing the actors in rehearsal suggests more elaborations or expansions of action than I am able to foresee with nothing but the script and the model of the setting before me.

Notations on lighting, tempo, offstage sound and music are also set down in the third (activities) column. These all concern the production's physical life.

In the last phase of his career Stanislavsky—of whose teachings and their influence I shall say more further on—

spoke of actions chiefly in terms of *physical problems.* This has been called the technique of physical action. Such actions as "to protect," "to flirt," and the like provoke physical impulses. Even a man sitting in a chair preoccupied by an unexpressed thought manifests minute "unconscious" physical activities: we detect them in his eyes, his breathing, his half-realized or suppressed desire to rise and changes of position of the head or body as he sits apparently "doing nothing" but thinking. The action, set down in the first column of the working script, may be translated into such problematic questions for the actor as "How will you prevent this or that person from approaching you?", "How can you get rid of that fool?", "What can you do to convince this man?" and so forth.

The disputes over such refined distinctions as to the best procedure in this matter so passionately engaged in by teachers and theoreticians may be of interest and importance but they are not vital to my present exposition. There are more ways of dealing with actors at rehearsal than have been dreamed of by readers of Stanislavsky's or anyone else's discourses. Stanislavsky himself said so.

At least four to six weeks have passed in the preliminary work I have described. The director has made himself ready for the first rehearsal. Let's get to it.

CHAPTER 8

Early Rehearsals

WHEN THE ACTORS are called for the first rehearsal, the director has, as we have learned, already done a considerable part of his work; the actors are only now beginning theirs. The director and playwright must bear this in mind. To overlook it will obstruct progress.

After greeting the actors and introducing them to one another, I ask the designer to explain the model of the setting. It becomes more meaningful and the actors' interest in it increases after the play has been read several times.

The actors have all read the script privately. Now for the first time they are to read it together. With permanent companies the actors become acquainted with the script through a reading by the playwright or the director, depending on which of the two is the better reader.

If the director and playwright have agreed on textual cuts

made at their early conferences, it is advisable that the actors take note of them before they begin their first reading. On this occasion it is preferable that they read from complete scripts rather than from individual part books or "sides." It troubles actors to cut lines which they have already committed to memory. There will be more cutting required at later stages of the work; in fact, there is almost always more cutting to be done than one suspects. The earlier the cuts are made, the better for all concerned.

Faced for the first time by the director, the playwright and the producer, the actors tend to suppress too overt an expression—of anything! They are "hiding." English actors at first readings are bolder and more fluent than Americans. This is due in some measure to the English actors' "professionalism"—which simply should be taken to mean more practice in the profession. Their facility is also due to the greater emphasis on speech and voice in their training.

Early in my career I used to instruct the actors on these occasions to *talk* the lines of the play to one another and to make themselves heard by the company around them. Speaking the lines as conversation, I explained, is the first step toward truth in acting. Whatever validity there may be in this explanation, what I really intended was to allay nervousness, to let the actors know that they were not required to impress anyone. (According to Equity regulations an actor not signed to a run-of-the-play contract may be dismissed on the fifth day of rehearsal.) But I soon learned that there was little point in giving the actors at the first readings any instructions whatsoever. They should be allowed to read in any way they will and should not be interrupted unless they become inaudible or strain to produce an effect. It is a routine joke with me to say, "If any of you are great right away, I shall have to fire you: it will leave me with nothing to do!" A well-chosen company—and I always assume complete confidence in the players I have cast—requires no special admonition.

Ten-minute breaks are taken after the reading of each act. The play of average length is read for the first time in little more than two and a half hours. We then retire for lunch which, according to the Equity contract, is to be not less than an hour and a half in duration. Since the tension of the first reading is tiring, I allow for a longer lunch (or rest) period. The company, I trust, will be comparatively relaxed when called back for the afternoon reading.

The time allowed for the entire rehearsal process differs with various companies. In certain European theatres a play may be rehearsed for twelve weeks or much longer. The actors in these theatres usually appear in other plays of their repertoire during this time. Rehearsals at such theatres rarely run more than five hours a day. I consider this the ideal length of time for daily rehearsals. Peter Brook rehearsed his *Midsummer Night's Dream* for eight weeks.

In our professional productions we allow four weeks of rehearsal for a "straight" play, five weeks for a musical. Equity demands that rehearsal time be limited to seven out of eight and a half hours daily. This may be extended to ten out of twelve hours during the week before the first public performance. The day prior to the opening night the rehearsal time is unlimited—always provided that twelve hours elapse between rehearsal calls.

If the producer chooses to prolong rehearsals beyond four weeks he may do so if he pays the actors full salaries or not less than the Equity minimum. But this can only be done if the actors have agreed to such an arrangement. Due to the present high cost of production, extension of the rehearsal period, without the support of paid performances, may prove exorbitant.

Even the four-week rehearsal period is not as much time as it appears to be. The first three weeks are computed on the basis of a six-day week. These first three weeks of seven rehearsal hours daily, conducted on a bare stage or whatever space has been procured for the purpose, must allow for cos-

tume fittings and the like. The next three or four days are
devoted to dress rehearsals on the sets, in costume and
makeup, with lights, etc. These are held in preparation for
either an out-of-town ("road") tryout or previews in town.
The previews or road tryouts are paid public performances.
During this time only four hours a day (except for the usual
two matinee days) are allowed for rehearsal.

It is necessary to keep this information in mind to understand some of the problems in craft and personal "psychology" which arise due to the pressures of time. The Group
Theatre's first production, Paul Green's *House of Connelly,*
was rehearsed for approximately twelve weeks, its second
play, *1931,* was rehearsed for eight weeks, and Sidney Kingsley's *Men in White* for ten weeks. All three plays were directed by Lee Strasberg. Because of altered circumstances I
was only permitted the regulation four weeks for all my
productions except for Odets' *Paradise Lost* (six weeks), the
same author's *Golden Boy* (five weeks) and, more recently,
O'Neill's *A Touch of the Poet* (five weeks).

The scheduling of my productions in regard to time is, as I
have said, typical of the commercial theatre. I have never been
obliged to postpone an announced opening. I should, nevertheless, quote a remark an actor who appeared in one of my
productions once made: "Harold rehearses a play as if there
were never going to be an opening night!" This says something about my "method": I refuse to create a sense of haste.
But for any but the most rudimentary script, four weeks of
rehearsals are insufficient. Apropos of this, I cannot refrain
from citing a Stanislavsky quip: "No matter how long one
rehearses one always needs two more weeks."

At the second reading of the play the actors may read
even less securely than at the first. It does not matter. They
are getting acquainted with the play and a little more accustomed to each other's voices and faces. They may even listen
better.

During both of the first day's readings, as already noted, I offer no advice. I make no comment; I listen and observe. I study the material: the script as read and the nature of the readers. My routine joke at the end of the day—by which time, to the actors' astonishment, I have hardly uttered a word—is to say, "You must admit that the direction today has been perfect." It is true! The director should shut up and allow actors and script to "merge" without interference.

This "treatment" is repeated on the morning of the second day. The actors even then may not read any more convincingly than on the first day, but they are more capable of listening to one another. They are now eager for word from the director. This, in my case, usually follows after lunch on the second day, that is, after the third reading. The actors are now sufficiently familiar with the script to gain something from a discussion of it.

Many directors and actors consider general discussion of a script superogatory. They want "to get to work" right away. This is particularly true of English actors; they wish to "get on their feet," that is, proceed to the staging immediately after the first or second reading. But I am speaking here of my customary practice. I have on occasion yielded to the habitual inclination of such an actor as, for instance, Ralph Richardson, who is somewhat discomfited by any talk which doesn't directly lead to blocking—the assignment of stage positions, crosses from one place to another, etc. Dogmatism in the theatre is debilitating.

My first talk deals with the character of the play we are producing, its general import, its relevance to the world we live in. In speaking of the "world" I include the actors themselves as part of that world. With a foreign play or an old play (out of a past epoch or such a play as Shaw's *Saint Joan*) I discuss its national and/or historical background. Apropos of Williams' *Orpheus Descending* I spoke about the South, which I had visited, read about and learned about from what

Williams had told me. For Miller's *Incident at Vichy* I read accounts of the Nazi occupation of France and made inquiries in Vichy itself, and I spoke about my findings.

My remarks may be sociological, psychological, "poetic." I avoid the dry sound of scholarship. The purpose of the talk is to arouse a feeling of the worthiness of our project, to create enthusiasm. The first rehearsals are the honeymoon period in our love affair with the play. The world of the theatre is the whole world, and nothing human is alien to it. No one need blush to approach production in this manner. Experience has taught me that the stimulation of these early exchanges bears fruit in the performance. They contribute to its "aura," without which it often remains arid, lacking in glamor.

I speak, too, of the play's style, the dramatist's individual touch, his habit of mind, his rhythm, the kind of acting his play demands. I illustrate this by references to the character of the writing, the play's structure. In the early years of my career I also spent considerable time analyzing each of the play's characters. This was not done with diagrammatic rigor. There was little specific mention of spines or main actions. I do not employ terms which may be meaningful only to me. The intention is to stir the actor according to his individual nature.

In speaking to actors about their parts some directors think it best to talk to each of them privately. This may be advisable at a later stage of rehearsal. But when describing the play's general lineaments and how the various parts constitute the play's general design, I prefer to address the company with everyone present. It enhances a sense of the collective character of the undertaking, for each part affects the other.

These first talks are a banquet of ideas: each actor can pick what he chooses from the fare. Authors and actors usually enjoy them and participate in them at my invitation. But they used to go on too long; there was too much to digest.

Some of the actors would note the gist of what I said, especially as it impinged on their own parts. I encouraged but did not insist on this. In productions subsequent to 1949 I have reserved many of my insights for those moments during the reading or the playing of scenes or whole acts when they might imprint themselves more firmly in the actors' consciousness. Nowadays my first "address" to the actors lasts little more than an hour.

We then proceed to readings with "interruptions." After a passage or a scene has been read I explain in what way my previous generalizations apply to what has just been read. These interruptions, which admittedly have often been too protracted, continue through the reading of the whole play. The actors begin to see the play and their parts in sharper perspective.

Something else I attempt to accomplish during this formative stage of work is to trace the progress of the play's inner action: how each segment and scene reveals the development of the characters' and the play's continuing action so that the pattern of the play as a whole becomes evident.

When one or more of these "interrupted" readings have been completed, the company reads the play once again without interruption. A certain experience of the play is achieved in this way. The actors are now prepared to "get on their feet" and "walk" the play. Through the readings the actors have acquired a solid *theoretical* knowledge of the play, though actually it is now something more than that.

Formerly I used to conduct the early rehearsals in the manner just described for a whole week. Later, due to an ever tighter rehearsal schedule, I reduced the period to three or four days. With *Golden Boy,* when a five-week rehearsal time was made available to me, the readings continued for two weeks! But they were, as we shall see, something more than simple readings.

Some directors, particularly in England, expect the actors to commit their parts to memory before rehearsals have begun. This may be necessitated by the fact that in the English theatre blocking commences on the first or second day of rehearsals. One director I know calls for a complete run-through of the play (with ad-libbed blocking) on the third or fourth day of rehearsal.

Though there may be nothing inescapably disastrous in such practices, I have never engaged in them, nor have any of the other directors whose first important productions were presented under the Group Theatre's auspices (Lee Strasberg, Elia Kazan, Robert Lewis) done so. We virtually forbade our actors to learn their lines prior to rehearsals. On the other hand, it is probably desirable for actors to do this in the case of plays by Shakespeare and other verse plays. But none of the directors just mentioned have directed these kinds of plays. We believed, and I am still inclined to believe, that actors learning the text by heart apart from actual work at rehearsal fixes preconceptions and hardens readings into set molds so that receptivity to their fellow players' impulses is impaired. The actors, under these circumstances, hardly listen to one another, and something mechanical in the acting results.

The actor must always remain resilient, be free and open to change and new adjustments. This becomes much more difficult to do if he has learned his lines before contact with other members of the company. He will abstract himself from the all-important human context, the "team." Still, I know that some actors who have memorized their parts before rehearsal manage to remain responsive to all the contingencies of production. In this as in other theatrical matters there is no "absolute."

The first rehearsals permit the director to learn something about the kind of direction which best befits each of the actors. He studies the actors' strong points and weaknesses. Some virtually demand direction; others are disturbed by too much talk even when it is good talk. Many like to discover everything—except for technical matters—by themselves. Talk, they feel, interferes with their creative process, their pleasure in discovery. They are often right, and their inclinations should be respected. I have known actors who were reluctant to do certain admittedly interesting bits of business because the director was the first to suggest it!

Not everything the cleverest director suggests is useful to the actor; the wise director recognizes this. Direction is not to be equated with giving orders. The teacher-student relationship is to be eschewed. I have occasionally been reproached for and indeed found myself guilty of doing too much for the actors or *saying* too much to them. I have had to learn to repress my natural volubility. Some actors—particularly Americans—may be equally disturbed by the mute director, one who too strictly keeps his council. Actors want help; they want to be worked with. This has recently become so marked a tendency that my hope is that the actor will take the initiative and strike out on his own. It is a matter of pride with the director to be able to inspire the actor; it would be a greater joy if the actor was able to inspire him.

On the other hand, the type of director actors call "traffic cops," those who confine their direction to the externals of the craft with here and there an "editorial" comment, must be deplored. A veteran English actor in the cast of *Tiger at the Gates* said to me, "You are the first director who has actually *directed* me since Granville-Barker." Many English directors, the actor went on to explain, believe their function to consist of little more than the arrangement of the physical elements of the production—blocking, grouping and the like. The actor is supposed to provide the rest by virtue of his talent. Such a division of duties is unsound.

I remember an occasion when a seasoned actor stopped me on my offering a suggestion about some seemingly small point at one of the early rehearsals. "You needn't tell me that," he admonished, "I know my business." I insisted no further. I decided to say nothing more to him for several days. Following a short passage of time the actor came up to me during a lunch break and complained, "You are directing everybody else; have you nothing to tell *me?*" He was ready to be directed.

Direction and acting compose themselves into a reciprocal exchange, a two-way relationship, a kind of marriage. The most important thing that should result from the initial work period is an understanding between actor and director; each learns how to put up with and deal with the other. This becomes increasingly vital in the subsequent stages of rehearsal.

CHAPTER 9

More Rehearsals

THE READING REHEARSALS of *Golden Boy* went on for two weeks. They did not, however, consist of daily repetition of the same thing. Every step in production entails another. As actors were wooed, prodded or inspired by the director, they became ever more imbued with the sense of themselves as characters in the play and with the play itself. They were possessed by it. During the second week, although they were still "only reading," they sprang to their feet and with "book" still in hand, accosted one another, pleading or threatening, warning or soothing, teasing or provoking—in other words, *acting*. Drama was already present. Very little time—approximately five days—was required to block the entire play.

The moral of this incident suggests a rule for rehearsal: **Do not move on to a second stage of work until the first has been**

satisfactorily completed. The first thing well done will naturally develop into the next. To work for everything at once—
immediately to achieve "tempo," for instance—while the actors are still seeking to make their actions true will induce
falsity.

One should not demand "pace" in the early readings. Perhaps, as I shall later explain, one should not insist on it at all:
it is a consequence, not a cause. Some of the best actors are
inordinately "slow" at the outset of rehearsals. It is a foolish
director who from the first whips his company with the command "faster, faster."

Before further pursuing this exposition I must pause to
remind the reader that there is an entirely different rehearsal
procedure which may be followed. There are in fact several.
But I shall confine myself to the mention of one which to
some slight extent I undertook, as, to a greater degree, Lee
Strasberg did, in the early Group Theatre years. It is the
method of improvisation, a method which calls for more time
than is ordinarily available to us at present.

There are at least two different types of improvisation. Before describing either of them it should be immediately stated
that improvisation does not signify "doing anything you want
to do." Improvisations should always be based on a plan or a
"scenario" the director has outlined, a goal or an objective he
seeks. What is left to improvisation is the path by which the
projected end is reached.

After the play has been read and its general dramatic line
has been established, the director, instead of going on to the
blocking of the scenes, asks the actors to improvise in either of
two ways and, at times, in a combination of both.

The first type of improvisation consists of positing imaginary situations which parallel the mood or action content of
a scene which occurs in the play. For example, one asks the
actors in *Awake and Sing* to improvise a typical dinner at the
Berger apartment. The improvisation will undoubtedly last
longer than the analogous scene in the play. It is important to

give such an improvisation a special dramatic "twist" by telling one of the actors—without notifying the others—of some disturbing occurrence during the day which affects the other members of the family and of which they had been unaware.

Through such an improvisation the actors learn something of the characters' customary behavior, their interrelation, their essential traits, their possible reactions in moments of surprise or consternation. The director then comments on the degree to which the actors have understood the nature of the character which they are to play.

An improvisation may involve a single character alone. In *Awake and Sing* I asked Morris Carnovsky, who played the grandfather, to sew the torn visor of his cap—a real, not an imaginary cap—and recount to his grandson some hitherto unrevealed episode of his life, something which might serve as a cautionary tale for the boy. Carnovsky profited more from this little improvisation than from anything I might have said by way of description or explanation of the old man's nature. The sewing of the cap was later used as a minor stroke of characterization in the performance.

A more elaborate improvisation emerged as one of the most impressive scenes of Sidney Kingsley's *Men in White*. A young woman is due to undergo surgery. Lee Strasberg thought the actors playing the surgeons and their assistants ought to witness an operation at a hospital. He then asked them to repeat what they had observed. The play script itself called for no more than a short scene preceding the operation, after which the curtain fell. The actors' improvisation or recreation of the operation procedure, the washing-up routine, the pulling on of surgical gloves, the handling of the instruments, was so awe-inspiring that it was incorporated in the production and lent it something close to grandeur.

Certain improvisations have only a peripheral relationship to the play. One of my first attempts at directing a play (it was never produced) dealt with the Russian Revolution. I felt the need to arouse in the actors some of the tensions of such a crisis. The improvisation took place on a quiet country road. I asked the actors to move in march formation carrying banners with insurrectionary slogans. Without warning the marchers, I instructed another group of actors to come out of hiding and assail them as the repressive military might do.

For the same play, and for similar reasons, I had the players enact a "scene" following an explosion in a coal mine with the miners' relatives gathered around the pit to learn the men's fate.

Such improvisations are of doubtful value, because to be at all truthful they might require as much rehearsal as would the doing of an original play. I mention them not only to indicate their limits but to move on to the second and more practical type of improvisation which Stanislavsky has described and which Lee Strasberg made use of with signal success on several occasions.

The play is done scene by scene following the basic situation and circumstances in each of them. To avoid the possibility of staleness through repetition the director adds ever new adjustments and circumstances designed to arouse new perceptions and responses within each situation. But the line of action remains identical with that of the play's text.

At a run-through of *Men in White*, after five weeks of rehearsal, the whole play was acted with hardly a word of the author's dialogue spoken. The words were almost all the actors'. But the play was essentially there. Sidney Kingsley was appalled at first, and then impressed.

Such improvisations necessitate true connection among the actors. It obliges them to listen: they cannot set their reactions mechanically. They cannot take the other characters' movements and manner of address for granted. The give and take among them is spontaneous, fresh, alive.*

The physical line of action under certain given circum-

* I am not at all sure that this type of improvisation can be employed to advantage in producing Shakespeare.

stances to which the director adds nuances and variations is the major substance of a staged play. Playwrights themselves recognize this principle. An anecdote I once heard is worth telling in this connection. The story has it that one day Racine entered his salon where guests were awaiting him. When asked what prompted his apparent elation, he replied, "I have just finished my new play: all I have to do now is to write the dialogue."

I shall have more to say later on about the approach to acting and directing just outlined. What must be immediately stressed, however, is this: there is and should always be a degree of improvisation in the making of a production no matter how traditional the rehearsal methods. If such a margin of freedom were not allowed, the theatre would be reduced to the mere recitation of lines in conjunction with the most primitive sort of illustration. And that, no matter how elegant, precise and intelligent the reading or the illustration, would hardly constitute theatre.

After whatever number of readings the director deems sufficient or has the time for, the actors "get on their feet": blocking begins. The stage manager and his assistants trace the ground plan of the settings, in accordance with the scene designer's working drawings, with tape, chalk or paint on the floor indicating where the entrances are to be made, where steps and platforms are to be placed, etc. In addition they "rustle up" benches, chairs, tables, couches, wherever they are able to find them. The same is true of such properties as dishes, cutlery, playing cards, firearms, swords and what not.

I refer to professional American productions where no permanent technical staff—carpenters, electricians, property men —is employed. In these respects, much of our professional theatre is miserably amateurish. In the run-of-the-mill setup under which most of my colleagues and I work, the use of adequate props, furniture, even such utensils as glasses, plates, forks and knives, entails payment of regular wages to stagehands at the union scale—a costly and more often than not a prohibitive item. Paper cups, knives, forks and all sorts of paltry substitutes take the place of what is actually needed. Couches and wooden benches which only approximate the dimensions specified by the designer as required for accurate staging are all the actors may work with. This is also true of armchairs, beds and the rest.

Such arrangements are extremely discouraging as well as inefficient. Imagine a love scene in which the actors are so constricted that every emphatic gesture they make puts them in peril of falling off their seats! The inadequacy of the furniture and most of the hand props leads to a waste of time in a specifically technical sense. One does not handle a paper goblet as one does silver, a stick is not wielded as a sword, slices of beef tongue are not cut, chewed and swallowed in the same way as fine meats. In all such instances timing of lines which accompany the various activities becomes mere guesswork. At the dress rehearsals when the proper paraphernalia is brought in, the matter of coordinating dialogue and business has to be rehearsed anew.

There is a comic side to all this: the actors who after a few days manage to achieve some ease in the use of the crude props provided at first become embarrassed at dress rehearsals when these objects have been replaced by the "real things."

Where the rehearsals occur on the stage of a theatre the lighting consists of a thousand-watt electric fixture which barely gives sufficient illumination to read by. The actors are immersed in a dismal atmosphere. If more light is demanded, it is made available—at a price, the price of an electrician's wage.

The director usually knows where he wants each of the actors to be discovered for the opening scene. The placement is often indicated in the script, though this, too, is subject to drastic change. Blocking in its barest outlines is not as complex a task as the inexperienced director may suppose; it is dictated in large measure by the designer's floor plan: doors,

furniture, essential props have been set accordingly. Much of
the placement may be altered when necessitated by previously
unforeseen business and movement. But such alterations, as
mentioned earlier, are not always feasible. That is why, whenever possible, director and designer are well advised to wait
on the progress of rehearsal before making the contours and
detail of the settings definitive. But occasions for such a procedure are extremely rare.

Manuals exist which lay down ground rules for blocking a
play. They instruct the director not to have several actors
stand in a straight line parallel to the "footlights," not to
have an actor walk on a "laugh line," even what foot it is
best for him to put forward on making an entrance! Certain
areas of the stage, according to these textbooks, are most desirable for the playing of love scenes, others for scenes of violence; crucial speeches should be read from stage center,
etc., etc. A director, highly regarded in his day and under
whose direction I acted in my nonage, always avoided having
scenes played at the center of the stage because he thought it
was "old-fashioned." It was the only technical rule he seemed
aware of and about which he was dogmatic! It should go
without saying that most such rule-of-thumb prescriptions are
absurd.

The audience's attention must be directed to the focal
point of interest in every scene. There are a number of means
by which this may be accomplished: gradations in the intensity of lighting is the most obvious. But there can be no strict
rules for blocking. Even "stage center" is not a fixed position:
all depends on the design of the floor plan—and the theatre's
architecture. In side seats of certain arena theatres, stage
center is at a considerable distance from the spectators. What
is most decisive in blocking is maintaining flow and variety of
movement. A fixed position within a limited area produces
visual monotony and decreases the audience's power of attention. All visible stage space should be used in the course
of an evening. Incessant movement, however, distracts.

It is my practice to remove virtually every property or piece of furniture which has no function in the play's action. During the early blocking session I sit on or very close to the stage. I move further back from it with the progress of rehearsals. The director ought to check his blocking from all parts of the house, although it is vain to hope for wholly propitious sight lines and grace of composition from every point.

Famous paintings and the manner of their creators often serve to inspire various directors in their stage pictures. Meyerhold spoke of finding the colors for his production of *La Dame aux Camélias* in Manet and Renoir. There was something of Brueghel in Peter Brook's staging of *The Visit*. Rembrandt's lighting is a frequent model. For study of dramatic movement, Gordon Craig recommended Giotto, Masiliano and Michelangelo; for facial expression and costume, Fra Angelico, Franz Hals, Teniers, Hogarth and Rembrandt; for Shakespeare, Carpaccio. But conscious "borrowings" of this kind, though legitimate, are alien to my habit.

As previously stated, some directors plan their blocking in advance of rehearsals. They map out every cross, change of position, move upstage (away from the audience in a proscenium theatre), downstage (toward curtain line). This may save time. Stanislavsky said he worked this way as a beginner. He gave it up later.

I concern myself with the climactic points of action: those movements or pieces of business crucial to my vision of the play. For the rest, to begin with, I allow the actors to ad lib their crosses and the moments they find most suitable for sitting, standing and pacing. Still, I regulate this "freedom" to assure myself that the blocking makes sense: that besides being conducive to the actors' effectiveness, it corresponds to the dramatic needs of the play and helps in the control of audience interest.

I remember an occasion when I was called in to redirect a play which had already opened out of town. During one of the rehearsals I asked an actress to make a cross at a different point than she had become accustomed to under the former staging. "But," the actress protested, "I feel so comfortable doing it the old way." "*You* may feel comfortable," I countered, "but the audience doesn't."

Looking back and recalling the actual conduct of my rehearsals I find that what I have just said is not strictly accurate. After the first "go" signal in blocking, I am careful to designate where I prefer the actor to cross, sit, stand, etc. I find that my suggestions in these matters are soon firmly established and rarely require change through the actors' request or because of my own dissatisfaction. Christopher Fry, who translated two Giraudoux plays I directed, expressed surprise that I made so few alterations after the initial blocking. John Gielgud, who directed Fry's *The Lady's Not for Burning,* kept revising his blocking almost daily, Fry said, and had on occasion to be stopped from doing so just before the curtain rose on the opening night.

Still, I warn my company and stage manager that my early blocking is by no means to be considered final: that I am prepared to alter it as I observe visual awkwardness or physical inconvenience to the actors. They themselves sometimes make suggestions for changes in blocking which are indisputable improvements.

A whole act may be blocked in rough outline in a few hours. This is particularly true of the ordinary realistic play. I have known directors who were able to block an entire play within two or three days.

After I have worked out my first blocking in patches, with repetition of each bit reasonably complete, I have the actors run through the whole act uninterrupted, except where they fail to remember what they had just rehearsed. The stage manager, having noted the blocking in his prompt script, reminds the actors of what had been previously set for them to do.

This run-through is followed by still another and then a

third. With each repetition the movement becomes more fluent. Then, often to the company's astonishment, I ask the actors to sit down and read the act through once more. My comments on the motivations of actions, scenes, lines, are now more minute. I try to stir the actors to a greater awareness of character traits or to the implications of certain actions which may previously have escaped them. They are now better able to understand the drift of my interpretive suggestions through having actually performed the basic externals of the act.

The company is then asked to run through the act again "on their feet." They apply whatever they are readily able to from the reading and discussion just held. I make still further suggestions. Still another repetition follows, but this time I stop from moment to moment to alter, refine, enlarge the earlier work.

This may go on for two or three days with just the first act. I have not yet insisted on any histrionic profundities or creative "heights." The actors have probably been rehearsing with book or "sides" in hand, although they have gradually absorbed their lines through the numerous readings. On the fourth day I expect them, through home study, to know their lines and to be able henceforth to rehearse without the "book." The act is run through once more, though recourse to the prompting stage manager is still inevitable.

What I have described is by no means an ideal procedure. It would be far more advantageous for the actor never to have a script in hand when he is actually trying to play a scene. This is possible only if he is allowed to improvise. In this case the blocking, to begin with, would perforce be loose, with little attention paid to precision in timing, etc. But we are not speaking of an ideal situation but one dictated by the limitations of time in the context of the ordinary American theatre organization.

Many directors, having blocked one act, go on immediately to the blocking of the next and then the next. They wish to view a rough sketch of the entire play without delay. This

mode of work has its merits but I half suspect that it is actu-
ated by fear. The director is being spurred by the producer
and the playwright, who are anxious to see "what we've got."
They are forever straining toward the semblance of a performance; they want to be sure they have a *show*. But hasten-
ing the process of gestation frequently produces a stillbirth.

I do not proceed to the second act till I've achieved a fair
"draft" of the first. There have been occasions when I've
withheld blocking of the last act till the fourteenth day of
rehearsal. This so alarmed one producer (not to mention the
playwright) that he reminded me that the tryout opening was
imminent. "Oh," I said, "I never rehearse the last act of any
of my productions." The jest was not appreciated till I drew
out my notebook in which the rehearsal schedule as I had
planned it showed that I was due to begin work on the final
act two days later.

The blocking of the last third of the play is usually the
least arduous for director and actors. Work on the earlier
parts of the play has already habituated them to the stage
layout and familiarized them with the interpretation and in-
terrelationship of the characters.

Suppose, then, that the first act has been run through
three days after the blocking rehearsals have begun. The evening before we are to block the second act (on the fourth day)
I ask the company to reread it at home because as we have
"neglected" the second act for three days it may no longer
be as fresh in their minds as it should be before blocking is
undertaken.

The same plan which obtained for Act One is adopted for
Act Two. We skip Act One for a day as we devote a whole
day to blocking the second act. Following this we resume
work on Act One while concentrating on Act Two. Soon
we begin devoting half a day to Act One and the second half
to Act Two. Finally we go on to the third act. When all three
run smoothly as far as the physical life of the whole is concerned, the rehearsals rise to a new level of study and effort.

But much more has been going on in the preliminary stages of rehearsal than just the perfecting of mechanics. The completion of one task, I repeat, achieves more than its specific aims. The measures taken to polish the externals are virtually inseparable from inner "psychological" considerations. It is merely a convenience for the sake of exposition to speak of both aspects of production as if they were distinct entities.

CHAPTER 10

Rehearsals Continue

IF THERE WERE little more to stage direction than blocking it would be a comparatively simple matter. Blocking by itself gives a production bone structure. The heart of direction, the brain, blood, nerve and spirit, give it life. People who have observed me at rehearsal have found me impatient with details, hesitant in blocking. Audiences and critics, however, have rarely complained about the mechanics of my staging. The finished product usually looks good—at least as far as blocking goes.

What chiefly concerns me is dramatic meaning, character, mood and feeling. This is essentially a matter of work with the actors, individually and collectively. Without the actor there is no theatre.

Apropos of the relation of the actor to the matter of blocking I am reminded of a story told me by Charles Laughton.

Ellen Terry was being directed by a "traffic cop" who instructed her as follows: "At the rise of the curtain you are noted at the table knitting. After a count of fifteen you rise, go to the window and look out. You then light a lamp on the mantelpiece. After that you return to your seat at the table and resume your knitting." "Yes," the actress responded, "and in the meantime I'll do all those things for which I am paid so much money."

There is, to be sure, the story of another actress, typical of certain English stars, which has quite another significance. The director asked her to pause after a certain phrase, then to stress a particular word in one of her speeches. "Young man," the actress said, "don't tell me when to pause and what word to stress. I shall pause when I please and stress what I choose." This kind of exchange recurred several times. The abashed director, his authority jeopardized, protested, "But Dame E., what am I expected to do?" "Don't worry, young man," the actress replied, "we'll find something."

"Oh," Molière exclaims in his play which shows him conducting a rehearsal, "how hard it is to lead those unruly creatures—actors!" Yes, indeed; but not really as unruly as the layman imagines. Unless an actor is perverse by nature or, as is more frequently the case, spoiled by show biz, he wants to be helped. Actors know that they cannot see their own performance (not on the stage, at any rate) and they hope for a trained eye, sympathetic as well as knowing, to judge and correct them. As a director I never find fault with, never "criticize," actors. I work with them, try to aid, if possible, inspire them.

I must recapitulate some of the items alluded to in the previous chapter. One advances from the general to the particular. During blocking sessions, while the actors still carry their scripts, they should not be asked to "give out," to act in any complete sense. They need only apply themselves intelligently to their tasks with just enough sense of the basic action to justify the moves they make, to understand why these are required. It is a mistake to exert pressure on the actor in the beginning.

One does well to assure the actor that if an indicated move is either inconvenient or uninteresting it is subject to change. The first steps are preliminary to the subtler aspects of the work. Some directors will not go on till each piece of business is perfected. I do not insist on this. I am chiefly intent on establishing flow and continuity.

I seldom encounter resistance. There are, of course, actors who find themselves at a loss unless told from the beginning precisely where they are to stand, sit, move, at each moment. This is not necessarily a sign of insecurity but the result of previous experience with directors who regard every rehearsal in the light of a complete performance. It is a way of work which is reassuring to many producers and playwrights. I am inclined to believe that it produces a certain stiffness, an absence of natural "breathing" in the actor.

One should not ask actors to speak to the last row of the house or to achieve pace from the start. The full voice, the right pace, come with the actor's familiarity with his part. With the progress of the rehearsals he becomes ever more imbued with the spirit of the play, gains confidence in it and in himself. One must simply make sure that sloppiness in technical matters does not become a constant. There are actors who whisper or mutter their lines at first. This may help them but is frustrating to their partners. I discourage the practice as it is antithetical to the give and take which is at the core of truthful acting—ensemble playing—but with certain very talented actors I am tolerant of it for a time.

"The actor is not a machine," Jean Vilar has written. "This is a truism that has to be shouted in people's ears. The actor is neither parrot nor robot. The director must assume from the start that his players have all the necessary talent." The actor gains confidence from such an attitude: it leads to freedom. Without freedom the actor remains a stick, no matter how polished.

Freedom, we all know, does not mean license. The actor cannot just do anything. " 'Anything,' someone heard Stanislavsky say, 'is the enemy of art.' " The actors' guide lines are the actions of each scene truthfully and completely carried out according to the given circumstances of the scene, the spine and characterization of his part and, above all, the spine of the play.

In directing Kazan in *Golden Boy* I explained that Fuselli, whom he was to play, was motivated by a drive to possession and power. The understudy, who played the part well during most of the play's London engagement, suggested an amendment to this interpretation. Wasn't it true, he asked, that Fuselli was fiercely possessive with everyone but the "golden boy" to whom he was strongly attracted? This was perceptive but, I pointed out, if emphasized it would prove false to the play's context. Even Fuselli's love for the boy was affected by his will to "ownership." How was this to be embodied?

The answer to the question illustrates a number of points about business and characterization which I have hitherto left vague. Joe Bonaparte expresses anxiety and dissatisfaction about the boxing racket. This occurs just before a match on which Fuselli, who owns "a piece of the boy," has bet heavily. Fuselli wants to soothe the boy while at the same time warning him against any "tricks." When Joe has calmed down, Fuselli manifests his pleasure by touching the boy's hand, a touch which is both a caress and an admonitory slap.

A single scene or passage may be repeated two, three or four times consecutively till it plays correctly. The same is true of each act. These reruns are of two kinds: one is stop-go, the other a straight run-through. The stop-go rehearsal is one in which the director interrupts the scene to explain what is amiss, how it is to be improved, what new adjustments ought to be considered. This constitutes the work on detail for director and actor. Even after a scene—twenty lines or several pages—has been repeated as many as three or four times the actor may himself request that he be permitted to run it through once again because he wants the satisfaction of feeling that he has mastered it. Some scenes are so difficult that the director will go over them innumerable times.

It is sometimes advisable to work on such scenes with only those present who are directly involved in them. The time taken for such rehearsals affords other members of the cast an opportunity to attend to their own needs—to study lines, be fitted for costumes, experiment with makeup or just rest. I am told that Kazan rarely permits members of the cast to sit out front in the house as observers. He doesn't want to make "critics" of them—critics, that is, of their fellow actors. Rehearsal may be called for an individual actor alone. This is done for intimate consultation, for "special treatment" of individual problems.

Should the director suggest his ideas or personally demonstrate them by "acting" them out? I believe such demonstrations dangerous. Yet they are inevitably resorted to. The peril in demonstrating to an actor how something is to be done is that it leads to imitation on the actor's part. If the director is a poor actor the result may be grotesque. If he is an excellent actor—Stanislavsky, Meyerhold, Reinhardt, for example—the actor becomes "crippled," hopeless of matching the director's brilliance.

An actor in *Tiger at the Gates* confessed he didn't know how to justify a crucial transition in his part with no more support than a single line to mark a total change of attitude. Throughout a long scene Ulysses has been telling Hector that he (Ulysses) can do nothing to avert the war; yet at the very climax of his argument he agrees to attempt doing so. The reason for the sudden change, I explained, is that as Ulysses speaks to Hector he is moved by Hector's passionately idealistic rebuttal. "Yes," the actor asked, "but how can I do this so the audience will understand that motivation?"

A pause was needed in which Ulysses' change from diplomatic regard to compassionate respect for Hector had to be *acted* before Ulysses could go on with the line expressing his conversion. I demonstrated the transitional moment. Silence ensued. "But I shan't be able to do that," the actor responded. I could not tell whether he meant I had acted skillfully or very badly. I only know that he finally managed to play the scene clearly and convincingly. I flatter myself that, in one way or another, I contributed some measure of assistance.

I demonstrate more than I believe fitting or desirable. (I was myself an actor for a brief period.) I usually preface my demonstration with an apology. "I'm going to do this badly," I begin, "don't imitate me. All I mean to do is to indicate an intention. It may prove clearer than anything I might be able to say. But *you must find your own way of carrying out the intention.*"

I rarely ask an actor to prove immediately that he has grasped the idea. "Work on it," I tell him, "it may take you a week to arrive at what we want." When the actor insists, as he frequently does, on effecting what I have asked for right away and fails, I reassure him, "Tomorrow will be time enough." Tomorrow is often a long time off.

In Miller's *Incident at Vichy* Hal Holbrook, an actor of gentle nature and benign appearance, was cast as a regular German army officer under orders from the Gestapo, a part for which no one considered him the "type." The character's troubled conscience sparked vindictiveness in him. I explained this over and over again. I demonstrated and demonstrated through readings and other means. When a director demonstrates by reading the actors' speeches he had best improvise the lines; instruction through exact readings of the text may be logically clarifying but rarely succeeds in evoking true responses in the actor.

For a while Holbrook made little progress. However, I saw him alone working hard in the corridor adjoining the rehearsal hall. Then one day he came to me and said, "I understand what you want. If you don't lose patience, I'll get it." A few days later he did "get it"—magnificently.

Generally speaking, the director should not read lines for

". . . the playwright is the director's closest collaborator."
The author with Arthur Miller during rehearsals for
Incident at Vichy.

"For my production of Robles' Montserrat *at the Habimah*
Theatre in Israel, the designer . . . was an artist whose work
I did not know. I therefore instructed him minutely on
every aspect of the set and costumes." The author's sketch
for the setting.

"*For Anouilh's* The Waltz of the Toreadors (*top*) *I
suggested that Edwards seek inspiration in Cezanne's and
Vuillard's colors. When in a similar vein I suggested
that Aronson make the set for Inge's* Bus Stop (*bottom*)
*look like an Edward Hopper painting, his rejoinder was,
'Why not like an Aronson?'*" (*Photo courtesy of
Ben Edwards; photo courtesy of Boris Aronson, by
Robert Galbraith*)

Top: *"It must seem constructed of metal and stone.
Its locale not too specific. . . . Something hard,
mysterious, 'Kafka-like desired.'" The model of Boris
Aronson's set for* Incident at Vichy. *(Photo courtesy of
Boris Aronson, by Robert Galbraith)*

Bottom: *"Ben Edwards' setting for my production of
Eugene O'Neill's* A Touch of the Poet *owed nothing to
any instruction from me. O'Neill's stage directions and
text were his sole guide." (Photo courtesy of Ben Edwards)*

Top left: *"In Odets' Golden Boy there was a difficult choice to be made in casting the role of Joe Bonaparte. He is a musically inclined youth who also happens to be endowed with a physique and the skill for boxing."* Luther Adler in the title role, with Lee J. Cobb, Phoebe Brand, John Garfield, Morris Carnovsky, and Frances Farmer. (*Photo courtesy of Alfredo Valente*)

Top right: *"The mood of this 'romance' is loneliness. Every element in the play, the physical environment (the setting), the heat, the 'love affair,' the 'sexiness,' must express the basic loneliness."* Morris Carnovsky, Eleanor Lynn, and Luther Adler in Rocket to the Moon. (*Photo courtesy of Alfredo Valente*)

Middle: *"Bessie (the mother) in* Awake and Sing *while chiding her husband and correcting her children's behavior (actions) is setting the table, which may be said to relate to her spine ('to take care of everything'). . . ."* Stella Adler as Bessie, with John Garfield, Morris Carnovsky, J. Edward Bromberg, Luther Adler, Sanford Meisner, and Art Smith. (*Photo courtesy of Vandam Studio*)

Bottom left: *"There is a peculiar turbulence in the air, a constant nervousness, everyone is impatient with the other, impatient with himself."* Richard Basehart and Joseph Wiseman in Uncle Vanya.

Bottom right: *"This play cannot be acted through the lines. A skein of emotional impulses must be woven. A web of odd sentiments which have only the 'logic' of feeling."* The Los Angeles Center Theatre Group's production of Uncle Vanya.

Left: *"Faced for the first time by the director, the playwright and the producer, the actors tend to suppress too overt an expression—of anything! They are 'hiding.' English actors at first readings are bolder and more fluent than Americans."* The author with Ralph Richardson and Mildred Natwick during the rehearsals of **The Waltz of the Toreadors.**

Below: *"Couches and wooden benches which only approximate the dimensions specified by the designer as required for accurate staging are all the actor may work with. . . . The inadequacy of the furniture and most of the hand props lead to a waste of time in a specifically technical sense."* Early rehearsals of **Truckline Cafe.**

Left: *"The first rehearsals permit the director to learn something about the kind of direction which best befits each of the actors."* The author with producer observe Kim Stanley and Helen Hayes during rehearsals of **A Touch of the Poet.**

"Dress rehearsals are among the most hazardous and troublesome periods in the production of a play. The rule 'one thing at a time' . . . is particularly applicable at this juncture." The author giving final notes during the dress rehearsal of the Japanese production of Long Day's Journey into Night.

actors. As just noted, a paraphrase may serve to suggest the action or feeling of certain speeches. Though for certain people—theologians of the Method—directing an actor by reading lines for him is a cardinal sin, it becomes mandatory at times and practically inevitable. I once apologized to Fredric March for presuming to read a line for him. "No! No!" he encouraged me, "your readings help me."

When I asked Stanislavsky, "Do you ever read lines for an actor?" he replied at once, "Of course, whole speeches sometimes. One does everything, *anything* to arrive at the desired result." And it is chiefly from Stanislavsky that the notion has arisen that a director's reading lines to an actor is harmful! Still, for the neophyte director I advise "proceed with caution." It is better to evoke than to command.

I have just quoted Stanislavsky to the effect that one does anything to arrive at a desired result. Directors have been known to take the most outlandish measures to achieve their ends. One might fill many pages with instances of directors' "tricks" designed to stimulate the actor when ordinary methods—explanations, improvisations, demonstrations—have not availed.

One such instance, unorthodox to say the least, occurred during rehearsals of my short-lived production of Maxwell Anderson's *Truckline Cafe* in 1946. I had cast a young actor of twenty-two. He had been recommended to me by Stella Adler who praised him highly as the most gifted of her students: Marlon Brando. I had never seen him on the stage but I trusted Miss Adler's judgment and went to "look him over" in John van Druten's *I Remember Mama* in which he played an adolescent. He was certainly interesting but the nature of his role in this play was so different from that of the returned G.I. in the Anderson play, who on learning of his wife's infidelity kills her, that I wasn't at all sure he would suit the part.

I had him read for the author, the producers (Elia Kazan and Walter Fried) and myself. He read poorly, his head sunk low on his chest as if he feared to divulge anything. Yet there could be no question: he was peculiarly arresting. We decided to use him.

He mumbled for days. I applied myself so strenuously to his problem (I really couldn't determine what it was) that after a particularly arduous session—he listened attentively— I cried out, "All the actors here are witnesses: you will be a star someday and I shall demand that you support me when I'm a broken down old director." We all laughed. But he didn't improve.

The author's agent and wife suggested I recast the part. Anderson was a gentle and fair man and told me about this. "What do you wish me to do?" I asked. "Do what you think best," was his reply. I said I had faith in the boy and I would continue to work with him. But I was worried: the boy couldn't be heard beyond the fifth row.

His difficulty, it seemed, was that he could not give vent to the deep well of feeling which I sensed in him. He could not overcome some inner resistance: he would not "open up." The use of affective memory—a term I shall explain in a later chapter—did not help.

One day I asked everyone in the company to leave the stage and retire to the dressing rooms. I turned to Brando and said, "I want you to *shout* your lines." (For this I chose the crucial scene in which the young man tells how he drowned his unfaithful wife, whom he still loved.) Brando raised his voice. "Louder," I ordered. He complied. "Still louder," I insisted. This was repeated several times and my command for ever greater vocal volume began to exhaust the actor and to rouse him to visible anger. Then I yelled, "Climb the rope!" as I pointed to a rope which was hanging from the gridiron above the stage. Without hesitation he began climbing the rope while I urged him to keep shouting his lines. The other members of the cast came rushing onto the stage, alarmed at the terrifying sounds they had heard while still in their dressing rooms.

When Brando let himself down, he looked as if he were ready to hit me. "Now," I said quietly, "run the scene—normally." He recovered his poise and did as I bid him. He "spoke up"—effortlessly. In a few days he played the "moment" beautifully. On opening night—and every night thereafter—his performance was greeted by one of the most thunderous ovations I have heard for an actor in the theatre.

I am not at all sure he wouldn't have come through without the "beating" I administered. I never again tried another such device—and I certainly don't recommend this method. But at the time it seemed a noble and triumphant experiment!

In the building of characterizations I draw, as I have already noted, from three sources: the dramatist's script, the actor's being, my own imagination. In speaking to an actor about his part in Odets' *Paradise Lost,* I remember inventing a long story about the character's past: the oppressive poverty, shame at his lack of education, embarrassment about his accent and foreign looks. As I spoke I observed tears shimmering in the actor's eyes. I later learned that without my realizing it I had described much of the actor's early youth.

Knowing the springs of an actor's temperament is an asset in developing inner characterization for him. The actor should be encouraged to recreate in his own mind an imaginary past for the character he is to play (and possibly a future). For whatever one imagines, no matter how fanciful, always has its origins in one's own experience. The imagined past the actor creates for himself may parallel the secrets of his own subjective being without the actor necessarily being aware of it.

The clues to outer characterizations are objectively numerous. It often happens that an observed external trait (even a particular costume or makeup) leads to a feeling for the inner man, though it is probably preferable to work from the inner characterization (dictated by the part's spine, etc.) to the outer. (I have heard that Alec Guinness appears to get the feel of a part by imagining how the character would dress his hair!) Then, too, the actor may begin with a model: a person he knows or has seen somewhere, a painted portrait, a newspaper photo. I remember a self-portrait by Paul Gauguin which suggested both an outer and inner characterization for a character who was not an artist or a Frenchman, but only an unhappy businessman.

The games people play, which consist of answering such questions about a person as "What kind of music is he like? What food? What town? What painter's style?" etc., may stimulate the actor in his search for a characterization. What prompted Odets to suggest that the professional arsonist in *Paradise Lost* be played with a Swedish accent? It may have sprung from some dimly remembered chance encounter in the past which made a sinister impression on him. I saw the same character with bright red hair, wearing a black leather finger protector! Was it the "devil" I had in mind? I'm not at all sure—and it doesn't matter, if the image works.

Racial origins may lend character traits (too often conventional) to the building of an outer characterization. Certain historical periods known through representative paintings may also contribute ideas for characterization. Illnesses, habits and occupations casually mentioned in the play's dialogue or in the dramatist's stage directions may be further hints to characterization. Chekhov tells us that Uncle Vanya on his first entrance wears a "fancy tie." The actor or director must ask himself why this one item of clothing should have been important enough for the writer to mention: what does it signify for the total characterization? There is something more to it than a manner of dress. Tolstoy tells us that Karenin in *Anna Karenina* is in the habit of cracking his knuckles. It is a sign of something more than just a tic which displeases Anna.

The director must not overlook variety and development in characterization. A characterization should *grow*. It is not something the audience is immediately to perceive which remains constant throughout the play as a static condition. A characterization must be seen to develop in stages and should only become perceptible in its entirety with the resolution of the play.

In the first act of *Uncle Vanya,* Voinitski has come to realize that he has wasted his life on behalf of his selfish and pedantic brother-in-law. In the second act he despairs. In the third act he rebels—ineffectually. In the last act he painfully resigns himself to his state.

Laurence Olivier has a penchant for disguising himself. He specializes in variety of nose shapes even when it appears uncalled for: the shape of the nose means something to him and will, he trusts, do something for us. Russian actors almost always employ some external feature to make their characterizations more vivid. (See the illustrations of Stanislavsky in a variety of roles to be found in his *My Life in Art,* each with a distinct and altogether different "face.") American actors, on the other hand, usually avoid sharp external characterizations. They consider them hammy. It rarely occurs to many producers that actors may invent special physical features. Such producers seek *the* type: the fat actor must play the fat man, the cadaverous-visaged character will be played by someone of that breed. Besides being a by-product of the commercial theatre's need for quick results, this shying away from overt physical characterization is part of a theatre thinking which is largely geared to realism, the "natural" rather than the expressively theatrical.

External characterization need not be strikingly graphic. Donald Cook played a jet set Frenchman of possibly aristocratic lineage in the Marcel Achard-Harry Kurnitz whodunit *A Shot in the Dark.* A practiced comedian with a talent for crisp delivery and timing as well as a dry humor, he was superb in the part when it tried out in New Haven. Unfortunately he died there of a heart attack. Walter Matthau replaced him. There was much head shaking; he was certainly not the "type."

The directorial task was to find some not too obvious facet of characterization which would convince the audience at once that here was a character who would behave and speak as the authors had him do. Since Matthau once mentioned that he was responsive to music, I asked him to choose the recording of a piece which struck him as "super-elegant." He was requested to play it for himself at home and then to walk rather than to dance to it. (I never inquired into what piece he selected.) His gait was ever so slightly altered at the next rehearsal. At the preview before the opening the producer asked that the "walk" be eliminated. I insisted that it be retained and Kurnitz agreed. Silently, Matthau glided onto the stage as if his feet were caressing the floor. The opening-night audience roared with laughter: the characterization had acquired a base.

There was no caricature in this. It became second nature to the actor. Such idiosyncrasies may be even more minute than Matthau's gliding walk. In Reinhardt's production of *Danton's Death* Vladimir Sokolov's Robespierre became memorable to me through his dry, staccato delivery of lines, but most of all through the two fingers he kept tapping ominously on the lectern in front of him as he drove home his arguments.

There is such a thing as an external characterization (or makeup) which overwhelms every other element of the portraiture and is therefore false. Funny accents sometimes have this effect. After the worldwide success of the Vakhtangov-Habimah Theatre production of *The Dybbuk* (part mystic romance, part social commentary), in which the actors' faces were rendered awesomely weird, the Habimah company was afflicted for years with mask mania: all roles were stylized to the point of distortion. This was so much a trademark of the Habimah company and others who modeled themselves on it that when I was asked my opinion of Israeli acting at a lecture in Tel Aviv I replied, "You have talented actors but many suffer from a certain peculiarity: if you tell such an actor 'You are to play a lawyer,' he will inquire eagerly, 'With a limp?' " It was therefore a really original stroke when an Israeli played Richard III without crookleg or hump.

The special walk which Matthau assumed in *A Shot in the Dark* might be set down in Michael Chekhov's terminology as a "psychological gesture." Chekhov explains that every person has some special manner of speaking or moving or watching which reveals something of his inner nature. When this remarkable actor played Chlestakov in Gogol's *The Inspector General* he seemed—especially after he had been mistaken for a V.I.P. by the local gentry—to be walking on springs. When he began to lie about his exalted position in St. Petersburg society he positively danced. I have found the discovery of psychological gestures for various characters of considerable value in developing character delineation not only because they are visually or aurally specific, but because if assimilated they lead to deeper insights.

The temptation to adopt the psychological gesture as a gimmick may be grotesquely illustrated by an incident in the direction of an actor who played a businessman in my Habimah production of *Montserrat*. For some time he floundered about without "finding" the part. The man, I told the actor, takes everything into himself, to his stomach as it were, and holds it in safe keeping there. The actor thereafter held his hands over his belly as if he were guarding his possessions in that spot. Now, he said, he knew how to play the part. But lo, one day I came to rehearsal and saw several other actors committed to the same gesture!

A play's action is fleshed in stage business. The elaboration of business, the byplay or outgrowth of action, is the chief attribute of drama in performance. It clarifies, intensifies, gives body to what is sometimes referred to as the play's *subtext*, the action believed implicit in the dialogue. It gives texture and vivacity to the play as spectacle. It is often hyperbolic and fanciful. The fame of certain directors and actors is founded on the imaginative quality or resourcefulness in their invention of business. Comedians often evince genius in this respect. As with everything else, business may be overdone, become too profuse.

Business may also be defined as the physical extension in minor activities of the major action in each passage or "beat" of a scene. In a production of a Danish play when Michael Chekhov cried out, "I shall defend myself," he used his fists, his feet, chairs, cutlery and every other available object to do just that. When Hume Cronyn in Molière's *The Miser* reached for the smoke from someone's pipe in order to "save" it, the audience appreciated the gesture as a crazy metaphor of Harpagon's avarice.

When Hermia in frustrated rage in Peter Brook's *Midsummer Night's Dream* jumped high onto a bar suspended from the flies and kicked her feet furiously she was very much like the "puppet" Helena called her.

Yelena's closing of the piano lid at the end of Act Two in *Uncle Vanya* (previously cited) tells us more clearly than words that her failure in life is the outcome of her constant obedience. When Julie Harris as Frankie in *The Member of the Wedding* spoke of her dream of going all around the world, she whirled herself around the stage imitating the sound as well as the slightly swaying motion of an airplane. She lent vivid substance to the thought I had expressed one day at rehearsal that children imitate what fascinates them. The written line could have been spoken as a point of information or as a yearning but Miss Harris made it *theatrical,* that is, dramatically visible. Eric Portman as Melody in O'Neill's *A Touch of the Poet* flinging his pistol into the mirror after momentarily posing in front of it while reciting Byron was a dynamic image of his self-contempt and defeat.

All such pieces of business, I repeat, may be planned in advance by the director, they may appear spontaneously during rehearsal or they may issue from the actor's response to a director's challenge when he says, "I need something unusual to be done at this point. Can you think of something?"

Every theatregoer speaking of a play or a performance he has enjoyed will remind you of what this or that actor *did* at a particular moment. The *doing* is more indelibly memorable than what the actor said. Though it was as long ago as 1926 I can still remember the German actor Albert Basserman as a famous painter in a play by Gerhart Hauptmann because while asking each of his several pupils such questions as "Have you read Goethe?," "Do you know Shakespeare?" and the like, he pinched the cheek of one, prodded the ribs of another. He was chiding and teaching them with respect, concern and paternal affection.

As rehearsals advance and take on genuine quality greater attention will be directed toward matters involving speech, timing and pace. A former reviewer on a New York daily newspaper could describe direction in no other terms than "fast" or "slow," the one signifying good direction, the other bad. It is silly to discuss the subjects of speech, pace and voice as if they were unrelated to all the rest. It is as much sheer ignorance to concentrate on these facets of acting and theatre art as to overlook them.

I pay close attention to them in the final weeks of rehearsal when the groundwork of the production has been laid and is nearly complete. If an actor has some special defect in speech, a disturbing vocal shortcoming or a disquieting mannerism (in which case one hesitates to cast him), one should do something about it as early as possible only if one is convinced that the fault may be corrected within the four weeks of rehearsal! Ordinarily, it should be taken for granted that an actor is adequately equipped or well trained in voice and diction. There are lamentable exceptions.

I find the question "How should one speak Shakespeare?"

somewhat absurd, as if it is of little importance how one speaks in a contemporary play. Laurence Olivier's speech and voice are as fine in Ionesco's *Rhinoceros* as in *Henry V*. Shakespeare doesn't call for a special type of speech; he demands besides an ear for language a particular emotional adjustment or style, in the way Pablo Casals asks his musicians to play Bach "with honor."

When the great Italian tragedian Salvini said that the three most potent factors in acting are "Voice! Voice! Voice!" he was enunciating a salutary apothegm—and an egregious simplification. It is like saying that to be a good pianist one must possess a good piano. There have been extraordinary actors with faulty or ruined voices (the Sicilian Giovanni Grasso of whom Stark Young wrote so beautifully comes to mind) and others with peculiarities of diction (Henry Irving), though, it is true, they are very few in number. Excellent speech and voice should be the stock-in-trade of every would-be actor before he embarks on acting as a profession.

Proper stage speech is largely a consequence of right thinking, of understanding the operative words in sentences, and partly of a feeling for language and literature and of being aware of sound and rhythm in relation to meaning. These in turn depend on the thorough execution of each of the play's actions or, to put it less technically, clarity of intention. Given a normal vocal instrument, actors need not shout to be heard: they need to know what they're talking about, what, *dramatically speaking,* they mean. Opera singers capable of producing magnificent sound and actors with "piped-in" voices are often unintelligible on the stage. They make no sense; they do not *act*. To fashion readings of elegance, euphony, grace and shapeliness are among the final tasks to which the director need devote himself.

Pace and tempo are usually taken to be synonymous with speed. They are not achieved by "going fast" but by change and variety of attack. But apart from this bald axiom, it should go without saying that pace is established through the nature of each particular action and the adjustment to it. I once saw an actor who made an exit prompted by the need to call a doctor for someone who had suddenly fallen ill. He moved at a pace which convinced me he wished the stricken person dead!

The director may well shout "Faster!" or—more rarely in the United States—"Slower!" and this may at times prove useful. But such commands are only short-cut remedies to correct a failure in understanding the nature of specific actions and adjustments. An actress in class once did a long speech from Shaw's *Misalliance* for me. Everything seemed right in regard to her understanding of content; her articulation and voice were unexceptionable. I asked her to increase the pace of her delivery. She frowned at this deviation from what she took to be my "credo," but she did as I bid her. When she was through, she agreed along with those present that her "fast" reading not only made the speech more entertaining but more "real." The reason for this, I explained, was that the rhythm of Shaw's thinking, his mental agility and the sparkle and fluent energy of his writing were attributes of his style, *part of his meaning*. Every play has its own basic rhythm, its ground tone. Reference to these aspects of the play should be made at the inception of rehearsal discussions but are to be insisted upon only during the final phases of production.

Then there is the question of *pauses*. In the early stages of his efforts an actor should be permitted to take his own sweet time and pause as often as he deems fit; if this threatens to become habitual he should be warned against it as an obstructive mannerism. The justification for such forbearance on the director's part is the recognition that the actor is still unsure of himself; he gropes for the "something" which still eludes him. He needs time to find himself in the part.

Some actors will protest that what makes them pause and pause again is that they are "thinking." Occasionally I retort with a long spiel of intellectual verbiage and then conclude with "You can't say I haven't been thinking as I spoke." The

actor's forethought should be done privately—at home.
Though rehearsals, as Vakhtangov once said, are the period
reserved for mistakes, it is also true that rehearsals are intended to reveal the effects of one's thinking. When the actor
retires for the day he should think over what has been said
and done during the day's rehearsal.

There is really no such thing as a pause on the stage. What
we call a pause, apart from breathing space and the "leap"
toward a stress, is the time when nothing is *audible* but during which we see or feel what is going on. It is a form of suspense; something *is happening* and we await the outcome:
what is going to be done or said next. If the audience's expectation isn't aroused, the pause is "dead air." A play's action
must never stop. When the actor is really thinking—itself a
specific action—we watch him with interest. This explains the
legitimate use of the close-up in film: the actor's eye is tell-
tale. The general imperative in staging, apart from variety of
movement, tempo and sound, is, as already noted, to keep
the audience's attention on the crucial points of action. The
placement of the actors, the groupings, the stage "pictures,"
should all be calculated with this end in view.

The first major run-through of the entire play usually takes
place approximately three weeks after the first rehearsal. Producers have urged me to hasten to the occasion. I have sometimes countered, "I'll show you two acts within twelve days
and will also go through the last act with the actors reading
from their scripts."

At this first run-through—a nervous time for everyone—we
find the director, the playwright, the producer and their various secretaries taking notes. For this latter occupation I call
on the services of one of the stage managers, an understudy or
a student volunteer. I mention this because I rarely take notes
in the early rehearsal period.

Following the first run-through the director, playwright
and producer (along with a stage manager seated discreetly
by their side) gather in conference, each with his own packet

of comments, criticisms, questions, suggestions and advice. On these occasions I say little; I listen. Many of the producer's and playwright's notes are already to be found in mine. I assuage their expressed and unexpressed fears, I promise to remedy the faults and rough spots they have complained about. By reasoned argument I am sometimes able to convert dissent into acceptance of directional details to which objections have been raised. I occasionally contradict certain criticisms so emphatically that my colleagues abandon their argument. Absolute conviction is rare.

I sometimes nod agreement to a criticism without the least intention of doing anything about it. There is no disdain in this. I know that certain "troubles" automatically right themselves through further rehearsal. Very often an objection which has been made is based on a momentary subjective reaction and will be forgotten by the very person who raises it.

I generally find my colleagues' suggestions helpful and I am grateful for them. Producers are not always dumb; some of them are quite smart, knowledgeable, even wise. The great majority of my production conferences have been carried on with the utmost cordiality and respect on everyone's part. The only time I am upset by criticisms or suggestions is when they are offered while I am still in the thick of work and I have not yet had time to observe the results. There is a proverb, "Never show a fool work half done." Playwrights and producers are rarely fools but their nervous impatience frequently provokes them to premature critical counsel. I am not a "temperamental" director, though in driving home a point I have been known to become vociferously oratorical. It's all fun—or should be.

Directors are sometimes dismissed after the first unfortunate run-through or after a disastrous preview or out-of-town opening. This has never happened to me. Other directors, disheartened or disgusted by their own or their collaborators' dissatisfaction, have resigned from a production *in medias res.* I never have.

The morning after the "big" conference the company is

given the notes agreed on by the "governing trio." When cuts have been recommended and approved by the playwright, the first order of business is to dictate them to the actors. Then all criticisms and suggested changes in staging (which may have to be specially rehearsed) are presented by the director alone. The director may ask the playwright to add something of his own personal views. If possible, the playwright should be encouraging. But he should never say anything specifically in the way of direction.

Work continues and after another three days there is another run-through and another conference, following the pattern just described. The intervals between these run-throughs are usually devoted to rehearsal of the more difficult scenes, the "rough spots" and to private work with particular actors. My usual practice is to do this polishing every morning of the last week and to run through the entire play every afternoon—for myself alone. Actors gain confidence, strength and fullness through repeated run-throughs. No amount of discussion or criticism is as productive at this point as playing the play.

The last run-through before the beginning of dress rehearsals is generally bad, unless an audience of friends is invited to witness it (this audience should not consist of theatre professionals). The guest audience at this point helps keep the company on its toes.

CHAPTER 11

Dress Rehearsals,
Previews, Tryouts

DRESS REHEARSALS are among the most hazardous and trouble-some periods in the production of a play. The rule, "one thing at a time"—the admonition not to correct everything at once—is particularly applicable at this juncture.

Though three or four days (a week for musicals) are supposed to be devoted to all the necessary adjustments prior to the first paid previews, the fact is that during these days the stage is largely given over to the carpenters, electricians, prop men, the designer and, if the designer does not light the show himself, to the lighting expert. There are also present dress-makers, milliners, hairdressers and wardrobe ladies as aides to the costume designer. They help the actors look presentable at the first dress run-through. The cast spends hours in trying on the costumes, wigs, shoes, etc.

While these technical matters are being attended to the cast is called to the theatre lounge, or to a large room in a nearby hotel, where the director goes over the notes made at the last run-through. Though the actors know their lines they may be asked and even wish to run them all once again. There may be some difficulty in remembering them when for the first time the cast finds itself in the play's setting.

English directors take pride in lighting their productions. In America lighting specialists have become prevalent. Certain scene designers—notably Joe Mielziner—do their own lighting. Very few directors do. A brief lighting conference attended by the director and the lighting staff usually precedes the dress rehearsal period. The designer and others responsible for the lighting have at an earlier time watched several run-throughs to familiarize themselves with the placement of the actors in the play's climactic moments. As soon as the "scenery" is safely in position, the light men begin their jobs.

I know what I want in lighting a play but I am unfamiliar with the precise designation, the number and the exact disposition of the lighting paraphernalia. For this reason I do not join in the preliminaries of lighting. I am confident of those in charge of the task; I am also sure that after several dress rehearsals the actors and I will find the stage too dark and the actors' faces in shadow.

It is a truism that designers are chiefly concerned, at first, with lighting the set so that it makes an impressive "picture." But one can hardly blame them for this. A play cannot be adequately lit till the actors are in place, and their figures, features and costumes closely studied in movement. Work on lighting therefore continues through most of the dress rehearsals—often disturbing the actors—and frequently goes on up to the last moment before the curtain rises on the official opening night.

I ask the actors, before the first dress rehearsal begins, to come on stage and occupy all the chairs and couches they are to sit on, to open and close doors through which they are to pass, to mount and descend whatever steps and platforms they are to use—in short, to acquire the habit of the play's physical environment. The request is hardly necessary; if they are at all experienced they will do this on their own. But it should be done even before they don their stage clothes. Each step—the testing of the set, the putting on of costumes, the application of makeup—should be separately effected before they all become part of a single routine. It is doing "one thing at a time."

The altered circumstances of dress rehearsal seem at first to be more of an impediment than a help. Time must be allowed the actors to achieve ease and comfort. Though the actors are acquainted with the set in its model, have moved within its dimensions, and have been informed where they are to find the needed props, they are usually "thrown" when they first encounter the set. They may even find the "real" settee designed for their playing somehow less convenient than the substitute bench which tormented them during the first days of rehearsal. The desk isn't quite high enough or it is too low, the chair not deep enough, the doorway not wide enough and so on. The complaints are sometimes well founded and alterations are made within hours or in a day or two. But the plain fact is that even when the actors declare themselves satisfied with the setting, the furniture, etc., the new conditions of the dress rehearsal discomfit them and time is required for complete adjustment.

Every marked change in the actors' working conditions affects them adversely. Not only laymen find this hard to understand, but even some producers and directors. For example: A producer who was entirely delighted with a run-through he had attended asked me to arrange for another on the following day to pick up the last bit of backing for the show from a lady who wanted to see the play before investing in it. I agreed to arrange for the special run-through. The only hitch was that this time the run-through would have to be held in a different theatre than the one in which the company had been rehearsing for more than two weeks.

The special run-through was a failure. The actors appeared ill rehearsed. The producer was bewildered. "What's happened? They were great yesterday. It was awful today." I explained that the change of theatre and stage was responsible for the difference. Though the man had produced many plays he still could not understand. Only a few theatre professionals learn from experience.

Whenever one makes a pronounced change in the conditions of performance—such as a change in spatial distance on stage and in relation to the auditorium—the acting will be disturbed though the actors themselves may not be aware of the cause. On this account I ask stage managers of companies on tour to have the actors speak some of their lines and run some scenes the night before the opening in every new town they play, no matter how long the tour.

Actors should be given the opportunity to wear their costumes before the regular dress rehearsals begin. The first rehearsal on the set should take place unencumbered by anything but the indispensable props. It should go without saying that the actors have tried on their costumes at a special "dress parade" onstage or in the costumer's shop at least a week before dress rehearsal time. (The actors of the Moscow Art Theatre wore their Roman dress for its production of *Julius Caesar* for many weeks prior to the play's opening.)

I prefer the actors to rehearse without makeup when they try their costumes on for the first time at the dress rehearsal. Makeup, even of the simplest kind, is another factor which contributes to their self-consciousness at dress rehearsals. "How do I look?" the actor asks himself, his fellow actors, the director, the designer. Even when satisfied that he appears no different than his natural self, he seems a little different to the other actors, a little strange. If the actor has put on a character makeup (a beard, a wig, a scar) or changed his hair style, he not only loses some sense of his own identity but even that of the character he has been working so carefully to create. After all, *that* person (the character) didn't look that way before! And if the actor seems strange to himself, he must seem even stranger to his partner. "Who is this man or woman I'm acting with: it's a new person, an unknown!"

Speaking of costume and makeup, I cannot refrain from telling one of my favorite theatre stories, not alone for its humor but for a point connected with the question of characterization. European actors, as already noted, are happiest in the disguise of pronounced characterization which often entails a change in facial and bodily look. Not so Americans. They prefer to appear "natural"—to be themselves. That is one reason why most American actors, particularly those who have embarked on their careers in the past twenty-five years, aren't adept at makeup and require assistance.

But to my story. In 1924 when Joseph Schildkraut played Edwin Justus Mayer's *The Firebrand,* a sex comedy presumably about Benvenuto Cellini, he was uncertain as to how that famous sculptor and rake should be made up. (Schildkraut's early theatre experience had been Viennese.) The author and director, never having thought of Cellini as anything but a darling playboy, as conceived by New Yorkers in the twenties, suggested that Schildkraut consult a portrait of the man in a book about Renaissance art. He did so. He was not surprised to find that Cellini was blessed with a formidable beard. On the evening of the first dress rehearsal he carefully applied that appendage to his face.

Rudolf Schildkraut, Joseph's father, himself a veteran of Max Reinhardt's productions and one of the finest actors of my theatregoing experience, had been present at several of the earlier rehearsals to keep a watchful eye on his son, who worshipped him. When the old man saw his Joseph at the dress rehearsal enter the stage for the first time as a bearded Benvenuto he rose from his seat and cried out in astonished German, "Beard! Beard! Where are you running with my son!"

There are makeups, costumes and characterizations which proclaim the actor's performance and run away with it. Period authenticity in costumes or makeup is of minor importance; what matters is dramatic relevance, not historical congruity. The criterion for judgment in these areas is the individual role and the actor cast for it. The habiliments worn in most productions which call for period dress seem to be fit for costume balls only. Costumes in the theatre must be, first of all, *clothing*.

When the actors run through the play for the first time in a complete dress rehearsal they should be warned to do very little in the way of acting. If they attempt to act in the full sense, they will frustrate themselves as well as disappoint the director. Despite all the good will possible, they will concentrate chiefly on overcoming the hurdles of setting, lights, costumes and makeup which have been supplied to aid them. No matter how well the actors speak, the director barely hears them. He, too, is chiefly conscious of the new faces, the lights, the costumes, which do not quite meet his expectations, or he is admiring a costume or makeup so much that he cannot see the actor. Usually nothing works as it should. The director may decide to stop the action because an actor has forgotten to shut a door (they were only imaginary doors before), and when he does close it, it opens again of itself. But there is no time to stop to attend to such momentarily trivial matters; the rehearsal continues, yet the director can't keep his eyes from the gaping hole that the open door cuts in the set.

A light cue is late or the light isn't of the right color or intensity, it doesn't hit the right spot, there is bad shadow on the leading lady's face and everything is either glaringly bright or, more often, dismally dark. The designer is busy whispering instructions to the electricians backstage; the costumer is exasperated because this or that actress didn't put on the right dress or has put on the right dress the wrong way. An actor complains that his jacket is too tight for him to make the telling gestures he did when he wore his own suit. Some scenes must be restaged for mechanical reasons and the curtain never falls at quite the right speed or on the right cue.

The occasions on which I have not found the first dress rehearsal exhausting and dispiriting have been rare. Technical notes are given the stage manager, as well as to various designers and the heads of the stage crew (carpenter, property man, electrician). Each of these makes his own notes.

The second dress rehearsal always begins later than the scheduled hour but it is usually a great improvement on the first. The technicians always require more time than anticipated to make the necessary adjustments. There are generally two dress rehearsals on the second day. The one called for two-thirty begins at four. If the stage crew is called between twelve and one the management is obliged to pay overtime; if the rehearsal lasts beyond midnight there is more overtime payment due. In any case, the crew must be paid for a minimum of eight hours a day.

And so on through the afternoon of the third day to the opening performance that night or, if one is lucky, on the night of the fourth day. The days before the first New York preview or the first out-of-town opening being hectic, the director's main job is to continue working as calmly as possible. If he is unduly nervous he must make every effort not to betray his condition. Nor must he try to "pep things up" with an impassioned speech about the seriousness of the occasion. I laugh the moment away by saying, "Tonight we rehearse the audience." The actors need not be reminded, as some silly producing fellows will, that they must do their best and a little better. Actors for the most part are responsible people.

If they are not a total bust these first performances out of town or at previews are always instructive. (Most "straight" plays nowadays are previewed in New York; the road or out-of-town tryout has become too costly.) If the play is a comedy, the actors may have learned through the presence of guests at the pre-opening run-through where laughs are to be expected. But there are always surprises: what tickles one audience may fail to amuse another. The duration of the audience's laughter is not calculable in advance. Then again the audience may laugh in the wrong places, and it is not always easy to understand what provoked the inopportune reaction. An ill-advised phrase or an incongruous gesture at a tense moment may give rise to guffaws. At the first preview of *Men in White* the audience found a passing reference to the moon funny. They understood only too well that an affair between a lonely intern and a pretty nurse was to follow. It took a while to discover that it was the word, not the scene, that had caused the "bad" laugh.

One soon learns which scenes drag, either because they need partial or total cutting or because they are not being properly played. Most such difficulties are readily overcome overnight or within a few days, provided director, playwright and producer maintain poise. Theatre folk are prone to alarm. They overreact to everything which in any way smacks of a setback or someone's displeasure. If a production at an out-of-town tryout receives an adverse review, even from a person everyone pretends to dismiss as a fool, a dangerous chain reaction is set up. What's to be done about this, that or the other? My own first decision, unless I agree with the reviewer's or the audience's reservations, is to do nothing.

As we approach that "moment of truth," the New York opening night, the number of people ready to proffer advice on the production increases. Everyone has an "idea." The playwright thinks you have cut too much, or too little. That actor is not playing as directed. One of the actors is miscast: fire him!

That astute agent, and the author's representative, Audrey Wood, confesses that after the first days of the Philadelphia tryout of *The Member of the Wedding* she advised Robert Whitehead, the producer, to postpone the New York opening: the show, she opined, was "not ready." The show opened on schedule in New York almost immediately after this advice was given—and was a decided success.

Judgments and criticisms on these occasions are not always misguided but the atmosphere in which they occur is overwrought. There is fierce, nerve-racking pressure—financial, egotistical and, worst of all, "corporative." Everybody gets into the act: show biz mentors, husbands, wives, boy and girl friends, other actors, other directors, other writers—experts all! It is my invariable practice to warn everyone concerned with the production against giving credence to these well-wishers and, if possible, not to listen to them at all.

It is panic time, and the director must keep his own counsel. There is no arrogance in this: he must realize that he knows the play and its problems better than anyone else. He should and will heed advice thoughtfully offered by people whose theatre knowledge or instincts he respects. But he must resist even the playwright and the producer if he believes them in error. He may "experiment," try new approaches. He usually has at least two weeks of previews or out-of-town performances (much longer with a musical) to do this. This gives him the opportunity to test a suggested change. The director should keep himself pliant, but he must not run scared. Presumption of infallibility is out of order because there is something unpredictable about the life of a play on stage before an audience. It is this "mystery" which is what makes play production so fascinating and frightening. The fright and the fascination (each is part of the other) are the cause of theatre superstition.

A director must cultivate the virtue of patience: patience with others, patience with himself. He must believe in himself and in what he is doing, but he must also know himself subject to error and gross miscalculation. What follows are some examples of what I am alluding to. It is pleasant to speak of those instances which refer to the production of *The Member of the Wedding,* for whatever difficulties we underwent in its making, we were rewarded by a happy ending.

There was Ethel Waters' trouble in remembering lines. It was not the ordinary trouble with a poor memory, but with coordination. When Miss Waters remembered the lines, she forgot the business; when she remembered the business, she forgot the lines. Julie Harris, who played opposite her, was very patient. (She is always generous with her fellow players.) Robert Whitehead, the producer, and I were worried. At the last run-through before the Philadelphia tryout Miss Waters was still far from having mastered the text.

I said nothing to indicate dissatisfaction or nervousness. I appointed one of the stage managers to go over the lines with her privately, repeating the exercise again and again and again. On opening night in Philadelphia (the coaching went on in her dressing room during intermission) she was still uncertain and occasionally "up" (stage slang for failure of memory), even though her acting was magnificent.

Though she gained confidence through enthusiastic notices, it took many days before she achieved verbal security. After returning to New York from Philadelphia, further rehearsals were called before the opening. Miss Waters suffered a relapse into uncertainty. I sought an explanation. She had pains in her stomach, she said. I reassured her: "You are simply nervous because of the approaching opening night." She then referred to the responsibility some actresses feel which is not entirely personal: she was referring to her race.

Still, this was by no means the knottiest problem which confronted us at the time. The Philadelphia opening ran till midnight. This was partly due to two scenes in a cheap barroom to which twelve-year-old Frankie, the play's central character, repairs, scenes which necessitated a mechanically difficult shifting of sets. One of the scenes was cut on the second night. I was strongly urged to cut the other as well. I objected. Increasing pressure was put on me, but I was obdurate. I argued that the barroom scene conveyed something of the town beyond the kitchen kingdom in which Frankie and her seven-year-old boy friend John Henry played together. The author, Miss McCullers, said nothing: she had no theatre experience. But everyone else, Robert Whitehead, his partner Stanley Martineau and their associates, pressed their point unremittingly. I was not to be moved.

Then one afternoon two local high school boys came to in-

terview me. They told me how much the play had moved
them. Their reaction was touchingly genuine. One of the boys
timidly asked if the scene in the bar was needed. I did not answer; I was convinced. That evening I cut the scene.

The audience plays a vital role in the theatre, but one
must be careful. There are those in the audience like the gentleman at the first New York preview of *The Member of the
Wedding* whom Robert Whitehead overheard saying to his
companion, "I don't see anything at all to recommend in this
show." An actor friend of Julie Harris' assured her in Philadelphia that she needn't be ashamed to appear in the show:
"It should run at least six weeks." But of audiences later!

During the out-of-town run of O'Neill's *Desire Under the
Elms,* Bob Whitehead one night declared himself a little unhappy about the performance. The actors were doing the right
things and the direction, too, was well conceived; still, he felt
a certain emotional hollowness in the production. There was
not enough "inner life." Would I do something about this;
would I not work harder? I nodded assent. Five days later
Whitehead returned from New York, saw the performance,
and was elated. He congratulated me. I never told him I had
done nothing. The fault which had disturbed him had corrected itself, as I knew it would, through further playing. Repeated performance is the actor's most valuable instructor, if
the play's interpretive foundations have been carefully
planned in the first place.

I have often been pleaded with, virtually commanded, "to
work harder." In most cases there exists a certain misconcep-
tion—I hesitate to say ignorance—about the solution of acting
problems by "hard work," a persistent hammering away on
the same nail. The director must work well, not "hard." After
prolonged effort, periods of rest and apparent nonchalance
are more salutary for the actor than hitting him again and
again with direction.

During the Philadelphia tryout of Arthur Laurents' *The
Time of the Cuckoo,* on a day when four hours of rehearsal

were available to me, I announced to the cast that they could take the afternoon off. I was going to hear the Philadelphia Orchestra, I said, and the actors were invited to do the same or anything else they pleased. Laurents may have been perplexed; he told me that Whitehead, hearing of this in New York, was furious. Well . . .

I call Bernard Shaw to witness. In a still unpublished letter dated July 11, 1905, to Arnold Daly, his first American producer, Shaw wrote: "Under the pressure of that awful responsibility, and the conviction carefully instilled by me that each member is the particular one on whom the whole performance depends, they all get into such a state that I sometimes have to beg them [the actors] to take it easy, and to remind them that, after all, a failure will not be the end of the world. The one thing they never feel is that they are working for an employer, or that they are simply to do what someone else conceives. When things go badly and a general terror that the play will not be ready on the night seizes us, I suggest golf and a holiday. As to saying 'we must work at this till we get it' such an outrage never suggests itself to me. The moment there is any difficulty I drop it. It [the solution] always turns up spontaneously two rehearsals later if it turns up at all; and if it doesn't, no grinding at it will make it possible."

Spoken like an artist of the theatre, not a shop foreman.

Part II

Part II

CHAPTER 12

The "System"

ANYONE WHO HAS HAD any contact with theatre folk in the past thirty years will know what the title of this chapter refers to: in America it has come to be known as the "Method." It is the overall tag for the teachings of Konstantin Stanislavsky, co-founder and co-director of the Moscow Art Theatre.

The moderately informed have surely recognized that what I have outlined in the foregoing chapters is a directorial procedure largely influenced by what I have learned from Stanislavsky's writings and from personal contact with him as well as with the most knowledgeable exponents and witnesses of his activities.

I do not propose to paraphrase even in the sketchiest fashion the material of Stanislavsky's three seminal books, *An Actor Prepares, Building a Character,* and *Creating a Role.* My purpose here is to dispel some of the misconceptions about the System, or the Method, which have resulted not only in twaddle but in malpractice.

We ought to remind ourselves that Stanislavsky did not establish his theatre with the System in mind. He had been acting and directing for a long time before the founding of the M.A.T. His aim was to set up a permanent company (a "collective") which would bring artistic probity to a theatre community infected by dead conventions and shabby and false methods or lack of method. Stanislavsky and his collaborator, Nemirovitch-Danchenko, a playwright and teacher of acting, proposed to bring art to the people, and by "the people" they meant chiefly the educated middle class of Russia and perhaps, too, the advanced working class of their day. By art, Stanislavsky, in particular, meant honest, heartfelt, moral expression.

Stanislavsky was acutely aware of inadequacies in his acting, though he was from the first an accomplished actor. Truth in acting was something he could recognize when he saw it or when he momentarily experienced it in his own playing, but he found it difficult to define and to capture. Was there no way, he asked himself, that the elusive mystery of acting could be made more than a matter of chance and happy accident? By close observation of great actors and by scrupulous examination of his own acting, he arrived at certain conclusions which he was able to formulate sufficiently to be of use as a system of training and of practical work in the theatre.

It wasn't till 1909, with the production of Turgenev's *A Month in the Country* that the System was consciously applied for the first time in the direction of a play. For those who still persist in thinking of the system as a "foreign" or "un-American" phenomenon, it is worth remembering that the actors of the Moscow Art Theatre were, to begin with, not only somewhat skeptical of it but resistant.

Still more astonishing was Stanislavsky's statement to Stella Adler in 1934 that the System had never been thoroughly practiced at the Moscow Art Theatre. It was only in the theatre's Studios, particularly in the Third Studio directed by his "prize pupil" Vakhtangov, that the System was consistently employed. And, be it noted, Vakhtangov's style was not realism. Some members of the Moscow Art Theatre company, Stanislavsky said, understood and appreciated the System but did not practice it.

I myself am convinced that the Stanislavsky System, or, if you will, the Method, has never really been practiced in the United States. It is understood by some, it is taught by many, but it has never been completely employed. It has influenced the American theatre more than any other outside of Russia and those countries in its artistic orbit. I am certain that its general effect has been far more beneficial than harmful. But I would also emphasize that its practical implementation has always and everywhere been sporadic and piecemeal.

The reason for this is simple. One cannot wholly follow Stanislavsky's precepts and procedures under the conditions which obtain on our stage: there is just not enough time. One has only to read Stanislavsky's suggestions on building a character to realize how complex are his demands and what protracted and arduous effort they require. Even in the Soviet Theatre rehearsals rarely exceed three months now, which does not compare with the time spent on rehearsals in Stanislavsky's day.

But we study the System and are right to do so. It is the only thoroughgoing formulation of the actor's craft. Its tenets are neglected at the theatre's peril. This does not mean that all good actors have been trained in the Stanislavsky "canon." It is, I repeat, from the study of great actors that Stanislavsky derived the basis of his lessons.

The System is not a style. As an artist, Stanislavsky was a realist, though it should also be recalled that in 1911 he set up a studio at his own expense to broaden the theatre's range, to progress beyond realism. He said:

Briefly, the credo of the new studio was that realism and local color had outlived their use. It was the time for the unreal on the stage. It was necessary to depict not life itself as it takes place in reality, but as we vaguely feel it in our dreams and visions, in moments of spiritual uplift. It was this spiritual state that it was necessary to portray, just as it was shown by modernistic painters on their canvases, by musicians of the new school in their compositions and by new poets in their poetry. The works of these painters, musicians and poets have no clear outlines, no definite and finished melodies, no clear thoughts. The strength of these works lies in the combination and blending of colors, lines, musical notes, and the euphony of words. They create a mood that subconsciously infects the audience. They give hints which compel the spectator to create a picture in his own imagination.

Meyerhold [whom Stanislavsky appointed to head the first attempt at a studio] knew how to talk of his dreams and thoughts and found good words for their definition. From the reports and letters I saw that we agreed in our fundamentals, and that we sought for things which had already been established in other arts, but not yet in ours. . . .

I saw no means of creating the things I felt in my own imagination, saw in paintings, heard in music and read in new poetry. I did not know how to incarnate on the stage those delicate shades of feeling which were hardly expressed in the much more developed medium of words. I was powerless to bring to life the things that interested me then and I thought it would take actors tens, hundreds of years, perhaps a whole new culture, to traverse the road that had already been traversed by the other arts. . . .

I believed that every generation had something of its *own* that could not be seen by the generation that preceded it. Perhaps that which we cannot find, which we can only desire, will be normal to them . . . the new art needs new actors with a new technique. . . .

The experiment failed. "A good idea, badly shown, dies" was his comment on this initial try at overcoming the limitations of his own realism. "But," he added, "we, Nemirovitch-Danchenko and I, already saw that we were at a crossroads, that we had to bring new blood into the company. . . ."

Though he adapted his system to the performance of opera, Stanislavsky never wholly achieved a new style. Still, the starting point or basic approach of the outstanding non-realists and even those who apparently opposed him stems from a core which he was first to enunciate and systematize. Vakhtangov and Grotowski have repeatedly affirmed this though their productions have aimed at different aesthetic objectives for which they discovered new or additional means.

Such a question as "Is X a technical actor or a Method actor?" makes me gag. The system *is* a technique, it is not an end in itself. Nor is it a *theory*. It exists and has value only in practice, in the work of the actor, the director, the company. What is called the "technical actor" is one who has mastered the peripheral attributes of acting: the problems of voice, speech and body and the various devices for effective projection. Stanislavsky does not neglect or reject any of these capacities but they are not central to his technique.

I have never spoken about acting without being asked: Can the System be used in comedy, in musicals, in farce, in fantasy, in the theatre of the absurd, in Brecht, in the non-verbal or ultra-contemporary theatre, whatever that may be. The question betrays a fundamental misunderstanding: the System wasn't conceived to produce a particular stylistic result, such as realistic truth; it is a means whereby a particular artist or group of artists may most authentically and completely manifest whatever they wish in the theatre.

One of the most unmistakably non-realistic theatre forms is the Japanese Noh. It is still appreciated by many Japanese today, most of whom barely understand a word of the archaic language it employs. It is preeminently a theatre of movement, song and speech which is closer to chant than to dialogue. It is one of the most abstract of theatre modes. When one reads the tracts of the actor Zeami (1363–1444), the Noh theatre "Shakespeare," one imagines one is reading Stanislavsky in poetic apothegms. "If, because the actor has noticed that old men walk with bent knees and back and have shrunken frames, he simply imitates these characteristics," Zeami writes, "he may achieve an appearance of decrepitude,

but it will be at the expense of the 'flower.' And if the 'flower'
be lacking there will be no beauty in the impersonation. . . .
The 'flower' consists in forcing upon an audience *an emotion
which they do not expect*."

The truth or the "emotion" of a Shaw play is not that of
one by Maeterlinck, Chekhov, Pirandello or Beckett. The so-
called Method director, unless he is an ass, will not aim at
the same objective for Shaw as for any of the others. Brecht,
influenced, he said, by the Noh theatre, did not seek to create
the kind of truth or the moods which Stanislavsky did, but
the System does not propose only one kind of mood or truth,
not even "emotion," in all plays. It only leads to ways and
means to induce assent of spirit, credibility and conviction on
any level desired.

The Method teaches the actor how he may discover in himself the causes which lead to proper effects. Such effects exist
in artificial comedy as in everything else. Realism, in its day a
new style, is the style fashioned to create a semblance of ac-
tuality. It might even be argued that it is the most extrava-
gantly artificial of all styles. For who but a yokel or a madman confuses a realistic play with real life?

When an actor exhibits sorrow or rage, nobility or exaltation, without our feeling something of their reality within
him, we who employ the vocabulary of the System say he is
playing the *result*: he is demonstrating what he wants to believe he is expressing. But unless we are guileless we fail to
believe him though his demonstration may be executed with
remarkable expertise. What he is doing may be superb imitation or illustration; it is not creation. Lightness, fancy, wit,
eloquence, vivacity, daring, may be as fraudulently exhibited
on the stage as the so-called deeper sentiments which the innocent or ignorant among actors and spectators associate with
the System.

The System comprises two main divisions. The first is
"the work on the self," the *training* of the actor; the other,
for which the System is specifically designed, is "the work on

the part," that is, within a production. Young people who study the System in theatre schools, colleges or studios are enlisted in the first of these divisions; in other words, they are hopefully equipping themselves to practice in the second.

We have no theatres, as there are in the Soviet Union and elsewhere in Eastern Europe, where the System is regularly part of production. Those of our actors and directors who have received some training in the System, and they are now legion, help themselves as much as possible with it—and, if wise, shut up about it.

When an actor mumbles, behaves in all sorts of unseemly and distasteful ways, grovels shamelessly, forces his soul grotesquely, cries out and roars to the point of unintelligibility, it is not because he is a "Method actor" but because he is a bad actor. No English or French theatre schooling has ever been as exacting in its insistence on vocal flexibility, control, euphony, clarity, force and beauty of speech as Stanislavsky. Reading the sections devoted to these subjects, in addition to the one on tempo-rhythm, in *Building a Character* and *Creating a Role,* one gathers the impression that the man must be exaggerating. The severity of the prescribed discipline is exhausting—even to read about.

I was convinced that Stanislavsky meant all he said on this score when he spoke with respect but unmistakable dissatisfaction about the actors' voices at the Comédie Française, a theatre which has always been regarded as preeminent in this respect. He himself, Stanislavsky added, could speak Pushkin's poetry as it should be spoken, but not Shakespeare's. His ideal for Shakespeare was the projection of something like an entire vocal score in itself, a thing of beauty but organic with the dramatic content and function of each speech and scene.

When Stanislavsky asked me which of the players at the Moscow Art Theatre I had most admired in the spring of 1935 and I named an actress who had played the leading role in Tolstoy's *Resurrection,* he dismissed the praise with a grimace and said, "But she speaks so badly."

My essay assumes that the director is dealing with capable actors who are not in production for pedagogic purposes. Still, I feel impelled to go on with these remarks on the System. I curse the day the subject was introduced to public discussion because certain of its aspects are the source of endless confusion among directors as well as actors.

The System is not nor was it ever intended to be a static body of knowledge. It kept changing not only through the practice of the epigones, but with Stanislavsky himself. He was always enriching it with new insights based on his experience as an actor and director. When Stella Adler complained that the System disturbed her, he said, "If it really disturbs you, forget about it. But perhaps you do not understand it." He then proceeded to rehearse a ten-minute scene with her for five weeks.

It may be useful to enumerate the three stages in the System's development. In the first, Stanislavsky's emphasis was on affective memory or the *memory of emotions*. I shall not discuss this in detail. For my present purpose it is enough to say, as I did in a brief discussion entitled "The Famous Method" in my book, *Lies Like Truth*, that in the exercise of affective memory the actor recalls some personal event in his past in order to generate true feeling in relation to a particular scene in a play.

I need only remark in this connection that in the cultivation and use of affective memory (interrelated with memory of the senses) Stanislavsky found the authentic stuff of life with which acting must be informed. Robert Edmond Jones defined acting as "a gradual half-conscious unfolding and flowering of the self into a new personality." In the memory of emotions Stanislavsky discovered the usable "roots" within the actor's person which might be guided toward the making of that new personality which is a particular role of a play.

The purpose and goal of this technique was to fulfill the *play*—not just the actor. Those who suppose that Stanislavsky was not concerned with the dramatist's work simply don't know what they are talking about or they have mistaken

Stanislavsky's apes for the man himself. Indeed, what Meyer-hold, Vakhtangov and others criticized in Stanislavsky was that he was too dependent on the mere interpretation of scripts. Over and over again Stanislavsky reiterates that the System exists for the "super-problem"—that on behalf of which the play was written, the dramatist's purpose.

In the United States the stress on emotional memory was embraced as a saving grace, as a universal answer. It became a fetish. It was what we all sought, were in need of: *feeling*. That is why the Method for many American actors is no longer a technique but a therapy. At a party I once heard an actress under the illusion that the System had great curative powers ask Grotowski if the Method mightn't be of inesti-mable value to a mentally disturbed person. Grotowski's im-mediate rejoinder was, "Such a person doesn't need a director, he needs a doctor."

After the initial insistence on the primacy of affective memory in lending substance to the actor's "living a role," Stanislavsky progressed to another means for arousing the actor's imagination and for stirring truthful responses in him. He spoke of the "magic 'if.'" When an actor found himself unmoved by a situation as presented in the script, he was asked to do whatever was called for by the scene *as if*—and here to interpose a substitute condition in the scene or "moment" which would make it come alive for him. The actor's imagi-native faculty—his unconscious, if you like—would awaken in him an emotion corresponding to what was required by the scene. For example: "You enter this hovel *as if* it were a cathe-dral," or "You listen to the proposal *as if* you were tasting peach brandy," "You address the man *as if* you feared he might attack you with a concealed weapon you suspect he car-ries."*

This new implement in the System led to its third stage,

* To quote Stanislavsky: "An actor must never say about the given action of his role, 'It could never happen to me,' or 'It could never happen in life,' but he must naively believe in that magic 'if' and freely and easily imagine he would do so 'if' he ever found himself in that circumstance."

one to which I have previously referred—the concentration on *physical problems*. This third stage finally became predominant in Stanislavsky's work with the actor but we should not overlook the fact that the three stages compose a continuum. Each is vital to the other.

"One must never speak of feeling to the actor," Stanislavsky says countless times. The prime element, the motive power of acting, the entire System, is based on *action*. By action Stanislavsky meant not only psychological action—the desire which prompts us to act—but the physical steps through which the desire may be aroused and fulfilled. "One must be a virtuoso in these physical actions," Stanislavsky told Stella Adler, "believe in what we do. But everything must be completely true—*to the very end*." Stanislavsky chose the physical actions implicit in the play. "For emotion," he went on, "I search in the *given circumstances* [the particularities of each of the play's situations] never in the feelings.

"If I try and do the psychological, I force the action. We must attack the psychological from the point of view of the physical life so as not to disturb the feeling. [I translate literally from the French he spoke.] *In each psychological action there is some physical element*. Search for the line, *in terms of action*, not in feeling.

"For example: I want to drink water but I am told there is poison in it. Before I drink, I question myself: 'Who has put it in, do I want to die, why should I drink, why should I die?' Your imagination must understand each of these things. . . . Do you see the character's life with your eyes (not your feelings)? How does the character get up in the morning? What was she like yesterday, what is the layout of her house?"

In his plan for the production of that highly emotional play *Othello,* and in his instructions to the actor who was to play the role, he wrote, "For God's sake don't think of the psychology, of the feeling, of emotion—work on the physical problem, the action."

Stanislavsky had always maintained that feeling, though

" 'tis a consummation devoutly to be wished," was most elusive and beyond conscious control. It could only be summoned by indirect means. He defined the System as a conscious technique to lure or awaken the super-conscious. To act means to will: one can prepare oneself to will solutions for specific technical problems.

All this has a special relevance to the *esthétique* of the new avant-garde theatre. In this theatre, we are assured by its exponents, life isn't "imitated." The actor doesn't interpret a character, he enacts "functions." Actors change from one "role" or "function" to another many times during a performance. Meaning is communicated through the various actions the actor is called upon to do. This leads to a particular style intended to embody something of our present mode of behavior. So be it! But this does not contravene the System, though it puts very special limits on it. I repeat: There is nothing in the System which dictates or necessitates a particular sort of play or performance—except an empty one. Most of the plays of the "new theatre" are certainly not the kind Stanislavsky would have cared about, but that is a personal, not an objective, consideration.

When we reduce acting to physical behavior alone (though that is just as impossible as totally abstract art) we are certainly in tune with the times: it is a social symptom. But action without motivation or without objectives other than itself, performed by beings without background or whose background is taken for granted as that of "anybody" in situations assumed to be common experience, rarely carries much impact—no matter how startling it may be. Such performances stir us to the degree that we might be stirred if a pistol were shot without our knowing who did the shooting, why it was shot and at whom it was aimed.

The removal of broad human scope from acting does not eliminate it, but it takes away much of its power to touch us. That is one reason the so-called new theatre has not yet produced any outstanding actors. Still, we may go so far as to admit that if the physical actions performed in such plays were dazzlingly, breathtakingly executed, they might produce the kind of exhilaration we sometimes experience at a bullfight or at an especially fine circus feat. We find perfection of this sort in certain dancers. But everyone familiar with the dance knows that the classical ballet as much as the modern dance calls for something more than physical aplomb.

The purport of my argument is neither to extol the virtues of the Stanislavsky System nor to uphold a traditional view of the theatre—neither is threatened by the new theatre—but to make clear that in the creation as well as in the judgment of theatre we must first of all understand what goal is being sought, what the artists are endeavoring to communicate. No holds are barred in the theatre, but we must believe in what we see and ascertain what value we attach to what we see and are asked to believe.

I believe in the Noh theatre, I believe in the great clowns. I believe Edward Villella's leaps, I believe Violette Verdy and Allegra Kent, Martha Graham, Merce Cunningham. I believe the superb acrobat. All have their reality—as well as deadly imitators. Whether we think of their different realities as an "imitation of life" or not matters little except to pedants: they are manifestations of life. What do we expect from the theatre? It is not merely a question of novel techniques for these must be ultimately judged by their contribution to our human needs, our aspirations, moral concerns and philosophies. These questions lead to the role played by the audience in the theatre.

CHAPTER 13

The Audience

WE HEAR MUCH TALK nowadays about the theatre of partic-
ipation, in which audience and players fuse and become part
of one another. The impulse which prompts propaganda
for that sort of theatre is a healthy one. It harks back to the
theatre's origins. Its recurrence now as a battle cry of the
younger generation has social meaning. But it should escape
no one that the theatre is and always has been the product of
such fusion. The theatre is inconceivable in any other terms.

Theatre is a particular mode of expression through which
a community realizes itself. The audience is the theatre's well-
spring, its leading actor. This is not a metaphor, it is a historical fact.

The theatre is an outgrowth of the rites of primitive communities engaged in prayer or invocation to the gods. These
communities beseeched the gods to supply them with those
things without which they could not live: rain, plentiful har-

vests, a successful hunt, *et al.* Every member of the community or tribe was involved. The gods were feared as well as
loved; along with pleas for sustenance there were magic cere-
monies of appeasement enacted in gestures of worshipful
praise. When the tribal pleas were granted, there were fes-
tivities. The communal rites developed ever greater variety
of form. Some of the rites were "reports" or symbolic reenact-
ments of the adventures, perils and triumphs attendant to the
tribal pursuits. Relief, fervor, ecstasy, as well as sheer pleasure, imbued these manifestations. Men cannot live without
venting the energy aroused by their deepest needs, desires
and drives.

Each tribe had its own identity; everyone shared in a common ground of anxiety, hope, appetite and faith. A leader always emerged from within the tribe. He may himself have
contributed to the ritualizing of ceremonial activities or
chosen a favored "qualified" person to help him do so. Rites
took place where it was natural or convenient for everyone to
participate in them. Whatever sites were selected for these
occasions were the first settings or stages, just as the leaders
of the tribal "performances" were the first directors.

Since language had not yet sufficiently evolved, primitive
men expressed themselves chiefly through gesture, mimicry,
movement and sound which became dance and music. With
the development of speech, magic words came into being:
poetry, "literature." Whoever extracted them from the welter
of tribal experience and ceremonial action was an embryonic
"playwright." Or perhaps the leader alone with the aid of his
subordinates chose the scheme of the "play" and determined
which of the spontaneous improvisations were most impressive as movement, sound and speech.

There may have been a time when there was no leader at
all—only the group unit. But not all its members could engage in the main pursuit: not all could hunt, plant seed,
gather crops, fight. They served complementary functions "at
home." The folk mass as a whole was therefore divided into

those at home and those who depicted their way of life through ordered celebration. Those who sat and watched—if they were capable of such passivity—must at least have swayed in sympathy with the "actors." The least directly engaged, let us say the old, were close kinsmen to those who were central to the ceremony.

It would have been unthinkable for a community which lived by the hunt to develop a rite centered on the need for grain or for one which depended on abundant rainfall to inspire themselves with the "play" of sun worship. The material and content of the various rites were always in accord with tribal needs. Art as such was not a consideration.

The foregoing is a wholly unscientific, crudely fanciful summary of what every history and book of anthropological conjecture tells us. What is almost never told us is the bearing such studies may have on our present understanding of the theatre. They proclaim the theatre's monistic essence, its oneness. The actor, the dramatist, the director, the designer, are interrelated in a single organism. They all originate in the community which they serve, they are all parts of the so-called *audience*. Actors are not born in Equity.

With the theatre's development from the unifying rite to the later mysteries and morality plays along with the street fairs, troubadours, clowns of the marketplace, and minstrels of all descriptions, to the theatres of sovereigns and nobility and then to the commercial theatre, the functions begin to separate, to assume independence and to arrogate to themselves special and divisive airs and privileges. The various craft unions of our contemporary theatre are signs of this baleful evolution. When each grouplet represents a separate interest, it becomes more inimical to the theatre as a whole. Monetary considerations, if nothing else, may force our new theatre groups to restore some of the lost unity by having actors, directors and even some playwrights serve as technical and administrative staff as well.

In our pluralistic society the audience is no longer homogeneous. The establishment in some countries of workers' theatres, political theatres, religious theatres, theatres for poets, guerrilla and hippie theatres, are attempts to recover harmony, to wed audience and players.

There is a practical significance in all this. It explains why a pleasant little comedy like John van Druten's *The Voice of the Turtle,* played by an excellent company headed by the enchanting Margaret Sullavan, succeeds in New York and fails in London with the same cast and production. The play, which had its New York premiere in 1943, dealt with the philanderings of an army officer on leave. The war with its daily devastation was no laughing matter to the English. They were not merely unamused by the play, they resented it. The audience was badly cast for the play. It rejected its part.

How explain the enormous success of Brecht-Weill's *The Threepenny Opera* in Greenwich Village beginning in 1954 after its failure on Broadway in 1933? Why, following its long New York run, did it fail once again when it was taken on tour in large theatres outside New York? The audience for a Macdougal Street theatre, though it is made up of people who come from different parts of town, is not of the same disposition as the Broadway audience: its financial estate is different, its social and intellectual physiognomy and its taste are dissimilar.

The Trial of the Catonsville Nine, about the destruction of draft board files by the Berrigan brothers and their followers, is acclaimed by public and press when produced at a small church only to collapse as a Broadway show. The audiences which pack the house for *Promises, Promises* or *Follies* are not likely to be attracted to a debate on the moral issues raised by the Berrigan action.

Strindberg, I venture to say, will never be a popular dramatist in the United States except in university theatres or with other special groups. Neither will Pirandello. Brecht has never been a success on Broadway, but he has been played in America more often than anywhere else in the world—played, that is, to audiences receptive to his art, which are found mainly in universities and in certain regional theatres. O'Casey's plays, by no means abstruse, have never enjoyed a long run in New York.

One reason, I believe, for the emergence of musical comedy as an eminently American theatre form is that productions of musical comedy unite talent of kindred nature and similar training in a form embodying American ebullience, commitment to fun, energy, industry and an optimism fostered by prosperity. Our musicals, if nothing else, are marvelous machines of entertainment. And that is what the big undifferentiated American audience wants above all in the theatre.

To everyone's astonishment, the Theatre Guild became a thriving organization in the twenties. There had been sophisticated, cosmopolitan people in New York prior to that period with a wider range of interests and tastes than the earlier American theatre had led us to suppose, but a theatre audience composed of such people became conscious of itself for almost the first time in 1915. When America was transformed into a world power in ever closer contact with Europe as a consequence of the First World War, its theatre entered a new stage in its history. A new audience formed itself through this development, an audience which brought about a "renaissance" in all our arts. The Theatre Guild was able to organize an audience on a subscription basis and attract large numbers of theatregoers for plays by St. John Ervine, Andreyev, Molnar, Shaw and O'Neill. Before 1914 such dramatists would have been caviar to the main body of our theatregoers.

"When the audience is not there," I once heard Jacques Copeau say, "the actors aren't there either." He was not referring to box-office receipts. A play achieves resonance when all its actors are bound together in a common faith and consciousness. The play receives its echo from the audience. To put it even more simply: if the audience won't play, there's no game.

What does this mean in the practical conduct of the thea-

tre? What has·it meant to me as a director? It has been basic
to all my practice. The playwright I choose to direct must be
"mine," and I, in a sense, must be part of him. We must be of
the same audience, of the same community, not in a parochial
way but in the widest sense of sharing a common vocabulary
of thought, feeling and ideals. In the broadest understanding
of this proposition, it applies to the plays of the past and to
foreign plays as well.

I do not cast actors on the basis of talent alone; I endeavor
to choose talents compatible with the playwright and myself. We know the sort of people we wish to address and to act
as our collaborators. Our audience is one which looks forward
to what we may have to say, with whom when we find ourselves in present conflict we hope to be able to persuade on
the grounds of common assumptions and proclivities. It is
this audience we believe it possible and desirable to move
and to please.

The theatre which scorns its audience is doomed, is, in fact,
no theatre at all. Does this connote conformism? Does it mean
that we follow the crowd or that Ibsen's "compact majority"
dictates the rules of our game and that we trip to its measure?
The man who believes that the audience (the *customer*) is always right, and he who believes the exact opposite by proclaiming the mass an ass, are both mistaken. The confusion
arises from ignorance with regard to the audience of which
they are part. They do not know to what segment of society
they belong. They are cut off from their fellow men, except
by the ties of animal need or, more appositely to our time,
money. Unless we are masochists, we always hope that our
audience is as large as we anticipate—or larger! I understand
what Goethe, as theatre director, meant when he admitted
that he hesitated to produce a play he felt had no chance of
success.

A director or a producer who believes he can count on an
audience of no more than a hundred people for ten nights
and finds such an audience is a success. Ionesco's *The Bald*

Soprano is a huge success in Paris: it has run for over ten years at a theatre which can only be described as minuscule. I scheduled Saroyan's *My Heart's in the Highlands* for a run of five performances under the Group Theatre's auspices; when we were able to extend its run to six weeks I found its success remarkable. I was disheartened when people who liked it bemoaned it as a flop. I could not help feeling sorry to find that such nice people's thinking was so tightly bound by Broadway calculations. "If a man does not act as he thinks," I have read somewhere, "he will end up thinking as he acts."

To the question often put to me in one form or another, "How conscious are you of the audience when you direct a play; if a situation arose in which you felt your own taste demanded one kind of direction and the assumed taste of the audience another, would you try to please yourself or the audience?" My answer always has been, "But I am one of the audience or, at any rate, a particularly conscious part of it." I choose a play for a certain audience, and the actors for that play. I do not consider myself alien to the audience. We are a family more or less in accord. I assume that the audience wants to see and hear what I do, that it will laugh when I do and be moved where I am moved. When I am disappointed by the audience's reactions, I try to understand the reason; I investigate the cause of the discrepancy.

If I am convinced that the audience is justified in its discomfiture or objection, I try to remedy the fault. When I believe I may override their objections, I persist on my path till proved wrong, though absolute proof is rarely possible. There are, after all, the previews or the weeks of tryout to test various solutions to unresolved problems. But I never proceed from contempt. At times I will allow myself to fail if failure is the cost of my convictions. I do not believe in gaining favor by self-betrayal. My normal attitude is exemplified by the incident of the two high school boys whose innocent and modest query about the barroom scene in *The Member of the Wedding* persuaded me to cut it.

No discussion of the audience should neglect the influence of the critic. It is not easy in our society for the critic to exercise his true function which is to serve as an enlightened go-between for artists and audiences. The reviewer on a large-circulation daily is chiefly responsible to the journal which employs him and its impact on the theatre profession *as a business*. His relation to theatre as an art and to theatre workers is, in the main, fortuitous. Ideally (and why not speak occasionally in that vein?) the critic should be something of an artist himself (*as critic*) with a particular aptitude for the "optics" of the theatre enhanced by experience and study. With innate sympathy for and understanding of the theatre's craftsmen such a person may serve as the audience's knowing eye and conscience.

When we speak of the theatre audience today we are referring to a conglomerate. Actually there is a great variety of audiences. The critic must know to which of these audiences he is most truly related or what sort of audience he would like to create. In his day Shaw helped create an audience for Ibsen and the then new theatre of England. In the fifties Kenneth Tynan waged a battle for John Osborne, Arnold Wesker, Bertolt Brecht and other writers, as well as directors and actors who were upsetting the West End theatre establishment.

We must judge a critic not so much by his particular opinions as by his standards. The chief issue is not the critic's separate likes or dislikes but what he believes and is as a man, what he strives for, in what sort of world he desires to live. I am distrustful of the critic who only wants "good theatre." Good for what, I ask, for whom? In what way is it good and what part of me is it good for?

The sound critic is not wholly "free." He is limited, as Shaw put it, by his prejudices. He must reveal them and "fight" for them. I have admired conservative, socialist, religious, Marxist, impressionist, analytic, anarchist and mystic critics. They have all been more useful in the formation of my own tastes and judgments than the affable creature who is equally and blandly, or even enthusiastically, receptive to everything. He signifies nothing because he stands for nothing: he merely fills space in a column which usually resembles pleasant or unpleasant chitchat. Such a person, at best, acts as a privileged consumer's guide.

The critic must know what a *play* (not simply its plot) signifies: he must be equipped to judge the script, the acting and the direction. Each of these has its own content, yet must be understood in relation to one another. He must be able to assess the "weight" and import of the theatre event as a whole. And he should be judged by his ability to see the play in the perspective of what lies "outside" the theatre, i.e., the world in which we live, the world which has brought the occasion into being. The critic most illuminates what he sees through the fullness of his own perception of life. That is how he may help make the audience a more creative participant in the theatre's festivity.

This has little to do with "raves" or "pans": they only concern show business. But who in hell thought of the theatre as a business in the first place? That is a sure way to eliminate it —even as a business!

CHAPTER 14

Questions and Answers

IN LECTURING on direction and related subjects I am asked many questions. Though most of my answers are implied in the foregoing chapters, I shall set down here a few summary replies to the questions most commonly asked.

1. *If the sources of the theatre are rooted in the community in which it is situated, does this not restrict the choice of plays to the narrow interests of the local scene?*

Though I deplore a theatre which neglects the patrimony of the past, I confess a predilection for the newly created. Not because the latter is superior to the old—obviously this is not so—but because the art of theatre, an art of *presence,* is also the art of the present. Shakespeare and other masters of the past are, as Jan Kott and others have pointed out, our contemporaries. Their greatness transcends the limits of time and

many cultural differences. In the *theatre* they reveal their con-
temporaneity only when they are felt and projected in response to our innermost needs. This is not to be construed to
mean that they must be made "topical," e.g., Julius Caesar as
Mussolini, Shylock as an East Side peddler or King Lear as an
example of latter-day nihilism.

The theatre is not a museum, a treasure house to commem-
orate ancient wonders; it is a vehicle for the manifestation of
the joys and travail of our existence. The greater the scope
and profundity of its revelations, the more universal it becomes. But it always begins with the *now*.

2. *What do you do about the resistant actor, the one who
disagrees with your interpretation of a part?*

Before answering the question point blank it is important
to realize that refractoriness in an actor has diverse, not always
immediately recognizable, psychological causes. Vanity may
enter into it, or a too-great susceptibility to criticism, a
fear of disapproval, a "star" complex, unfamiliarity with the
director's mode of procedure and other peculiarities.

Every director invents or improvises "tricks" to deal with
the individual actor's hang-ups. An actor in whose talent Stanislavsky believed lacked self-confidence. He was always breaking down with a sense of inadequacy after his finest flights.
Stanislavsky instructed his company to prepare placards on
which were inscribed something like "Y is a superb artist."
Whenever Stanislavsky noticed that an attack of inferiority
tremens was about to overpower the actor, he would call on
the others to parade around the despondent man. This always
produced the desired effect: the actor felt refreshed.

In directing Thomas Mitchell in the touring company of
Death of a Salesman I found that no matter how brief a remark I made about some small point, he would elaborate with
extended comments of his own to show me not only that he
had understood what I had said, but that he understood more
and better. After all, he was a veteran actor and director many

years before I had begun my career. I realized that if I betrayed impatience or attempted to silence him he would resent it. On the other hand, if I let him continue to interpolate
his disquisitions at every bit of direction I proposed, the rehearsals would deteriorate into hours of futile discourse.

I ceased offering him any direct guidance. I would turn instead to whomever he was playing a scene with and say something like this: "You are annoyed because your father [Mit-
chell] has just reprimanded you," or "Willy [Mitchell] has
begun to plead with you so touchingly that you answer in
kind," or "You see in Willy's face the clouds of anger gather
and you try to calm his impending fury." In other words, I
directed Mitchell through his partners in the scene. The
stratagem worked.

But my principal maxim in cases of personal difficulty with
an actor is: Never, never, never win an argument with him,
never persuade him that he is "wrong," just get him to do
what you want! The director who beats an actor down by the
force of his own authority does so at his own cost. The direc-
tor-martinet is an obsolete phenomenon today—and should be.
A director who insists that he is always absolutely right is indulging his own ego. Much rehearsal time is wasted through
such indulgence.

Still! When an actor tells me that he differs with me, I usually say, "Don't talk, *show me*." If his demonstration fails to
convince me, I explain why what he has shown me doesn't fulfill the play's or the scene's demands. Or I choose two or three
other possible directives, not previously proposed, which he
may follow. The actor more often than not will then turn
back to the directorial suggestions which he had initially rejected.

Though I am given to close analysis of all the interpretive
problems which may arise at rehearsal, I am aware that too
much cerebration of this sort tends to be redundant and obstructive.

In casting *The Time of the Cuckoo,* I had Katina Paxinou in mind for a certain part. Arthur Laurents, the author, had reservations on this score. We chose another actress: Lydia St. Clair. But the Paxinou image persisted in my thinking. I directed Miss St. Clair as if the Greek actress were playing the role. After the first major run-through Miss St. Clair said, "I'm bad in this role. If you want it acted as you have directed it, you should have cast Katina Paxinou." "I never thought of such a thing," I lied. "Please show me how you would prefer to play the part." She did, and was excellent. Thank heavens she "won"!

The actor is seen on the stage, not the director. It is also important to realize that there is a moment—very late in the rehearsal or preview period—when the actor knows more about the part he is playing than the director. The director must be ever vigilant in seeing that the actor doesn't become sidetracked in his performance; he must be kept "in line." But the role is finally the actor's possession.

An actor, after due compensation of course, may be dismissed. I have very rarely had recourse to this method of improving the quality of a production.

3. *Does the director call additional rehearsals after the play has opened?*

He should. It is difficult to keep a production in shape after three months of playing. We rejoice in a long run, but it is artistically debilitating. A director should check on his production *at least* twice a month.

I say this glibly, but the truth is that during my first years as a director I positively loathed seeing one of my productions after it had opened; I was nearly always disappointed at my failure to accomplish all I had hoped to. But since then self-discipline has prevailed.

Apropos of this, I recall speaking to the brilliant Czech director Ottomar Krejča about his beautiful production of *The Three Sisters*. Though I admired it, I found much in it subject to cavil. A year later, on seeing it again, I told him that I now liked it much more. "Ah, but we've been working on it ever since we opened," he said. The play, to begin with, had been rehearsed for many months. It was in repertory.

Kazan once told me that after six months of a continuous run actors are unable to retain either the glow or the just proportions of their original performance: they lose their resilience. I agree.

There are exceptions. I saw Walter Huston in *Desire Under the Elms* four times over a period of twelve months. Each performance was better than the previous one. One day after many months of playing in *Awake and Sing* I noticed Stella Adler examining the "book" of her part. I asked her why. "I'm looking over the notes I took at rehearsal," she answered. "I'm trying to see if I've lost something of the original intentions and if there are new ways of recharging the 'battery.'"

4. *Are there any ground rules you bring to bear for comedy versus tragedy versus "straight" drama versus fantasy, etc.?*

The basic tenets of direction remain the same for all productions. Only emphases change, that is, styles. Before I undertook the direction of my first independent production, *Awake and Sing*, Elmer Rice advised me to direct it "for comedy." Several other established theatre people told me I must stress the pathos. I found both counsels meaningless. I directed the play for the qualities I perceived in it—without "labels." The results depend on the choice of actions, adjustments and characterizations. What counts is the director's vision and temperament.

In the direction of musicals, certain technical considerations are extremely important: they have to do with concision, overall rhythm and proportions in the relationship of music and dance to dialogue. There are directors who are peculiarly suited to the task. I have directed only one musical: Rodgers' and Hammerstein's *Pipe Dream*. It was not a success: serious mistakes in casting were made, and the piece itself was far from the team's best. Would the outcome have been happier if George Abbott, let us say, had directed it? He is adept in the field, but *Me and Juliet,* the Rodgers and Hammerstein musical which preceded *Pipe Dream,* had also been a failure.

5. *Can a good director handle anything from* King Lear *to* Burlesque?

Theoretically, yes. Actually, I doubt it. An artist's limitations are integral with his talent. I can't truly say which of my productions I regard as the "best." Was it *Awake and Sing, Golden Boy, The Member of the Wedding, The Waltz of the Toreadors, Bus Stop, A Touch of the Poet, Tiger at the Gates, Incident at Vichy,* or—? Perhaps one of my failures was as good as any of these. What is the "best" anyhow? I work as scrupulously on plays I do not particularly admire as on those which I do.

6. *How have you managed to direct plays in such languages as Japanese and Hebrew, of which you are totally ignorant?*

Apart from the use of an interpreter, my methods do not change in these cases. Technique sustains me. After several readings and the repetition of scenes for a week or two, I begin to associate the foreign sounds with the script in English (or with *Monserrat,* in French). I am able to detect errors in readings and even, incredible though it may seem, faults in diction. This was no doubt also Tyrone Guthrie's experience in Israel with *Oedipus Rex.*

7. *Do you assume that for any play an ideal production is at least in theory possible?*

No; a production is ideal only in relation to its director's vision of it and to a particular spectator's taste. "A play," Vakhtangov said, "must be directed with a view to the company and the audience to whom it is to be presented." I have seen productions which have troubled me in regard to interpretation but which I respected for the excellence of their craftsmanship and their imaginative originality. A play is new with every fresh view of it. We would all be horrified, I am sure, if we were able to see *Hamlet* as it was done at the Globe Theatre in the Shakespeare-Burbage production!

8. *Do you ever lose your temper?*

Very rarely. Usually it does little good—unless the temper is feigned and is suitable to a particular situation and actor. (Directors are often expert "hams.") But an atmosphere of genial cordiality coupled with earnest effort serves best. Blame, recrimination, anger, a display of anguish, are hardly ever in order.

9. *Can an actor direct as effectively as a good nonacting director?*

An actor had better not direct a play in which he appears himself—unless his role is a subsidiary one. But what of Stanislavsky or Orson Welles? There are many notable exceptions. Should a playwright direct his own play? Those who are qualified should. Bernard Shaw, Noel Coward, George S. Kaufman and Bertolt Brecht directed their own plays with signal success. Each in his own way was a consummate theatre craftsman. Very few contemporary playwrights are, though some believe themselves to be. Ask their actors.

10. *Should a director have acting experience?*

It is most advantageous, even if the director should not have proved to have been a good actor. The more general theatre experience the would-be director acquires during his apprenticeship, the better. I frown on those who, having just graduated from a theatre school, attempt direction on an ambitious scale.

11. *How much of an "academician" must a good director be?*

An intelligent person need never fear learning. The more extensive the director's general study, the more equipped he will be for his profession. "Direction," Meyerhold said, "is the broadest specialty there is." But one must learn how to translate one's knowledge into theatre. Direction is not achieved solely through verbal concepts. For stage embodiment words alone do not suffice.

12. *Can directing be taught?*

To a certain extent, yes. It certainly can be learned. But a college course alone is inadequate for the purpose. One should attend many, many rehearsals of many different sorts and eventually take some active part in them. It is best to study direction under a variety of theatrical auspices. Assistant stage management and, later, stage management in several productions under different directors provide good schooling. Working for or directing a stock company, a community theatre or a modest but professional experimental group is also a valuable preparatory step. A theoretical approach alone will not do.

The simplest answer to the question is: you can learn directing if you have a talent for it.

13. *Should theatre people be aware of sociological or political problems?*

The answer is the same as to question eleven. The director today, particularly with a permanent company, tends to become an educator as well as a director. The theatre is not a school, but work in it should constitute a schooling. I applaud Tyrone Guthrie's dictum: "Unless you're a rounded citizen, you're a square theatre person."

14. *What other "lines of work" are comparable to directing?*

Directing is often compared to conducting an orchestra. The parallel is only partially apposite and there is one very important difference. While a conductor knows the exact properties, possibilities and limitations of each instrument, the director is never certain with the actor whether he is to be stroked, scratched, plucked or thumped!

15. *Are "stars" easier to work with than "unknowns"?*

An experienced and talented actor is easier to work with than an unpracticed one. He knows more and has more to offer. The amateur or novice is often extremely touchy and cocksure when he is not self-conscious. (But children are sometimes "born" actors.)

After years of work with the Group Theatre's acting com-company I found Fredric March, Melvyn Douglas, Julie Harris, Maureen Stapleton, Michael Redgrave and several other stars most amenable and appreciative of direction. The test of the actor is innate creative resourcefulness which is intimately associated with receptivity to suggestion. Perhaps I've been lucky, perhaps I've known how to choose the right people.

16. *What are the chief qualities a director must have?*

The first of these surely is the ability to deal with people. "Direction," a French critic has said, "is criticism transferred to action." Yes, but the director, I repeat, does not influence by verbal explanation only. There are eloquent directors and some who are very nearly mute. In one way or another the director must impress his company, make it feel that he merits his leadership and their confidence.

The director does not achieve his effects only by means of physical staging, the visible and audible signs of his invention, knowledge and skill. I have observed many directors in rehearsal. Even in the case of those who said little and seemed to be "doing" less, I could detect their imprint in the completed production. There is something of a mystery in this of which the director himself may not be conscious. It is an emanation which we inadequately designate as "personality." It goes beyond the demonstrable specifics of the craft.

Did not Reinhardt's productions breathe a Viennese gaiety, a baroque sensuality and glamor, a peculiarly mid-European warmth, a cordially humorous Jewish skepticism? Was there not something of the cunning necromancer, the diabolic magician, in all of Meyerhold's productions? Guthrie's wide-

ranging playfulness, his vaulting freedom, his amiable mis-
chievousness, shines through all his work. We cannot fail to
recognize the muscular energy added to common sense in
Kazan's best efforts on the stage, or the adventuresomeness,
the love of prestidigitation and the bravado in Orson Welles'
stage exploits.

The director's essential qualities as a human being, which
he perhaps unconsciously communicates, cannot be pinned
down. There are no lessons for acquiring this inalienable personal touch. This is only another way of saying that a director
must be a creative person, he must be *somebody*. Otherwise
he is only a journeyman.

But we must never lose sight of my first proposition: It is
not the director alone who shapes the production, he employs everyone's talent. He chooses those whom he may be
able to inspire and those he believes will aid and inspire him.
As a leader, he must be a knowing follower. Like all good artists, the director must also be a canny plagiarist.

17. *What should a director avoid or prevent?*

Though the director must at all times leave himself open
to suggestion and be prepared to accept correction, he must
never release his command. Though a collaborator in a collective effort, he must always remain at the forefront of his
troupe. He must not permit the playwright or the producer
to speak to the actors about their roles—unless he requests
them to do so. It is confusing to actors to receive direction
from several sources. Moreover, playwrights and producers
rarely employ the actor's vocabulary, that is, they seldom
know what is exactly the right thing to say to the actor and
the right moment to speak. The director and his company
develop a common language through their long and intimate
exchange during rehearsals.

Previews and out-of-town tryouts are the periods at which
the actors are most vulnerable and susceptible to infection
even by the most kindly or innocuous comment. Actors will

listen to almost anything at such times. They should be quar-
antined from friends and relatives.

I directed Morris Carnovsky in Odets' *Night Music* in the
role of a New York detective, the fount of wisdom in the play.
He was to speak his lines, I told him, in a gravelly voice and
to apply a makeup that would give him an almost bestial look.
He chose the bust of a grim Roman emperor as his model.
The combination of compassionate sentiment in the dialogue
with the forbidding mask contributed to an unusually interesting characterization. Odets was most favorably impressed.

A friend or a relative—perhaps an out-of-town critic—found
the voice and the makeup "unsympathetic." Slowly and un-
knowingly Carnovsky began to modify both. It took me a
while to realize that by the time the play opened Carnovsky
had gone back to his own natural, clearly benevolent and
dignified physiognomy.

Still another example of interference from an outside
source came to my aggrieved notice after the opening of *Golden Boy*. Luther Adler, it struck me, had lost something of
the boyish innocence with which, as directed, he had endowed
his part. When I questioned him about this he told me that
an actress whom he greatly and justifiably admired had reminded him that he was playing an *artist*. I winced in pain.
All through rehearsal I had insisted that Joe Bonaparte was a
kid who might conceivably become an artist. If he were already an artist (how does an artist behave?), the play's story
might be considered incredible. Actors and directors must
protect themselves from the hot air of chance guidance.

18. *Do you place more emphasis on the eye or the ear in
your productions, that is, are you more visually or orally
oriented?*

As this question is put, I cannot answer it. Certain directors
compose beautiful or striking tableaux or visual patterns. I
never consciously attempt to do so. I direct for the idea or intention of each scene and for the play as a whole, and seek
whatever combination of means will best convey them. I di-

rect for the actor and through the actor: he is body and voice, movement and feeling, and something more than all these. The actor, like the production itself, is an indivisible totality. I do not conceive a production in "departments." I seek the integration of all the theatre's elements to form a unified effect and meaning.

Speaking of his production of Beaumarchais' *Marriage of Figaro,* Stanislavsky said, "The style was hardly French: it is impossible for Russians to achieve a true French manner. There were crudities in the acting and in some of the staging. Not all the actors were well cast. The sets weren't all they should have been. But somehow the production worked, it was alive." The same must have been true of the first Moscow Art Theatre production of *The Seagull*—which made history.

Perhaps the overall answer to the question should be stated hyperbolically: The director should listen with his eyes and see with his ears.

19. *What are the director's special satisfactions?*

For all his preparation and particular competence the director works "blindly." He cannot really be sure as he concentrates and polishes each bit what effect the play will ultimately produce. There are occasions when it never comes to life till the audience has acted with, on, or in it!

The director experiences his greatest satisfaction the moment he realizes that he has contributed to the magic of a birth, and that what has been born possesses something of the nature he hoped it might have.

20. A sixteen-year-old student once asked me, *"What is the worst thing that happens to a director?"*

My answer was: "You see from all I've told you how thoughtfully, how painstakingly, how sincerely and how knowledgeably I labor on a production. Yet for all that my efforts to bring about the hoped for result may be in vain. The magic doesn't happen. I fail."

"What do you do then?" the candid youth asked.

"I forgive myself."

Part III

Part III

Rocket to the Moon

by CLIFFORD ODETS

(First presented by the Group Theatre at the Belasco Theatre, November 24, 1938.)

The mood of this "romance" is *loneliness*. Every element in the play, the physical environment (the setting), the heat, the love affair, the "sexiness," must express the basic loneliness.

The loneliness is also a social phenomenon. Stark's office, his practice, his daily pursuits and habits, his income and his marital life create his need for Cleo or someone like her. These are all part of the play's poignancy.

The setting must suggest a kind of mystery. Always the feeling of night, of secrecy, a hidden place, an enclosure, "mysterious" sounds: the gurgle of water from the cooler, the hum of the electric fan, rain.

The spine of the play: to seek love (search for love).

Spine: to make things (his life) approximate the condition of love.

He has always been poor; his childhood was spent in an orphanage. He has had to accommodate himself to the "reality" of lower-middle-class inevitability. "Aren't you always right?" he says to his wife.

But even after he has accommodated or accepted this sort of reality, he somehow resists it. He suggests that with his father-in-law's aid he might open a new office with new equipment. "All night I didn't sleep thinking about it," he says, but when his wife demurs, he weakens. "Let's forget it, Belle." Nevertheless, he keeps pressing his point. When Belle rejects his arguments he surrenders, "You win, you win!"

His lower-class timidity overcomes him, both here and at the end of the play. "It's settled."

His life is a long forgetting: "I came over to the water cooler," but he has forgotten his objective. "I wanted *to do* something." "I have a bunch of answers for that, but I won't give them . . ." because they won't avail. He even kids his ineffectuality. To his wife's remonstrances he replies, 'Yes, m'am."

He has forgotten the struggle that has made him forget. He has almost forgotten his child's death.

He is embarrassed by his own and other people's emotion. It is too sharp a reminder of the feelings welling within him —feelings and impetuses which he has suppressed or have been suppressed in him.

His *smile* is the sign of his embarrassment.

He is boyish, sometimes almost childishly jubilant. He is naive, and on a mature emotional level, inexperienced. He is guileless, lacking aggressiveness. His perpetual state of economic disadvantage makes him habitually neglectful of himself: he doesn't eat on time, for instance.

There is withal a certain stubbornness in him. Though he

renounces many things, he depends on his desires. What he has desired was something to help him toward love.

He is irritable, but his irritability, being without positive consequences, gives way to depression. After Mr. Prince, his father-in-law, leaves him, he admits to himself all the secret desires he has denied in Mr. Prince's presence.

Mr. Prince depresses Stark because he sees in him a completely despairing man, and Stark isn't that as yet.

Stark's naiveté is the result of his continued surprise by the evidence of life. He is amazed that his old, financially successful father-in-law should have wished to be an actor. He thinks of a secretary as a simple employee but Cleo, his secretary, opens his eyes to himself.

Stark doesn't believe that Mr. Prince has ever been a faithful husband. He envies Prince, jealous and attracted to him because of his sexual freedom.

He defends his own status quo because he has accommodated himself to his own defeat.

Stark's relation to Cleo: in the first act Stark doesn't really see Cleo. He notices Cleo as a woman because Prince has done so.

In the first scene of the second act his (Stark's) questioning of the girl begins to arouse his sexual interest in her. "Life must be very pleasant for you," he says. That is because he sees in Cleo the possibility of fulfillment. She is in conscious quest for love, therefore closer to it, and through it, to life in general.

His inactivity has become a habit. His unhappiness is a habit.

Finally, he dares to love her. Life has forced this upon him. Cleo teaches him the insufficiency of his way of life. She urges him to change this. She makes him realize how wrong his wife's pushing him about is. He protests; he is jealous. He's afraid to lose her. He takes her.

He is unable to change his condition. His life's "reality"

is too strong and he ends defeated. But somehow because of his desire (implied in his spine) and his experience with Cleo he has been brought closer to life and love. Forever after, even if he "forgets," he will be a deeper, perhaps an ennobled man.

CLEO SINGER

Spine: to seek love—the essential action of the play.

Her quest is not simply the desire for a mate, a sexual partner. All the men offer her that. She wants a release from the drabness of her surroundings—physical and spiritual. She wants a free world of true contact with everything which is humanly worthy. Though "lost," she is richest in aspiration and in the experience of her aspiration.

Her lying is a lyric flight to an imagined world of beauty and a free life. She admits she lies, doesn't know anything; she likes "big" words, high-sounding ideas, because they move her beyond herself toward the world she yearns for. Still, they leave her empty as the people who use them are empty. She wants them concretely embodied in real people and actions. Someday, somewhere, she hopes to find them.

When she lies in a sort of daydream, she "dances."

To begin with Cleo thinks of Willy Wax as an "artist." But soon she realizes he loves only himself—not even his art, only himself in art.

BELLE STARK

Spine: to keep her man "right," in order, safe and secure in their small world.

Background of emotional insecurity, quarrels. She too is an "orphan." Her father and mother did not speak to each other. She turned against her stern father. But she wants a father.

She wants safety, steadiness. She has become "practical," conservative, she wants everything to proceed on an even keel.

Her relation to Stark is based on admiration for his fundamental kindness and fineness . . . but he must be made "steady" (her father was a gambler, a bankrupt).

She can't stand adversity. She wants to save money, to keep things neat. She wants the world's "respect." Her thoughts are turned toward keeping Stark a good provider and making him a less perfunctory, distraught lover. When she is able to arouse him in this respect she sends him back to his job again.

The loss of her child makes her feel inferior, a feeling she hides even from herself. She imagines her husband blames her for the loss, but she never talks to him about this.

She, too, is hungry for love. Through frustration, everything centers on *her* man. Cleo's yearning for love extends beyond a man. Only her husband exists for Belle.

She is secretive about her feeling, she is *lonely*.

She is proud of her ability to make Stark work and keep in line.

"No man deserves me!" Because I am competent, intelligent, practical, faithful, warm, protective, "romantic."

She is insensitive, through her exclusive concern with her own problem or her husband's. Only their world is real to her.

She is jealous of other women. Disapproves of them. (Jealousy isn't nice: lacks pride.)

"Your terrible wife": she realizes that she nags . . . feels superior and inferior. Coquettish: "You like me anyway, don't you?"

She wins her battle. But she will forever be locked in her dilemma.

She is suspicious of everyone who deals with her husband, including her father.

MR. PRINCE

Spine: he wants to find something to *do*.

"I like to do some good to a man who needs it, a lovable being"—a real connection.

He has no "philosophy." He learns only by a certain type of practical experience (success, etc.). But he has learned that the "right" answer is wrong.

He began as an "idealist," married a good-looking girl . . . then he encountered frustration of the sex impulse in marriage. No warmth. Only work was a release. Frustration of his vaulting imagination. There is a bit of the aesthete in him. He likes beautiful fabrics, colors, opera, music . . .

He broods a good deal. Lives in his past. "How did I miss my boat, a man of my fire. What did I do with my life! Where was my mistake?"

He has a sense of failure, the paradox of his failure.

Love is the only thing which really interests him. But being worldly-wise, he got "stuck." The result is cynicism. He doesn't altogether believe in anything. Yet he doesn't quite believe in his own cynicism, his own "fake" or that all there is is a fake! Yet what is there? What is the truth? He, too, is embarrassed (like Stark) but he knows one must *do* something, one must take the leap into life, unafraid. And somehow, if you're lucky, you'll have lived. But he didn't live.

He is still a sort of idealist. (Why didn't he have extra-marital affairs? Because he was honest, because he was baffled. Because just sleeping with a woman doesn't interest him even now. He was faithful, he was "stuck" even in that regard. Yet he doesn't really know what kept him faithful.)

His energy seeks an outlet. He's generous with money. He is given to large gestures, a certain panache. He is shrewd because as a businessman he has learned that there is nothing sure but money and the power it gives.

He appears to be a misogynist—because of his bad marital experience. But he loves women: tenderness, warmth, beauty. He needs companionship.

Frustration: he wanted to be an actor. He laughs at this, it is only a symbol for the kind of life he desires. Occasionally a cry is torn from him, the cry of a deeply suppressed longing.

He "resents" his age. He doesn't like being old when he's still young! It hurts him when Cleo says he's old. But being both proud and "sensible," he takes no notice of this. He toys with the idea of declaring his desire for her. He wants, wants, wants to live. And laughs at this. But thinks about death.

He dislikes himself. But he is too strong to allow any sense of inferiority in himself. He sees the fraudulence in himself and in others. This is *his* honesty.

He's still potent. And he hasn't been with a woman for a year. He is almost morbidly curious about sex. His humor and gaiety are edged with sexual repression. His cynicism is hearty. He's mischievous.

He's clownish. His alert and disturbed mind has no coherent and definite object. He has thoughts and sentiments unworthy of himself, thoughts he would be ashamed to acknowledge. When these thoughts show, he pretends he is only joking.

In the end, he bursts forth—*fights*. He has found something to do: he's even willing to buy Cleo. He's realistic about it: "I'll leave you money, give you what you dreamed about." But he's missed the boat.

Perhaps he'll commit suicide.

COOPER

Spine: to solve a problem. (If he can solve this problem he will be able to find love.)

But he is a man unused to and ill equipped for problems.

He is boyish, good-natured, almost jovial. He is never sore. A well-liked American middle-class boy. All the fellows at high school and college liked him. Never gives trouble. Always optimistic.

He doesn't do anything besides work.

He is bewildered, helpless, without protest. The heat enhances his inner discomfort.

He can hardly believe his bad luck: it has stolen in on him imperceptibly.

He worries about his creditors. But hardly believes they will *insist* on collecting—is surprised and hurt when they do. Expects everyone to be as considerate as he is.

Background: two great shocks in his life. (a) *His wife's death.* He's utterly helpless without her. He doesn't know what to do with a kid. He's a man who should be married and have someone to take care of him. (b) *Unemployment*—loss of his practice. Puzzled and intimidated, frightened by the unexpected breakdown. Hysteria.

He's also sentimental. If he weren't fundamentally healthy, he would be maudlin.

He jokes a lot, kids.

His drinking is a minor offense. He doesn't think he drinks much; he slips into the drinking habit.

The last thing he does in the play is to kiss Cleo.

FRENCHY

Spine: to keep going.

Poor. Intelligent, independent. Lives on his energy.

Without direction because he lacks love, hasn't found any "real" love. He's turned away from any true contact with women, except as sexual playmates. He doesn't like "janes" or conniving girls. He's looking (but not very hopefully) for a *real girl,* a girl for this tough world.

He loves Stark because he is without malice, helpless, lonely and tender.

He (Frenchy) also is lonely. He's attracted to Cleo, looks for her whenever he enters. "You're like a magnet." He's jealous of the Cleo-Stark relationship, partly out of his desire for her, and partly because of his concern for Stark's well-being.

If it were not for his desire to avoid becoming entangled in the mess of life he would become a bum. But now he works at his job. Lives "animal-fashion"—eats, sleeps, observes people, reads a bit. He is alone a good deal of the time.

He's something of an "anarchist" because most of his reactions to life are negative. He's waiting for a world in which he can safely connect himself with people. But now responsibility is too much for him. He's a lone wolf.

He hates phoniness, pretense and softness (as exemplified in Wax).

He is a little shy . . . arising from a fear of any connection which is not effected on his own terms. Yet he longs for connection.

I see him wandering, hovering, lolling about, breezing in, retiring with regret, yet hurriedly.

WAX

Spine: to please.

The inferior man's sense of *superiority*. This is constant even when he disparages himself.

Terribly nervous. Never contacts others except to make himself liked. He actually *sees* no one.

Eager to succeed, to get ahead, to make himself known in the rat race. This has made him overwork himself. He suffers constant strain, tension.

He cannot really enjoy his work, only his dream of it (a bit forgotten). He is sustained by his illusion that he is better than anyone else. He has no time for *devotion* to a woman. His only concern is with getting ahead and reassuring himself. He tries to impress everyone (himself included) and to please young girls.

He envies genius—chiefly among the deceased or the foreign. He's observant, even keen, malicious or sweet by turn —according to his egotistic need.

A very hard worker. Eats in. Stays alone a good deal of the time. Doesn't frequent places like Sardi's or the Algonquin. Quasi-contemptuous of ordinary theatre folk. "Kind" to radicals, but not one of them. Has heart-to-heart talks with promising young writers, musicians. Laughs a little at "arty" groups, minority communities, etc.

He rather likes Stark. He's no threat to his ego: Stark is poor, honest, and reads Shakespeare!

DIRECTOR'S NOTES FOR

The Member
of the Wedding*

by CARSON McCULLERS

(First presented in New York, January 5, 1950, at the Empire Theatre by Robert Whitehead, Oliver Rea and Stanley Martineau.)

What is the audience to enjoy?

The poetry of first impulses expressed naively, sweetly, directly. The first "shoots" of life and emotion (adolescent longing) appreciated by grown-ups thinking back on the purity of their first contact with life.

The production style: poetic—which means concentrated: every moment visually significant of the inner state.

The spine of the play: to get "connected."

It all happens in a hot summer atmosphere. The world is "dead"—the people suspended. Everything is slightly strange, not altogether real.

"Lets us have a good time," says John Henry. He seeks

* First published in *Directors on Directing*, edited by Toby Cole and Helen Krich Chinoy, Bobbs-Merrill Publishing Co., 1953, rev. ed. 1963.

"connection" but there's so little to connect with in this environment.

People who seek connection and aren't able to—ache. Frankie aches all the time. Her sobbing in the first act is the climax of an ache delicately indicated all through . . . part of the loneliness inherent in the main action.

(Frankie has no one to talk to about her resolve—so she talks to strangers: the Monkey Man or to a cat. . . . She wants connection with the whole wide world of experience.)

A stage direction reads: "Frankie scrapes her head against door." These strange gestures of children make one think that they are reenacting man's past living through the ages—animal-like, weird, primitive. More of such "gestures" must be invented for Frankie. "Flying around the world together"— Frankie will "fly" through the kitchen.

A mighty loneliness emanates from this play. It is as if all the characters were separated from the world—as if the world were only a mirage in a vaporous space making wraiths of the people.

THE SPINES FOR THE LEADING CHARACTERS

FRANKIE

Spine:—to get out of herself.

Getting out of herself means *growth*. . . . She has "growing pains": she is both tortured and happy through them. . . . The juices of life are pouring through her. She is a fragile container of this strange elixir.

Growth twists and turns her—as it does us—gives us new shapes. Frankie twists and turns. The play is the lyric drama of Frankie's growth. At the end of the play, she runs or twirls out—"to go around the world." She has achieved her aim— imaginatively. She is ready "to get out of herself."

THE MAIN CHARACTERISTICS

(1) Frankie is tomboyish. (She puts on no shows with kiss-

ing. Her father is a "widowman" with his nose to the grind-stone. She has no mother, no "social" environment.)

(2) Frankie is crazy with first love: literally head over heels: the love of the *wedding*.

(3) She is intense. She's trying to see underneath every-thing, seize its essence, "cozen it in her mind"; she even tries to seize the atmosphere of heat as a unique experience. "The kitchen's the hottest place in the U.S." she says.

Thus she is a "poetic" character. She is terribly aware of every little thing: Berenice's fur, Frankie says, has "a sad, fox-wise face."

(4) All the above produces an awkwardness that is weird an occasionally graceful.

(5) Frankie is hostile. You hate what you can't connect with and want to hurt it. Or you want to hurt yourself for failing to make the connection.

(6) She is given to self-examination. She is self-absorbed in relation to her desire for connection and wanting to "get out."

(7) Her torture comes from a sense of a past vaguely re-membered, troubled and painful—and the future—wondrous, void, unrealized and therefore frustrating. "I have this feel-ing," she moans.

(8) She is imaginative. Her mind and spirit leap: they stretch, lift, dart, fly . . . to whatever place she wants to go. When the destination is too vague, she explodes or drifts in all directions.

(Remind Julie Harris: The main action makes her a very active character. She is straining to get out. When she fails, she has one sort of emotion; when she almost succeeds, an-other.)

Frankie is fascinated by Honey. He is romantic, exciting, lightfoot. He's been "out."

BERENICE SADIE BROWN

Spine: To do her deed (work) . . . "normally." For her to live is to be connected.

A woman who is naturally and easily connected. Once she was connected with Ludie Maxwell Freeman. He died. "It leaves you lonesome afterward." After that, she sought connection with scraps and bits of what she loved—even to a madman. Now she's alone, relatively unconnected. But she manages somehow to connect with her community, with T. T., with Honey, with John Henry—but some people she doesn't desire connection with (Mrs. West, "them Germans and Japs," Mary Littlejohn). Of John Henry she says, "We enjoys him." It's as simple as that. Everything is approached without fuss, without sentimentality, without "eloquence."

She is plain—direct, earthy, quiet. Hers is the poetry of the "prosaic!" She's basic: "Two is company," she says.

Her life: "We just talks and passes the time of the day"—that's enough.

"Stop commenting about it," she tells Frankie. She does not need to "comment" to make things real to herself.

"Sunday will come." Sufficient unto the day—

When people want to go away from her—John Henry or Frankie or Honey—she just lets them go.

Unnaturalness ("freaks") give her the creeps.

She rarely tries to prevent anything from happening that seems to have to happen: when Frankie wants to take a splinter out of her foot with a kitchen knife, when Frankie smokes, when Honey needs a stimulant, when Frankie rushes out to the town, she cautions, but does not fight. ("I'm just trying to head this thing off, but I see it's no use.")

This is her wisdom: the acceptance of the pain and sorrow of life. All this is, as she puts it, a "thing known and not spoken."

Her movement is quiet, solid, strong. Her eyes look deep with a slight slanting glance—so that she may see better out of her one good eye.

And suddenly—she, too, feels the loneliness, the fear, the terror of life . . . and needs consolation from John Henry or anyone else. This pain of life is always sensed by her, but she lives on despite it. She knows the irony of life—John Henry's death—she didn't believe he was sick—a rebuke to her "practicality," to her too-sensible nature.

She ends alone—tragic, majestic, patient, waiting—while Frankie dashes out joyously to learn—some of the things Berenice knows.

This contrast in their destinies (that of Frankie and Berenice) must be clear in action at the end. They change "colors" —Frankie becomes more "extroverted" and "superficial" at the end. Berenice more quietly profound than ever.

JOHN HENRY

Spine: To learn to connect.

The pathos of the child is that it imitates the process of life as it beholds life being lived. There is mystery and comedy in this, too.

The child repeats a pattern of behavior without realizing its significance. The child has hardly any conscious tastes, appetites, or desires (they all seem automatic).

The child develops conscious appetites and ideas through imitation.

Hence it is likely to imitate bad things as well as good, it might kill or die almost as easily as live and love. The environment teaches the child through its tendency to imitate, its capacity to be formed unconsciously.

The child's imitation is a species of attachment: hence the child appears to be "loving." It loves to repeat what it sees and hears—and since most life is an effort to "connect," the child is always learning to connect and so grows to be a man.

"Me too" is the keynote. But since this is just the sign of a desire to follow or imitate a pattern without any reason or justification beyond what appears to be merely an imitative impulse—it strikes us (grown-ups) as funny.

John Henry says "how pretty" about Frankie's dress, but repeats Berenice's less flattering description; that is, he imitates

Berenice, attaching himself or reflecting her . . . so that Frankie calls him a "double-faced Judas."

The child reflects life: it reflects connection, attachment, but it has to learn to develop a conscious connection which it doesn't possess at first.

The child's lack of consciousness makes much of its behavior seem meaningless and mysterious. Hence there is something sad as well as funny, and, from a conscious point of view, oddly pathetic about the child.

The child is fragile: death is "natural" to it . . . it is always close to death. The "realest" thing John Henry does is to say he is sick, but because he says such things as a reflex he is not taken seriously.

A child is like the light of a flickering candle—bright, gay, pretty, sad, extremely sensitive to the atmosphere around it— easy to intensify or to extinguish.

Frankie wants to get out of herself so that she can connect, even more with the world. Berenice connects because she has learned to live and John Henry is learning the process in the unconscious way of a child—but he stops (dies) before he has gone very far in the process. . . . In a word, he presents the image of the fragility of the whole process—hence our tender feeling toward him. How susceptible he is (the life process) to destruction—disappearance—"the ghost in the arbor with a little silver ring!"

The first step in connection after imitation is attachment, and from the attachment, "love" develops, which we observe in John Henry's consolation of Frankie and Berenice.

When the child's connection is sharply cut off, it becomes afraid—"scarey." It has become used to the connection. The child isn't a bit lonesome (as John Henry says) but comes running to get together—connected—with what he has become used to.

The child "studies" to be a man. Observe the rapt look of a concentrated child. This "study" is the essence of the child's activity—the study and the action that follows—sometimes slow and hesitant, sometimes sudden as if inspired.

ADDAMS (FRANKIE'S FATHER)

Spine: To keep in touch.

He can barely make it. . . . His connection is faltering, bleak. "Marriage is a sacred institution," he says, but it's a long time since he's been married. He keeps on going, but he has connection only with memories and the little mechanisms—watches—to which he has set, automatic responses.

Life is queer, a little strange or "funny" to him—he has a trace of humor. Life is sad for him because its objects are dim, sweet because he realizes no evil, sour because he's pushed into a corner and his area of nourishment is limited.

He's widowed of life. "A good provider," he works without aim. He pets life (Frankie) in passing, and wanders off into bleakness—and rest.

All that remains to him is his "white superiority." Even his porter doesn't show up to work for him. People don't pay attention to him—because he's not there for them. ("Answer me when I call.")

Handling people who are "alive" embarrasses him. He's "evasive"—constantly clearing his throat in embarrassment.

A baffled man.

JARVIS

Spine: to make the simplest connection . . . with the first thing that's nice—a girl.

He's an ordinary boy—rather unimaginative—his father's son—proper, good-natured, conventional, cautious—pleasant and inconspicuous—except to Frankie and people who admire his looks.

He smiles a lot, friendly, even sentimental, normally affectionate, but without much expression. He is comparatively mute"—awkward in expressing his feelings. Affectionate gibberish is the best he can manage in response to Frankie's adoration.

T. T.

Spine: to make as much conncetion as he can find.

Modest, resigned, soft, unhappy. He hasn't enough energy for his unhappiness to develop into resentment. He is acquiescent.

He is self-effacing, "understanding," honorable—"understanding" in a mediocre, practical way. Hence his deaconish fat. "Respected"—walking in a state of grace. He is almost "womanish" (or eunuch-like).

He would take a blow, quietly, hurt, unangry. ("I'm not particular—whichever way is convenient.")

He's even afraid—or at least shy—of being unseemly in front of Frankie. . . .

Yet he is not obsequious—honorable in a way, dignified, understanding and kindly—slightly depressed.

HENRY BROWN

Spine: to force connection—(or die).

Rejected, humiliated, his only connection is through violence, hostility (defiance) or mad escape ("snow," liquor, the protection and romance of jazz).

He is depressed and crazed by his own violence.

He's always on the verge of breaking loose or getting into a stupor of sadness—followed by an outbreak toward escape. He's repentant about hurting John Henry—for a second—tries to make up for it by playing with him, giving him money.

He has a kind of hysterical lyricism about him (his movements are dance-like in their nervousness).

A kind of terrified joy in being pursued. He takes a kind of mad pleasure in his violent connection through pistol or razor. . . .

DIRECTOR'S NOTES FOR

The Autumn Garden

by LILLIAN HELLMAN

(First presented in New York at the Coronet Theatre, March 7, 1951, by Kermit Bloomgarden.)

First impression: There is an atmosphere of unsentimentally expressed *regret* in the play. It is not the regret of a beautiful past but of a past which is vague and an immovable present. The air is still: there is not even an anticipation of a new tempest. Perhaps hopeful of one—timidly so. There is also the regret that nothing is likely to happen. . . . The dead end of the middle-class spirit.

Everybody is so "nice." That is as near as these people can get to love.

(1951—the year of the national nervous breakdown!)

The spine of the play: to "fill out" their lives.

NICK

Spine: to rub himself up into things.
Psychological gesture—one form or another of cuddling.

To get tied up, lean on, mess with, so that he can "fill out" his life, which he finds inadequate.

He pats everybody, kisses everybody, wants to be sweet to everybody . . . so that they will be nice to him . . .

He tries to embellish every situation. He likes to make matches, go to parties, where he can "cuddle."

Such people are sentimental, nostalgic. Because they imagine they were happier, "fuller" *then*—long ago—they try to recapture that lost fullness.

He *flatters:* which is a way of "rubbing up" and being "rubbed."

Hates to be bothered. Hates to be bored: nothing to "rub" into.

He loves Nina in his way, but most of all he loves her response to him. It gratifies him that he can arouse her. He plays the whore with her. She's the woman he's most used to lean on, to fulfill himself with. She can stand him longer than anyone else.

He's an "enthusiast," a perennial boy.

CONSTANCE

Spine: to realize a dream.

Psychological gesture? Carrying a tray—with love. Turning away delicately.

Only the consummation of the "dream" will fill out her life. Her dream of the beautiful life is based on childhood ideals, "notions" of the past.

She's a dignified lady—and a little girl. A hero-worshipper. She idealizes or romanticizes everyone.

She hides, like a hurt and forgiving child, unwilling to know about wicked or ugly things.

She is a secondary mother to Crossman, Nick, Sophie and the others.

She is credulous and vulnerable.

She tries to avoid truth: she lies, and being essentially good and honest, she retracts the fib.

She has more delicacy than vitality.

If she were able to love she would still love Nick.

The play's situation furnishes Constance with her last chance. She *flutters* toward it like an eager and awkward bird.

She likes music, Renoir, and all pretty things. . . . There is a certain real purity in her withal. She is one who serves. . . . She is a woman of another era. She falls into attitudes and poses that are too picturesque to be true. Still, she is sincere. She was brought up to see, think, behave that way through books, pictures and training in decorum.

CROSSMAN

Spine: to probe or "understand."

Psychological gesture: the manner in which he indicates "No, thank you" or his indifferent compliance.

He began with nothing, fell in love, failed. Hoped that love would fulfill him. But now he feels that his life has been wasted. He feels "empty." He took recourse in reading. When that proved insufficient he satisfied himself with sensation (sex) and drink.

He has no objective. But *understanding* is left to him; studying, observing, interpreting. He finds a certain vengeful satisfaction in exposing pretense, sham, foolishness—some of which he feels ruined him. In his "punishment" of others he is vicariously punishing himself. But his greater contempt is for the others: this is his "compensation," his little claim to wisdom.

He has become bitter and stoical. While he mocks Sophie, he understands and tries to help her. He is obliquely kind to those who need kindness: Griggs, Constance.

His understanding leads him to realize his failure. He is not, however, aggressive or nihilistic: he is too gentle for that. He "refuses" everything and will quietly disappear when his friends and the broken machine of his body disappear.

He resents Constance's foolishness a little as he does the maintenance of hoax or self-delusion in his community. Still, "he is doing the best he can."

Plays with a paper knife(?) A kind of scalpel or dagger. His posture is symptomatic of his refusal. But he still shows signs of emotion—for instance, when he is told that it is only his drinking which causes him to unburden his heart.

NINA

Spine: to follow Nick.

Psychological gesture: her laugh. Hurt (half-closed) eyes.

Following Nick is the only way she knows of "filling" her life. This is bitter for her because of what Nick is. She has contempt for herself but cannot help doing what she does.

She's a puritan; she's a little ashamed that her sexual urge keeps leading her back to Nick. So she punishes herself and him by her contempt. She pays "too heavily inside. . . ."

She has breeding, intelligence, yet the best she has been able to find is Nick. Therefore she laughs at herself, at Nick whom she sees through, at the paradox of the situation which deeply wounds her.

She accepts her life "manfully": her instinct tells her that Nick can't help himself, isn't responsible, is even a little pathetic and, after all, needs her protection.

She is "Boston"—therefore, according to Nick, "cold." But because she is of so proper a family she is attracted to Nick as an "artist," a bohemian with gallant manners, warmth, gaiety, boyish enthusiasm, a sense of adventure.

She knows more about art than he does but she isn't able to *do* anything. She was not trained to be anything but a "lady."

She woos him with gifts. . . . She appreciates Crossman and Griggs. She tries to save herself by contact with these nice men. After all, she is better off!

She has humor, even wit, crossed with asperity, nervousness and "trembling" . . . which she controls.

Nick is a cheat about money. He is paid for pictures he never paints, then has an affair with the lady who commissioned the picture. This is one of the real scandals and shames of her life. With all this, a certain weariness or disgust.

GRIGGS

Spine: to free himself.

Psychological gesture: he looks into space.

Free to be the man he believes himself to be, the man he promised himself to be, the man who was comfortable with himself. He has never lived his life.

An idealist: he wanted to be a serious man, the man who was his serious mother's son.

He's grieved or pained—more than shocked—by his wife's frivolity.

Very upright—disciplined—no self-pity.

With Rose: it's as if he were constantly talking to a deaf person or one who very successfully pretends to be deaf. He does not know how to master her.

He is shy, a man who cannot easily formulate the imponderable but real emotions within him.

His only companion—a fellow sufferer—is Crossman. He's kind to all the "outsiders": the young, the foreign, the abused, the defeated.

A way to freedom is to think straight and true, and though even this is no longer easy, he works at it.

He's a little stronger than Crossman because he has a goal, and he began with something real to him: a serious way of life, serious thoughts.

He's not neurotic. . . . He has a curious protective feeling in regard to his wife, for she is a victim of her own foolishness and of the environment which made her foolish.

His patience, of which he is a victim, is a heavy burden to him.

His desire for freedom is now his only passion, that and the contemplation of what this freedom might mean: thinking, studying.

When Rose is broken, he feels he has to protect her; she must be spared. He is trapped by his kindness.

Perhaps he was afraid of his freedom, for freedom is hard. It is easier to be a victim: it absolves one from responsibility.

ROSE

Spine: to play at life as a "charming" woman.

Psychological gesture: twittering, fluttering.

Life for her consists of doing all the things a charming, well-brought-up lady is brought up to do, to think, to say.

She is a lively kid who needs attention, flattery. She must "mix," fly, flirt, be the life of the party, dance, dress . . . (No wonder she has a bad heart!)

Nothing has a true meaning: only the form, the display and the energy have.

She is deserted by everyone because she has never attracted anyone on a serious level—except for her superficial sensuality: eating chocolates and drinking champagne.

As she senses her advancing age, she becomes pathetic. Poor little butterfly!

When she "flutters" she believes all is well because it has always been considered delightful. She fluttered so much she couldn't tell what was going on, not even what people thought of her. This became auto-intoxicating.

She really has no idea, because she has no capacity to understand, what Griggs really wants.

Her children don't like her any better than Griggs does; she doesn't know anything about them, except that they think her a silly nuisance.

Though seriously ill, she flirts with Nick.

She has the most old-fashioned feminine "wiles," gestures, manners—to the point of caricature. She coquettes about her "heart murmurs" as if they were an attraction. . . . If she flirts with a man, she thinks he likes her (Nick is like that too) and they—the man and she—have something in common.

She really doesn't understand her illness, but she is truly scared, like a kid who fears being left alone.

MRS. ELLIS

Spine: to fight the lie (get things straight).

Psychological gesture: a skeptical look, a rejecting look.

She says witty things, but she is not witty.

An intelligent woman who married an empty man, and was thus cheated of fulfillment. She became neurotic. She does not have either Nina's sensuality or her puritanism. She saw the emptiness of life around her, Carrie's failure, her son's inadequacies and the nullity of it all.

She resents fraud. Being old, she does not feel herself too involved. She won't stand for any sentimental messiness. This is her consolation and "revenge." She is cynical without being harsh.

She doesn't kid herself; she doesn't want to be kidded and despises those who kid themselves: they are weaklings and fools. She observes and keeps cool and clean, which is her consolation.

She is "neat" in her relation to life, patrician. Her environment, like Nina's, was empty but she was not talented enough to evade it. So she became a "loner" with social graces. She is thoughtful. She doesn't crack jokes for the sake of fun.

Her main concern now is that the young—Frederick and Sophie—be given a chance.

CARRIE

Spine: to hold onto the last thing remaining to her—her son.

Psychological gesture: an alternation between "proud carriage" and her head bent as if pleading.

A woman who has always been squelched, almost "fractured." She tries to resist, but she has no strength and always ends a victim. She needs help. She is soft and without inner resources.

She was always *correct*. And being so made her seem strong, but nothing in her was strong enough to overcome a neutral husband, a domineering mother-in-law, a weak son.

She has no real convictions or knowledge. She treats her son as if she were his governess, schoolteacher and lover. She suffers from a kind of frustrated reticence.

She probably wants her son to marry Sophie because their love isn't "romantic," a genuine attachment. For this reason she believes she can control the boy.

FREDERICK

Spine: to escape into another world. Away from mama and even grandma.

Psychological gesture: he "ducks"—broods and smiles tentatively.

A masculine and youthful counterpart of Nina, Carrie, and Mrs. Ellis, in their various struggles to free themselves from the limitations of their "old society."

But no one encourages even his talent for appreciation. He is always under pressure because he is financially dependent and emotionally immature. Sensitive though.

He likes Sophie because she exerts no pressure on him, nor is she herself under pressure. She is his "equal" but he is in trouble with her. He is attracted to Payson who is "free"—and wants to join his free world. There is hero-worship in this.

He respects his grandmother's brightness and will power. He is sorry for his mother, though dependent on her.

Europe is an "ideal" (a fantasy) with him.

Sophie treats him as his mother should have.

Like Nina, Frederick knows his own inadequacy and impotence. . . . He's rejected even by Payson.

A tender, lost character.

SOPHIE

Spine: to *do* the best she can.

The affirmative or positive in her role must be stressed to counteract the shyness which under the circumstances may be thought to be her "character."

Her action must be straightforward, clear, never cloying. More *action* than characterization.

Sophie is a "mother" to Frederick. Being a mother is not a submissive action. It is vital and purposeful.

A sense of humor is constant in a person of alert intelligence. She is never passive. She likes to laugh.

She is curious, interested, trying to learn and understand. She is never frightened or pathetic.

She'd rather be thought guileless, shy, than not. It gives her greater freedom . . . people bother her less. She will find her way—in time.

She is not a waif—she is spirited.

Her "meanness" comes from her logic, her rationality. Both these qualities are exasperating to her American guardians.

LEON

Spine: to keep out of trouble; to have fun.

His humor is based on a scorn for his white employers.

DIRECTOR'S NOTES FOR

Tiger at the Gates

by JEAN GIRAUDOUX
in a translation by CHRISTOPHER FRY

(First presented by Robert L. Joseph and the Playwrights Company, in association with Henry M. Margolis, on October 3,
1955, at the Plymouth Theatre, New York. This production was
first presented in London at the Apollo Theatre, June 2, 1955.)

Costumes: lightweight. Don't use too much material. Actors
must be able to move freely.

Setting: provide places to sit all over stage—but no ordinary
chairs.
Laundress passes on the lower (stage floor) level.
Hector's entrance on the topmost level as high as possible.
The middle level is the main playing area.

Style: The play is a passionate comedy. Passionate by virtue of the basic content. Comedy in the writing. There is a
certain detachment in Giraudoux's manner: sunny, playful,
witty. Behind a sly grin and an "uncaring" mode of speech,
we must feel a tragic sense of life—without tears.

People are forces in this play: graphic symbols; they stand
out in strong relief. Each posture, position, move, must be
sharply defined.

Theme: the play is about the struggle against Destiny (the Tiger). Destiny is reality: the natural world without morality. Beautiful like the face of Helen. Pitiless, without mind or soul.

The struggle is between the idealists—Hector and Andromache—who combat Destiny and those who yield to it, gaily like Paris, stupidly like Demokos and Priam, and those who want to see only the pretty side of Destiny (Helen). Helen herself is on all sides and no side . . . except that she is magnetized by what is pretty.

War is a paroxysm of reality with two faces: the face of Helen and the backside of an ape.

The spine of the play: to struggle with the forces of chaos; to make sense of them.

HECTOR

Spine: to quell the "Tiger."

A full man; a fighter. But not a fanatic idealist.

He has begun to hate war, but not because he has no feeling for it. He is tender, but capable of rage. He is tolerant but inclined to savage disdain which becomes murderous anger: he kills Demokos.

There is integrity in him: not the integrity of the one-tracked mind. His integrity is a matter of control and the balance of opposing impulses. Profoundly serious, he has humor, irony and wisdom.

He has returned to Troy converted, a changed man. He was not always the Hector we first meet. He is a romantic who once romanticized war, but his romanticism has now been tempered by a new maturity.

A man of strong will. He is resolute through moral conviction.

He's capable of sensuality. He sees "two charming buttocks," but that's not all he sees!

He moves with sudden resolution, a hawk looking straight into the sun.

He has intimations of doom but he must fight even this. He will not resignedly accept fate. He will stand up and combat the "Tiger," even if the chances for victory are slim.

He is also a shrewd politician: as exemplified in the scene with Busiris.

ANDROMACHE

Spine: to sustain (support and aid life-forces) . . . but she needs help.

Exemplifies womanly love and loyalty. She trusts Hector. She is *giving.*

But unsure of herself in all else. Easily depressed, and out of love, moved to fear.

"I don't understand abstractions."

She sustains Hector, but needs to be sustained.

Admires Hector's idealism which is at the core of his "fighting" spirit.

She is real, not just an image of noble womanhood. . . . She admits that she'd prefer Hector a little less good!

To put it in the vulgate: Andromache is "nervous." (Helen is like an element of nature, a diamond or a bit of marble.) Andromache palpitates.

HELEN

Spine: to respond (and conform) to the physical or natural forces of life.

She is ruled by the beauty of the physical world which is not bound by morality or ethical direction. Her beauty and the beauty which attracts her has its own soulless, implacable life.

She has a kind of sweet abstractedness. . . . If she were not so serene, playful and fundamentally strong, she might be called silly or vapid.

"I leave thinking to the universe."

Though powerful, she is essentially passive.

She knows and enjoys the pleasures of others: in a sense she is *cold*. She has no pity and is equal to anything—high or low. She defends herself against those who attempt to engage her on a moral level.

PARIS

Spine: to enjoy "Destiny" (in its physical, injudicious manifestations—Helen!).

He is very "fresh." A good-humored, good-natured playboy or sportsman. He's neither deep nor passionate. An average sensual man. He doesn't like to be "possessed" by a woman: hence his feeling for the "remote" Helen.

The most physically active of the characters: leaps, springs about.

Given to boyishly "wicked" jokes. A nice chap with very few convictions. He has no idea of why Hector should want to prevent a war. He doesn't think about war. If it should break out, he will fight it and take his chances with it with little sense of its horror.

He listens distractedly to the philosophic arguments. If he participates in them, it is with a certain detached amusement.

He passes responsibility by: in fact, rejects it. It hardly exists for him.

A male flirt! He's occasionally "cute" ("I suppose you wouldn't like to take just one look at Helen").

He has little imagination. He kids Troilus about Helen. He doesn't anticipate Helen's later interest in Troilus. . . . He's bright but not very intelligent.

CASSANDRA

Spine: to expose the "fraud" (in French: *démasquer*) Destiny.

She's "on" to Destiny; in other words, she distrusts it.

She mocks. She has sensibility and intelligence. Sharply humorous, even biting. Disabused.

She's an artist (like Mary McCarthy?). A lance-like brain. Most often contemptuous. Acid.

Often cryptic: "Your wife is going to have a child." (She intimates that this is both good news and bad.)

Peering into people's faces, she grins. What is she grinning about? She sees the frailty, the fraud, the self-deception. It "amuses" her.

She taunts her brothers. She's the sister "in the middle." Not honored like Hector, not spoiled like Paris.

Is she a little "jealous" of Helen? Helen is a nuisance, and men, the idiots, are crazy about her. But that's "life." Destiny (the Tiger) is a whore.

The ending confirms her bitter prediction and she, too, must suffer the slings and arrows!

HECUBA

Spine: to unmask men (as instruments of a stupid Destiny).

We are dependent on men and men are fools. A realist, disenchanted but not rebellious.

She's not "bitter" or mean. She respects Andromache; she is tender with Polyxene. She realizes, as does Cassandra, that Destiny imposes its hoax on men. Hecuba's barbs are directed toward men's weaknesses.

A strong person. She has borne much and will bear more. No pettiness, she is not personal in her contemptuousness of men's follies. . . . Occasionally a vast hatred bursts forth from her with sibylline incisiveness as in her description of war.

She is "on the side of the angels." Cassandra no longer believes in "angels"!

She probably loved Priam, but being a man, he is foolish. Zeus forgive him. There's no fool like an old fool!

PRIAM

Spine: to defend the way things are by "ennobling" (romanticizing) them.

The "Tiger" is nothing but a splendid animal.

An old sensualist posing as a lofty, dignified lover of Beauty. (A French academician!) He commands a rhetorically passionate eloquence. He wants Helen to remain in Troy because of the "kick" and prestige involved. Her presence gives the men of his generation a renewed life. They see only Helen's pretty face; Hector sees the danger in her.

Like the Mathematician, he, too, might cry over *La Femme et La Beauté*. He is something of a lecher along with his august manner. He puts garlands over the graves of fallen soldiers.

His most sincere moment is his defense of war: voicing a conviction which is the heritage of the best days of his youth.

DEMOKOS

Spine: to fight for the romanticized Tiger.

Destiny is always benevolent: one shouldn't combat it. The official romantic and therefore reactionary. Vigorous, lusty and venomous. Sullen outbursts of heroic aestheticism. Philosophical *and* violent. He is sentimentally priapic. Like the French poets and politicians who tremble when they speak of *la patrie*.

He is part of a government which works. Such men would rather be drowned in blood than acknowledge that the world they knew—which worked so well—has to be changed.

He is a consummate orator and demagogue. The rhetorician of official patriotism.

Priam is warm: married, a father; Demokos is frustrated. He sublimates through poetry and mistresses. He's a killer at heart: the violent chauvinist. Very conceited, as are most bad poets. Something of a ham.

He's over sixty. Helen is his last tremor . . .

War furnishes him with an opportunity to inspire the nation: he will write.

ULYSSES

Spine: to face Destiny (the Tiger) as it presents itself—with grace, strength, reasonableness.

Very composed, business-like, shrewd, a realist with an eye on fate. He doesn't trust fate too far. . . . He has a sense of humor. His "anger" and calls for vengeance are dictated by his duty as a general and statesman: they are not very personal. Skeptical rather than cynical.

He's willing to gamble (occasionally) on idealism or humane considerations, though he doesn't believe they will work.

AJAX

Spine: to engage in action for its own sake. Thus, the Tiger's accomplice.

He is the willing, boisterous, almost joyous instrument of Destiny because he is by nature a bully and a troublemaker: a bulldog who is pleased with the chaos of existence: drinking, roistering, killing and laughing . . . he has a good time getting angry, getting drunk, etc.

He's baffled by Hector, then won over. He admires courage, grandeur ("guts"), "class." He laughs a lot: soldier's humor. Rough, but not really ill-natured. Born the "lieutenant" for great men: Ulysses, Hector.

A *follower:* he enacts the motions of destiny; he wants to reconcile Hector and Ulysses because both are great . . .

He tries to take Andromache but desists because he is impressed by Hector's nobility and fears Hector's sword, which he knows Hector will thrust efficiently.

MATHEMATICIAN

Spine: to complete (extend) his life.

He's a deprived man; physically weak, sex-starved. He wishes to compensate for all this. He needs a greater share in what Destiny (fate, the Tiger) has to offer: excitement, sex, even war.

When he speaks of Helen he becomes terribly excited, fanatically inspired: he weeps. When he speaks of war he uses violent epithets: which is all the violence he is capable of. He comes close to having a stroke in describing Helen. He screams the epithets—exalted!

BUSIRIS

Spine: to rationalize Destiny (therefore to falsify it).

In this way he puts himself at ease with life. Unimaginative. Stiff.

He has a tic: his nose twitches.

To be impressive, he speaks dryly. To be persuasive, he speaks unctuously. All pose. The basic motive is self-preservation.

THE TOPMAN

Spine: to assert his pride and patriotism.

In the prowess of Paris' penis he finds the symbol of his patriotic pride. It is somehow a testimony of his own strength. Very much like people who say "our whiskey is the most potent, our women the most beautiful," etc.

A baritone!

ALPIDES

Spine: to admire the world.

"Oh, the things I've seen." Naive, astonished. (His voice breaks.) He can't get over the miracle of what he has beheld from the crow's nest. He's wide-eyed, lyrical . . . a light tenor!

TROILUS

Spine: to begin living (to start the Tiger stirring).

Young desire. Growth and its pains. Passionate and shy. Ambitious and ready for renunciation! Reckless and timid. The desire for life causes the drama and the enchantment of living.

ABNEOS

Spine: to play a role in the drive of Destiny. (There is an element of hysteria in all the old men.)

Such men—fat, grotesque, senile, always offer the silliest suggestions in an officious manner, which are taken seriously because they reflect the surprising stupidity of the most intellectually backward people. They are stuffy, self-important, noisy. Gossips. When there is a sign of trouble they are the first to holler "murder" and call for a lynching.

IRIS

Spine: to charm and play-act.

She is the pretty messenger of the gods.

She is three different ladies in one. (She imitates three different feminine stage stars.)

(a) Aphrodite . . . simpering and cute.

(b) Pallas Athene . . . serious.

(c) Hera . . . *grande dame.*

POLYXENE

Spine: to cling and to give to all.

A budding Andromache. . . . She echoes love, wants to help. Imaginative.

She absorbs, listens, imitates, wishes to please. Her eyes are always on Hecuba or anyone who shows the most feeling.

Because of this she is used in the conflict by Andromache to move Helen to pity: but Helen cannot be moved. And Polyxene does not understand what she is called on to say.

DIRECTOR'S NOTES FOR

The Waltz
of the Toreadors

by JEAN ANOUILH
translated by LUCIENNE HILL

(First presented by Robert Whitehead and Robert Stevens at
the Coronet Theatre, January 14, 1957.)

The spine of the play: to seek "romance" (the romantic
life), "la belle vie," prettiness, sensuousness, dreaminess, softness.

There's a mood of "regret" in this play. A smile when the
mouth is salty, the eyes moist, the heart full!
Sex and love—in confusion.
Soul and the flesh . . .
Morality and practicality . . .
The humdrum and the Dream . . .
Romance and Reality . . .

Setting: The French bourgeois home—somewhat humdrum in contrast to the lovely garden and landscape outside
(Bonnard).

The more bittersweet the regret, the more the comedy will emerge.

The audience is to enjoy the irony of confusions, the tears of our disappointments and the laughter of our folly.

THE GENERAL

Spine: he wants to "give his all"—romantic fashion.

He's a softy, a big "kid," an elderly youngster. . . . He was brought up on dreams, even in the army: the battle for *la patrie,* etc.

Naive about sex, love, etc. Bewildered and sometimes credulous, despite himself.

He likes dancing, gypsy orchestras, and tends to reject everything plain or bad or real (his children, for example). He loves a *good time.*

Even his picture of the Moroccan campaign is "operatic": replete with naked Arab girls, etc. His "culture" is academically romantic in painting, poetry, music; but his daily life is petty bourgeois in its practicality.

Because he's a kid, he's still afraid of his wife—reality harasses him. He romanticizes his women, falls in love like a moon calf of military background.

(A sentimental animal: a dog.)

He's forever wishing, longing, dreaming, regretting that life is so different from his dreams.

"There is one who never hurt me: true, I never lived with her" . . . and when all the blustering and little "adventures" are over, there is fear: "I'm alone, and I'm afraid."

When he explains the drabness of bourgeois existence he offers romantic reasons for abiding by its ritual.

MLLE. DE STE.-EUVERTE

Spine: to transfigure the world to her idea of the beautiful.

A storybook romantic: she sees life as the mild romantics

describe it. But there is a certain practical side to this: it leads her to what she wants, to her objective—a young man, love, marriage.

Her posture and demeanor express the single-mindedness of a person who brushes off everything that is not to her purpose. She is as "intrepid as an Amazon," a little middle-class Amazon. Hers is a *hard delicacy*: very French. She is willful, determined, decoratively romantic and entirely proper.

Almost everything she does has a practical core, following the straight line of her will.

She has a slightly solemn manner: "proud." There is a practical purity in all she does. She is, in her special way, *perfect*.

THE GENERAL'S WIFE

Spine: to possess everything: husband, household, lovers.

She was poor—on the fringes of respectability. Her mother, a dresser at the opera. Gounod held her hand. (What a dream!)

She is the fiercest of romantics, she wants all and is willing to kill herself to have it.

A vulgar woman of fantastic energy and will. Enough to bellow Wagner in a small-town theatre and to work herself up to the Paris Opera; to marry a promising officer, to acquire lovers, to hold her husband even when he has lost his appetite for her, to bring up children (teaching them economy) and to maintain a fine house.

In a sense, she is the most romantic person of the lot: she has stopped at nothing to realize her "dream" and ideal. . . . She wants to possess her husband's thoughts.

The person who desires to possess all becomes possessed: capable of anything. Such a person can make herself sick, climb down vines. Her inner energy is boundless. She becomes pure will. She is a demon of strength and imaginative projection. Since, after all, she cannot possess *anything*, she screams with the pain and frustration of her effort. Anguished, horrified and horrible, pathetic finally in the knowledge of her failure. . . . When she cries out that her heart is shrinking, it *is* shrinking!

DOCTOR BONFANT

Spine: to live (enjoy) life as it comes, as it is. (That is realistic romance. The doctor is a realist.)

Life is acceptable as it is . . .

An amused, skeptical, yet a friendly and tolerant person. He's an understanding *observer*. The action of observation is central to the characterization.

He always has a slight smile on his face.

He's patient, modest, in normal health. He's almost *tender*.

GASTON

Spine: to find (the ideal) *life*.

He's a beginner in hope. He looks forward, "dreams" of life. (He sings Italian romances in the garden where he reads the classics.)

He pants for life: undercover, in dark hallways . . .

(The General sometimes clasps his hands as does Gaston: it is a romantic gesture of innocent imploring and waiting.)

Something delicate, young, fragile, in everything he does no matter how physically virile.

He's "under wraps" through shyness. Life has hidden from him, it has been closed off. His feelings and behavior are solitary and "secret." . . . He's not effeminate.

An element of quiet surprise in everything he does.

Obedient, honest, upright—not at all stupid.

ESTELLE (THE REDHEAD)

Spine: to get what she wants from everything.

Her mother in little. Aggressive. She is the initiator.

She does the asking, she does the spying, she makes the resolutions.

A little grasper, with some of her mother's vulgarity, "sensuality" and shrewdness.

SIDONIA

Spine: to get what is morally due her.

The "bigot." The file. The shrew with *right* on her side.

EUGÉNIE (THE MAID)

Spine: to do her work so that she can live her own private life.

She's seen everything, suffered everything, knows everything, observes everything. But she understands only what relates to her job.

Her bosses bore or disgust her; her real life is somewhere else. She is like most "permanent maids": *bonnes à tout faire.*

She's not at all perturbed or excited by the accident in the house. "Maybe she wanted to kill you," she says. This interests her somewhat but does not alarm her. It would be one more mess she would have to clean up.

MADAME DUPONT-FREDAINE

Spine: to live it up.

She has a sweeping good time. A successful, much pleased woman. All the men play up to her and she has what she wants. She's queen of a small comfortable world.

FATHER AMBROSE

Spine: to please the world: to encourage everyone to like the world, God, himself and the life of the town.

A jolly little man, an accommodating man. A man pleased with small comforts as if they were great comforts.

He flatters his flock . . . treats everyone as a child. What are his little comforts? White wine, the events of the day, playing the part of the wise, all-knowing, friendly, forgiving person. . . . He's not at all stuffy. He wants to win over everyone to his or her own joy: a simple, peaceful life to his or her own measure.

THE MAID

Spine: to respond to the call of life. Innocently and readily. Life's no problem!

A Touch of the Poet

by EUGENE O'NEILL

(First presented in New York by Robert Whitehead at the
Helen Hayes Theatre, December 8, 1958.)

The characters are immigrants in a new country: they
want—

The spine of the play: to make a place for themselves.

This play, written as realism, is a kind of parable. Its tone
is objective, sober, almost detached. There is a quality of dignified but sympathetic understanding in it. Under the rather
stoic surface is a sadness, a tenderness, a warmth, even regret.
The author says, "I'm sorry. But this is how it was." He's too
mature for bathos, but his heart is touched. He soberly exam-
ines the "moral" of what he has recalled. It is a strong man's
play. It has pity in it, but it is not soft.

CON MELODY

Spine: to retain his sense of himself, his Ego.

He has the personality he assumes. He is not a fraud but he overacts his personality because circumstances are depriving him of it. . . . The falsity, the pretense, creates the pathos of his situation: he has to exaggerate what he is. That is why he is absurd to the outside eye. When one is solitary one cries out for a reflection. Those who "reflect" him are his unaware wife, his carping, down-to-earth daughter. He is of foreign origin; his alien disposition ignores trade, labor and the democratic spirit of the times. He finds it necessary to seek his true self (the image of it) in a mirror. He wants to assure himself that he is present, that he exists as he knows himself to be.

He feels guilty. But he fights this sense of guilt: it would make him acknowledge that he is not what he would have himself be, what indeed he is. This would mean to forsake his past, his accomplishment, his being. But who can forever persist in denying the world's evidence—which is entirely against him? He therefore clings to the remnants of his past in Cregan and in the tattered rabble, the lowly Irish who were once his subordinates or "vassals." He *needs* Roche, O'Dowd and Riley—mocking and shabby ghouls though they be. They play his inferiors to cadge drinks. At least he can subdue *them.*

He is the lord of the mirror and several cowed derelicts whom he despises and who, at best, fear him.

His wife loves him. She sees him as he was and, to a degree, still is. She is the earth which bore him and above which he has tried to rise. She represents for him the old sod, the lowliness of his origins—which he has abjured. He holds on to her and looks down on her.

He is "grand" and ridiculous, a sorry, funny, pathetic character. He is finally crushed, demolished and perhaps "saved." The seed must rot before it brings forth new fruit.

What else must he retain in order to preserve his personality as he conceives it and as he wishes the world to view it?

(a) His mare. She contributes to his inner power, vibrant and bounding, physically real.

(b) His uniform: the colorful sign of his former position and abiding personality.

He must ignore his lack of money, his plain abode, his want of credit. He makes phantoms of them; when we make a phantom of reality we ourselves become phantoms. He is a phantom major.

He hates England that has forsworn him. He hates Ireland from which he has escaped in order to become "free." He only accepts America as an Idea—something poor and uncultivated now but which may in the future become worthy.

He is constantly apologizing about his drinking. But liquor helps him forget the present reality, inspires him with a renewed sense of himself and arouses him to undignified outbursts because of the contradiction. Drink is the crossfire in which he burns.

Byron has written *his* (Con's) *truth* in ringing and melancholy words: "Among them but not of them." This was and is true of him everywhere. It is the state of mind of every intelligent and rebellious *emigré*.

He barely understands the nature of his pose. (Why must he pose at all, since the pose is a metaphor for the truth? But since posing is ludicrous, he has to apologize for that too.)

His wife is his solace and his support, but she smells of the rank earth above which he wishes to rise. He loves her but cannot embrace her.

His daughter challenges him so he must scorn and correct her. Yet he is attached to her and is proud of her, for she is strong and fair. She is the future America which may ultimately redeem him. (The immigrant is frightened and shamed by the assimilated first generation and also resentful of it.)

His *gallantry* is not sexual; it is an expression of pride,

pride in the exercise of power, of grace or ornamental passion. It is an attribute of the acquired cultivation of his natural gifts.

Only his having been subject to a beating and the humiliation of it makes him *know* that he is the dust and dirt of the country, that he is riffraff, one of the rabble, comrade and companion of the Cregans, Roches, O'Dowds of the vicinity.

After his beating he trembles and shakes with the aching memory of what he was and imagined himself to be. He is in a fever as if a sword were being withdrawn from his body which cuts and tortures him in the process.

Thus he arrives at his new credo: "It's to hell with honor if you want to rise in this world."

The "world" (America) has won, has triumphed over him. What world? The coarse world without honor, glamor or any aspiration beyond gain and material satisfaction. . . . He'll no longer be lonely with his ideals and dreams.

NORA

Spine: to give (devote) herself (with its joy and sorrow).

For her, her husband is God. He's a *gentleman* . . . beautifully strong. He can do no wrong.

Her *place* is with her husband. She is weak and rheumatic when he deteriorates, spirited and well when he flourishes. ("There's no slavery in it when you love.")

Hers is the love story of the play. She plays all the actions of love, every nuance and color of it, in high and low, in smiles and tears.

She has the energy and strength that love bequeaths. The role must not become passive.

Because she's a simple and honest peasant she realizes that her husband's dreams are dreams. Yet they are dreams he needs to live; she therefore sustains them, that is, their reality.

Her drama is that she loves what she has been taught to be ashamed of loving: she has become a renegade from the

Church, her religion. She is hurt by this, but not shattered. Her love is strong within her, though she cannot altogether "justify" it. She's at a loss to explain the contradiction.

The end is tragic for her. After his defeat, she has Melody back, but he's "dead" now, a crippled man. Her victory is bitter; she will suffer it as all else, forever wondering what it all meant. A pitiful, sweet, grand and confused child of nature is what she remains. Her only conviction and task is that one must do all for love.

SARA

Spine: to win her place.

She speaks of her marriage as ". . . my chance to rise in the world and nothing will keep me from it" . . .

Also, "We'll get on in the world—for I'm no fool either."

First-generation American: between the old and the new—which way?

Proud, almost imperious. Her father's daughter . . . she has spunk, energy, courage. Willful, a fighter.

She's opposed to the old country and her father. She's going to be an *American*. But the old has its hold on her through her father; his glamor, pride, "style."

She's practical: she wants to take care of the money. Not such a fool, she says, as to be in love, but . . .

The first-generation American is always a little ashamed of and antagonistic toward parents from "the old country." So Sara with Con.

(The American woman of the pioneer period: "Oh, if I was a man with the chance he had, there wouldn't be a dream I'd not make come true.")

She thinks Harford's dreams are "crazy" because she knows what people are like.

But she's still young; she has to learn everything—her sensations are "new."

For all her boasting she's still a little in awe of, even obsequious with, Deborah.

Still, her father is grand, handsome, independent, proud and "like Napoleon," if he would only be that way truly. For that is her dream: to be *great,* strong, above the mob.

The pride, will and capacity to dream beyond their station destines the new Americans to conflict . . . conflict of similar personalities facing two different sets of conditions and needs.

The contact with love transforms her, softens her, completes her and brings her closer to her mother and to *her father.* With less resentment and self-confidence she is more prone to understand him. . . . Her dream has changed to a dream of love. (Will she become like Deborah?)

She gathered strength from her father's pride and background. When he is broken, something in her—some mainspring—is injured. She will be weaker because of her father's defeat. That is why she cries unconsolably at the end.

DEBORAH

Spine: to escape the place she has found—"transcendentally" in her self-made prison and dreams.

She has a place but she "never goes out at all but stays home in her mansion reading books, or in her garden."

She sees the world ironically with a wistful, resigned irony. . . . Life will take its course—fate is implacable—the country will follow its historical necessity.

She wanted to be a great man's delicate treasure: "*Josephine.*"

Her big speech is her swan song. "I shall never again venture forth to do my duty." She has told Sara to beware of New England's puritanic idealism. It crushes whatever stands in the way of its ideals whether it be "poetic," political or material.

CREGAN

Spine: to find a place to settle.

A certain sturdiness and dependability. The honest worker. Trustworthy henchman.

He's on the loose. The worker without a steady job. He needs a base, seeks a boss, a homestead. He's not without toughness, an ability to endure tribulations—with the help of a little liquor.

He's a dependent, a supporter.

MALOY

Spine: to get along (live, work in an inferior position).

Another variation of the *Immigrant.*

He's an average mick. Gets along. Doesn't like to be patronized or bossed. He looks for the flaw in those who treat him shabbily in order to preserve his pride and ward off the taunts of his superiors—to hold his own. His malice and cunning are a defense against "oppression." But he's not a bad lad. Grateful for all favors. Responsive to Nora's kindness, to all friendliness.

He has a kind of crush on Sara and is a little afraid of her . . . which is part of her attractiveness. Because she scorns him, he would like to get back at her—but not meanly.

Shrewd and observant, as he must be to live and work in a humble job in a rather inimical world.

GADSBY

Spine: to carry out the important mission of the ruling class.

One of the settled, the assured. He has a right to his place. He is polished, decorated by the place he has come to occupy. He shines with position. He is a little apprehensive when he faces the unfamiliar roughness of the new elements that have come to New England. But he cannot but believe that his sovereignty, as part of the "establishment," will ward off all inconvenience and trouble.

He has the manner of a surgeon, sure of his craft, with the oiliness of a prosperous businessman who has the protection of his even stronger superiors. He would be really hard if his authority were all his own.

THE BOTTOM RUNG—THE TAIL OF SOCIETY— THE UNAMBITIOUS AND "WORTHLESS" IMMIGRANTS

ROCHE

Spine: to bluff his way through.

Loud-mouthed, blustering. Empty windbag. Talks as if he were important as long as he feels protected. Stupid. Envious. Rather cowardly. Fawning. He brays and prates.

O'DOWD

Spine: to squirm through.

Slippery, snivelling. A sneak. He snickers as high as he dares.

He would be a spy if he were bright, but he isn't.

He also thinks he's funny, a "sport." He cadges everything.

RILEY

Spine: to settle in a dream.

He's in "air," nowhere . . . far gone. Altogether without roots except in some distant memory. He has passed out of the real world. He dwells in a mist. His look turns toward whatever is warm, attractive, lively. But he has no hope of anything beyond his contemplation and the direction of the stimulus.

His only true expression is *a song* which he sings as if prompted by the spirit of another planet.

Heartbreak House*

by GEORGE BERNARD SHAW

(Produced by Maurice Evans and Robert L. Joseph at the Billy Rose Theatre, October 18, 1959.)

FIRST NOTES

This *crazy house* is a truth house—for adults.

There is a certain "childishness" in this play.

The play of a bunch of brilliant kids not as old as the people they impersonate—much wiser and gayer and more crackingly articulate than such people would "normally" (naturalistically!) be.

A charming, surprising *harlequinade*. (An intellectual vaudeville.)

Make them funnier—"nuttier"—than Shavian "realism" (or literalism) usually permits.

"The house is full of surprises," the Nurse says. The Cap-

---

*First published in the *Tulane Drama Review*, Volume V, Number 3 (T 11), Spring 1961. © 1961 by the *Tulane Drama Review*. Reprinted by permission. All rights reserved.

tain's whistle, the sudden entrances and exits are Shaw's clues to this.

Another character says, "Something odd about this house."

The style tends toward a bright-minded whackiness. A puppet show! (Shaw jokes about bowings, introductions, greetings, etc.)

"We are under the dome of heaven."—The garden outside should be very much part of the first act "interior." (Variable nonrealistic lighting.)

Sound—"a sort of splendid drumming in the air." Later air raid is compared to Beethoven. Ideally the air raid should be orchestrated—use musical instruments—on a Beethoven annunciatory theme—but not the motto of the 5th!

SECOND NOTES (ON FURTHER READING)

Shaw's characters are ideas—conceptions of people, theatrically and comically colored. The adverse criticism of certain critics who say that Shaw's characters are merely puppets spouting ideas should be made a positive element of the production style.

They may be made as puppet-like as the nature of the play's dramatic structure and the audience's taste will allow.

Mangan says he wants to get "to hell out of this house." Everyone in the play wants somehow to escape his or her condition. All are dissatisfied with it . . . it's a crazy house, driving them crazy!

All in a sense are "crazy," not true to themselves, not what they seem or pretend to be. So everyone is somehow odd, a *clown*—disguised, masked. Outside is "the wide earth, the high seas, the spacious skies"—waiting.

"In this house," says Hector, "everybody poses." "The Trick is to find the man under the pose."

This is the director's job as well:

(a) What is the pose?

(b) What is the man or woman under the pose?

These English in *Heartbreak House* do not behave as English people do: an Irishman has rendered them! They are more impish, more extrovert, more devilish, devilishly *comic*.

Hesione is a "serpent"—she has mischief in her—not a "proper" lady. She's the cat who swallowed the canary, an intelligent minx. Mentally speaking she *winks*.

An element of "ballet-extravaganza" throughout—as if everyone were "high."

The audience is to enjoy: ideas as color, comedy, and "show," or intelligence as clowning.

They are all aware that they are living in a looney world, which they are expected to take seriously—but can't. As they progress they become aware of the need to act mad in order to approximate reality. To achieve their liberation—their world must be destroyed.

Some of the madness demands that they hide it—which is the greatest madness. Thus they speak of "form," of not making scenes—while they are always making scenes. (Lady Utterword.)

They want to burst the bonds of the old times—convention —"to get the hell out." Thus the comic outbursts. (Prelude to England's "angry young men.")

RANDOM NOTES CONTINUED

Shotover roars.

The world's askew (the set to begin with).

They are all flying off the handle: the "handle" being the old steady values, the desire to get the hell out of a situation which no longer supports anybody. The "handle" supplies the form—which these people no longer can grip. Lady Utterword still wants to hold on with her unseen husband Hastings Utterword. (A "wooden" handle!)

The movement of the play is not placid, polite (or Chekhovian!). It is rapid, hectic, almost "wild." (The actors are asked by Shaw to sit on tables, etc.)

Mangan "not able-bodied." Has aches and pains—presses his liver when he is irritated.

Randall—curly hair ("lovelocks"—like the fop in the film of *Kipps*).

The spine of the play: to get the hell out of this place.

This "hell" suggests some of the explosive quality desired in the playing—the element of *opéra bouffe* involved.

THE CHARACTERS

SHOTOVER
THE SAGE OF HEARTBREAK HOUSE

This "sage" has fed himself on rum, worked hard with his body, his fists, and his wits. The rugged person on whose hard work and tough life the house was built. But this sage has a mask—a Pose—as important for the actor as his wisdom—indeed more important. It is the mask of the Drinking Devil—almost the "debauchee" with his West Indian Black wife.

Bluff, gruff, hardy—also shut off from anything but his own thoughts and "ways." (Modern England was built by such men: born 1818 . . . in their prime in 1865.)

His dismissal of everything secondary comes from his urge to get at fundamental reality—to run the ship—to find the means to set the boat on its due course. This requires the "seventh degree of concentration."

To drive toward *that* goal (the seventh degree, etc.) is his spine—his prime motive or action. (To scare people into doing what he wants, or to be free of their nonsense, their blather.)

He wants to go on with his quest; his energy is great enough to do so, but at eighty-eight, he knows it's late. Therefore he's wistful too. Despite himself he has to relax into a resignation which is a sort of "happiness." This is his pathetic side.

(The clearing and cleaning up necessary to achieve the "seventh degree" will entail a certain amount of destruction —dynamite. He is prepared for that too.)

He moves with nervous energy, sudden shifts of pace, to absolute quiet or concentrated energy—as when he sits down to work on his drawing board.

I'd rather he looked like old Walt Whitman than Shaw!

ELLIE
THE NEW LIFE OR YOUTH IN HEARTBREAK HOUSE

She wants to find Port. (A goal for her life.)

The Pose is the Sweet Young Thing: the well-bred ingenue.

The real person is eager, intelligent, with a strong will and capacity to fight.

The House is bewildering, heartbreaking: all the facts she learns are upsetting. . . . She encounters hidden or masked wisdom in the Devil—the ogre Shotover. So she ends bravely in a sort of exaltation—"greater than happiness."

In the transition between these two aspects of her character she is miserable, hard, calculating.

Then she "falls in love"—differently—with life itself, in all its danger in the person or symbol of Shotover.

This is the Education of Ellie.

Shotover's dreams and ravings—his wisdom and idealism—are the most real things in the world to her—new blood.

She knows her strength (the last curtain), so she *looks forward* to another air raid . . . as toward the prospect of a new world, a fresh start!

HESIONE
HEARTBREAK HOUSE IS HER HOUSE

The Eternal Woman! (And an "actress" by nature.) She wants to make life beautiful, to keep it romantically beautiful.

She wants to get out of the house too (they all do) because she knows its madness . . . yet she likes it here—the adventure, the uncertainty, the fun . . . like an actress who understands the theatre's absurdity and deception but at the same time enjoys its warm charm.

She is loving but so intelligent that she occasionally is sharp—in the face of hypocrisy, or stuffiness.

Hushabye (the Soother!). She loves company, the "menagerie." She sees through her husband, admires and laughs at him. . . .

She is active . . . yet "lazy" . . . likes to fall asleep when unoccupied because she enjoys all agreeable sensations and experiences. She is not a particularly good housekeeper . . . not thrifty . . . not very neat (show this through business at the very outset) . . . the maid takes care of "all that."

She likes to gossip . . . so she's socially endearing. Frank, open, *Enthusiastic,* likes to tease affectionately.

She's a flirt—for fun. It is also gracious, it keeps things "interesting."

Something of the improvident Bohemian—with very little care for money.

"You are your father's daughter, Hesione." (She's got the Devil in her too.)

She has temperament and temper too—like an actress!

She is changeable—with swift alternations of mood.

LADY UTTERWORD (ADDY)
THE FINE LADY OF HORSEBACK HALL

Conventionality is her mask and protection—the sense of "form" in the "Colonel's lady" manner.

Her reality beneath the mask is a hunger for experience . . . her desire to escape the prison of her class convention. This expresses itself secretly, stealthily, unobserved . . . except in unguarded moments of hysteria.

"The first impression is one of comic silliness." She has the English "twitter."

Her "form" makes her appear more stagey than Hesione (who is real theatre!). Addy is what we call theatrical theatre of the old *very* English school (1910).

She swishes quite a bit.

Her way out of Heartbreak House is to run off to India, to the garden, to tea, to fashionable behavior.

She wants to cultivate, hold on to the "manner" which "saves" her and perhaps gives her the best of both worlds—that of feeling and that of decorum: the one utterly private, the other a "style."

A consciously picturesque *flirt* . . . but her flirtatiousness rarely goes any further than that—titillation plus elegance, and a slight touch of danger.

When all is said and done she is very practical: she sticks by her husband, Hastings—the "enduring" Englishman.

HECTOR
THE INTELLIGENT MAN WITHOUT EMPLOYMENT IN
HEARTBREAK HOUSE

He wants *to get* out—*somehow* . . . but there's no place to go. He cannot see the goal. Therefore he wants everything destroyed! He has no task. For this reason he dreams up exploits, philanders, plays "parts," dresses up (in "crazy" costumes), becomes decorative . . . even in his intelligence.

Like Ellie he's trying to find—a port, but he knows of none, foresees none.

"I am deliberately playing the fool," but not out of worthlessness, out of aimlessness.

He's a dilettante—forced to be one—yet he has the energy and intelligence to be something more.

Debonair and cool like a practical madman. A bit of a show-off. This gives him an identity. . . .

But this is his pose . . . the real man is dissatisfied, unhappy.

A pretty woman is a challenge to him: it leads to an activity of flirtation, the semblance of impressive action. He is telling

the truth—or part of it—when he says he doesn't like being attracted—for it arouses him without leading anywhere. He is a
civilized person, not a lecher. Thus he is a romantic without
a cause.

He sees futility in all positions and arguments—even that of
the anarchist . . . he hasn't even the confidence to feel superior
to anyone.

He curses women because they are the only thing left for
him to deal with . . . yet he knows they are only distractions
for him.

He wants "beauty, bravery on earth." But he cannot find it
around him or in him—except as a senseless activity.

The "saddest" character in the play, and he behaves like an
ass and a liar . . . though he often speaks honestly and even
wisely.

MANGAN
THE "STRONG MAN" OF HEARTBREAK HOUSE
("NOT A WELL MAN")

He wants to get in everywhere—and to get the hell out too.

The big "capitalist"; the sharper, the practical man, the
man who counts in business and in politics. All of this is the
Pose.

The real man is wistful, twisted, rather frightened and a
somewhat resentful child . . . the most "cheated" or frustrated person in the house.

He's "aggressive" . . . yet he is always caught off guard. He's
sure an aggressive manner is the way to success, but he becomes unsure when his success is challenged or his aggressiveness doesn't impress.

Except in a very limited sphere, he's always out of his element, shaky—unhappy.

So he's always *forced* to pose—except when he believes it's
particularly clever of him to tell the truth about himself.

"I don't quite understand my position here"—is the keynote. He never does—anywhere outside his office.

In the end he has a "presentiment" (of death) because he's insecure, a "worrier."

Afraid of women—gullible—an easy prey for them. Shy with Ellie, mooney with Hesione.

Like all lower-class folk who have arrived in the upper middle class he has an excessive sense of propriety—or priggishness.

He's full of unaccountable resentments (a source of comedy in this)—secret and almost ludicrous hostilities. He gets sore and vindictive in spurts. One can hardly discern the source of his irritations.

The craziness (or "unusual circumstances") of this house bursts the bubble of his pose . . . he collapses into tears, a hurt boy.

MAZZINI DUNN
THE INEFFECTUAL INTELLECTUAL IN HEARTBREAK HOUSE

To be helpful to all (in Heartbreak House) is the "spine." Mazzini has "moist eyes," always smiling—except for moments of total consternation, and even then there's a little smile. He is obliging to everybody.

He feels a bit inferior, insufficient, guilty. Thus he wants to make up for it by being helpful. He regards everyone as somehow better, cleverer, stronger than he. He admires everyone.

(From the actor's standpoint: a sweet zany.) Shy and modest because of all this. But sweet: there is nothing cringing or undignified about him. He accepts his humble position.

He loves his wife as he does Ellie but he feels indebted to them—as to everyone else.

He is credulous, gullible . . . the world is always a surprise to him; he smiles with wonder and admiration. He really doesn't understand evil.

He thinks all one has to have is the right influences and inspirations to become good, loyal, strong.

(Key lines: "How distressing! Can I do anything I wonder?" "Think of the risk those people up there are taking"—

in reference to the bombers in the air raid. "And the poor clergyman will have to get a new house.")

RANDALL

To act as if he were the one proper—immovable—person. The "imperturbable," the superb English gentleman. Ornament of all diplomatic circles.

That is the Pose. Unruffled, exquisite, the last word in smoothness. Narcissistic.

The real man: a bundle of ragged nerves, a spoiled, almost hysterical baby.

He believes himself a romantic character, so impressive in bearing that no matter what he does he must somehow appear dashing and right.

He's always play-acting till his "hat" is knocked off . . . then he screams like a helpless kid.

The most absurd of all the characters . . . the most "typically" British—in the old-fashioned comic sense. A "cultured" dandy, super-sophisticated. He will still look and be a kid at sixty-five.

His nerves will always show through his *sang-froid*.

His eyelids flutter . . . a bit effeminate.

He has no real passions or convictions. Therefore he needs his adoration for Lady Utterword. All his convictions have been absorbed in his pose—which is his class pattern.

BILLY DUNN

He reverses all values in *Heartbreak House*.

To get out, make out—anyway he can.

Shaw's intention with this character is to illustrate the total topsyturvydom of Heartbreak House. A sense of guilt hovers over Heartbreak House. Its inhabitants no longer believe in the old justice. The criminal no longer believes in his crime: it's just another way of earning a living.

Because of all this Dunn behaves like a clown—now contrite, now shrewd, now crooked, now pious, now immoral, now joking: for all these poses serve him. (A "ham" actor.)

The real man is the poor bloke who couldn't make it either in Heartbreak House or in Horseback Hall, and therefore preys on both—preferably on the former, since he would simply be given a tanning in the latter.

He ends in a terrified attempt to escape—in vain.

NURSE GUINESS
THE LEVELER

To wait it out—with a minimum of worry.

She's an "anarchist"—she doesn't care because she does get along.

"Quite unconcerned," says Shaw. She's quietly brazen.

A CONCLUDING STATEMENT*

Sitting at the back of the auditorium at a Washington performance of *Heartbreak House,* I was delighted to hear a spectator whisper to his neighbor, "Shaw certainly wrote wonderful gags." Why "delighted," why not dismayed? Shaw a gag writer: blasphemy! But I *was* delighted because the spontaneous remark in ordinary American meant that the person who had made it was glad to be attending a "laugh show."

Everyone nowadays refers glibly to Shavian wit. But in relation to *Heartbreak House*—not well known because infrequently performed—there is a tendency to become solemn. Shaw himself is largely responsible for this, first, because he called his play a Fantasia in the Russian Manner on English Themes, and, second, because in his Preface he cited Chekhov's plays as models.

In directing the play the first thing I told the actors was

---

* Published in the Souvenir Program sold in the theatre a few days after the opening.

that both the phrase "Russian manner" and the name Chekhov were to be disregarded in connection with *Heartbreak House:* they were altogether misleading. True, the name *Heartbreak House* signifies in Shaw's words "cultured, leisured Europe before the [First World] War" and Chekhov's plays deal with the educated middle class of the late nineteenth century. It is also true that in Russia Chekhov's plays —despite their melancholy—are construed as comedies, but there most of the resemblance between *Heartbreak House* and Chekhov ends.

The only other parallel between the work of the two playwrights is that Chekhov's world was destroyed by the Revolution of 1917 and the folk in *Heartbreak House* drifted into the First World War and if not destroyed were terribly shaken. Also the emphasis in this Shaw play—as in those of Chekhov—is not on the plot but on character and atmosphere.

What makes *Heartbreak House* utterly different from Chekhov is its unique style. Shaw's play is extravagant, full of capering humor which verges on the farcical. One of the characters refers to the environment he finds himself in as "a crazy house" in which one's mind "might as well be a football." The fact that this "crazy house" is also a truth house— a sort of distorting mirror which exaggerates the features of the people who enter it gives the play its human and social relevance but it does not distract from the topsy-turvy fun that my Washington playgoer enjoyed so much.

Years ago when there was still some resistance to Shaw—as we all know the greatest playwrights of our time encountered resistance as they came on the scene—certain critics complained that Shaw's characters were not people but puppets. There is no need to deny this. Shaw's characters *are* puppets— unnatural only in the sense that they reveal the truth about themselves more directly, more pointedly, more eloquently, more wittily than people in life are able to.

The director's task then was to combine the "fun" aspect of

the play—its arch frivolousness—with its basic intent. The setting had not only to disclose a place but make a comment—smilingly suggestive of the author's mood. The clothes had to be costumes. The characterizations had to be tipped from realism to a kind of gay picturesqueness. Gravity had to be avoided, except as fleeting reminders that we were still dealing with a truth about life—our lives. This slight duality—a sort of "gayed up" seriousness, part game, part prophecy—is only a reflection of the text itself which begins as a comedy of mad manners and ends with an air raid by an enemy never named or even hinted at throughout the course of the play.

What was Shaw's purpose and why did he write *Heartbreak House* in this peculiar way? The play exemplifies a typical Shavian "trick." *Heartbreak House* is all carefree talk and horseplay—apparently devoid of dark portent; then it bursts for a moment into a scene of shock and ends ironically on a note of almost languid peace. "Nothing will happen," one of the house guests says. Something does happen and something more fatal may yet happen—expected, almost hoped for, by certain of the characters.

These "charming people, most advanced, unprejudiced, frank, humane, unconventional, free-thinking and everything that is delightful," are content to drift. No matter what inner qualms they may have, no matter what emptiness or discontent they occasionally experience, they have settled for the happiness of dreams and daily pastimes. For all his sharp teasing, Shaw is tolerant of them. Only, says he, in earnest jest, if you go on like this without "navigation"—that is, without plan, purpose and preparative action—your ship will "strike and sink and split."

The thought or warning which informs the play—stated in a frolic of entertaining word and postures—is wholly appropriate to our day and our theatre. Though the people of *Heartbreak House* are English, it is not merely a play about a certain class or a certain country. Time has turned it into a play about practically all of us, everywhere.

DIRECTOR'S NOTES FOR

Incident at Vichy*

by ARTHUR MILLER

(First presented by the Repertory Theatre of Lincoln Center
at the ANTA Washington Square Theatre, New York City, on
December 3, 1964.)

*An Impression of My First Reading of the Script (July 11th,
1964):*

The Play: A medallion or emblem engraved on metal or
stone. When the curtain rises (there is no curtain at the
ANTA Washington Square Theatre) two pauses: one in
which the characters remain immobile—arrayed as if in a
"memorial tablet" or "frieze" in commemoration of the dead.
Then they move as living characters—slowly. There is a long
wait of anxiety. They are in a hell of expectancy, uneasiness,
bewilderment, wonder.

Business? The Prince gives the boy's ring to Leduc. (This
business and an accompanying line were not in the original

* First published in the *Tulane Drama Review*, Volume IX, Number 4 (T
28), Summer 1965. © 1965 by the *Tulane Drama Review*. Reprinted by permission. All rights reserved.

script. I suggested it to Miller who added the line and business at rehearsal.)

The Old Jew is a "chorus"—his behavior is a spiritual pantomime. He's praying . . . he's waiting, he despairs, he pleads for mercy (of God). His gestures and attitudes are an unconscious running commentary on what is being said.

The others (in their silence) must run the gamut of indifference, self-absorption, fear, horror, a desire to interrupt, to object, to stop the conversation, to watch what is going on in the office behind them, etc.

August 12th: Conversation with Boris Aronson about the setting. It must seem constructed of metal and stone. Its locale not too specific. (Originally it was called "a police station." Changed by Miller to "a place of detention.") The fact that the play presumably takes place in Vichy is not important. A first sketch rejected as rather too decorative—though macabre. Something hard, mysterious, "Kafka-like" desired. A "no-man's land" enclosure.

Casting. Bob Whitehead suggests Joseph Wiseman as the Actor, David Stewart as the (Communist) Worker. I prefer Wiseman as Leduc the Psychoanalyst, Stewart as the Actor. An actor outside the Permanent Company suggested for the Prince. I prefer David Wayne. All my casting unanimously accepted by Whitehead, Kazan and Miller.

Early Notes (Before Setting Down Character Description):
The Prince [Von Berg] is distracted, hesitant, uncertain as if slightly "gaga." He is puzzled. Diffident. Then deeply troubled.

The characters have been detained. Confined. "Imprisoned." Why? They do not know. They question: why? why? why? The first action is to learn, discover the reason. They are worried and confused, and they "hope"—a concomitant of anxiety.

How explain their detention?

Because they are Jews? Is the Business Man a Jew? Is the Gypsy a Jew? Is the Prince a Jew?

And if they are Jews, does that mean they must die? Why?

What can save them?

Believing in the Working Class Revolution? Belief in Art? Belief in God?

Or must they fight?

All this resolves itself to "What's to be done?" Is there no hope? What? What? What?

The answer is to take responsibility. The "revolt" of responsibility without any guarantee except the belief that each must help the other.

This suggests that the spine of the play has to do with the anguished (bewildered) quest: an attempt to discover the answer to the question, the meaning of and "remedy," for *evil*—which consists, Leduc (the Doctor) says, in "the fear and hatred of the 'other.' "

Apropos of this Leduc asks, "Is there a reasonable explanation of your sitting here? But you are sitting here, aren't you?"

The Actor exclaims, "But an atrocity like that (burning Jews) is beyond belief." To which the reply is, "That is exactly the point."

All (except the Gestapo "Professor," the Police) *ask questions.* The Police and the Gestapo have the answers—through their superiors. Even the self-torturing Major asks a question: Why is he allowing himself to do what he is doing? He asks, "Why do you deserve to live more than I do?

How many ways are there to "act" tension, anguish?

Begin rehearsals quickly, with simple and clear actions, not fully expressed. Do not attempt "big emotions" at first.

They stand up when it is impossible to remain seated.

"Does anybody know *anything?*" This is the key to the spine and mood of the play. (The play might be called "The

Waiting Room." They are waiting for an answer to a question to which there is no "answer."

The spine of the play: To find the answer (to the "trap" = evil), the way out of the dilemma in which they are imprisoned.

VON BERG (THE PRINCE)

Spine: to learn (*see*) the situation fully for the first time.

He *doesn't know the answer.* He doesn't even know the question. He's vague, confused. He has lived apart from the central reality.

Life has passed him by; he's out of the mainstream. Hence his diffidence, sense of frustration, which brings him close to tears. Very gentle and polite.

"Bewildered." His first question is a clue: Excuse me. Have you all been arrested for being Jewish?" And his second remark: "I'm terribly sorry. *I had no idea.*" Very shaken by the discovery.

Long silences of "confusion." He's trying to puzzle it all out . . . he's intuitive (romantic) rather than intellectual. Almost "sweet," naive. ("I am Viennese.")

He's modest: the nobleman is a forgotten man, a relic. "Vulgarity" is the supreme sin. It bespeaks coarseness, lack of feeling.

He considers things very carefully, speaks diffidently unless intuitively certain. He's always apologizing.

His final action is explained only by the fact that he is a man of feeling, not of calculation. His is the pure impetus of the truly moved person, the basic impulse of love. Even in the Major's office he is not yet aware of what he will do a minute later.

He wants to believe the best = he hopes for amelioration. That is why it takes him so long to realize the worst.

He asks the cardinal question of the play and of our time: "But what is left if one gives up one's ideals?"

He grieves for the world . . . his final gesture is not intended by him to *prove* anything: it is a spontaneous burst of his innermost self.

Psychologic gestures:

(*a*) A timid and pained movement of hand to inquire or learn.

(*b*) Lowering of head in pain or shame.

(*c*) A suddenly fierce resolve and affirmation.

LEDUC

Spine: to see it through to the end . . . intellectually and physically.

His is an *active* mind. It seeks to find answers which work. It is a "fighting" mind. It is a firm, unhysterical mind, courageous, with the will to accomplish an end.

Reason is a weapon to be handled with care, caution, and respect. It can liberate. There is the thrust of a blade in this man's spirit but it is controlled by his humanism. He has passion but it is not indiscriminate; it is held in check by his professional training and the discipline which that entails.

Hence he is willing to fight, to kill, if that is the only way out. He tries to understand, to plan. Remember: he was a soldier, an officer.

He is inclined to "pessimism," through a scientific or objective recognition of the facts. But—less consciously—he desires a "mitigation" of the facts. He is more moralist than he realizes. (Perhaps this is his "Jewishness.") Though reason (rationalism) prevents him from hoping excessively. He is "appalled" by Von Berg's action, though he has admitted to the Major that he would be ready to escape alone.

"Come on, we can do something" is fundamental to his character.

"I am being as impersonal as I know how to be." It is not easy but the impulse *to understand* is constantly present.

His "scientific" assurances place him against a blank wall which even he cannot bear or altogether accept. Hence his tension, his ultimate bafflement. He is less "released" than Von Berg. (Von Berg's inexplicable, unreasoned action is more meaningful and more valuable finally than Leduc's knowledge and confirmed data. Leduc may learn something his reason could not reveal to him.)

When Leduc tells Von Berg that man is full of hate of the other, this "dreadful truth" is a form of self-crucifixion . . . a desire to put some terrible blame on himself.

Psychologic gesture: control; the desire to point out . . . with a thrusting finger of examination and diagnosis; then, grasping his head to lessen the agony of his own contradictory pulls.

LEBEAU (THE PAINTER)

Spine: to ask the question.

With all this, bespeaks of fear, anxiety, hope, confusion, and final fatigue.

An innocent. He feels "guilty" somehow—because he is innocent. (His "escape"—coffee!)

The average man of sensibility. Knows he can't understand—but thoroughly honest about it. (The artist!) He is certainly frightened because he has no answer: in this respect he is the most "normal" person of the lot. ("You wouldn't have any idea what's going on, would you?") He's hungry, nervous, he wishes he were somewhere else, he is almost ready to die of tiredness. It's all torment, but not "pessimism." He's simply a feeling person of our time.

The surprise, the indignity, the madness of having his nose measured!

He's in sympathy with almost everybody who is "nice." Observe how he speaks to the Gypsy.

Likes to talk, to "philosophize." He is the artist without many fixed ideas, only feelings and the heritage of a liberal culture.

"What kind of crew is this? The animosity!" This is the natural man (or artist) who resents or is offended by "closed" people—the Business Man *et al.*

Alternates between trembling fear and sweet hope . . . "nervous" hope.

"Good papers." Oh, the little things that can give one courage, a sense of stability. *Repetition* of self-assurance.

No realist he. He can only paint what he imagines. He has a need to be with others, to feel himself with others, but the others, being more "practical," hold back.

Psychologic gesture: arms apart, questioning the world. Then dropping them in discouragement.

BAYARD (THE WORKER—ELECTRICIAN)

Spine: to stand by and save himself by his answer or social conviction.

His conviction—the triumph of socialism—keeps him erect, sustains, fortifies him. (His costume, typical of the French worker, should have some of the "stiffness" of armor!) He has earned his answer by a life of work and struggle.

He's watchful, alert, ever "on the ready." He's learned how to take care of himself, fight if need be.

He's helpful: to Lebeau for example. Wishes to cooperate, work with others. He's not impulsive; he's strong, contained. Somewhat "didactic" in the leftist manner. Not entirely without humor. But downright!

(Use of French popular gestures.)

There is vigor (quiet or explosive) in all his utterances.

Psychologic gesture: shoulders set, jaw tight, clenched upright fist.

MONCEAU (THE ACTOR)

Spine: to live by the ideal of his cultural environment, his "public." He's a bourgeois idealist: as an artist I serve the public, my country, humanity. This is my justification and my support.

A certain dignified hauteur. A certain *histrionic* "simplicity." A conscious pose of modesty.

Still there is *le geste, panache,* the courage and pride of the stage. Dresses conservatively offstage with only a hint of the theatrically self-conscious. There is here the mixture of the academic (French Establishment) and the discreetly Bohemian. He's tense withal.

It is the bourgeois in him which assumes the "sensible" attitude in everything. But like so many actors of this kind, he is not altogether secure, though usually in an optimistic frame of mind. He vacillates and may at times be superstitious. . . . Still he clings to his ideal to the end.

He has eloquence, a forensic ability both French and theatrical.

Psychologic gesture: he stands at attention with a tendency to throw his head backward employing graceful gestures (*noblesse*).

THE MAJOR

Spine: to carry out orders.

But he has been wounded and he is no longer sure of his ability or desire to carry out orders. But what else is there for him to do?

So he is "caught" too . . . sickened by the compulsion to follow orders. Still he tries not to listen to the voices of his doubt or guilt. He fights them off as symptoms of weakness. He almost hates himself for suffering from these symptoms and hates those who provoke them in him. He would like to prove that he has no cause to harbor any doubt.

He hates to talk to the prisoners, tries to avoid them. Tries, because of his ambivalence, to "appease" Leduc, and failing that, to subdue him as the embodiment of his guilt. For a man with his job he suffers the fatal weakness of feeling!

He's at the breaking point. He wants to calm himself with drink, which only stimulates the pain of his various wounds. When he fires the gun, it is a signal to himself and the others: *Schluss!* Shut up, you Jews; shut up, my soul! Get on with the job: we're all under orders anyway.

Like many Germans, he is a semi-disciplined or controlled hysteric.

He's "tempted" to break ranks, to defy the Professor. This is the specific and immediate cause of his tension. The debate

with himself is carried on through his confrontations with the
Professor, Leduc, even with the Old Jew!

After his scene with Leduc he resumes the procedure of
examination, savagely confident that he will now be able to
follow the Gestapo orders. He very nearly "glories" in the fact
that he shall succeed in doing so.

Psychologic gesture: stands with clenched teeth, tight fist,
trying to carry on with power; determined eye, and yet he is
never wholly secure.

THE PROFESSOR

Spine: to carry out or perform the answer.

The Enemy ("evil") is anyone or anything standing in the
way of the Third Reich. He functions through will, science
and force.

(He dresses very correctly. Like a "polished" university
bureaucrat.)

He is *absolute*. His certainty makes him dangerous, quietly
fierce. He's in command.

Psychologic gesture: cold imperious eyes (he wears glasses);
straight-backed, efficiently spare in gesture and movement.

THE WAITER

Spine: to worm out of trouble.

The most defenseless of all the characters. Timid, always
"friendly," obsequious, terrified by his humble position. (He
feels superior to the Gypsy only.) He makes friends through
café and *croissants*.

Perhaps he is an emigré from Poland . . . previously terrified there. Now he hates "irregularity." He finds comfort
only in the quiet nest of the bistro or café where he works. He
leans on people, looking to the strong for protection (his
native-born French boss, the important customers including
the Major). He tries to smile his way out of trouble. Always
seeking to be reassured by authority. A "schnook."

He's the only one who tries to flee in terror and is seen to be beaten. The only one thoroughly cowed. (He's naturally very pale.)

Psychologic gesture: smiling and crouching away as if ready for flight, that is, when he's not leaning on someone for protection; looks as if he were always prepared for a slap; compensates by always trying to ingratiate himself.

MARCHAND (THE BUSINESS MAN)

Spine: to do important work. To be in the center of activity. (Should be rather comic in effect.)

He is annoyed, indignant at his being detained. He's carrying on the business of the world, of France in the moment of its need.

He puts people "down" because he is right. Condescension is natural to him. He knows the answers.

Obsequious in a "reputable" manner to authority. He's "above" the situation. He sounds as if he were giving orders reasonably yet with a touch of indignation.

(The French bourgeois knows how to fix and correct everything. He always complains about the government and the powers that be.)

Psychologic gesture: impatience; sits on edge of chair; pushy in his desire to get on; he throws his weight around; waddles with impatience, walks rapidly.

POLICE CAPTAIN

Spine: to get even.

Vengeful because of hurts—real and imagined—suffered all his life. People have been getting away with murder: now men of my sort have a chance to get rid of all the vermin—wipe them out.

The knowing smile of a mean twirp. Squints, grins with malice and "shrewdness." He is at once "sneaky" and obsequious in regard to the Germans.

Cutting voice.

Psychologic gesture: a malicious smirk on his face like a

man about to play a dirty trick or discover something which will justify his pleasure in punishment; walks with noiseless tread.

GYPSY

Spine: to disregard it all.

He's used to being arrested. He's a vagrant. Indifferent. He's waiting for—what? He's disconnected from the others, from their problems.

He's sure he'll get out of the jam somehow . . . hardly concerned. The others are all "strangers," "outsiders." They are hostile forces of nature to be avoided, not to be fought with. One must deal with them as best one can.

He doesn't laugh; he grins. Not a grin of amusement but rather a protective coloring. It may look idiotic or sinister. A mechanical response. "If it were possible I'd like to cut your guts out"—is his secret thought.

His voice whines a bit on "No steal." "Fix." The "whine" is not an expression of sorrow but rather a plea or an assurance made for the thousandth time.

Psychologic gesture: he abstracts himself from his environment, generally turned away from the others.

BOY

Spine: to take care of his mother.

The son of Polish Jewish parents. He's been in trouble most of his life. Worked hard, concerned only with protecting his mother. (Father died in 1932).

Intelligent, aware, sensitive. Quietly trying to survive. Taut, attentive and spunky. His main idea: "How can I get the money to my mother if I fail to get out?" His courage is an extension of the love for his mother. That is why he attempts to "jail break."

Psychologic gesture: he's bent over in the pose of "The Thinker," turned toward the corridor door—*the way out.* (The Gypsy is turned away in the opposite direction: he has no intention of escaping. The boy is straining toward the only point of egress.)

FERRAND (THE CAFÉ BOSS)

Spine: To get along.

In an incomprehensible world which he has long given up questioning or understanding. He is all "adjustment."

Trying to please the customers, the powers that be, always scurrying and in a sweat.

Weeps with fright, with sorrow, with impotence: inability to help, fear of becoming "involved."

Psychologic gesture: the hurry and bustle of service.

DETECTIVES

Spine: to ape the Captain.

Without an opinion. They have no business with an opinion. They are the "mutes" of the world, those who stand by and do not interfere with superior force.

THE OLD JEW

Spine: to endure *in faith.*

He has been in hiding. He is dragged onto stage. He is neither hero nor victim. He has become "resigned" since he has no weapon against evil except faith, which is something between himself and the Almighty. He does not fret over trouble. He is inured to pain to the point of death. He is above fear, he will not break under torture. For him, endurance itself is meaningful. He is aware of the "atmosphere" around him. He prays . . . he remembers, he sighs in sorrow, he pleads (with God) that he may come to understand, he falls in a faint. He "resists" in his spirit.

He is not the "abject" Jew though he may be the eternal wanderer" or the eternally pursued. Sorrowful or exalted he may be but not "little," martyred but never degraded. His eye accuses his tormentor.

DIRECTOR'S NOTES FOR

Long Day's Journey into Night

by EUGENE O'NEILL

(Directed with an American company for the Kumo Theatre, Tokyo, 1965.)

FIRST IMPRESSIONS

Guilt—a keynote
↓
Apprehension—suspense
↓
More guilt
↓
Self-accusation

The characters are
sustained by no faith

The eyes of each character are on the other.

Foghorn—a desolate sound of aloneness.

Loneliness—everyone is alone with his or her own secret and guilt.

The play is a self-examination, a search into oneself and

into others. Through understanding to find forgiveness, relief, the connection of love which may overcome loneliness.

Long Day's Journey (self-examination) into Night (the darkness of the self). The journey to self-discovery. The search for the true self which has somehow been lost.

Mary: "If I could only find the faith I lost so I could pray again!"

Later, "What is it I'm looking for? I know it's something I've lost."

The spine of the play: to probe within oneself for the lost "something."

TYRONE

Spine: to maintain his "fatherhood"—the tradition (the crumbling grandeur).

He is a *positive* character: he wants to sustain the structure of his home and family, above all, his wife whom he still loves. If she were well, he thinks, all would be normal. There would be no suffering, no crises. He hopes and hopes—so that that he may not see the failure of his whole life, his part in that failure, his guilt.

He still clings to his religion: his faith in the theatre, his world. (He takes pride at never having missed a performance.) His gods are Shakespeare and Edwin Booth. . . .

But the tradition has been shattered in the struggle for existence in the dark days of America's Gilded Age. . . . Tyrone is "redeemed" by the discovery of the past in his son.

Tyrone's heartiness is something more than a sign of physical health. It is part of the fortitude in his *struggle* with poverty, his *struggle* to educate himself, to lose his brogue, to learn Shakespeare, to become a stage star. (The theatre is his religion.) But he has betrayed his religion through his fear of poverty. He wants land, which means security to him ("the farm"). He seeks roots, lost in the departure from Ireland and in the effort to grow new roots in the new and different American "soil."

It is hard for him to admit the least fault or guilt in himself. He can't even admit that he snores, that he drinks too much, that he is greedy. He does not, at first, understand his faults as a consequence of his background and situation. He must maintain his self-respect to be a father, a god, a leader, a man.

(American children of immigrants rarely understand their fathers. They are always disappointed in them. They do not appreciate the hardships of their fathers' struggle as immigrants or as "pioneers": *Desire Under the Elms, A Touch of the Poet.*)

"Socialism," for Tyrone, means destruction of the tradition. His sons blaspheme against the theatre, Shakespeare, etc.

He shuns "Wall Street"—the forces, which without his realizing it, have conspired to ruin him. He doesn't understand his life—or his country. Hence, his constant self-contradiction, his absurdity.

He's a good man, a soft man. He always yields to his better nature, to sentiment and affection. Like most actors, he is susceptible to compliments. He's an "old-time" actor: life was composed of work on the stage, stage lore, companionable drinking, dreams of glory, celebration of success.

MARY

Spine: to find her bearings, her "home," to seek them (for they have somehow been lost).

Her bearings? Her religious faith, her peace of mind, her beauty, her womanliness, which have been abused by the neglect of a man who has *his* bearings in the theatre and its people.

She feels the loss as a guilt. Is she to blame? She justifies herself, rationalizes, but she still feels guilty, inadequate to her ideal.

"You haven't a nerve in you," she tells Tyrone. She admires this and resents it. She sees this as a strength which has hurt her. . . . He is insensitive (unaware) of what he has done to her. It makes him a "preacher," in his own way, a "fanatic," intent on maintaining the respectability of the family and his position. She's a "romantic," he a "classic" personality. The "classic" person cannot comprehend faltering or weakness. The "romantic" cannot forgive the unreality (rigidity) of the "straight line": its unbending determination and sense of direction. That sort of character seems inhuman. Still, it is awesome in its justness, its power. That is why Mary defends Tyrone against the boys' accusations: you must *respect* him.

She is all contradiction, because she struggles against things she does not fully understand, as the loss of her ideals, the causes of her illness, the fact that she finds "excuses" for her sickness.

She would be "lost," even if she were not addicted to drugs. The theatre, which sustains Tyrone, means little to her. She has "lost" her children who have their own and new problems—besides their horror of her illness. They have lost her protection; she has nothing to protect them with. They are caught between their father and mother, neither of them capable of giving them what they require: moral, spiritual support.

Tyrone wants a home, a solid home; he didn't have one as a boy. But his only home is the theatre and the bars he goes to —which are an extension of the theatre. That is why he has never created a home for Mary, a home in which the mother is the center, the queen. She is an appendage. He is a "guest" in the house; she merely the caretaker. This is one reason for her loneliness.

Isn't there some defiance in her addiction to dope? She not only escapes through it but she punishes the others through it for their "neglect," their lack of understanding. "We can't forget," she says. She means: I am condemned, I am guilty, there's no hope for me. I'm bad and I must continue to be bad because you have made me so. You have left me no other course.

There is *childishness* in her, innocence. She has not grown up to mature understanding, to any degree of impersonal objectivity. Her wisdom is unconscious, intuitive.

The more pressure put on her, the greater her pain, the greater amount of dope she takes.

Her resignation and "acceptance" of Tyrone's faults is like an accusation to him. It increases his sense of guilt and his resistance to it. . . . What keeps her going, the last vestige of stamina, is her husband's love and need of her, his fidelity. That is why she still loves him—despite everything.

The wedding gown is the symbol of what she has lost; her innocent, trusting, confident past.

EDMUND

Spine: to discover or understand the truth (thus to help).

He is the strongest of the four. "I'm trying to help. Because it is wrong for you to forget. The right way is to remember."

After his father's long confession he says, "I'm glad you told me. I know you a lot better now."

He's *independent.* . . . He went away to sea, to discover, to learn. . . . He's more just than anyone else. He slaps Jamie for being cruel. When he hurts his mother it is to help her by making her face the truth which may save her.

He is without self-pity. He feels the need to find some saving truth. All of O'Neill's quest for transcendence is in Edmund's description of his mystic experience at sea: he even speaks of God—*meaning*.

JAMIE

Spine: to free himself from guilt.

To do this he finds it necessary to denounce the fraud in others, to sneer at life's double-cross: this to him consists of his mother's loss of innocence (her vice), and his brother, who came between his mother and himself. He confesses the evil in himself as a way of alleviating the burden of his guilt.

He's the guiltiest in his own eyes. Can't free himself. Must blot himself out. He despises himself for everything. No pride in himself, a loser to himself.

The sneering and denunciation of everything (including the stage) is a way of proving that he is *not* as guilty as he feels, that he is *justified* in his cynicism.

He humiliates himself through sex with the most unattractive whore.

"If she'd [his mother] beaten the game, I could too." He wants to pass out with his brother: to accomplish either a double redemption or a double suicide.

"Caught her in the act with a hypo." As if she had "*deceived*" him.

He loves Edmund—a kind of compensation—for Edmund is clean, healthy in his spirit. But Jamie is also jealous of him. For if his brother is good, then he is not, is wrong about everything. Yet he wants to absolve himself of this guilt—jealousy of his brother. Hence his confession: his one positive act.

The actor should perhaps think of Mary as his sweetheart and all the others as people guilty of her "downfall."

DIRECTOR'S NOTES FOR

Uncle Vanya

by ANTON CHEKHOV
translated by ALEX SZOGYI

(Produced at the Mark Taper Forum, Los Angeles, California,
August 13, 1969.)

IMPRESSIONS

There is a peculiar turbulence in the air, a constant nervousness, everyone is impatient with the other, impatient with
himself. There is self-contemplation which ends in annoyance
with the other. "No exit."

"I am dissatisfied with life like you, Uncle Vanya, and we
are both growing peevish" . . . "I have no light in the distance."

Yet there's an underlying warmth, kissing. The intimacy of
it all. Truly Christian.

They all talk about what they want to do and always fail to
do what they wish.

Still there is a great reverence for life, a faith in life just as
it is, though so terribly sad.

They all speak from the unconscious. . . . The deepest feelings are somehow entangled in the most nondescript, insignificant remarks and things.

The people are a queer lot—eccentric.

This play cannot be acted through the lines. A skein of emotional impulses must be woven. A web of odd sentiments which have only the "logic" of feeling. Even the violence—the shooting—is ordinary!

Act One—The landscape, the outside "world."
Act Two—Domestic (night).
Act Three—Conference.
Act Four—"Buried: the grave." "Peace" and quiet! We shall endure.

The spine of the play: to make life better, find a way to be happy.

They are not satisfied with life; therefore they are grumblers—

"I want to live, I want success," the Professor says.

"How will we live through the winter . . ." (the years!)

"I don't like this house; it's some kind of labyrinth . . . one can't find one's way in it . . . nobody can find anybody."

"What do I do with myself? What do I do?"

"Give me something to comfort me!"

"If I could only live out the remaining years of my life in some new way."

"They, those of the future, may perhaps find the way to be happy but we—."

VANYA

Spine: to find some way—some positive way—to live through the suffocation of his life.

A man of delicate sensibility. He is intelligent: a would-be artist of continental stamp. (He wears a "fancy tie"—"bohemian.") He's moral. Has a sense of justice. Self-observant. What, then, is his "weakness"? Self-sacrificing, overidealistic. He lacks aggressiveness, ego. No self-confidence. ("I'll shut up and say I'm sorry.")

"I know my chances for a little reciprocation [from Yelena] are almost nil. . . ." (Astrov does try to have an affair with her. Vanya defeats himself.) His idealism consists of too much consideration and regard for the other person. "Help me make peace with myself."

Everything in him is tentative—he's never certain . . . he cannot push through.

The symbolic (and actual) symbol of his defeat is the Professor who represents mediocrity in power, and selfishness.

His tentativeness comes from too great an awareness of the other person's situation: "That may be . . . that may very well be . . . everything may just very well be."

He drinks because "it makes you think you're alive. . . ." He still yearns to get on. Hence the violence and the ineffectuality of his most active gesture—the shooting. And the other effort: his attempt to woo Yelena.

Yet he's shocked by pessimism: Yelena's thoughts about the world going to pot are "distasteful" to him. . . . He advises her to be adventurous, "jump in head first."

When he has fired at the Professor he cries out, "What am I doing! What am I doing?"

End: there's nothing left but to go on as before, "to work!"

ASTROV

Spine: to do what he has to—despite everything.

When called away—his visit interrupted—he says, "What can I do? I have to go."

He accepts what Vanya isn't able to: he's more down-to-earth. He sees through his own contradictions. This makes him ironic. His perceptions are negative, his actions are positive: he accepts life as it is.

He's an objective idealist, less abstract in his thinking than Vanya. He hopes for amelioration, even if only in two hundred years! "We'll have played some part in this." His soul is filled with pride when he sees a birch tree growing from the seed he planted. Then, dismisses it all with apparent cynicism.

He has no hope for himself as an *individual*. "My personal life . . . there's nothing good about it."

"I work—and I keep getting beaten down by fate, but *I don't stop*." (This is the essence of his spine.)

He doesn't love anyone (except the old Nurse) but he responds to beauty and he suffers guilt at the death of a patient.

YELENA

Spine: to obey and to justify her obedience—as the only thing she can do. (Her spine is weak in relation to the play's spine, almost negative.)

She is shy. . . . She is the worst failure: she is beautiful, a potentially passionate woman. Yet she's repressed herself—she's not strong enough to act, to dare. Raised in gentility without courage. Everything is potential in her, nothing realized. She's languid because she doesn't hope to accomplish anything.

She has given up. "Wait, in five or six years, I'll be old too."

She can't stand scenes, ugly situations, violence. "Several times I've been on the verge of tears. . . ." She wants peace (quiet). Everything to be accepted without squabbling. She is an honest, good person, meaning no harm.

When she speaks about Astrov she becomes lyric; we realize that she's a feeling person. She's not a bore, but *effaced*.

Once she's expressed herself, she has an impulse to play the piano, but because her husband says "no," she obeys and desists.

Faced with Vanya or Astrov, she always tries to escape. . . . All she is capable of, except for one kiss, is to take Astrov's pencil as a reminder!

SONYA

Spine: to serve everyone with love.

She is constantly attentive to every little need of the people around her.

She scolds and corrects those who behave foolishly or self-ishly: this, too, is service, for she hopes they may improve. A sturdy person, a worker.

She is open, intelligent, tender and *smiling. Resolute* withal, not just "nice." She's on to her father and treats him as he should be treated for his own and everyone else's good. Yet she protects him from Vanya's hostility.

She's happy when she can declare herself, when she can express her feelings as with Astrov and later with Yelena. She cries with happiness when she's opened herself to someone in friendship or affection.

She always wishes to hope, to live in hope.

THE PROFESSOR

Spine: to improve things for himself.

He's unfortunate: he believes in his superiority, in the importance of being a professor, especially a professor of art . . . but he is not famous, he is unloved, he hasn't enough money, he is getting old and he has gout!

So he insists on having everyone take care of him, serve him. He tries to preserve his superior attitude. Vanya is a nonentity to him, the doctor knows nothing, his wife is too young. He wants everyone to appreciate his cleverness: he acts like visiting royalty. But he's sure that he behaves with largesse and that he harbors charitable feelings toward everyone.

His manner of dress shows that he takes care of himself.

Even his illness is more important than the ordinary person's complaint because Turgenev also suffered from it.

He summons his family to a conference with regal imperiousness. His joke about the "Inspector General" is that of a superior being clowning before his inferiors.

He can't face any real resistance. He retreats from a quarrel. He's a coward in the face of life.

He leaves as he came, not having learned anything—except that Vanya is impossible and that the others should work (which they do, while he only prates about it).

TELYEGIN ("WAFFLES")

Spine: to keep himself attached to these people (the family).

He's inspired by something other and more than mind—the guitar expresses him. He's sad and happy in his "uselessness."

He knows the meaning of bliss . . . which is simply to be alive next to good people on the land and in the house his family owned.

He upholds or exemplifies the old (basic) morality. He feels close to Marina, always sits beside her. This establishes his social position, his "throne."

He doesn't think he's *seen*: he's inconspicuous. "If you deign to take notice, I have dinner with you every day." (But Sonya says, "Telyegin is our helper, our right hand.")

He follows people like a little dog: the attachment of a faithful dog.

He kisses Vanya when he sees Vanya's upset. . . . "I can't stand it," he says when Vanya becomes violent through frustration.

The Marina-Telyegin relationship is embodied in Act Four when they are winding the wool together. (His *attachment*.)

"Hey you *sponge*." But said as an insult, it gives him "a bitter feeling."

"Yes, my friend" to Astrov. Everyone is his friend, he's everyone's friend. Note the first stage direction: "Telyegin plays his guitar quietly."

MARINA

Spine: to help everyone (including animals!) to live.

The part must not be played stolidly. She has a sly humor, forbearance and saltiness. She's the "earth."

She calls the Professor "my little fellow." She is tender with him, treats him like a child. All these "children" have to be scolded sometimes, but above all, understood and loved.

When Sonya is frightened and heartbroken she seeks comfort in Marina.

She uses the word "Christian." It means a good, well-ordered, decent way of life. "We're all sponges on God."

She knows and appreciates that "all of you work hard."

"May the Lord forgive us all" are her concluding words—as she keeps knitting a stocking.

MARIA (MAMAN)

Spine: to side with learned authority: there is dignity and safety in that.

She enters with a book. We see her last with a book.

(I see her as thin, boney. A blue-stocking, old-fashioned Russian style. Wears a pince-nez with a ribbon.)

Complacent amidst woe. She's satisfied, nothing touches her. A "liberal" pillar of society.

Her essential character is expressed when she scolds Vanya, "*Jean,* don't contradict Alexander. Truly he knows better than we do what is right and what is wrong."

A psychological gesture: she beats her hand on the arm of a chair in reproof of Vanya, "listen to Alexander."

At the final curtain: "Maria writes notes in the margin" of a book.

THE WORKMAN (THE DOWNTRODDEN)

Spine: to *do* (depressed but without complaint).

There is a certain dignity in his deference to the doctor and the others. . . .

Part IV

Actions	Adjustments	Activities
To advise	Strongly, urgently.	
To hear the results	Perhaps he has already become convinced of his wife's guilt and is now ready to take the fatal step.	

268

The Waltz of the Toreadors[*]

by JEAN ANOUILH

Act I, Scene 2

DOCTOR: Then you must make haste, General. One good honest explanation. Cut to the quick before gangrene sets in. Hurt if you must but do it without flinching. And then start again afresh. Crossing the threshold of that door seems like flying to the moon, but in fact all it requires is this one step.

(GHISLAINE *appears at the door*)

GHISLAINE: I can't stand it! I must know!

* Adapted by permission of Coward, McCann, & Geohagen from *The Waltz of the Toreadors,* by Jean Anouilh. Copyright © 1953 by Jean Anouilh and Lucienne Hill.

Actions	Adjustments	Activities
To fight off being rushed	This is the nervousness of the man on the verge of doing something he wants to do but fears.	
To fight for her due (her spine)	Impatient! A real Woman.	
	More reasoned urgency— harassed.	
	Powerful (with heart)	Urgent
	becoming tearful—	fast tempo
	Exasperated!	
	Icily tearful (insulted) Harassed! Women are nuts —so unreasonable ("I adore you"— nervous reassurance)	This stops her! (She stands rigid) Swinging his head and body.

GENERAL: *(Slightly on edge)* Dammit all, Ghislaine, you've waited seventeen years, surely you can contain yourself for an extra ten minutes!

GHISLAINE: No I can't, not even for ten minutes.

GENERAL: I must have time enough to make her confess, and inform her of my irrevocable decision. She is an invalid, dammit. I owe her consideration. Don't *you* be cruel, too.

GHISLAINE: I bore her cruelty and respected her love so long as I believed her faithful to you. Now I know that she dared to betray you I shall know no pity, Leon, and no patience. Either way, should you be capable of hesitating still, I have a little revolver with a mother of pearl handle which you may remember, here in my reticule. I shall end this life within the hour, without ever having known more of love than your vain promises, Leon.

GENERAL: Give me strength! All I ask is a moment to set my life in order. Go back into the morning room and be patient. There are some magazines on the table.

GHISLAINE: Magazines! Like at the dentist's! You have wounded me for the first time, my dear.

GENERAL: My beloved! Who said anything about a dentist? Anyhow, you aren't the one who is going to have the tooth out. *I adore you!* Just one moment.

    (He pushes her gently but firmly back into the morning room)

Actions	Adjustments	Activities
	A rapid sugges-tion (under pres-sure)	He's holding his head in agitated confusion.
To remind him	Stands his ground —as a way of urging the Gen-eral on.	
	Stops. Convinced.	Turns to go. Stops for a second —he goes very quickly (count of three or four).
To tell alarming news	that he has hardly been able to grasp.	
	Also alarmed! Stronger—dis-covery of an amazing feat.	
	He's about *to* *deny* the possibil-ity.	
Frantic!		Rapidly
		a count of one or two.

Time is getting on. Suppose you spoke to her first, Doctor?

DOCTOR: That might prove a little awkward considering those letters. Suppose she falls into my arms? There'll be no end of explaining to do then.

GENERAL: That's true. Stay here though will you, and if I cry out "Help" come in.
(*He goes into his wife's room, and rushes out again almost at once, distractedly waving a letter*)
Doctor, she's not in her room!

DOCTOR: What! Is there another way out?
GENERAL: Through the window, by hanging on to the wisteria.

DOCTOR: In her condition—
GENERAL: She left this letter on the table.—"I heard everything. Men are all cowards. Whatever they may have said to you, Leon, I have never loved anyone but you. I can walk when I want to. I am going. You will never hear of me again." Good God! Does she mean she wants *to kill herself?*

DOCTOR: (*Looking at his watch*) The railroad crossing! She spoke of it! It's two minutes to, the train goes through at five past!
GENERAL: The pond! You go one way—I'll go the other!

Actions	Adjustments	Activities
		The General downstage—the Doctor through rear door.
To "discover"	A desperate secret! A desperate resolve. *Almost* grand—then very quiet, quick, intense.	
		Tearfully. With little half-dry sobs or gulps.
	Sighing— "Disgusted" (with a little tearfulness) A moment to decide—with her hand on her mouth.	

(They both rush out. GHISLAINE *comes in almost at once)*

GHISLAINE: I too heard everything. *You love her still,* Leon! Only one way out.
(She sits at the desk and begins to write rapidly, calm but dabbing away a tear through her veil) (Murmuring)
Leon, here is my last letter to you—
(Her voice trails away, she continues to write. GASTON, *the secretary, is heard outside the window, singing his Italian love song. The ditty continues throughout the writing of the letter. When she has finished,* GHISLAINE *leaves it on the General's desk in a prominent position)*
There. On his papers. That's all. It's the simplest thing in the world.
(She rises unhurriedly, picks up her reticule, draws out the revolver with the mother of pearl handle, presses it to her heart, and pulls the trigger. Nothing happens. She looks at the gun in surprise, pulls out a catch, pushes another, blows into the barrel and fires again. Still nothing. Sighing)
Seventeen years you too have been waiting.
(She throws away the gun, looks at her fobwatch and mutters)

Too late for the train. The pond!
(She runs to the door, but changes her mind)
No. Not in the same place as her, for Heaven's sake!
(She darts a quick look round the room)
The window! With a little luck . . .
(She takes a run at it, swings her legs over the

Actions	Adjustments	Activities
To find out	Startled—but not too much so.	
To complain	Dismay! and almost annoyance.	
Not too excited.		
	Surprised! Life is a surprise! Servant girl's annoyance. (Inefficiency of the "master" rather than fright is expressed.)	
To try to do something	He's very worried . . .	
	A young boy's excitement. Practical! Strong!	
To examine and fix	All tremulous— worried for her— for himself. At sixes and sevens—worried.	
To get consoled— solace	"It helps me"—a bit sensuously Very nervous.	

balcony and drops. The singing ends abruptly in a loud hiccup. The stage is empty for a moment, then GASTON *enters carrying a senseless* GHISLAINE, *closely followed by the* MAID)

MAID:	Goodness gracious sir, whatever's the matter? You hiccupped fit to raise the dead!
GASTON:	I was rocking quietly in the hammock when this lady comes tumbling down on my head.
MAID:	Well fancy that! Maybe she wanted to kill you?
GASTON:	Herself more likely. Besides I don't know her from Adam. She's fainted.
MAID:	And the Doctor just this minute left. The man as good as lives here half the time, and the one day we have a suicide he's out!

GASTON:	(*Slapping Ghislaine's face*) For God's sake go and fetch something.
MAID:	What?
GASTON:	Well *I* don't know—ointment, smelling salts—iodine. . . . Anything.
MAID:	I'll make her a good strong cup of coffee. (*She goes*)
GASTON:	No blood, anyway. (*He feels her all over*) No bones broken, apparently. No bumps. Madame! Madame!
GHISLAINE:	(*Weakly*) Mademoiselle.
GASTON:	Mademoiselle—I beg your pardon. Are you feeling better?
GHISLAINE:	(*Murmuring*) Leave your hands where they are, Leon.
GASTON:	(*Turning away in embarrassment*) Excuse me, but you are making a mistake.

Actions	Adjustments	Activities
	Stronger.	
To become aware of what is really happening	After this quiet—trying to straighten it out with himself and for others. Hysteria! Sweet hysteria! A nervous outpouring of her thoughts and feelings . . . a mixture of staccato sobs (like pre-orgasm) coquetry included.	He flutters his hands as if he hadn't realized what he had been doing.
To gush out her desires		
		—fluttery
	To himself (but almost turned out to audience with a kind of frightened apologetic smile turns back for the kiss)	
		Her arm goes round his neck in a big swing
		she's a determined girl . . .

GHISLAINE: (*Crying out*) Leave your hands Leon—all over me—or I feel I shall swoon again—your hands quickly!—I'm going—

GASTON: (*Looking in panic at his hands*) My hands? Oh dear, I can't very well let her faint away again. Not that it's at all unpleasant, and I am such a lonely young man. Besides I'll mention it when I go to confession.

GHISLAINE: Oh how good it is! You are touching me at last, Leon! You thought me strong—and I was strong —I had to be, but oh how long they were all those nights on my own! Before I met you I was alone too, but I never knew it. It was on the morrow of the Saumur Ball that my bed suddenly seemed wide—that next night and all the nights for seventeen years. And all the wicked thoughts—you don't know! I shall never tell you. I struggled alone. No one was to touch me until you finally came. Your arms are strong and gentle your hands, gentler even than at the Saumur ball. Kiss me, now that you know I am going to die. *What are you waiting for, Leon my death!*

GASTON: The lady is obviously making a mistake, but seeing that she may be going to die—(*He kisses her*)

GHISLAINE: (*Has the time to sigh*) At last! (*A long kiss*) (*Enter the* GENERAL, *carrying his unconscious* WIFE *in his arms. He stands rooted to the spot at the sight which confronts him*)

Actions	Adjustments	Activities
		Music—overture —fanfare, and then sensuous, grave music.
To invite	With pleasurable eagerness and curiosity	
To refuse	With trepidation —almost sullenness	
	A little sharply	

Tiger at the Gates*

by JEAN GIRAUDOUX

Act II, Scene 1

> *A palace enclosure. At each corner a view of the
> sea. In the middle a monument, the Gates of
> War. They are wide open.*
> *(Helen. The young* TROILUS*)*

HELEN: You, you, hey! You down there! Yes, it's you I'm
calling. Come here.

TROILUS: No.
HELEN: What is your name?
TROILUS: Troilus.
HELEN: Come here.
TROILUS: No.

Actions	Adjustments	Activities
To flirt	Wheedling—coaxing—with satisfaction	Troilus: need not play with childish timidity. The adolescence shows through the passionate virility.
To "hide"	A little *assertive* Teasing . . . (as if it were naughty) To give up As to a child—dog —man!	
To "take"	Half "angry" More commanding—archly An outburst (yet shy—fifteen) Coquetting Telling him! Sharp Stronger Passionately (grown-up)	
To study	A delectable, interesting creature	

HELEN: Come here, Troilus!
(TROILUS *draws near*)
That's the way. You obey when you're called by your name: you are still very like a puppy. It's rather beguiling. Do you know you have made me call out to a man for the first time in my life. You will pay for that. What's the matter? Are you trembling?

TROILUS: No, I'm not.

HELEN: You tremble, Troilus.

TROILUS: Yes, I do.

HELEN: Why are you always just behind me? If I walk with my back to the sun and suddenly stop, the head of your shadow stubs itself against my heel. Tell me what you want.

TROILUS: I don't want anything.

HELEN: Tell me what you want, Troilus!

TROILUS: Everything! I want everything!

HELEN: You want everything. The moon?

TROILUS: Everything! Everything and more!

HELEN: You're beginning to talk like a real man already; *you want to kiss me!*

TROILUS: No!

HELEN: You want to kiss me, isn't that it, Troilus?

TROILUS: I would kill myself directly afterwards!

HELEN: Come nearer. How old are you?

TROILUS: Sixteen. Alas!

HELEN: Bravo that alas. Have you kissed girls of your own age?

TROILUS: I hate them.

HELEN: (*Yes!*) But have you kissed them?

Actions	Adjustments	Activities
To talk about himself	There is a certain masculine egotism in this.	
To tantalize	Staunchly Play with him	Holds on to his hand—she wants to pull away (twists around him—circles)
		He pulls away—retreats—almost ready to beat himself or her.
	Very graciously—into his eyes	Music ends
To have fun (make fun) To have fun too	Blithe energy—almost gaiety Playfully	
	Mock-seriously	

TROILUS: Well, yes, you're bound to kiss them, you kiss them all. I would give my life not to have kissed any of them.

HELEN: You seem prepared to get rid of quite a number of lives. Why haven't you said to me frankly: Helen, I want to kiss you! I don't see anything wrong in your kissing me. Kiss me.

TROILUS: Never.

HELEN: And then, when the day came to an end, you would have come quietly to where I was sitting on the battlements watching the sun go down over the islands, and you would have turned my head towards you with your hands—from golden it would have become dark, only shadow now, you would hardly have been able to see me— and you would have kissed me, and I should have been very happy. Why this is Troilus, I should have said to myself: young Troilus is kissing me! Kiss me.

TROILUS: Never.

HELEN: I see. You think, once you have kissed me, you would hate me?

TROILUS: Oh! (*Older*) Men have all the luck, knowing how to say what they want to!

HELEN: You say it well enough.
           (*Enter* PARIS)

PARIS: Take care Helen, Troilus is a dangerous fellow.

HELEN: On the contrary. He wants to kiss me.

PARIS: Troilus, you know that if you kiss Helen, I shall kill you?

Actions	Adjustments	Activities
	Teasing—serious	(The boy is ready to kiss—kill or jump over the parapet)
	Tossing it all off —the game is done	
To put him up to a prank	With delighted energy	
To assert himself	But now melancholy self-awareness—reverse egotism Egging him on	
	Big—(but "down") Excited teasing, playful challenge With a shocked reaction—pleasant and disturbing	Touches his mouth
To provoke (arouse)	A kind of sensuous and grave provocation (provoking to Paris and perhaps to Troilus)	

HELEN:	Dying means nothing to him; no matter how often.
PARIS:	What's the matter with him? Is he crouching to spring? Is he going to take a leap at you? He's too nice a boy. Kiss Helen, Troilus. I'll let you.
HELEN:	If you can make up his mind to it you're cleverer than I am. (TROILUS *who was about to hurl himself on* HELEN *immediately draws back*)
PARIS:	Listen, Troilus! A committee of our revered elders is coming to shut the Gates of War. Kiss Helen in front of them; it will make you famous. You want to be famous, don't you, later on in life?
TROILUS:	No. I want nobody to have heard of me.

PARIS:	You don't want to be famous? You don't want to be rich and powerful?
TROILUS:	No. Poor. Ugly.
PARIS:	Let me finish! So that you can have all the women you want.
TROILUS:	I don't want any, none at all, none.

| PARIS: | Here come the senators! Now you can choose: either you kiss Helen in front of them, or I shall kiss her in front of you. Would you rather I did it? All right! Look! . . . Why, this was a new version of kiss you gave me, Helen. What was it? |
| HELEN: | The kiss I had ready for Troilus. |

Actions	Adjustments	Activities
To make it part of the game		Troilus is leaving—stops when Helen addresses him—and then goes.
	More provocation	
	Calling—surprised—eager —"amorous"	
To become aware		
To seize an opportunity	Also his sort of flirtation	He rushes in eagerly—as if to "catch" her and stop her from leaving.
To stop this	Annoyed—and an element of jealousy (Troilus, etc.)	
To oblige	She likes to respond to every flattery	
	His concentration is part of a sexuality	
	"Coquettishly," "poetically"	
	A little let down —dry—flat	

PARIS: You don't know what you're missing, my boy!
            Are you leaving us? Goodbye, then.

HELEN: We shall kiss one another, Troilus. I'll answer
            for that.
            (TROILUS *goes*)
            Troilus!

PARIS: (*Slightly unnerved*) You called rather too loudly,
            Helen.
            (*Enter* DEMOKOS)
DEMOKOS: Helen, one moment! Look me full in the face.
            I've got here in my hand a magnificent bird
            which I'm going to set free. Are you looking?
            Here it is. Smooth back your hair, and smile a
            beautiful smile.
PARIS: I don't see how the bird will fly any better if
            Helen smooths her hair and gives a beautiful
            smile.

HELEN: It can't do me any harm, anyway.

DEMOKOS: Don't move. One! Two! Three! There! It's all
            over, you can go now.

HELEN: Where was the bird?
DEMOKOS: It's a bird who knows how to make himself invis-
            ible.
HELEN: Ask him next time to tell you how he does it.

Mlle. Colombe

by JEAN ANOUILH

(Produced by Robert L. Joseph and Jay Julien; opened at the
Longacre Theatre, January 6, 1954.)

November 2, 1953

Dear Boris:

On re-reading the script of our play, I was struck by the fact
that many of the characters act like *clowns* and then I realized
that in the commedia dell'arte sense they are all clowns.
Julien is a "Pierrot"—*Colombe* is a "Columbine"—and the
rest are "Pantalones" and "Dottores," etc. The play is, as the
commedia dell'arte plays so often are, a kind of tragic farce
and pure theatre. It is, in fact, a sort of serious *circus*.

This leads me to believe that the play should be made as
colorful as possible in costume and setting, in turn romantically gay and romantically sad. It must be heightened to a
thoroughgoing theatrical picturesqueness. The shabby element, which also exists as part of the atmosphere, may be
minimized in behalf of the picturesqueness. We should see

the theatre with the eyes of Colombe, who thinks of it as a fulfillment of everything she desires. If we see the theatre too
realistically, we would be seeing it through Julien's eyes and
that is not desirable.

The color should not be garish, but rather *light* and
tasteful in the French manner. In *Colombe,* the theatre is the
world, the world which Anouilh loves and despises at the same
time because it is a place of beautiful illusion and terrible
cynicism, in contrast to Julien's inner world which is asceti-
cally pure and bleak. I want the set to be the most glamorous
of many seasons. I intend to heighten makeups, color of hair
and characterizations in line with this feeling I have about the
play.

Perhaps what I say here is more useful to the costume designer than to you, but I think you ought to know how I
sense the atmosphere of the play. One thing is sure, I am not
going to have a realistic production.

Love,
Harold

The Creation of the World and Other Business

by ARTHUR MILLER

(To be produced by Robert Whitehead; early fall, 1972.)

October 11, 1971

Dear Boris:

The Creation of the World and Other Business is a philosophic comedy or a comedy with philosophy. It is even more philosophy than comedy if we understand "comedy" not as rib-tickling jokes but as a special way of presenting vital matter.

The reason I insist on the "philosophical" aspect in this play is not intellectual but *theatrical*. I explain later on.

Though it is not strictly necessary for the purpose of this letter which is to guide you in my concept of the play (also Miller's), I shall summarize the play's philosophy in the simplest terms.

The *dramatic struggle* in the play—what the text calls the

"issue"—is what *principle* or *power* shall rule the world or who and what force must dominate in the world.

There are two principles: God, in every sense, the Father: powerful, benevolent, warm, hearty and sometimes so perplexed and confused by what he has created—the Family of Man—that he makes terrible mistakes and is rarely altogether sure he has done the right thing by his Family and his own intention. He is, in short, like every father and also like every great Artist—passionate, powerful, exalted and never sure his own work is as good as he wishes or thinks it is—and therefore he is in need of both praise *and* criticism.

Physically he is massive, commanding, sometimes unctuous, quick-tempered, irate and given to changing his mind—variable. He is also as cute as a bear, playful and "sensuous" like a man in love with his large brood of troublesome kids. He is *Love*—which is also variable and can be turned to fierceness and tremendous mischief. Love is not "sweetness and light," it's the surge of all creative force which sometimes deviates toward destructiveness but always aims at tenderness, harmony and passionate coherence. The author is on his side not because God is always "right," but because without him there is *Nothing*. It is he who created Life and the author is for an acceptance of life even in its ferocity. Man (who is in God's image) also has this desire, need, passion for the creative life force.

Lucifer is Reason, the corrector of God's possible errors in logic. Lucifer is the Awakener who sees the Father's and the Artist's errors and believes that he is "smarter" than Him—which he is—even more persuasive, because more logical—pure intelligence, in fact. Without the Awakener to challenge God and thus Man we should all stagnate. He is witty (whereas God is only kind, warm, or angry), he is keenly perceptive, lithe, handsome, with an electric mind. He knows his "weakness" (dryness of heart) but he believes he is right because he can *prove* it. He is in all of us, as is God, and his reason often triumphs or seems to because he is much more plausible than God, who at times is all "mixed up," as are Fathers and Artists.

I see Lucifer as slender (God is heavy), quick of mind and limb, a veritable *dancer* in body and spirit, a ham actor, a clown, a flirt, a lady's man, a killer of utmost fascination. God is a bass, Lucifer a tenor. God is ponderous, slow-moving, Lucifer quicksilver and varicolored—as the fireflies in the play who twinkle in the night as Lucifer's charming helpers.

Adam and Eve, Cain and Abel, are the pawns and instruments at the mercy of the two mighty forces which rule the *World*. Adam, good-looking, healthy, between thirty-five and forty, is the good ordinary man, who sides with the Establishment. He is *obedient* above all to God's will, knowing it is good—even if he hasn't the intelligence to understand Him. His heart is on God's side. He is moved by emotions more than thought—for this reason he suspects Lucifer and loves God, who like him is all *feeling*. He favors God's order. He has a good heart and partakes of God's *fatherliness*. He belongs to and with God—but he is of this earth. There is nothing "mystic" about him, but he is both superstitious and trusting.

Eve is the ingenue (Act I), she is the tormented one (Act II), she is the Mother who despite everything perpetuates the race and for which whatever we think of her frailty we must bless her—if we believe in the acceptance of God which is the Acceptance of Life—horror and all!) . . . She is attracted by Lucifer because he *is* attractive and brilliant, she is changeable and is also with God as she is with that other father, her husband Adam, and above all, despite pain, she wants *to give birth* to the race. She is the Earth Mother—she who bears us and bears with us. She so loves life that she will let her children play with her and even make love to her. For she lives through her children.

She should be between twenty-eight and forty: not "beautiful" (Hollywood style) but truly womanly. Hers is the glory and the anguish of life.

Cain is forever seeking righteousness and fearful of his own potential corruption. He is the average good man who suspects that he is no good at all. He is always eager to *"make good"* and wants assurance of it from some power that is above suspicion. He wants life to be fair to him, to be just and respectful of his good deeds and to reward him. When he is not rewarded, he sees no reason to believe in anything. But this, too, torments him. Therefore he *needs* religion: it is his only support. He needs God though God "betray" him.

He will go into the world, ever smiling as a man of the world, but gnawed by a sense of his own unworthiness, for he knows that he has killed and may kill again. He is forever torn between Heaven and Hell, God and Lucifer—he is what most of us are. . . . The actor who plays the part should have some of this Dostoevskian torment and "twistedness" in him: lean, a little devilish, as if he were related to Lucifer. He is inwardly restless and violent.

Abel is the pure, simple soul, loving, innocent, credulous and willing to accept everything at its face value—he doesn't speak of God or need him for he is without guile or guilt. He plays with his mother but he will not mount her with fierce desire as Cain does. He only wishes to love and to be *loved.* The desire to be *loved,* to win approval, is his "weakness"—which leads him to trouble.

THE PRODUCTION

I said this is a philosophical comedy. Which means that whatever else we accomplish, the *Words* and *Sense* of the play are more important than the Spectacle. If the *Words* aren't clear, striking, ringing, or if they are interfered with by any other stage element, the play as *meaning* will fail.

Therefore we must consider how to make the speakers stand out above everything else. The setting and background must be beautifully *Simple.* (When the world was created, it was bare. There wasn't very much there!) No matter what mechanical complexities are involved, to the spectator, the audience, the stage must look simple—even to the point of "bareness." We must forget the *Setting*, once we have admired and felt its tone. The setting should not express the play but serve as a background for it as well as a "machine or podium for the actors."

Therefore: (a) It should be or represent what the Germans call an *Erdball*, the globe, a *circle*, the WORLD itself. This circle should be made the inner frame behind which the action takes place and in front of which, if possible or desirable, Lucifer may step out of God's reach and soliloquize. But everything is contained within the *Circle* which is the World and which has the perfection and completion of circularity—no matter what terror occurs within it.

(b) The sky is important. It should be limpid, blue or cream white with occasional shots of red when storm and strife are indicated. All the colors, including that of the grass, should be on the lighter side of their vibrations, almost pastel. Delicate and very often transparent so that bushes, trees (as sparingly used as possible) may be employed as masking and when desired (as in Act III when Abel's bloody body is discovered) make visible what is behind it.

(c) Places to sit and lie down are boulders, rocks, stone protuberances—but not too many. Clear space must be provided on the forestage—most of the boulders upstage a bit—so that characters can move freely or dance: there are two real dances in the play: "God's waltz" with Eve and its distortion by Lucifer with Eve, Cain and Abel.

(d) The upper—heavenly level—should be circular too—a lateral half-moon going from its center upstage to downstage right and left. It must carry the throne for God and lesser seats—not chairs or thrones—for the angels (six or seven of them). Since God and Lucifer hold forth there, the upper level must be solid enough to support *nine* actors. This platform used only in Act I; first scene should either be lowered from the "flys" or rise from below. It must go out of sight in Act I, Scene 2.

(e) The Total Effect and Style is *Magical*. Thus God and Lucifer never enter or exit but appear and disappear—materialize or dematerialize mysteriously. God does walk off with the Family in Act III and comes in normally. Lucifer should sometimes seem to shoot up from below suddenly. God descends from above. This is also true when the Angels come down or return to Heaven. (Remember: Eve says Lucifer has come out of the mist.)

(f) Speaking of Magic: the electrician, the Light Designer or a person who is a magic specialist must know how to make fire sparks or smoke come out of blows, delivered by Lucifer and the Heavenly Creatures—just as the winds, animal noises and whatever not are created electronically.

(g) *Nakedness:* The simplest solution would be thin tights over naked bodies. On these may be drawn "leaves" (or nature spots) so that the tights look like the filmy waters of the lakes and the leaves which float or are shadowed on them. Adam's penis may be dimly perceived under the tights, which should also be true of Eve's breasts and pubic hair, or they may be shadowed over by one of the painted leaves.

I wouldn't want the "costume" for nakedness to be too clever or "original." Let us get as close to real nakedness as possible without competing with *Oh! Calcutta!*: embarrassing neither to actors nor to audience. The tights should be easy to slip off and be replaced by the large fig leaf between I and II.

(h) There is a tree of knowledge on stage with *an apple* (or two). But the script speaks of figs and pomegranates. Would these be on less conspicuous bushes or trees?

(i) The change from 1 and 1 (I hope it can be made in *one* minute) should be mostly a change of white or silvery blue light to sombre hues. The tree of knowledge can be rolled off with only scrubby bushes and rocks remaining. Perhaps the green grass of the ground cloth can through lighting lose its hue and seem ashen, dusty.

(j) A costume note: Lucifer when he first appears is in electric or steel blue—a *Radiance*.

General notes:

Let's not worry about too much *realism*.

Don't try to express everything in the play *scenically*: it will complicate matters and get in the way of the *all* important Words which express all the play's nuances. We are only there to help project them. The play is a dramatic debate—it is a *literary* play, essentially: the *writer's* play. The play's "Hebraic" quality is in the language. It will be in the intoning of some of the prayers, invocations, etc. It can be expressed, too, in the rough simplicity or rudeness of the *costumes* and props (such as the "throne" in Heaven).

Makeup, too, should highlight certain features: the handsomeness, Lucifer's wicked wit, the devil's torment in Cain, the gravity and awesomeness of God's body and *eye,* etc.

The lighting should be the most elaborate and complex of all the scenic elements. The *watchword* is *Simplicity*—plenty of *Air* on stage. *Gentle* colors.

Except for the Altar, rocks for reclining and other properties essential to Action, we must make it seem that there is really not much "scenery" at all—otherwise willy-nilly we shall move into the "musical" or "operatic" area. The sky can become "angry," "bloodshot," etc. But the effect, I repeat, must always return to a certain lightly tinted calm, an evaporating, a disappearing, a beautifully fading calm: the *Heavens* always return to serenity. Life goes on . . .

A raked stage is desirable. The last disappearance of God and Lucifer on either side of the stage will be helped by this—and they should "go out" magically, too—so to speak, forever.

None of this is easy: but it must never occur to the audience that it was difficult, that our solutions are complex and hazardous.

Good luck,
Harold

P.S.: We must try to make the play a two-act play. One minute after Scene 1; fifteen minutes between Scene 2 and Act III. Make very few changes between 2 and 3. If you want a deeper tonality for the ground cloth (earth) in the now Act II (formerly Act III), O.K., but your worry about the change of tone between the Beginning and the End is not altogether well-founded. The play is beautifully *unified*. There is as much seriousness as comedy in Act I—though it is not as strongly marked as at the end. The play is also—like the *world*—and the framework of the set—*circular*. It keeps coming back to its single theme: *who and what shall rule the world*. It is finally *Man* who is always closer to God's Love than to Lucifer's Reason—and that is why the world will roll on in perpetuity unless Reason (the Atom Bomb and other brilliant devices of reason) blow us all to Hell—which neither I nor Miller nor the play really believes to be our Destiny!

P.P.S.: The specific physical actions, pieces of business, are clearly marked in the text and may be followed literally. I need not repeat them. If any special idea occurs to me which affects you, I'll let you know.

Index

Contents

DEDICATION

This book is affectionately dedicated to my fourteen-year-old daughter, Danae, who continues to be one of the great joys of my life.

A Message to Parents

How would you like to be thirteen years old again, by the wave of a magic wand? I can almost hear my adult readers answering that question in one booming voice: "No Thanks!" Everyone in our culture wants to remain young, but not *that* young! And why not? Because we grown-ups remember our adolescent years as the most stressful and threatening time of life.

Most of us recall the scary physical changes that were occurring during those early years. We also remember our sexual anxieties and the guilt that was associated with our strange new desires. We have not forgotten the self-doubt and feelings of inferiority which seemed unbearable at times. And of course, we recall the emotional vulnerability to practically everything throughout adolescence . . .

vulnerability to failure, to ridicule, to embarrassment, to parental attitudes, and especially to any form of rejection by members of the opposite sex. There's no doubt about it: adolescence was a turbulent voyage for most of us "old folks" (i.e., those over thirty!).

From this perspective, it does seem strange that we parents are so reluctant to share our youthful experiences with our own children. Preteenagers could profit from what we have learned *because we've been where they're going.* Nevertheless, we typically keep our memories to ourselves and permit our boys and girls to sail into the same troubled waters with no preparation or orientation or warning. The result is often disastrous. As I stated in a previous publication, "The primary reason adolescence is so distressing is because youngsters do not fully understand what is happening to them. Many of their fears and anxieties and discouragements could be obviated by a simple instructional program."*

Where would such an educational effort begin, and what content would it cover? The book which you hold in your hand is addressed to those questions. It was written specifically for boys and girls between ten and fifteen years of age, and is expressed in language that they can understand. This book describes the typical "adolescent experience" and discusses the delicate issues without flinching, including masturbation, menstruation,

---

Hide or Seek, Fleming H. Revell, 1974, p. 108.

sexual morality, parent-child conflict, drug abuse, conformity, and, most importantly, the "canyon of inferiority."

The final chapter may be the most beneficial, which was taken from a recorded conversation with four teenagers. These young people participated in an open discussion designed to explain to younger readers what they can expect to feel and experience in the years ahead. That recorded session, which took place in my home, was a meaningful time of sharing feelings and fears and hopes and dreams. I think your child will find the text interesting and helpful.

Not only was the final chapter taken from a tape recording, but this entire book originally appeared in the form of a cassette tape album by the same name. The six tapes in the *Preparing for Adolescence* album represent quiet conversations between my listeners and me, with one cassette being devoted to each of the six chapters in the book. The album is available through bookstores (or can be ordered from the address provided on the final page of this text). Also available is a *Preparing for Adolescence Growth Pak*, which includes the six tapes, this book, a workbook for students, and two instructional tapes addressed to parents.

Let me conclude this statement by citing an analogy. Each September, football coaches across America bring together the boys they hope to mold into a team. They drill the players on funda-mentals—on blocking, tackling, throwing, and catching. For two weeks or more, this grueling practice continues day after day. Finally, the night of the game arrives amidst tension and expectation. The stadium is filled with screaming fans and the opponents are waiting on the field. Before leaving the locker room, however, the coach gathers his team for one last reminder and word of encouragement. You see, he knows that there will be little opportunity to teach or guide once the game has begun. His final words are vitally important, and in fact could even change the outcome of the game. After his remarks have been delivered, he sends his team out to do its best.

A parent who is preparing his child for adolescence is functioning much like that football coach. Since childhood he has been systematically teaching the "fundamentals"—getting the youngster ready for the approaching contest. They drilled and practiced throughout the elementary school years, continuing into junior high. They rehearsed the proper spiritual attitudes and moral values and they worked especially hard on building self-confidence. Finally the moment of truth arrives, and a concluding instructional session is held.

"Don't forget what we've been teaching you," Dad says.

"Watch out for the tackler I told you about," warns Mom.

"Do a good job, son. We believe in you!" they both shout.

Junior nods affirmatively and runs onto the field. His parents stand glassy-eyed on the sidelines, knowing that their coaching job is almost over.

They have made their contribution, and the outcome now depends on the bony kid in the backfield.

Do you get the message? If you have a youngster in the preadolescent age, you should capitalize on this final "coaching session" prior to the big game. You must take this occasion to refresh his memory, provide last-minute instructions, and offer any necessary words of caution. But beware: if you let this fleeting moment escape unnoticed, you may never get another opportunity.

Preparing for Adolescence was designed to help with that important assignment, and I'm confident that you will handle it properly. Knute Rockne would be proud of you!

James C. Dobson, Ph.D.

The Secret of Self-Esteem

1

You are about to read a very personal book about an important time of life known as adolescence . . . those years between childhood and adulthood. Some of you are nine, ten, or eleven years old now, and you're just beginning to think about growing up. You're not sure what's coming, but you're excited about the experience and want to know more about the details. This book is written for you.

Others of you are already teenagers, and these concepts will be important for you too. Whether you're looking forward to your teen years or are already involved in them, you'll soon understand a little more about the questions and problems that are likely to occur in the years immediately ahead.

But why make such a big deal about adolescence? Why should we go to the effort to learn about this period of life? Well, very honestly, growing up will not be the easiest thing you'll ever do. It was not easy for those who are now adults, and you won't find it simple either. It's always difficult to grow up, because life presents many new demands when you enter a new phase. You don't remember it, I'm sure, but before you were born you were curled up nice and cozy inside your mother's warm body. You could hear her heart beating steady, soft, and secure, and you were safe and warm and comfortable in that world that God had provided. All your needs were met and there wasn't a care in the world. You had nothing to worry about and not a single concern.

But when the proper time came, you were rudely pushed out of that perfect little pocket, whether you liked it or not (nobody asked you!), and you entered this cold world where a doctor picked you up by your heels and whacked your behind. (That was some kind of welcome for a new fellow in the neighborhood!)

As a matter of fact, while you were hanging there, looking at all those upside-down people all around you for the first time, you probably would rather have gone back to that protected little world you just came from. But you simply couldn't stay in your mother's womb if you were going to grow and develop and learn.

The Challenge of Adolescence

In a way, moving into adolescence is like that. You've been in the very warm, secure world of childhood. All your needs have been met by your parents: they were there to put a Band-Aid on your big toe when you stubbed it on a rock, and they kissed away your tears when things didn't go right. You played most of the time, and life was pretty rosy and comfortable. But you can't stay in that childhood world forever, any more than you could remain in your mother's body. There's something better ahead for you—the excitement of growing up, of becoming an adult, of having your own family, of earning your own living, of making your own decisions, of being independent. This is the natural, necessary process of moving from childhood to adulthood.

Unfortunately, however, you can't just *suddenly* mature. First you have to wiggle out of your secure world of childhood, and that is where the difficulty often begins. There will be times when life will whack you on the behind, so to speak, just as it did before. And you may even feel that you're hanging by your heels once in awhile. There will be some new fears and some new problems, and the world won't be quite as safe as it used to be. But it's an exciting world, and it will be even better if you know what to expect.

With that introduction, then, I want to describe some of the new experiences that are about to occur. You'll soon have some of the most thrilling moments of your life (and some of the scariest, too!). We will be talking about the things that teenagers worry about most—the events that are most often upsetting. I want to help you get better acquainted

13

with your mind, with your feelings, with your emotions, with your attitudes, with your body, with your hopes and dreams, with who you are, with where you're going, with how to get there, and with the things you're likely to face in the years ahead. We are going to face these issues head-on; nothing will be considered too sensitive or too delicate to discuss, as long as it's relevant to those of you between twelve and twenty years of age.

As you read this book, I hope it will make you want to discuss these issues further with someone in whom you have confidence. Let this be just a beginning; start to ask your own questions, to express your own concerns, and to make growing up a very personal event in your life.

The Dark Canyon

Let's begin by playing a mental game for a moment. Imagine yourself driving alone down the highway in a small car. You've just come through a little town by the name of Puberty, but now you're back on the main highway, and over on the right you see a sign that says "Adultsville, eight years straight ahead." You're clipping along the highway at about 55 miles an hour, heading for this great new city that you've heard so much about.

But as you round a curve, you suddenly see a man waving a red flag and holding up a warning sign. He motions for you to stop as quickly as possible, so you jam on the brakes and skid to a halt

14

just in front of the flagman. He comes over to the window of your car and says, "Friend, I have some very important information for you. A bridge has collapsed about one mile down the road, leaving a huge drop-off into a dark canyon. If you're not careful, you'll drive your car off the edge of the road and tumble down that canyon, and, of course, if you do that you'll never get to Adultsville."

No Backing Up

So what are you going to do? You can't back up because your car has no reverse gear. *None* of the cars that travel on this highway can go backward. That's like trying to back up on the freeway—it just can't be done. So you ask the flagman, "What am I going to do?" and he says, "Well, I have this suggestion for you. Go ahead and drive down the road, but go slowly and carefully and keep watching for this ruined bridge. When you get to it, turn to the right and go south for about a mile or two. Then you'll find a place where you can get around the canyon and back onto the main highway again. You don't have to fall down that hole—you can drive around it—so good luck and drive carefully."

Now let me explain the meaning of this story. The automobile you're driving represents your own life. It has your name on the door. In fact, it has all of your characteristics, and you're driving this sports car down the highway of life toward adulthood. And you see, *I* am that flagman standing beside the road. I'm waving the banner back and forth, and holding up a warning sign, and motioning for you to stop. I want to warn you about a problem that lies down the road—a "canyon" that *most* teenagers fall into on the road to adulthood. This is not a problem that affects just a few teenagers; nearly everybody has to deal with it one way or another during the adolescent years.

After I've motioned you to stop, I lean in the window of your car and tell you that many other young people have wrecked their lives by plunging down this dark gorge, but I can show you how to avoid it—how to go around the danger.

The Agony of Inferiority

But what is this problem which so many adolescents face at this time of life? What is it that causes so much hurt and pain to young people between twelve and twenty years of age? It's a feeling of hopelessness that we call "inferiority." It's that awful awareness that nobody likes you, that you're not as good as other people, that you're a failure, a loser, a personal disaster; that you're ugly, or unintelligent, or don't have as much ability as someone else. It's that depressing feeling of worthlessness.

What a shame that *most* teenagers decide they are without much human worth when they're between thirteen and fifteen years of age! It may have happened to some of you even earlier, but in most cases the problem is at its worst during the junior high years. This is the canyon I was talking about—that dark hole in the roadway to adulthood that captures so many young people.

Recently I was interviewed by the editors of *Teen* magazine for an article they were writing on the subject of inferiority. The editors of this magazine knew that most teenagers face this problem. I tried to tell their readers that this is an unnecessary crisis: you can go around the difficulty and avoid it if you know what to expect. But if you simply drive your car down the highway full speed ahead, without thinking about the dangers and without being aware of them, you too can fall victim to this same feeling of worthlessness. It doesn't make sense that we should all have to suffer the agony of defeat. We *all* have human worth, yet so many young people conclude that they're somehow different—that they're truly inferior—that they lack the necessary ingredients for dignity and worth.

Ronny's Problem

Some of you know that I often work with young people who have these kinds of problems (as well as physical problems). I've been on the staff of a children's hospital for ten years. But I previously served on a high school campus, and there I worked with many teenagers who were struggling with some of the feelings that I've been describing to you.

One day I was walking across the grounds of the high school after the bell had rung. Most of the students were already back in class, but I saw a boy coming toward me in the main hall. I knew that his

17

name was Ronny and that he was in his third year of high school. However, I didn't know him very well. Ronny was one of those many students who remain back in the crowd, never calling attention to themselves and never making friends with those around them. It's easy to forget they're alive because they never allow anybody to get acquainted with them.

When Ronny was about fifteen feet away from me, I saw that he was very upset about something. It was obvious that he was distressed, because his face revealed his inner turmoil. As he came a few feet closer, he saw that I was watching him intently. Our eyes locked for a moment, then he looked at the floor as he came closer.

When Ronny and I were parallel, he suddenly covered his face with both hands and turned toward the wall. His neck and ears turned red, and he began to sob and weep. He was not just crying—he seemed to explode with emotion. I put my arm around him and said, "Can I help you, Ronny? Do you feel like talking to me?" He nodded affirmatively, and I practically had to lead him into my office.

I offered Ronny a chair and closed the door, and I gave him a few minutes to get control of himself before asking him to speak. Then he began to talk to me.

He said, "I've been going to school in this district for eight years, but in all that time I've never managed to make one single friend! Not one. There's not a soul in this high school who cares whether I live or die. I walk to school by myself and I walk home alone. I don't go to football games; I don't go to basketball games or any school activities because I'm embarrassed to sit there all by myself. I stand alone at snack time in the morning, and I eat lunch out in a quiet corner of the campus. Then I go back to class by myself. I don't get along with my dad, and my mother doesn't understand me, and I fight with my sister. And I have nobody! My phone never rings. I have no one to talk to. Nobody knows what I feel and nobody cares. Sometimes I think I just can't stand it anymore!"

Ronny Is Not Alone

I can't tell you how many students have expressed these same feelings to me. One eighth-grade girl named Charlotte felt so badly about herself and about being unpopular that she didn't want to live anymore. She came to school one day and told me she had taken all the pills that were available in the medicine cabinet in an attempt to do away with herself. But she didn't really want to die, or else she wouldn't have told me what she had done. She was actually calling for help. The school nurse and I got her to the hospital just in time to save her life. Both Charlotte and Ronny are among many thousands of students who are overwhelmed by their own worthlessness, and sometimes this even takes away their desire to live.

Some young people feel inferior and foolish only occasionally, such as when they fail at something very important. But others feel worthless *all* the time. Maybe you're one of those individuals who hurts every day. Have you ever had that big lump in your throat that comes when you feel that nobody cares—that nobody likes you—that maybe they even hate you? Have you ever wished that you could crawl out of your skin and get into another person's body? Do you ever feel like a complete dummy when you're in a group? Would you ever like to descend into a hole and disappear? If you've ever had those kinds of feelings, I hope you'll finish reading this book, because it's for *you*! I wish Ronny and Charlotte could have read what I'm writing when they expressed such feelings. I wish they could have recognized their true worth as human beings. They had, you see, driven into the canyon of inferiority and were groping in the darkness below

Why?

Now let's ask a very important question. Why do so many teenagers feel inferior? Why can't American young people grow up liking themselves? Why is it common for people to examine themselves and be bitterly disappointed with the person God has made them? Why is it necessary for everyone to bump his head on the same old rock? These are very good questions, and I believe there are good answers to them.

Mother Nature's Damage

As young people grow up in our American society today, there are three things that teenagers feel they *must* have in order to feel good about themselves. The first of these, and by far the most important, is physical attractiveness. Did you know that about 80 percent of the teenagers in our society don't like the way they look? *Eighty percent!*

If you asked ten teenagers what they are most unhappy about, eight of them would be dissatisfied with some feature of their bodies. They feel ugly and unattractive, and they think about that problem most of the time. They also believe that the opposite sex doesn't like them. The girls feel too tall and the boys feel too short, or they feel too fat or too thin or they're worried about the pimples on their faces or about the freckles on their noses or the color of their hair, or they think their feet are too big or they don't like their fingernails.

No matter how minor the problem is, it can create great anxieties and depression. Most teenagers examine themselves carefully in the mirror to see how much damage has been done by Mother Nature, and they don't like what they see. Since none of us is perfect, they usually find something about themselves that they don't like. Then they worry and fret about it, wishing they didn't have that flaw. Can you imagine being depressed and miserable over something as silly as having a nose that is a fraction of an inch longer than you think it should be?

What Kind of "Friends"?

One reason teenagers become so sensitive about their tiny flaws is because their "friends" have teased and embarrassed them during their early years. Unfortunately, boys and girls are often brutal to one another, hurling insults back and forth like poison darts. I knew a third-grade girl, for example, who received a note at school from another girl who apparently hated her. She had done nothing unkind to the writer of the note, but this is what it said:

> Awful Janet
>
> Your the stinkest girl in this world. I hope you die but of course I suppose that's impossible. I've some ideals.
>
> 1. Play in the road
> 2. Cut your throad
> 3. Drink poison
> 4. Get drunk
> 5. Knife yourself
>
> Please do some of this you big fat Girl. we all hate you. I'm praying Oh please lord let Janet die. Were in need of fresh air. Did you hear me lord cause if you didn' will all die with her here. See Janet we're not all bad.
>
> from Wanda Jackson*

Have you ever received a note like that? More important, have you ever *written* that kind of note? Young people are easily hurt, and the pain from this kind of message goes very deep and lasts a long time. It may even be remembered after Janet is grown.

---

*Quoted from *Hide or Seek*, Revell Publishers, 1974. Used by permission.

"Pee Wee" and "Gorilla"

One of the most damaging games played by teenagers is to create unkind nicknames that draw attention to anything different or unusual about a person. In this way they put a spotlight on the feature that the victim most wants to hide. You may have been given a nickname or teased about your body at some time or another. If you're a small boy you may have been called "Runt" or "Pee Wee." If you're a big girl you may have been called "Moose" or "Gorilla." If you have large ears they may have called you "Dumbo." You see, *no one* has a perfect body and *everyone* has something that can be made fun of. Even Farrah Fawcett—Majors, the Hollywood beauty, said recently that she thought her mouth was too large. (I never really noticed.) At least Farrah was able to talk about her imperfections. Most people try to conceal theirs in shame.

To illustrate further, let's suppose that Charlie is a healthy boy, ten years of age. He has a strong body, a sharp mind, and a loving home. He has been blessed by many good things in life, and he experiences very few problems. Then one day a group of students on the playground begins teasing him about his big feet. They call him "Snowshoes" and "Duckfeet." It's all done in fun, I guess, but Charlie takes it very seriously. He becomes extremely sensitive about the size of his feet, and thinks everyone is laughing behind his back. He tries to hide his feet under his desk at school, and insists that his mother buy him shoes that are three sizes too small. Eventually, Charlie may become depressed and disinterested in living instead of being a happy fellow who enjoys the advantages God has given him. This illustration may sound unreal to you, but please believe me, I know many "Charlies" who have been made to dislike themselves over very minor flaws.

If you're not yet a teenager you should know that you're likely to be dissatisfied with your body in the future. If your concern is great, it may cause you to be shy or very easily embarrassed. Or it may lead you to be the opposite—loud and angry— because you feel foolish and you think nobody likes you anyway. There's just no way to estimate the amount of pain and worry that teenagers feel over the way they look.

At Seventeen

This concern was expressed in the words of a popular song written by Janis Ian. She actually won a Grammy Award in 1976 for this song entitled "At Seventeen."* The words are reproduced below so that you can see how feelings of inferiority are reflected throughout this song.

I learned the truth at seventeen
That love was meant for beauty queens
And high school girls with clear-skinned smiles
Who married young and then retired.

The valentines I never knew,
The Friday-night charades of youth,
Were spent on one more beautiful;
At seventeen I learned the truth.

---

*Lyrics by Janis Ian
© 1974 MINE MUSIC, LTD. (ASCAP).
Used with permission.

And those of us with ravaged faces
Lacking in the social graces
Desperately remained at home,
Inventing lovers on the phone
Who called to say, "Come dance with me,"
And murmured vague obscenities.
It isn't all it seems at seventeen.

To those of us who knew the pain
Of valentines that never came
And those whose names were never called
When choosing sides for basketball.

It was long ago and far away;
The world was younger than today
And dreams were all they gave for free
To ugly-duckling girls like me.

I am not personally acquainted with Janis Ian, but I'm sure of one very important fact about her: she too has been down in the canyon of inferiority. It would have been impossible for her to write the words of this song without having felt inadequate when she was younger. She speaks for millions when she describes "those of us with ravaged faces" (those with pimples and blackheads) and "those whose names were never called when choosing sides for basketball." I hope *you* will never be included in this vast group of discouraged people who learn so many painful lessons "at seventeen."

Who's Dumb?

The second characteristic that young people don't like about themselves is that they feel unintelligent (or dumb). This feeling often begins during the very early school years, when they have trouble learning in school. Either they have a hard time learning to read, and they start worrying about this problem, or else they blurt out answers that cause everyone to laugh. They gradually start to believe that everybody in the classroom (including the teacher) thinks they're stupid, and this brings the same old feelings of inferiority.

The more often a student fails in school, the more discouraged he is likely to become. He will probably be called unkind names by his classmates, such as "Stupid" or "Dummy" or "Lamebrain." If these insults are too painful, he may lose all interest in school and even quit trying. This causes a vicious cycle to develop: his refusal to work results in more failure, which brings more ridicule in the classroom, which produces less motivation to try, which results in further failure . . . and round and round it goes. Finally this individual reaches the awful conclusion that he has a defective brain and is certain to fail throughout life. It is a terrible experience to believe that you have no human worth.

Parents, too, can accidentally make their children feel they aren't very smart. Adults are human beings too, and they get impatient and tired, just like you do. This may cause them to become upset and call their children insulting names, which are remembered for a lifetime.

So children often grow up thinking they're stupid and dumb, and this is the second reason why inferiority is so common among junior high and high school students.

The Measure of Money

The third value that young people use to measure their worth is money. You see, they think the wealthy family is more important than the poor one, and to be accepted and popular they have to dress a certain way, or their family has to have a particular kind of car, or they have to live in a big house in the right part of town, or their father has to have a certain kind of job. The young person who can't afford these things sometimes feels inferior and inadequate. Everybody else has sweaters to wear, but he has to wear shirts that are worn around the edges. This financial problem is not as common now as it used to be, simply because today more people have the necessities of life. However, some families still live in poverty, and those children who can't afford to be like their friends sometimes feel inferior because they are poor.

Beauty, intelligence, and money are the three attributes valued most highly in our society. And when junior high students first discover that they are lacking in one (or all three) of these characteristics, they begin sliding downward in despair. For them, the "bridge" has collapsed and a dark canyon looms below.

Now if you're one of those young people who *already* feels bad about life—if you feel miserable about yourself and would like to escape somehow, to just run away from it all, or if you've been hurt when someone said unkind words, let me give you several suggestions that may help you.

1. Recognize that you are not alone.

First, begin observing the people around you and see if you detect hidden feelings of inferiority. When you go to school tomorrow, quietly watch the students who are coming and going. Some will be smiling and laughing and talking and carrying their books and playing baseball. Unless you take a second look, you'd never know they had a care in the world. But I assure you, many of them have the same concerns that trouble you. They reveal these doubts by being very shy and quiet, or by being extremely angry and mean, or by being silly, or by being afraid to participate in a game or contest, or by blushing frequently, or by acting proud and "stuck-up." You'll soon learn to recognize the signs of inferiority, and then you'll know that it is a *very* common disorder! Once you fully comprehend that others feel as you do, then you *should never again* feel alone. It will give you more confidence to know that everyone is afraid of embarrassment and ridicule—that we're all sitting in the same leaky boat, trying to plug the watery holes. And would you believe, *I* nearly drowned in that same leaky boat when I was fourteen years old?

2. Face your problem.

The second suggestion that I hope will be helpful for you is to face the issue of what's bugging you. Look squarely at the thought that keeps gnawing at you from the back of your mind or from deep within your heart, causing a black cloud to hang over your head day and night. It would be a good idea to get alone, where there is no one to interfere with your thoughts. Then *list* all the things which you most dislike about yourself. Nobody is going to see this paper except the people to whom you choose to show it, so you can be completely honest. Write down everything that has been bothering you. Even admit the characteristics that you dislike, including the tendency to get mad and blow up (if that applies to you).

Identify your most serious problems as best as possible. Do you get frustrated and angry at people and then feel bad later? Or is it your shyness that makes you afraid when you're with other people? Or is it your inability to express your ideas—to put your thoughts into words? Is it your laziness or your unkindness to other people, or the way you look? Whatever concerns you, write it down as best you can. (You're probably going to need a big stack of paper, because most people can find too many things they don't like about themselves.) Withhold nothing from this writing assignment. Then when you're finished, go back through the list and put a checkmark by those items that worry you the most— the problems that you spend the most time thinking and fretting about.

Find a True Friend

Now you're ready to take some action to improve your circumstances. It would be a good idea to select someone you trust, a person in whom you have confidence. This should be an adult who understands the problems of young people. Perhaps it will be your parent—or your teacher or counselor or pastor. You will know the right person. Take your list to that trusted leader and go over it with him or her, discussing each one of your problems. Talk openly about your feelings, asking your friend to make suggestions about changing the things that concern you.

It is very likely that many of the problems you face have been conquered by other people, and you may be able to profit from their experience also. In other words, there could be an easy solution available. Maybe you don't have to go through life struggling with the same concerns that have troubled other people. Your first step, then, is to map a strategy, a plan of action, a way of solving your problems. You'll feel much better for having discussed your worries openly, and you just might discover some successful solution.

The Fire of Commitment

But how will you handle the remaining items on your list that can't be changed? What can you do with the more difficult problems that defy solution? *It would be wise to remember that the best way to have a healthy mind is to learn to accept those things which you cannot change.* There will always be circumstances which we wish we could rearrange or remove. However, the happiest people in the world are not those who have no problems, but the people who have learned to live with those things that are less than perfect.

Let me suggest, then, that you take your remaining list of "unsolvable problems" to a private place where a small fire will not be dangerous. Perhaps you would like to have your counselor-friend present for this ceremony. Then burn that paper as a symbol to God that the problems are now His. Your prayers should contain this message to Him (stated in your own words):

> Dear Jesus, I am bringing all my problems and worries to you tonight, because you are my best friend. You already know about my strengths and weaknesses, because You made me. That's why I'm burning this paper now. It's my way of saying that I'm giving my life to you . . . with my good qualities along with my shortcomings and failures. I'm asking you to use me in whatever way You wish. Make me the kind of person You want me to be. And from this moment forward, I'm not going to worry about my imperfections.

God Knows and Cares

I'm sure that you will find great warmth, love, and acceptance from God when you pray that prayer. By doing so, you are saying, "I want Your will for my life, not because I'm a superstar or superman or superwoman, but because You promised to help those who admit their weaknesses. I'm depending on *Your* power and *Your* strength to make something beautiful out of my life." The Bible teaches us to reveal this humble dependence on the Lord, and He will honor it!

Did you know that God sees you when you hurt? He knows those deep fears and frustrations that you thought no one understood. He knows the longings of your heart, and He's always there during those moments when a little tear pushes out of your eye and down your cheek . . . those times when you feel totally alone. In fact, God loves you and me so much that He actually sent His only Son to die for us. Now that's real love at its greatest! I'm convinced that Jesus would have died for me (or you) even if I had been the only individual in the whole world. That's how much He cares for us.

If God can love us that much, just the way we are, why can't we accept ourselves? That's probably the best question of the year.

Something Beautiful, Something Good

Bill Gaither has written a song with the words, "Something beautiful, something good; all my confusion He understood. All I had to offer Him was brokenness and strife, but He made something beautiful of my life." God can do that with *your* life. If you read the Bible—and I hope you do—you'll learn that God does not choose the superstars and the miracle men to do His work. All through the ages He has selected ordinary people with human flaws, people who were less than perfect, to do His jobs. When Jesus was choosing His disciples He didn't select the most powerful and popular men in the country at that time. He chose ordinary fishermen, and even a tax collector who was hated in his community.

Send Somebody Else

You may also remember the story of Moses and his experience with the burning bush as told in the book of Exodus. God was speaking to Moses through the bush and said something like this: "Moses, I have a very important job for you to do. I want you to tell Pharaoh that I have commanded him to let my people go."

Well, Moses felt inferior and inadequate, just as so many people do today. He gave this kind of answer to the Lord: "God, couldn't You send somebody else? When I get to Pharaoh's palace I know they're going to laugh at me. They could even throw me into prison. I think, Lord, that perhaps you ought to send somebody else." And then Moses told God what was *actually* bothering him—he admitted the reason he felt inferior: "And besides, Lord, I didn't want to bring this up, but you know that I stutter. I'm not eloquent of speech . . . my words don't come out right. When I try to talk at an important moment, the words get all tangled up. Lord, I'm not the man for the job. I'd rather stay home, if you don't mind."

In the fourteenth verse of the fourth chapter of Exodus, the Bible says, "The anger of the Lord was kindled against Moses." The Lord was displeased at Moses for using inferiority as an excuse. You see, God intended to go with Moses and help him. That's why He didn't want Moses to hide behind an excuse of inferiority. The Lord doesn't want *you* to use this excuse of inferiority either, because He will help you to accomplish what He tells you to do. When you return to school tomorrow and find yourself afraid of other students—afraid they're going to laugh at you or leave you out—just remember that you're not by yourself. You have with you the power of the God who created the entire universe. He can make something beautiful of your life, if you'll allow Him to take charge.

3. Compensate for your weaknesses.

Are you ready for the third suggestion? There's a very important word that you ought to understand, and it's called *compensation*. Compensation may be a ten-dollar word, but it has a very simple meaning. It means *to make up for your weaknesses by concentrating on your strengths*—in other words, to *compensate* for your weaknesses. Returning to the unsolvable problems on your list which bother you the most, you can *balance* those weak areas by excelling in some other abilities.

Not everybody can be the best-looking person in school. If this is your situation, say "All right, so what? There are a lot of other people in the same boat, and it doesn't really matter. My worth doesn't depend on the arrangement of my body. I'll put my effort into something that will help me feel good about myself. I'll be the best trumpet player in the band, or I'll succeed in my part-time job, or I'll raise rabbits for fun and profit, or I'll make good grades in school, or I'll see how many friends I can make, or

I'll learn how to play basketball as well as possible, or I'll become a good pianist or drummer, or I'll just see how pleasant a personality I can develop (that's one that nearly everybody can work on), or I'll learn to play tennis, or I'll become a seamstress, or I'll draw or paint and express myself through art, or I'll write poetry or short stories, or I'll become a good cook." Or maybe you could become highly skilled at entertaining small children and become well-trained as a child-care worker.

You see, there's success waiting for *you* if you'll just look for it. You can learn to make the most out of what you have, and that's the first step toward developing self-confidence and acceptance. It doesn't hurt nearly as much to be rejected by other people when you know that you're successful at doing something. So develop a skill that will make you proud of yourself, and gradually you will start to have a better self-concept. You will begin to like yourself a bit more, and when you like yourself better, so will other people.

4. Have genuine friends.

This brings us to the fourth suggestion: *nothing helps your self-confidence more than genuine friends*. When you know that other people like you, it's much easier to accept yourself. You don't have to be beautiful or highly intelligent or wealthy in order to be liked by other people. "The best way to *have* a friend is to *be* a good friend to others." That's a very old proverb, but it's still very true.

How can you make new friends quickly and

easily? You must remember that the people you deal with every day have exactly the same problems I've been discussing with you. Understanding that fact will help you know how to get along with them and earn their respect. Never make fun of other people or ridicule them. Let them know that you respect and accept them, and that they are important to you. Make a conscious effort to show this kind of affection for people.

But you can't be a phony about showing respect to others; it has to be real. People will see right through you if you're phony. Learn to protect the reputation of other people, and they will do the same for you. Be sensitive to their feelings; they have the same needs that you do. Be kind to them; don't ever be sarcastic or catty. You may think you're getting away with insulting other people or laughing at their mistakes. But you'll get it back; they won't forget your insults. They may not hit you in the nose (or maybe they will!), and they may not cry or run away, and they may not even say anything when you treat them unkindly. But they'll probably try to hurt you in return the next time they have a chance. They'll gossip about you or try to get other people not to like you.

Friendship Pays

Fortunately, the opposite is also true. When you've befriended someone, they will remember your generosity and look for ways to return your kindness. You'll be surprised at how many friends you can make by being understanding, by "covering" for other people when they make a mistake, by standing up for them when others are trying to make them feel foolish. You'll find that this sensitivity leads to friendship, which leads to greater self-confidence.

One of the most important responsibilities in the Christian life is to care about other people—to smile at them and to be a friend of the friendless. You see, God wants to use you to help His other children who feel inferior. He said, "Inasmuch as you do it to the least of these my brethren, you are doing it unto me!" If you'll start living this kind of Christian life as recommended in the Bible, I know you'll find that your own self-confidence will grow, and that God will bless you for it. The Lord honors those who obey Him.

God's Values

Let me stress again that the attributes which our society values most highly—beauty, intelligence, and money—must be seen from the Christian point of view. These are *man's* values, but not *God's* values. The Lord doesn't measure your worth the way people do. He emphasizes in His Word that each of us is worth more than the possessions of the *entire* world. This is true just because we are human beings—not because of the way we look, or to whom we are married, or what our parents do, or how much money we have, or how much we have accomplished in life. Those earthly factors don't make the difference at all.

Did you know that the Bible tells us that God actually hates the three things which our world values most highly? Luke 16:15 states, "For that which is highly esteemed among men is abomination in the sight of God." He despises those things which we treasure, because they get in the way of our self-confidence, and they interfere with the work we ought to be doing for Him. Those phony values could keep you from being a good parent or employee or business person. More importantly, these false values can interfere with your Christian life, making you feel that even God doesn't accept you as a person. The temporary values of beauty, intelligence, and money represent a method of estimating human worth, and that's why God hates them. His method gives eternal worth to every one of us, and that includes *you* and *me*!

In summary, I must speak to those of you who have not yet suffered from feelings of inferiority. I hope you will remember my illustration of driving a car down the road. You don't have to fall into that black hole; you don't have to tumble into the canyon with all the other wrecked cars at the bottom. You can drive around this dangerous drop-off. Don't let it happen to you. Don't listen to the little voice inside you which says, "You're not really worthy; you're a failure; there's something wrong with you; you're ugly; there's something wrong with your mind; you're different; everyone is laughing at you; they think you're a fool; you're going to be a failure in life; everything will go wrong."

Don't believe it! Steer your car around the canyon of inferiority. God will help you do it!

Everybody's Doing It

What does the word "conformity" mean to you? Is it just a mysterious word in the dictionary, or does it relate directly to your daily living? Though you may never have used this word before, you'll need to become very familiar with its meaning. It will play an important role during the adolescent period of your life.

The word "conformity" refers to the desire to be just like everyone else—to do what they do and say what they say, to think what they think and wear what they wear. A conformist is someone who is afraid to be different from the majority; he feels a great need to be like everyone else. To conform means to accept the ideas, the fashion, the way of walking, and the way of talking that is popular at the time. In our society, there is *tremendous* pressure on all of us to conform to the standards of the group.

The Orientation Blues

Conformity is not only a problem among adolescents. Let me give you an excellent example of conformity which took place in a group of adults. When I first joined the staff at Childrens Hospital in Los Angeles, I had to go through an "orientation session." An orientation session is a meeting that employees are required to attend when they begin a new job. It's a training period prepared by the employer to acquaint each person with the organization that has hired him. But unfortunately, these meetings are usually boring—it almost seems that they're planned to be dull! The speakers talk endlessly about Blue Cross Insurance and retirement programs and the proper use of the telephone and similar topics that are terribly monotonous. Knowing this, I dreaded going through the orientation session at the hospital.

Nevertheless, I arrived as expected at nine in the morning. There were twelve new employees in the room that day, and it just happened that I was the only man there. The eleven women appeared to be young, and I guessed that most of them were secretaries or clerks, probably starting their first jobs. The atmosphere between the people that morning was "icy." In other words, the women were strangers to each other and they seemed frightened and tense. They came in quietly and sat around a large, horseshoe-shaped table, but no one talked unless spoken to. If one of the young ladies had anything to say, she leaned over and covered her mouth so others would not hear.

The Coffee Hope

I could see that there was one possibility of keeping us all awake for the next two hours, and that was for the director to offer us plenty of coffee—it was our only hope! And sure enough, a large coffeepot was percolating on a table in a corner. However, nothing was said about coffee. I can only guess that the pot had not been plugged in until a few minutes earlier, and it was not ready. However, it was obvious that all eleven women were thinking about that coffeepot, because every time it chugged, they would turn and look at it. What's more, there were colorful donuts arranged on the table, and the aroma filled the room. But the goodies were never mentioned.

The orientation lady stepped to the front of the room and began her long-winded speech. She spoke in a dry, monotonous voice, and attacked the first subject on a 42-item list. She talked for over an hour, but still nothing was said about coffee. The women yawned sleepily, leaned on one elbow, and glanced periodically in the direction of the coffeepot.

Finally, after an endless presentation, the leader said, "Okay, we're going to take a break and get some coffee now." However, she wasn't about to send all eleven ladies to the coffee table at the same time. Instead, she thought she had a better idea. She turned to a lady at one end of the table and said, "How would you like to slip back and get a cup of coffee?"

Well, this young lady was very shy, and she wasn't sure she wanted to be the first to go. She obviously knew that there are many ways a person can get "hurt" doing anything in front of eleven other people. She could trip on her way to the coffee table, or the spigot could stick on the coffeepot, or she could burn herself coming back. I watched her as she looked around the room and considered the risks of accepting the coffee. In a moment, she dropped her eyes and said, "No, thank you, I don't believe I'll have any."

I *knew* she wanted a cup of coffee. What she planned to do, it was clear, was to wait until everybody else had gone to the refreshment table, and then she could quietly get a cup of coffee with no risk! That way her ego wouldn't be in any danger. I found her amusing, but just watched her quietly from the opposite side of the table where I sat.

The Coffee Terror

The orientation lady then turned to the next girl and said, "Well, okay, how about you? Would you like to have a cup of coffee?"

But you see, the second girl faced all the same risks that scared the first young lady, plus a new one. The group had now "spoken" through that first individual and said, "We're not drinking coffee today." Only one "vote" had been cast, but it was unanimous. This pressure on the second girl was also too great, so she said, "No, thank you." That made the vote two to nothing!

The coffee invitation was then extended to the third girl. "Will you have a cup of coffee?" said the leader.

"No, thank you," said the employee.

The pressure then became enormous. It was clear that no one was expected to drink coffee or eat donuts. To my amazement, all the other women refused the offer of refreshments one at a time. Each said, "No, thanks" when their turn came to reply. But when the invitation was made to me, I said, "I believe I'll have a cup."

Would you believe that when I got up to get my cup of coffee, *eleven women followed me to the table!* I looked over my shoulder and here they came. As a gentleman, I felt I should step back and let the ladies go first, and it took me fifteen minutes to reach the goodies table!

Isn't it amazing how terrified we are of each other? We won't even get a cup of coffee if it's not socially acceptable at a given moment! We're terrified that somebody will laugh at us or ridicule us, or that we might make a mistake in front of others. Even such a completely insignificant thing as getting a cup of coffee can be frightening if we think the rest of the group doesn't want us to do it. This causes us to limit our behavior to those acts which are completely safe and totally beyond ridicule. We do that to eliminate the chance of anyone laughing at us.

The Fear of Flared Pants

This pressure to conform is so strong in some people that they feel uncomfortable if they are different in *any* way at all. If flared pants are "in" for boys, woe to the fellow who doesn't get the message, and wears tapered pants! If a girl walks funny or talks with a lisp, she may be laughed at every day. If Fords and Chevrolets are popular at high school, a person had better not buy a Plymouth. That would be an insult to the entire student body! You see, any little deviation, any change at all in what the group declares "this is what we do," becomes a breach of etiquette. They point at the offender and talk disrespectfully about him, making him feel very uncomfortable.

I want you to understand that this pressure to conform is at its worst during adolescence. That's why teenagers often move in "herds," like a flock of sheep, as we will see.

The Card Game

A team of doctors decided to conduct an experiment to study the ways in which group pressure influences young people. To accomplish this, they invited ten teenagers into a room and told them they were going to evaluate their "perception," in order to learn how well each student could "see" the front of the room from where he sat.

Actually, all the teenagers were very close to the front of the room and everybody could see quite easily. What the doctors were *actually* studying was not the students' eyesight, but the effects of group pressure.

The doctors said, "We're going to hold up some cards at the front of the room. On each card are three lines—Line A, Line B, and Line C—each of a different length. In some cases Line A will be the longest; in other cases Line B will be the longest, and in still other cases Line C will be the longest. Several dozen cards will be shown with the lines in a different order. We'll hold them up and point to Line A, Line B, and Line C on each card. *When we point to the longest line, please raise your hand to show that you know it is longer than the others.*" They repeated the directions to be sure everybody understood, and then raised the first card and pointed to the top line.

The Object of the Game

What one student didn't know was that the other nine had been secretly informed earlier to vote for the *second* longest line. In other words, they were told to vote wrongly.

The doctors held up the first card and pointed to Line A, which was clearly shorter than Line B. At this point, all nine students cooperated in the scheme and raised their hands. The fellow being studied looked around in disbelief. It was obvious that Line B was the longest line, but everybody seemed to think Line A was longer. He later admitted that he thought, "I must not have been listening during the directions. Somehow I missed the point, and I'd better do what everybody else is doing or they'll laugh at me." So he carefully raised his hand with the rest of the group.

Then the researchers explained the directions again: "Vote for the *longest* line; raise your hand when we point to the *longest* line."

It couldn't have been more simple! Then they held up the second card, and again, nine people voted for the wrong line! The confused fellow became more tense over his predicament, but eventually he raised his hand with the group once again. Over and over he voted with the group, even though he knew they were wrong.

This one young man was not unusual. In fact, *more than 75 percent of young people tested behaved that same way. They sat there time after time, saying a short line was longer than a long line!* They simply didn't have the courage to say, "The group is wrong. I can't explain why, but you guys are all confused." A small percentage—only 25 out of 100—had the courage to take their stand against the group, even when the majority was obviously wrong. This is what group pressure does to an insecure person!

The Power of a Friend

Another very interesting characteristic was revealed by this study. *If just one other student* recognized (voted for) the right line, then the chances were greatly improved that the fellow who was being studied would also do what he thought was right. This means that if you have *even one friend* who will stand with you against the group, you probably will have more courage too. But when you're all by yourself, it's pretty difficult to take your stand alone.

Now this raises an interesting question. Why is social pressure so great during adolescence? Why are we so afraid of being rejected by the group? Why must we do what we're told by those of our same age? Why can't we be independent? Well, the answer to these questions goes back to the subject of inferiority.

You see, when you feel worthless and foolish—when you don't like yourself—then you are more frightened by the threat of ridicule or rejection by your friends. You become more sensitive about being laughed at. You lack the confidence to be different. Your problems seem bad enough without making them worse by defying the wishes of the majority. So you dress the way they tell you to dress, and you talk the way they tell you to talk, and all your ideas are the group's ideas. You become afraid to get a cup of coffee, or to raise your hand for what you know is right, or to express any of your own views. Your great desire is to behave in the "safest" way possible. These behaviors all have one thing in common: they result from feelings of inferiority.

Dean Martin once said, "Show me a man who doesn't know the meaning of the word 'fear' and I'll

49

show you a dummy who gets beat up a lot!" In this case, however, it's not really a fear of getting "beat up" but a fear that the group is going to reject you— the fear of not being invited to a party . . . the fear of being disliked . . . the fear of failure.

The Teenage Choirs

If you want to confirm the existence of this conformity, look around you. The next time you hear a teen choir singing in your church or school, look closely at the young people involved. You'll notice that all the girls have exactly the same hair-style! If it's fashionable to have long natural hair, then every girl will comb her hair straight down to her shoulders. There will be *very* few exceptions. Perhaps none of the girls will have the courage to curl her hair. On the other hand, if the popular style is curly, or ratted, or back-combed, all the girls will look exactly the same. It is obvious that they have worked hard to try to look just like their friends.

About a year ago a teen choir was singing "The Battle Hymn of the Republic" in a Miami concert. That is a very emotional song, and a person can get carried away while singing, "Glory, glory, hallelu-jah! His truth is marching on!" There were about sixty teens in this choir, and as they were singing, one girl in the front row became so emotional that she fainted. The director saw her fall, but he didn't want to wreck the performance, so he continued to lead his choir. Several adults gathered around the unconscious girl and helped her regain her senses.

However, when that one young lady passed out, the possibility of fainting was planted in fifty-nine other impressionable heads.

About six seconds later another young fellow turned white, then buckled and disappeared from the back row. At that point, the "suggestion" of fainting became even stronger. Each singer was thinking, "Is it going to happen to me? I do feel rather dizzy!"

Sure enough, a third young man sailed off the end of the risers and hit the floor with a thud. Then it began to spread like wildfire ... numbers four, five, and six! By the time the choir reached the final phrase ("His truth is marching on"), *twenty* kids lay flat on their backs! That is conformity at its peak!

The Pressure of Conformity

This group pressure can be even more ridiculous at times. We adults have been told by television advertisers that we must look exactly alike. We're warned, for example, that "the wet-head is dead." That means that nobody uses hair oil anymore, and if you use it as you did during the fifties and sixties, there must be something wrong with you.

Old people are made to feel uncomfortable because they are aging. Isn't that foolish? There are more than four billion people on this earth, and every single one of us is growing older. There isn't a single person on earth who isn't aging! (The moment you stop aging you are in deep trouble!)

Nevertheless, adults are made to feel inferior over the normal signs of aging. This great pressure acts to force us all into identical blocks, making us robots instead of human beings.

Think About the Problem

Now let's think about some important questions. Why will this subject of conformity be important to you as you go into the adolescent years? Can you see any reason why peer pressure could be dangerous to you? Do you see any ways it could get you into trouble a little later? How does conformity hurt you right now? How does it keep you from doing what is right? How could it interfere with your life?

The reason conformity is so dangerous is that it can cause you to do things that you know are wrong. This is what happens when you don't have the courage to be different from your friends.

Can You Say No?

Suppose you're in a car with four other young people, each about fifteen years old. You're driving around at night, looking for fun, when the driver reaches into his pocket and retrieves a bottle with some little red pills in it. He takes one pill and pops it in his mouth, and then hands the bottle to the guy sitting by the door. He laughs and takes a pill before handing the bottle to the three of you in the back seat. You are the last one to be handed the bottle, and all four of your friends have taken the pills.

As it is handed to you, what are you going to say? You know that those capsules are called "reds," and that they are very harmful to the body. You don't want to take them, but you don't want to be laughed at either. You hesitate a moment, which causes the fellow beside you to say, "Come on, Sissy. Whatsa matter? You scared? Hey, guys, we've got a mama's boy back here! He's afraid daddy will find out. Who would have thought that Jackie-Boy was a big chicken! Come on, Baby Face. Try it, you'll like it!"

Your hands tremble a bit, and you notice that your palms are moist. Then the other boys begin to tease you too, because they want you to do what they are doing. The pressure is enormous. Your heart is pounding. You don't know what to say. You just feel foolish. Maybe you should just try it once to see what it's like. That probably won't hurt much. So you give in. You pop the pill. What a relief to be one of the boys again!

You'll find that the next time drugs are offered, it'll be a little easier to take them because you've done it before. Then you start getting the habit, and soon you'll be seriously hooked on narcotics, all because of the pressure of conformity. This explains the most important reason why drugs are being used by teenagers every day throughout this country. Thousands of young people are permanently damaging their bodies and their lives this way. The human body is very delicate. It can be easily hurt so that the rest of a person's life is spent in pain. Or if the individual "overdoses" on drugs, he can actually kill himself while trying to have a little fun.

I talked to a thirteen-year-old girl the other day who takes ten to twenty reds every day of her life. Her body is so wracked and ruined from these narcotics that she will never be healthy again. What a *shame* to destroy a youthful body in this way! How unfortunate that she didn't have the courage to reply to the person who first offered her drugs, "Why should I wreck my body? It's the only one I have!"

Other harmful behaviors can also be traced to the pressure of conformity. Why do you suppose teenage alcoholism is such a serious problem in this country? Why else would cigarettes continue to be smoked by young people, even though they know that the habit has been proven to shorten life, contaminate the lungs, increase the risk of cancer, and damage the blood vessels? Why do teenagers pick up that first cigarette and inhale the filthy smoke into their pink lungs? It usually begins by a "friend" offering a weed to someone who has never smoked. He says, "Would you like a puff?" And unfortunately, the nonsmoker lacks the guts to say, "No way!"

The Courage to Lead

It will be helpful for you to think about these issues *before* you face a crisis with your friends. Recognize the fact that they are under the same pressure that you feel. They're tempted to take drugs or smoke or drink for the same reason you are—simply because they're afraid to be different. They're afraid that the next time their admired friend (the one who owns the car) decides to pick up some guys for a joyride, he won't include them because they're not much fun to be with. So he acts like a jellyfish and does something that makes no sense whatever.

How much better it is to show that you have confidence in yourself when the pressure is greatest. You can say, "If you guys want to do something crazy, go ahead. But I think it's stupid!" That's not being childish. That's a way of showing that you have the courage to oppose the group when they're wrong.

I'll tell you something else: most teenagers respect a guy or girl who has the courage to be his own person, even when being mocked and teased. An individual with this kind of confidence often becomes a leader. He has shown that he doesn't feel as inferior as the other followers. He's not made of putty inside. Instead, he has the guts to stand up for what he knows is right.

And one other thing: he is likely to influence others who are looking for that one friend who will increase their confidence. (Remember the experiment with the cards?) He might make it possible for someone else to oppose peer pressure too.

The Pain of a Handicap

The pressure of conformity is not only harmful to young people who take drugs or smoke cigarettes or drink alcohol. It is especially damaging to those teenagers who *can't* be like their friends. In the high school where I served as a counselor, for example, there was a blind student who could not accept the fact that she was different from the other students. Her way of dealing with her blindness was to deny that it existed. She refused the help of a special teacher who was hired to work with her. She wouldn't do the work the teacher gave her to do, nor would she talk to this specialist. She even tried to walk without the use of her white cane or a seeing-eye dog. She put her shoulders back and walked down the sidewalk of the school as though she knew where she was going. One day I saw her heading in the wrong direction, but before I could stop her, she walked right into a post. Nevertheless, she simply refused to feel her way around. You see, this unfortunate young lady just could not accept the fact that she was different from "normal" students. Consequently, she suffered from great feelings of inferiority.

I have seen deaf children refuse to wear a hearing aid which would have made it possible for them to hear and learn in school. One second-grader refused to wear "that thing in my ear" because it made him feel foolish. He would remove it as soon as he left home each morning, even though he could hear very little in the classroom.

I know one little four-year-old boy whose glasses were lost at home. His family looked all over the house but couldn't find them. The child didn't seem to know where they were either. Finally he confessed, "Mommy, I have something to tell you."

She asked, "What?" and he replied, "I can find my glasses for you."

They went out in the backyard, and he retrieved them from a hole in the ground! This four-year-old had buried his glasses because they made him feel different! This is the discomfort felt by those who can't conform. They need our understanding and kindness.

A Boy Named Jeep Fenders

I was not always sensitive to the feelings of children who couldn't be like their peers. In fact, I had to learn to be kind to others during childhood. When I was nine years old, I attended a Sunday school class every week. One Sunday a new boy named Fred visited our class. I didn't stop to think that Fred might be uncomfortable as a stranger in our group, because I knew everyone and had many friends there. He sat quietly looking down at the floor. During the morning class I noticed that Fred had very strange ears. They were shaped in a kind of half-circle, like this: Ꙩ . I remember thinking how much they looked like Jeep fenders. Have you ever seen the fenders on a Jeep, which go up and over the tires? Somehow I managed to see a resemblance to Fred's ears.

Then I did a very unkind thing. I told everyone that Fred had "Jeep-fender ears," and my friends thought that was terribly funny. They all

laughed and began calling him "Jeep Fenders."
Fred seemed to be accepting the joke pretty well.
He sat with a little smile on his face (because he
didn't know what to say), but it was hurting him
deeply. Suddenly Fred stopped smiling. He exploded
from his chair and hurried toward the door, crying.
Then he ran out of the building and never came
back to our church. I don't blame him. The way we
acted was vicious, and I'm sure God was very displeased with me, especially.

However, the important thing to understand
was how ignorant I was of Fred's feelings on that
day. Believe it or not, I didn't really intend to hurt
him. I had no idea that my joke made him feel
terrible, and I was shocked when he ran from the
classroom. I remember thinking about what I had
done after he left, wishing I hadn't been so mean.

Why was I so cruel to Fred? It was because no
one had ever told me that other people were as sensitive about being teased as I was. I thought I was
the only one who didn't like to be laughed at. The
teachers of my many Sunday school classes should
have taught me to respect and protect the feelings of
others. They should have helped me to be more
Christlike.

That is why I'm writing these words to *you*
today. I want you to know that others feel just like
you do. They get the same lumps in their throats
when they're being teased, and they also cry when
they're alone. You have *no business* making them
feel worse than they already do, particularly someone who has a handicap or a strange body feature

which makes him seem odd or strange. If a person's nose is too big, he already knows it, so don't talk about his nose. If he is too tall or short or fat or thin, don't make fun of him, don't give him a nickname, don't call attention to the feature he's already sensitive about, and don't give him any other reasons to feel bad. He has enough problems already.

The Daily Gloves

I'm reminded of a second-grader named Jeff whose teacher came to me a few years ago to help solve a riddle. She had noticed that Jeff always wore big, thick leather gloves to school every day. He was rarely seen without those gloves, even on the warmest days of the year. He obviously wasn't using them just to keep his hands warm. Of course his teacher would make him take them off when he came into the classroom, since he couldn't hold a pencil with the thickly padded fingers. But the moment Jeff went out to recess or lunch, he put on the gloves again.

Jeff's teacher just couldn't understand the reason for this behavior. Why was he so in love with those gloves? They weren't new or expensive; in fact, they were all scratched and dirty. But in talking to me about this problem, Jeff's teacher casually mentioned that he was the only black child in a classroom of white children. Then Jeff's behavior suddenly began to make sense. He was bothered by being different from his friends, as you and I would have been.

You see, when Jeff wore a long-sleeved shirt, trousers, shoes, and socks, *the only part of his skin that he could see was his hands.* By wearing those gloves, Jeff couldn't see his own black hands! His black skin certainly didn't make him inferior, but it made him feel unusual because he was the only non-white child in his room. He was embarrassed by this difference and tried to cover it up.

We need to understand friends like Jeff who feel inadequate and inferior. In fact, if we really love others as much as ourselves, we will give as much time and attention to helping them avoid pain and ridicule as we do ourselves. We will think about them as often as we think about ourselves. We will befriend the person who is a little different, or who is new at our school, or who is a foreign student with a strange accent; or who is in some kind of an embarrassing position. The Bible says that when you help that kind of needy person, it is as though you were doing it for Jesus Himself! *More than any other concept, this is the meaning of Christianity!*

God's View of Conformity

This brings us back to the principles of the Bible, which should guide our behavior in virtually every area of life. The Scriptures speak very plainly about the dangers of conformity. God in His wisdom knew that social pressure could keep us from doing what is right, and He spoke strongly against it.

Romans 12:2 warns, "Be not conformed to this world [in other words, don't let the world squeeze you into its mold], but be ye transformed [made into something new] by the renewing of your mind, that ye may prove what is that good and acceptable and perfect will of God." That is written in the King James Version of the Bible. Now let me read the same verse from *The Living Bible:* "Don't copy the behavior and the customs of this world, but be a new and different person, with a fresh newness in all you do and think. Then you will learn from your own experience how his ways will really satisfy you."

Another Scripture (First John 3:13) states it even more pointedly. It says, "My brothers, don't be surprised if the world hates you."

It is obvious from these verses (and many others) that God does not want us to follow the whims of the world around us. He expects us to say to ourselves, "I am going to control my behavior, my mind, my body, and my life. I will be like my friends in ways that don't matter, such as wearing fashionable clothes when convenient. But when it comes to being moral and obeying God and learning in school and keeping my body clean and healthy, then I won't let anybody tell me what to do. If they must laugh at me, then let them laugh. The joke won't be funny for very long. I'm not going to let *anything* keep me from living a Christian life. In other words, "I will not conform!"

The Courage of a Christian

I hope this discussion will help you to brace yourself against the pressures around you as an adolescent. And I also hope that you'll keep your pressure off other people (especially the handicapped) so they will be able to be happy and secure too. That will require Christian courage and confidence on your part.

I heard a true story of a young man who was a very courageous young Christian. After graduating from high school, he entered a state university near his home. During the first few weeks of class, a godless professor asked his class if any students considered themselves to be Christians. It was obvious that the professor intended to embarrass anyone who raised his hand. This young man looked around and saw that none of the two hundred students was going to admit his faith. What should he do? He either had to admit his Christianity or deny it, like Peter did when Jesus was about to be crucified. He suddenly held up his hand and said, "Yes, I'm a Christian."

The professor made him stand in front of the class and said, "How could you be so stupid to believe that God became a man and lived here on earth? That's ridiculous. Besides, I read the Bible and it didn't say a thing to me."

This young man looked right at the professor and said, "Sir, the Bible is God's letter to Christians. If you didn't understand it, that's what you get for reading somebody else's mail!"

Wasn't that a courageous answer? (That's the kind of reply I always think of later, when it's too late to say it.) Whether or not you can think up clever answers to disbelievers doesn't matter much.

What *does* matter is that you protect your faith in God and be willing to be identified with Him.

As you get out of high school and into college, some people may try to make you feel foolish for trying to live a Christian life. When that happens I hope you'll remember our discussion about conformity, about group pressure, and about the commandment of God Himself: "Be not conformed."

Something Crazy Is Happening To My Body

3

Let's turn our attention now to another new experience which will occur during the adolescent years. I'm sure you've noticed that adults are not just bigger than children, but their bodies are very different from those of boys and girls. They're shaped differently and they work differently. For those of you between ten and thirteen years of age, I want to discuss how your bodies will soon make this dramatic change from childhood to adulthood. Those of my readers who are teenagers will already have experienced some of the physical changes we'll be presenting.

The Big Boss Upstairs

The growing-up process is a wonderful and

interesting event. It's all controlled by a tiny organ near the center of your brain called the *pituitary gland*. This little organ is only the size of a small bean, yet it's called the master gland because it tells the rest of your glands what to do. It's the "big boss upstairs," and when it screams, your glandular system jumps. Somewhere within your own pituitary gland is a plan for your body. At just the right time, it will send out chemical messengers, called hormones, which will tell the rest of the glands in your body, "Get moving, it's time to grow up." In fact, those hormones will have many implications for your body during the next few years of your life.

There are several reasons why you ought to understand this aspect of physical development. First, if you don't know what is about to happen to your body, it can be pretty terrifying when everything goes crazy all at one time. It's not unusual for a teenager to begin worrying about himself. He wonders, "What's going on here? Do I have a disease? Could this be cancer? Is there something wrong with my body? Dare I discuss it with anybody?" These are unnecessary fears that result from ignorance or misinformation about the body. When young people understand the process, they know that these changes represent normal, natural events which they should have been anticipating. So I'm going to tell you exactly what you can expect in the period of early adolescence. There's just no reason for you to be anxious over these rapid physical changes.

Preparing for Parenthood

What can you expect to happen during early adolescence, and how will it all take place? The most important change that you will notice is that your body will begin to prepare itself for parenthood. Now I didn't say that you are about to become a parent (that should be years away), but that your body is about to *equip itself* with the ability to produce a child. That's one of the major changes that occurs during this period. The correct name for this time of sexual awakening is *puberty*. (Do you remember reading in the first chapter about driving your "car" through a little town by that name?)

A Boy's New Body

First let's discuss what happens to boys, and then we'll talk about girls. During puberty, a boy begins to grow very rapidly, faster than ever before in his life. His muscles will become much more like those of a man, and he'll get much stronger and better coordinated. That's why a junior high boy is usually a much better athlete than a fifth- or sixth-grader, and why a high school boy is a better athlete than a junior high boy. A dramatic increase occurs in his overall body size, strength, and coordination during this period.

Secondly, hair on a boy's body will begin to look more like the hair of a man. He'll notice the beginnings of a beard on his face, and he'll have to start shaving it every now and then. Hair will also grow under his arms for the first time, and also on what is called the pubic region (or what you may have called the private area), around his sex organs. The sex organs themselves will become larger and more like those of an adult male. These are evidences that the little boy is disappearing forever, and in his place will come a man, capable of becoming a father and taking care of his wife and family. This fantastic transformation reminds me in some ways of a caterpillar, which spins a cocoon around itself and then after awhile comes out as a totally different creature—a butterfly. Of course the changes in a boy are not that complete, but he will never be the same after undergoing this process of *maturation* (the medical word for growing up).

Rapid Changes

These rapid changes are just around the corner for many of you. The frightening thing for some kids is that they occur very suddenly, almost overnight. The pituitary gland quickly begins kicking everything into action. It barks its orders right and left, and your entire body seems to race around inside, trying to carry out these commands.

Everything is affected—even your voice will be different. I'm sure you've noticed how much lower your dad's voice is than your own. Have you ever wondered how it got that way? Was it always deep and gruff? Did it always sound like a foghorn? Can you imagine your dad in his crib as a baby saying "Goo, goo" in a deep voice? Of course not. He wasn't born that way. His voice changed during puberty, and that's what will happen to yours, too. However, an adolescent boy's voice is sometimes an embarrassment to him until this deepening process is finished, because it doesn't sound very solid. It squeaks and screeches and wobbles and cracks for a few months. But again, this is nothing to worry about, because the voice will soon be deep and steady. A little time is needed to complete this development of the vocal cords.

Solving Skin Problems

As I've stated, practically every part of your body is affected in one way or another by puberty. Even your skin will undergo major changes, whether you are a boy or a girl. In fact, this is probably the most distressing aspect of all the physical events that take place in early adolescence. One study of two thousand teenagers asked the question, "What do you most dislike about yourself?" Skin problems outranked every other reply by a wide margin.

Skin eruptions occur primarily as a result of an oily substance which is secreted during adolescence. The pores of the skin tend to fill up with this oil and become blocked. Since the oil can't escape, it hardens there and causes pimples or blackheads. You might expect to have these imperfections on your skin for several years, although some cases are milder than others.

When you get numerous pimples and blackheads regularly, the condition is called acne. If this happens, it will be very important for you to keep your skin clean, minimizing the oil and dirt on your face. It is also important to watch what you eat, since certain greasy foods are thought to contribute to the difficulty. If the problem is severe, you should ask your parents to take you to a *dermatologist*, who is a doctor specializing in skin problems. He will advise you on the best method of treatment.

Teenage Fatigue

Another physical problem occuring with both boys and girls during puberty is fatigue, or lack of energy. Your body will be investing so many of its resources into the growing process that it will seem to lack energy for other activities for a period of time. This phase usually doesn't last very long. However, this tired feeling is something you ought to anticipate. In fact, it should influence your behavior in two ways.

First, you must get plenty of sleep and rest during the period of rapid physical growth. That need is often not met, however, because teenagers feel that they should not have to go to bed as early as they did when they were children. Therefore, they stay up too late and then drag through the next day in a state of exhaustion. Believe it or not, a twelve- or thirteen-year-old person actually needs more rest than when he was nine or ten, simply because of the acceleration in growth.

If your parents are also reading this book, I

would suggest that they let you sleep on Saturday mornings if possible. It is often difficult for mothers and fathers to permit their overgrown son or daughter to lie in bed until 9:30 A.M. when the grass needs mowing. However, they should know that he is lying in bed because he needs more sleep, and they would be wise to let him get it. *Then* he can mow the lawn when he awakens, with a great smile of gratitude on his face!

Second, the foods you eat will also be very important during adolescence. Your body has to have the raw materials with which to construct those new muscle cells and bones and fibers that are in the plans. Hot dogs and donuts and milkshakes just won't do the job. It will be necessary for you to get a *balanced* diet during this time; it's even more important than when you were six or eight. If you don't eat right during this growth period, you will pay the price with sickness and various physical problems. Your body *must* have the vitamins and minerals and protein necessary to enlarge itself in so many ways.

The Beauty of Womanhood

Now let's talk about the many changes girls will experience during the years of puberty. A girl's body goes through even more complex changes than those of a boy, because it has to prepare itself for the very complicated task of motherhood. The way a woman's body functions to produce human life is one of the most beautiful mechanisms in all of God's universe. Let's look at that process for a moment.

All human life begins as one tiny cell, so small that you couldn't see it without a microscope. This first cell of life is called a zygote, which begins to divide and grow inside the mother's uterus.

The uterus is a special place inside the mother's lower abdomen, or what you may have called the stomach. Actually, it's not in the stomach at all, but below it. The uterus is a special little pouch that serves as a perfect environment for a growing and developing embryo. (An *embryo* is the name for a baby in its earliest stages of development.)

All the baby's needs for warmth and oxygen and nourishment are met constantly by the mother's body during the nine months before his birth. Any little slip-up during those very early days (the first three months especially), and the growing child will die. The embryo is extremely delicate, and the mother's body has to be in good physical condition in order to meet the requirements of the growing child.

In order to meet these requirements, a girl's body undergoes many changes during puberty. One of those important developments is called menstruation, which you've probably already heard about. This is a subject that girls will need to understand thoroughly in the days ahead. Most schools provide this information to girls in the fifth or sixth grade, so what I'll tell you now may just be a review of what you have seen and heard elsewhere. However, I feel it is important for boys to understand this process too, although they are seldom informed properly.

72

The Growing Life

When a woman becomes pregnant—that is, when the one-celled zygote is planted in her uterus after having a sexual relationship with a man, her body begins to protect this embryo and help it grow. It has to have oxygen and food and many chemicals which are necessary for life. The substances are delivered to the uterus automatically, through the mother's blood. But since the uterus has no way of knowing when a new life is going to be planted there, it must get ready to receive an embryo each month, just in case it happens. Therefore, blood accumulates on the walls of the uterus in order to nourish an embryo if the woman becomes pregnant. But if she *doesn't* become pregnant that month, then the uterine blood is not needed. It is released from the walls of the uterus and flows out through the vagina—that special opening through which babies are also born.

Every 28 days (this number varies a bit from person to person), a woman's body will get rid of this unnecessary blood which would have been used to nourish a baby if she had become pregnant. It usually takes about three to five days for the flow to stop, and during this time she wears a kind of cloth pad to absorb the blood. This process is called *menstruation*.

There are some very important attitudes that I want you to understand through this discussion. First, menstruation is not something for girls to dread and fear. Since the subject of blood causes us to shudder, some girls get very tense over this process happening to them. They start worrying about it and dreading its arrival, and some do not want it to happen at all. But actually, menstruation makes possible the most fantastic and exciting event that can ever occur—the creation of a new human being. What a miracle it is for a single cell, the zygote, to quietly split into two, then four, eight, and sixteen cells, and continue to divide until trillions of new cells are formed! A little heart slowly emerges within the cluster of cells, and begins beating to the rhythm of life. Then come fingers and toes and eyes and ears and all the internal organs. A special liquid (called amniotic fluid) surrounds the baby to protect him from any bumps or bruises the mother might receive. And there he stays for nine months, until he is capable of surviving in the world outside. Then at just the right moment the mother's body begins pushing the baby down the birth canal (the vagina) and into the waiting hands of the physician.

The Beauty of God's Design

The most beautiful aspect of this incredibly complicated system is that it all works *automatically* within a woman's body. It's almost as though the Master Designer, God Himself, were standing nearby, telling her what to do next. In fact, did you know that this is precisely what happens? We are told by King David, writing in the Psalms, that God is present during this creation of a new life.

Let's read his description of that event (Psalm 139:13-15):

> You made all the delicate inner parts of my body, and knit them together in my mother's womb. Thank you for making me so wonderfully complex! It is amazing to think about. Your workmanship is marvelous—and how well I know it. You were there while I was being formed in utter seclusion!
> —*The Living Bible*

Not only did God supervise David's development in his mother's womb (another word for uterus), but He did the same thing for you and me! He has also scheduled each day of our lives and recorded every day in His book. That is the most reassuring thought that I've ever known!

So you see, menstruation is not an awful event for girls to dread. It is a signal that the body is preparing itself to cooperate with God in creating a new life, if that proves to be His will for a particular woman. Menstruation is the body's way of telling a girl that she is growing up . . . that she is not a child anymore . . . and that something very exciting is happening inside.

Know the Facts and Be at Peace

Now, girls, please don't worry about this aspect of your health. You will not bleed to death, I promise you. Menstruation is as natural as eating or sleeping or any other bodily process. If you feel you are abnormal in some way—if you're worried about some aspect of menstruation—if you think you're different or that maybe something has gone wrong—or if there's some pain associated with your menstruation or you have any question at all, then muster your courage and talk to your mother or your doctor or someone in whom you have confidence. In about 98 cases out of 100, the fears will prove to be unjustified. You will find that you are completely normal, and that the trouble was only in your lack of understanding of the mechanism.

Other Changes to Anticipate

Now, obviously, other things will begin to happen to your body at about the same time as menstruation. You will probably have a growth spurt just prior to your first menstruation. (Incidentally, the average age of first menstruation in American girls is now about twelve-and-one-half years of age, but it can occur as early as nine or ten years or as late as sixteen or seventeen. The age varies widely from girl to girl.)

During this time your body will become more rounded and curvy like your mother's. Your breasts will enlarge, and they may become sore occasionally (boys sometimes experience this soreness too). This doesn't mean that you have cancer or some other disease, but simply that your breasts are changing, like everything else in your body. Hair will also grow under your arms, on your legs, and in the pubic region, as with boys. These are the most obvious physical changes which take place, and when you see them happening you can kiss good-bye to childhood—it's full speed ahead toward adulthood!

The Bridge of Late Maturity

There's another important matter that I must discuss with boys and girls. Your road to adulthood not only passes over the canyon of inferiority, but it also crosses the shaky bridge of *late maturity*. What I'm talking about is the anxious feelings that occur when a person doesn't grow up as quickly as he expected, or as soon as his friends develop. These changes of puberty that I've been describing may occur as early as nine or ten years of age or as late as seventeen or eighteen, but *each boy and each girl has his or her own timetable*. Again, the age of development is supervised by the pituitary gland in the brain, which has everything under control. However, these individual timetables cause a lot of unnecessary worry among those who are either ahead of their friends or behind them. The age of puberty really doesn't have much meaning, but it can become a source of great worry and concern.

For example, let's suppose you're a thirteen-year-old girl whose body has not yet begun to change. You still look like Little Red Riding Hood; none of your adult features have begun to show up. As you look around at the other girls in your class, you notice that some of them already look like women. They're wearing bras, but you clearly don't need one.

Then you start worrying about what's occurring inside. "Is there something wrong with me? Why haven't these things happened to me yet?" Then you turn fourteen, and still nothing changes. Your body is just sitting there yawning at you, and you're really getting concerned. You lay awake at night wondering if you'll still look like a child when you're fifty years old. Your girlfriends are talking to each other about menstruation, but you can't share in the conversation because you know nothing about it. You feel different and odd, and you worry until you're almost sick with anxiety.

No Peach Fuzz

Or suppose you're a fifteen-year-old boy who has the same problem. You aren't nearly as strong as your friends, and since you haven't had your growth spurt, you're one of the shortest boys in your class. In fact, you're even shorter than most of the girls, because girls start their puberty growth before boys. The other boys are starting to shave, but you don't even have peach fuzz on your face. You pick up the telephone to talk to the operator, but your voice is so high that she thinks you're a girl. She says, "Yes, Ma'am." That may be the worst insult that's ever been thrown at you!

But the most painful thing of all is that the other guys have noticed that you're still a little boy, and they've begun to tease you. When you're in the locker room, they call you nicknames and make fun of the fact that you don't have pubic hair or that you're still short and scrawny.

What are you going to do if this happens in the next few years? Are you going to crack up? Will you grind your teeth and bite your nails and chew your tongue? I hope that won't be necessary in your life.

There's Nothing Wrong with You

Let me make a suggestion for those of you who grow up a little later than your friends. The main thing to remember is that *there's nothing wrong with you*. It's just as healthy to grow up later as earlier, and there's no reason to fear that you will never mature. Just hold steady for a year or two, and then the fireworks will all begin to pop for you, just as for everybody else! I can promise you that this is going to happen. If you don't believe me, take a look at all the adults around you. Do you see any of them that look like children? Of course not. *Everyone* grows up sooner or later.

Certainly it's never much fun to be laughed at by your friends, but if you know you'll be different for only a short time, maybe you can stand it. Most importantly, don't you be guilty of making another person feel bad about himself if you happen to grow before he does!

The Sex Appetite

As your body starts to change, you'll notice that

you're beginning to be more interested in people of the opposite sex. Suddenly girls begin to look great to boys and the boys start appealing to the girls. How do I know this will happen? How can I predict it so accurately? Because sex will soon become an "appetite" within you. If you missed your breakfast this morning, I can predict that you'll be plenty hungry by two o'clock in the afternoon. Your body will ask for food. It's made that way. There are chemicals in your body that will make you feel hungry when you haven't eaten.

In the same way, some new chemicals in your body will begin to develop a brand-new appetite when you're between twelve and fifteen years old. This will not be a craving for food, but it will involve the matter called sex, or the male or female aspects of your nature. Every year as you get older, this appetite will become more and more a part of you. You'll want to spend more of your time with someone of the opposite sex. Eventually this desire may lead you to marriage. Marriage is a wonderful union for those who find the right person. However, let me offer a word of caution on that subject.

One of the biggest mistakes you can make with your life is to get married *too soon*. That can be tragic. I want to stress that point in your mind. For two people to get married before they are ready can be a disaster. Unfortunately, this happens all too frequently. I will say more about this subject later in the book, but I strongly advise you not to get married unto you're at least twenty years of age. *Half of all teenage marriages* blow up within five years, causing many tears and problems. I don't want yours to be one of those broken homes.

Pretty Girls and Fascinating Boys

Now let me describe for you the feeling that sex will bring in the next few years. Boys will become very interested in the bodies of girls—in the way they're built, in their curves and softness, and in their pretty hair and eyes. Even their feminine feet may have an appeal to boys during this time. If you're a boy, it's very likely that you will think often about these fascinating creatures called girls, whom you used to hate so much! In fact, the sexual appetite is stronger in males between sixteen and eighteen years of age than at any other age in life.

Girls, on the other hand, will not be quite so excited over the shape and the look of a boy's body (although they will find them interesting). They will be more fascinated by the boy himself—the way he talks, the way he walks, the way he thinks. If you're a girl, you will probably get a "crush" on one boy after another. (A crush occurs when you begin to think that one particular person is absolutely fantastic, and you fantasize about the possibility of being married to that person. It is not uncommon to get a crush on a teacher or pastor or older man. Usually crushes are constantly changing, lasting only a few weeks or months before another one takes its place.)

81

Plain Talk About Sex

Now we need to talk very plainly about the subject of sexual intercourse. Remember what I told you at the beginning of this book. I'm going to be treating you like adults and withholding *no* subject that is relevant to you. Therefore, you must understand the importance of sexual relationships between a man and woman.

Sexual intercourse is the name given to the act that takes place when a man and a woman remove all 'their clothing (usually done in bed) and the man's sex organ (his *penis*) becomes very hard and straight. He puts his penis into the vagina of the woman while lying between her legs. They move around, in and out, until they both have a kind of tingly feeling which lasts for a minute or two. It's a very satisfying experience, which husbands and wives do regularly. You probably already know about sexual intercourse as I described it. But did you know that a man and woman do not have intercourse just to have babies? They do it to express love for each other and because they enjoy doing it. In this way they satisfy each other. They may have sexual intercourse two or three times a week, or maybe only once a month; each couple is different. But this is a fun part of marriage, and something that makes a husband and wife very special to each other. This is an act which they save just for each other.

God's Gift of Sex

This appetite for sex is something that God

created within you. I want to make this point very strongly. Sex is not dirty and it is not evil. Nothing that God ever created could be dirty. The desire for sex was God's idea—not ours. He placed this part of our nature into us; He created those chemicals (hormones) that make the opposite sex appealing to us. He did this so we would want to have a family of our own. Without this desire there would be no marriage and no children and no love between a man and a woman. So sex is not a dirty thing at all; it's a wonderful, beautiful mechanism, no matter what you may have heard about it.

However, I must also tell you that God intends for us to control that desire for sexual intercourse. He has stated repeatedly in the Bible that we are to save our body for the person we will eventually marry, and that it is wrong to satisfy our appetite for sex with a boy or girl before we get married. There is just no other way to interpret the Biblical message. Some of your friends may tell you differently in the days ahead. You may hear Jack or Susie or Paul or Jane tell about how they explored each other's bodies. They'll tell you how exciting it was, and try to get you to do the same.

Decide Now

Let me state it more personally. It is very likely that *you* will have a chance to have sexual intercourse before you reach twenty years of age. Sooner or later that opportunity will come to you. You will be with a person of the opposite sex who will let you know that he or she will permit you to have this experience. You're going to have to decide between now and then what you'll do about that moment when it comes. You probably won't have time to think when it suddenly happens. My strongest advice is for you to decide *right now* to save your body for the one who will eventually be your marriage partner. If you don't control this desire you will later wish that you had.

Venereal Disease

God's commandment that we avoid sexual intercourse before marriage was not given in order to keep us from having pleasure. It was not His desire to take the fun out of life. To the contrary, it was actually His *love* that caused Him to forbid premarital intercourse, because so many harmful consequences occur when you refuse to obey Him.

You've probably heard about venereal disease, which is caused from having intercourse with someone who has caught it from another carrier. Syphilis, gonorrhea, and other diseases are very widespread today. Our country is having an epidemic of these diseases, and they have a damaging effect on the body if they go untreated. But there are other consequences for those who have premarital sex. They run the risk of bringing an unwanted baby into the world by this act. When that occurs, they face the responsibility of raising a human being—a little life with all its needs for love and discipline and the stability of a home—but they have no way to take care of him or meet his needs. That is tragic.

The Sin of Impurity

But just as serious are the changes that take place within a person's *mind* when he has intercourse outside the bonds of marriage. First, and most important, his relationship with God is sacrificed. Premarital sex is a sin, and a person just can't be friends with God if he is going to continue to sin deliberately and willfully. First John 1:6 says, "If we say we are His friends but go on living in spiritual darkness and sin, we are lying" *(The Living Bible).* It's as simple as that. Furthermore, nothing can be hidden from God, as you know, because He sees everything.

Sin always has a destructive effect on a young person. But I believe the sin of premarital sex is especially damaging to the person who engages in it. He or she loses the innocence of youth, and sometimes becomes hard and cold as a person. It's also likely to affect his or her later marriage, because that special experience which should have been shared with just one person is not so special anymore. More than one person has had a sample of it.

So you see, there are many obvious reasons why God has told us to control our sexual desires. What I'm saying is that God has commanded us not to have sex before marriage in order to spare us these many other effects of this sin. In fact, the *worst* consequence is one I have not yet mentioned, relating to the judgment of God in the life to come. We are told very clearly in the Bible that our lives will be laid bare before Him, and He will know every secret. Our eternal destinies actually depend on our faith in God and our obedience to Him.

Self-Stimulation

Let me talk with you now about a related subject called masturbation. This is something you may have heard about from your friends. If not, you will hear it soon. Masturbation is the act of rubbing your own sex organs in order to get that same tingly feeling that you would have if you were participating in intercourse. Most boys do this at some time during adolescence, and so do many girls.

Many rumors surround this act—scary stories about what happens to people who do it. Some people say that masturbating will make you go crazy. Others say it will keep you from being able to have a child later on. Still others say it will make you weak and sickly. You may hear all kinds of drastic warnings about the consequences of masturbating. Well, I can tell you right now that not one of these stories is true. They are all falsehoods. If masturbation made people go crazy, there would be a lot more crazy people in the world than there are!

Still, the subject of masturbation is a very controversial one. Christian people have different opinions about how God views this act. Unfortunately, I can't speak directly for God on this subject, since

His Holy Word, the Bible, is silent at this point. I will tell you what I *believe*, although I certainly do not want to contradict what your parents or your pastor believe. It is my *opinion* that masturbation is not much of an issue with God. It's a normal part of adolescence which involves no one else. It does not cause disease, it does not produce babies, and Jesus did not mention it in the Bible. I'm not telling you to masturbate, and I hope you won't feel the need for it. But if you do, it is my opinion that you should not struggle with guilt over it.

Why do I tell you this? Because I deal with so many Christian young people who are torn apart with guilt over masturbation; they want to stop and just can't. I would like to help you avoid that agony. The best I can do is suggest that you talk with God personally about this matter and decide what He wants you to do. I'll leave it there between you and Him.

Nocturnal Emissions

One other thing that bothers boys during adolescence is the occurrence of "wet dreams." Doctors call these *nocturnal emissions*. This refers to the fluid which comes out of a boy's penis occasionally at night. The fluid is called semen, and contains millions of cells so tiny that you can't even see them. One of these cells could become a child if it were injected into a female and combined with her egg cell. (That would compose the zygote which we discussed earlier). This semen sometimes is released

87

during a nighttime dream; then the boy finds the stain on his pajamas the next morning and begins to worry about what is going on. However, this event is perfectly normal. It happens to almost all boys, and is nothing to worry about. A nocturnal emission is just his body's way of getting rid of the extra fluid that has accumulated.

The Questions of Fear

Have you noticed how many times I've said in this chapter, "It's nothing to be concerned about; it's normal; don't worry"? The reason behind my reassurances is this: most young people become frightened about their own sexual development. As I stated in my book *Dare to Discipline*, teenagers often worry about the following kinds of questions during the early part of puberty.

1. Are all these changes supposed to be happening?

2. Is there something wrong with me?

3. Do I have a disease or an abnormality?

4. Am I going to be different from other people?

5. Does this pain in my breast mean I have cancer? (Remember, I mentioned that the breasts sometimes get sore during adolescence.)

6. Will I be able to have intercourse, or will there be something wrong with me?

7. Will the boys laugh at me? Will the girls reject me? (It's very common for people to feel they're not going to be attractive to the opposite sex and

that nobody will want them because they are not as pretty or handsome as they wish they could be.)

8. Will God punish me for the sexual thoughts that I have? (I told you that you're likely to think about the opposite sex often during these years. When this happens you may feel guilty for the thoughts that occur.)

9. Wouldn't it be awful if I became a homosexual? (A homosexual is someone who is not attracted to the opposite sex, but who is attracted to the *same* sex. It's a boy's interest in boys or a girl's interest in girls. Homosexuality is an abnormal desire that reflects deep problems, but it doesn't happen very often and it's not likely to happen to you.)

10. Could I get pregnant without having sexual relations? (This is another possibility that some young girls fear—that they could find themselves pregnant even if they haven't had sexual relations. I want you to know that this *never* happens; it's an impossibility. Only one time in all of history did this occur, and that's when the virgin Mary, Jesus' mother, became pregnant even though she had never had sexual intercourse. Jesus was conceived or planted in her uterus by God Himself. That's the only time in the world's history that a human being has ever been born without the father doing his part by providing half of the cell that becomes the zygote.)

11. Do some people fail to mature sexually? (Any system of the body can malfunction, but this one *rarely* fails.)

12. Will my modesty be sacrificed? (It's common during the early adolescent years for you to become extremely modest about your body. You know it's changing and you don't want anybody to see it. Therefore, you may worry about being in a doctor's office and having to take off your clothes in front of other people.)

No Need to Fear

Let me say it one more time: these kinds of fears are almost universal during the early years of adolescence. Nearly everyone growing up in our culture worries and frets over the subject of sex. I want to help you avoid those anxieties. Your sexual development is a normal event that is being controlled inside your body. It will work out all right, so you can just relax and let it happen. However, you will have to control your sexual desires in the years ahead, and that will require determination and will power. But if you can learn to channel your sexual impulses the way God intended, this part of your nature can be one of the most fascinating and wonderful aspects of your life, perhaps contributing to a successful and happy marriage in the years ahead.

I Think I've Fallen In Love

Today it is very common to hear someone talking about "falling in love" with another person. But have you ever stopped to ask yourself what these words actually mean? What changes take place in the minds of men and women who have fallen in love? How can they know when that love is genuine? Can they be fooled, thinking they are "in love" when they aren't? What is necessary to keep their love alive?

Can you answer these questions about the meaning of love? Most young people cannot. In fact, there is great confusion among teenagers about this important subject. It is my belief that the high divorce rate in our country results, in part, from the failure of newlyweds to understand what love is, what it is not, and how to make sense out of their emotions.

This subject of romantic love may not be very interesting to you now. You might even think it is rather silly. However, unless you are a very unusual person, you are likely to become extremely attracted to members of the opposite sex in the years immediately ahead. And as you get older, the possibility of marriage will present itself. Girls usually start thinking about marriage several years before boys do, but sooner or later young men begin to "dig" the same idea. That's when some fascinating events start to unfold.

The Ecstasy of Love

Most people in their early twenties (or before) begin searching for the perfect numan being with whom to spend the rest of their lives. And when they find someone who seems to fit that general description, they tumble head over heels into sheer ecstasy. There is no feeling in the world quite like it. They can hardly take their eyes off each other and they want to be together every moment of the day. They spend their hours picnicking in parks and walking in the rain and sitting glassy-eyed by a crackling fire. They even invade one another's dreams at night. Believe me when I say "falling in love" is a thrilling experience. I know—I've done it hundreds of times!

This exhilaration of romantic love is so captivating that it leads naturally to the question of marriage. A starry-eyed couple seems to reason, "If this feeling is so neat, why don't we spend our entire lives together?" So they begin making plans for a wedding. They set the date and call the preacher and order the flowers. Finally the big night arrives with the bride nervous and the groom bewildered. The bride's mother cries through the ceremony and her father is pale and tense. The bratty little flower girl refuses to walk down the aisle, and the groom's sister butchers a sentimental song about eternal love. But somehow the couple says, "I do," and the preacher pronounces them "man and wife." Then they march down the aisle, each flashing 32 teeth, as they head for the reception room.

There is noise and laughter and kisses for the bride as the people file by to offer best wishes to the new Mr. and Mrs. They eat the nuts and choke down the cake and talk about their own weddings. At last the bride and groom run from the church in a shower of rice and confetti, and drive off to start a new life. As they leave, they hear the groom's sister crooning, "They've only just begun. . . ."

So far, so good. Everyone seems happy and excited. But for this grinning young couple, serious trouble lies ahead. Almost from the first day of the honeymoon, something changes in their relationship. That tremendous excitement and enthusiasm begins to fade a bit. Marriage itself takes on a new look. Instead of being something they hoped they could capture if they were lucky, it now becomes a lifetime entanglement that has sprung a trap in reverse. They wonder silently whether this is what they really wanted, or whether they've made a hasty

93

decision. The awful thought occurs that they might have stumbled into the biggest mistake of their lives.

Scratching and Clawing

The third day of the honeymoon brings the first real fight. The couple disagreed on where they should eat dinner and how much money they should spend. She wanted to eat at a romantic restaurant, and he thought they should have a hamburger at Ronald McDonald's. It was a minor argument, but some harsh words were exchanged that further damaged the romantic feeling with which they began. They would learn to hurt each other more effectively in the months ahead.

They had only been home from the honeymoon about a week when the first all-out battle occurred. Insults were hurled back and forth like nuclear warheads. Deep feelings of hurt and resentment then raged on both sides, followed by long periods of icy silence. The husband left home for two hours and his wife called her mother. From then to the bitter end, we see two extremely bitter and unhappy people who cry themselves to sleep at night. And what is worse, they may have produced another member of the family by that time . . . a toothless little guy who has to have his diapers changed every 45 minutes. This toddler will grow up in a broken home and will never fully understand "why daddy doesn't live here anymore."

The Tragedy of Divorce

Now obviously this pessimistic description of marriage isn't accurate in *all* cases, but it does happen far too often. The divorce rate in the United States is higher than that of any other civilized nation in the world. In fact, it is known that *50 percent* of all teenage marriages end in divorce *within the first five years!* What a tragically high percentage! It means that *half* of all the people who thought they were "in love"—those who were tremendously excited with each other—quickly become disillusioned, bitter, unhappy, and broken. And we must ask ourselves, "Why?" Why is this happening? How do all these people get misled? What caused the flame of love to flicker and go out? How did their mutual affection turn into such hatred and anger and conflict just a few months later? These questions are extremely important to *you*, if a similar disaster is to be avoided in your own life. To answer them, we must examine the meaning of romantic love more closely.

Beliefs About Love

We'll begin our study by measuring how well you already understand this concept of marital love. I have developed a short quiz to sample your knowledge and beliefs on this important topic. May I suggest that you take a sheet of paper and number it from 1 to 10. Then answer the following questions, True or False.

_____ 1. I believe that "love at first sight" occurs between some people.

_____ 2. I believe that it's easy to distinguish real love from infatuation.

_____ 3. I believe that people who sincerely love each other will not fight and argue.

_____ 4. I believe that God selects one particular person for each of us to marry, and that He will guide us together.

_____ 5. I believe that if a man and woman genuinely love each other, then hardships and troubles will have little or no effect on their relationship.

_____ 6. I believe that it's better to marry the wrong person than to remain single and lonely throughout life.

_____ 7. I believe that it's not harmful or sinful to have sexual intercourse before marriage if the couple has a meaningful relationship.

_____ 8. I believe that if a couple is genuinely in love, that condition is permanent and will last a lifetime.

_____ 9. I believe that short courtships, six months or less, are best.

_____10. I believe that teenagers are more capable of genuine love than are older people.

Answers to the Questions

The quiz you have just taken is not intended to

be a highly scientific test. In fact, some people might even have different opinions about the correct answers to each item. However, let me give you my views regarding the ten questions and the explanations behind them.

Instant Love?

Question Number 1: "I believe that love at first sight occurs between some people."

There are individuals who believe that romantic love occasionally hits two strangers like a bolt of lightning the moment they first see each other. There they are, just walking down the sidewalk or sitting in church, and Zappo! Their eyes pop, their ears ring, their toes curl, and they have "fallen in love."

I hate to sound unromantic, but that kind of instant love is an *impossibility*. You can't love someone whom you do not know, someone who is a total stranger. I can't deny that some very strong feelings may occur the first time you see a particular member of the opposite sex. He is handsome (or she is pretty) and you like his eyes and the sound of his voice and the confidence he displays. Everything about him is appealing, and you feel a powerful attraction toward this new dreamboat. You may think, therefore, that you have fallen in love with him from the first moment you were together. But in reality, you have fallen in love with his *image*— you don't even know the real person. You're not acquainted with his thoughts, habits, hopes, fears, plans, skills, abilities, or manners. So you can't say you love that *total* person when you've only met his outer shell.

Confusion in Music

Many teen songs show that the writers did not know the difference between genuine love and the temporary feelings described above. One popular song, for example, contained this phrase: "Before the dance was through, I knew I was in luv with yew." Come on now, that's not love! During the course of the dance this young fellow merely had a few warm thoughts and figured he had somehow slid into romance during the second stanza! But beware: *any feeling that arrives during one dance might just disappear during the next.*

Another songwriter penned these words: "I didn't know just what to do, so I whispered 'I love you.'" Now isn't that weird? The idea of making a lifetime commitment on the basis of confusion seems kind of silly to me! Yet that is what often happens. There's an awkward moment between a boy and a girl, and he isn't sure of himself, so he says, "I love you." His girlfriend gets shook up and thinks, "Fantastic! This guy's falling in love with me!" So she returns the compliment, and they hustle down the road toward disaster.

The Partridge Family recorded a song which stated, "I woke up in love this day, went to sleep with you on my mind." There's the error again. The singer had fallen in love sometime during the night. Isn't that sweet? Don't you see how this kind of love is *nothing more than a frame of mind*? It came overnight, and it can leave overnight.

There are dozens of examples showing confusion about love in today's teen music. However, the song that gets my vote for having the dumbest lyrics of the century was popular during the sixties. It was sung by a rock group named "The Doors." They recorded a number entitled "Hello, I love you, won't you tell me your name?" Will someone explain how you can love a person about whom you know absolutely nothing? What nonsense!

"How Can It Be Wrong When It Feels So Right?"

Let me repeat that the *feeling* of romantic excitement can occur instantly between a man and woman, as it did for those writing the songs mentioned above. Furthermore, those feelings can sometimes gradually lead to genuine love upon which a successful marriage can be based. In most cases, however, this momentary enthusiasm will be stone-cold-dead in twelve months. That's why it's so dangerous to make any lifelong decisions on the basis of any temporary emotion.

Debbie Boone once recorded an immensely popular song entitled, "You Light Up My Life." In it was the phrase, "It can't be wrong when it feels so right." Unfortunately, I could show her many bitter divorced people who once felt marvelous about the relationship which now haunts them. Some of them were fooled by "love at first sight."

Real Love or Infatuation?

Question Number 2: "I believe that it's easy to distinguish real love from infatuation."

I hope you marked this item "false," because it is definitely not accurate. The emotional explosion which occurs during infatuation makes it difficult to think clearly about *anything*. It is one of the most exhilarating events in human experience, being more fantastic than a roller coaster ride or a trip to Disneyland! Someday you will know what I mean. When it happens to you, however, there are two important facts about infatuation which you should remember.

First, "puppy love" or infatuation is highly *self-centered*. Let me explain by offering an illustration. When I was in college a number of years ago, my parents traveled throughout the year. Therefore, I had no place to go when school was not in session. During the summer months, especially, I had to stay in the school dormitory while the other students went home to visit their parents. I usually got a job nearby and would return from work each evening to my quiet, boring room. A couple of other guys also stayed in the dormitory, but I didn't know either of them very well. Consequently, I usually spent a very lonely summer during those college days.

As you can imagine, I would begin to get excited near the end of August each year, anticipating the return of my friends in September. Finally they would arrive, and the old dormitory would again rock with laughter and noise and fun. Those were great days. But I was even more anxious for the *girls* to return to school. I hadn't had a date since May, and I couldn't wait for the "crop" of young ladies to show up for classes. Therefore, I was ripe for love every autumn. I would fall hopelessly in love with someone . . . anyone . . . on September 12th of each year. There was no question about it happening—the same thing occurred four years in a row. Each September my world would suddenly turn upside down: I couldn't sleep, I couldn't eat, and I couldn't study. (In fact, studying was one of the first things to go!) It was a truly thrilling event, as predictable as Thanksgiving or Christmas.

Don't you see how self-centered my "love" was each September? I would tell my friends, "*I* can't believe how fantastic this is. *I* never felt this way before. This is the greatest thing that ever happened to *me*." There can be little doubt about it—I had not fallen in love with a girl, but I had fallen in love with *love!* The young lady for whom I had "gone bananas" was merely a prize to be won . . . an object to be captured. She was usually forgotten and replaced the following January.

Genuine love is very different from this temporary infatuation. Instead, it is focused on another human being. It brings a deep desire to make that person happy . . . to meet their needs and satisfy

101

their desires and protect their interests. Real love is best described as being unselfish in all aspects, even if a personal sacrifice is required in the relationship.

Short-Lived Infatuation

The second fact about infatuation which you should know is that it *never* lasts very long. If there is one message in this chapter which is more important than all the others, this is it! Let me repeat it: that exciting feeling between two new "lovers" *never* continues for life. It can't last, simply because human emotions are constantly changing. Even when people *genuinely* love each other, there are times of great closeness, times when they feel nothing for each other, and times when they are irritable and grumpy. Emotions are like that, swinging regularly from high to low to high to low. (We'll return to this point later.) Therefore, it is *impossible* for a married couple to maintain that peak of intensity with which their relationship began.

Why is it so important to understand the temporary nature of early romantic love? Because some young people plunge quickly into marriage, before their emotions have even taken the first dip into apathy. They're still in the first "fever" on the wedding day. Unfortunately, however, they receive a great shock during the months (or days) that follow when they awaken one morning without that exciting feeling down inside. It is wise to understand that the "fever" of love can easily turn into a rash in the months that follow.

Surprisingly, each of the sad young couples who eventually stand before a judge in the divorce courts thoroughly believed themselves to be "in love" at the beginning. They didn't always hate the person they married. There was a time when their happiness seemed to be above any hardship or difficulty. But their good feelings disappeared like snow on a warm day, melting and running toward the gutter.

What's the Difference?

Even for those who know that infatuation is self-centered and temporary, they may eventually confuse it with genuine love. How, then, can they tell the difference between these two "conditions?" How can they interpret their own feelings? How can they avoid making a disastrous mistake?

To my knowledge, there is only *one* way to distinguish puppy love from the real thing: give yourself time to test your emotions. You will gradually come to understand your own mind and know what is best for the other person. How long will this process take? It differs from person to person, but in general, the younger you are, the longer you should wait. As I stated earlier, it is my opinion that teenagers should not get married until they reach their twenties, and only then if they have been sweethearts for at least two years. This recommendation is not offered for my purposes or to impose parental wishes on teenagers. Rather, it is suggested to help prevent some of the painful divorces which bring deep wounds to so many young people today.

No Arguments?

Question Number 3: "I believe that people who sincerely love each other will not fight and argue."

The answer to this third item may surprise you. (In fact, the average person misses at least three or four of these ten questions about love.) The statement above is false. People who genuinely love each other still have differences of opinion. They still disagree. They still become irritable. They still fight and argue on occasion.

Let me describe a common scene which brings conflict between a loving husband and wife. The father drives home from a bad day at the office. He parks his car in the driveway and walks wearily into the house. His wife meets him at the door, and she is equally tired. The children have been wearing on her nerves all day. She tells her husband that the washing machine is broken and there is water all over the floor and everything has gone wrong. On their desk is a big stack of bills that the family is unable to pay. Both the mother and father are on edge and grumpy. Under these circumstances it's very easy for people who actually love each other to find themselves arguing and fighting. Besides, there are honest differences of opinion about important subjects. They may disagree about how to spend their money, where to go to church, and many other issues that divide them. But even in the midst of these struggles it is still possible for them to love each other very deeply.

Let me state it more strongly. I have seen very few marriages which are so harmonious and stable that the husband and wife never have this kind of disagreement. You can expect some conflict in your own marriage even though you are deeply in love with your mate. More specifically, I would predict that the first year of marriage will be the most difficult twelve months of your first decade together. It will be a time of adjustment; you'll have to decide how your marriage is going to function and who will spend your money and where you'll go on vacations. These issues may heat your emotions and set off some pretty serious conflicts in your home.

Work on Your Differences

If this occurs, don't think your marriage is doomed, or that you've necessarily made a big mistake. What it means is that both of you must compromise and seek solutions to your problems. That's the difference between a good marriage and a bad one. Both have moments of struggle, but in a healthy relationship the husband and wife search for answers and areas of agreement because they love each other very much.

What, then, is a "bad" marriage? It is one where each partner loves himself more than the other person, where these attitudes lurk in the mind:

"I married you because I thought you would be good for me," or, "I married you because I wanted someone to help me take care of my home," or, "I married you because I hoped you would earn a lot of money for me." You see, when marriage occurs for selfish reasons, then the routine arguments become more serious. They no longer reflect differences of opinion, but become fights to the death. Each person then tries to hurt the other person, who has become a bitter enemy.

Dreams of Marriage

Question Number 4: "I believe that God selects one particular person for each of us to marry, and that He will guide us together."

I have great faith in God, and I believe that all of the important decisions of life should be preceded by prayer and requests for divine guidance. Our heavenly Father, in response, is very loving and merciful to those who seek His help; He will reveal His wishes and influence on all important decisions. Nevertheless, the answer to Question Number 4 is "false." In fact, those who believe that God automatically puts the right people together are in danger of making a tragic error in judgment. They may think the first person with whom they are infatuated is the lover sent by the Lord, and off they tear into forty years of conflict.

I'll never forget the unhappy fellow who told

me he was awakened by a powerful dream in the middle of the night. It seemed to say, "Go marry Susan." Ralph had not been praying for God's leadership, yet he thought this order came directly from the Lord. The next day he called Susan (whom he had dated only two or three times) and said, "God told me to marry you!" Susan felt she shouldn't argue with the Almighty, and she accepted. Their marriage has been most unhappy and unfortunate, appearing to be a mistake from a human point of view. Neither partner now believes that God actually spoke to Ralph in the middle of the night, but that his *own* impression fooled him.

Let me stress that it is *extremely* important for you to choose your marriage partner very carefully. The Lord has given you good judgment, and He expects you to use it in making the decisions of life. It is possible, in my opinion, to love Jesus and be a good Christian, yet make a hasty decision to marry the wrong person. God doesn't sit in heaven with a list of names, saying, "Let's see. I'll take Jack and put him with Nancy." In other words, our heavenly Father does not operate a routine matchmaking service for those who call themselves by His name!

Before you settle on a plan to be married, I suggest that you take the matter to the Lord in prayer. Ask Him to guide your paths in this vitally important decision. I'm sure He'll answer that request. But this kind of prayer is similar to one in which you are asking God to heal a disease. Just because you are a Christian doesn't mean you'll never get sick. God can heal that disorder if you ask

Him (and if it is His will to do so), but *He isn't obligated* to help you if you don't ask Him.

Happy Hardships?

Question Number 5: "I believe that if a man and a woman genuinely love each other, then hardships and troubles will have little or no effect on their relationship."

Again, the answer is "false." Love is like life—it is delicate and fragile. It can be broken and crushed and ruined. The death of a family member, or sickness, or poverty can severely damage a genuine loving relationship.

I'm on the staff of a children's hospital, where some very tragic events occur every day. I see little children in great pain and sickness. I see boys and girls who have cancer and heart trouble and various deformities. Some are in the process of dying, others have brains that don't work properly, and still others have been born with strange physical malfunctions. These problems often make their parents feel guilty, even though they are not to blame for the sicknesses. Sometimes the guilt of having a diseased child is so damaging that a home can actually be destroyed by it. This is only one example of how a love relationship can be affected by one's circumstances and environment.

Someone said, "Love conquers all." That is not always true. It is important to know that you have to work to keep love alive; you have to protect it and maintain it, just like you would a delicate flower. This point is so important that I want to come back to it in a moment.

Wait If You Have To

Question Number 6: "I believe it's better to marry the wrong person than to remain single and lonely throughout life."

Once more, the correct answer is "false." I think it is much better to still be looking for the right person than to be involved in a bad marriage, even though being single may mean being lonely.

It is a wonderful blessing for a man and woman to be happily married, enjoying each other's friendship and perhaps raising a child or two. However, God did not intend for everyone to fit this pattern. The Apostle Paul even said that it is better for some people not to get married, especially those who are called to carry heavy responsibility in Christian work. Therefore, it is unwise to seek marriage at any cost.

People who fear they won't be able to get married are sometimes willing to accept any invitation that is offered, even if it comes from someone they don't love. That can be tragic. It is far better to remain single than to spend your lifetime scratching and clawing and fighting with a mate when you should never have married in the first place.

Sex Before Marriage?

Question Number 7: "I believe that it's not harmful or sinful to have sexual intercourse before marriage if the couple has a meaningful relationship."

I certainly hope you know by now that the above statement is absolutely false. Nevertheless, many people in our society have decided that the old rules no longer apply. "Everything has changed," they say; "now there's a new morality. There's nothing wrong with having sexual relations— with exploring the body of a person of the opposite sex—provided both of you seem to like each other." This is the most dangerous of all of the mistaken ideas about love, because it has many terrible consequences.

God's view of sex outside marriage is abundantly clear. If you are a Christian and if you believe that the Bible is the guide for your daily life, there can be no doubt about what is right and what is wrong. Let me read to you directly from *The Living Bible*:

> Honor your marriage and its vows, and be pure. [Marriage is a promise to be faithful to one person throughout life. God expects us to honor that commitment, not only after marriage, but before.] For God will surely punish all those who are immoral or commit adultery (Hebrews 13:4).

This same message appears repeatedly throughout the Bible, and it is obviously what God wants for our lives. Consider the following advice

offered by King Solomon, one of the most brilliant
men who ever lived:

> I was looking out the window of my house one day,
> and saw a simple-minded lad, a young man lacking
> common sense, walking at twilight down the street
> to the house of this wayward girl, a prostitute. She
> approached him, saucy and pert, and dressed seduc-
> tively. She was the brash, coarse type, seen often in
> the streets and markets, soliciting at every corner
> for men to be her lovers.
>
> She put her arms around him and kissed him, and
> with a saucy look she said, "I've decided to forget
> our quarrel! I was just coming to look for you, and
> here you are! My bed is spread with lovely colored
> sheets of finest linen imported from Egypt,
> perfumed with myrrh, aloes and cinnamon. Come
> on, let's take our fill of love until morning, for my
> husband is away on a long trip. He has taken a
> wallet full of money with him, and won't return for
> several days."
>
> So she seduced him with her pretty speech, her
> coaxing and wheedling, until he yielded to her. He
> couldn't resist her flattery. He followed her as an ox
> going to the butcher, or as a stag that is trapped,
> waiting to be killed with an arrow through its heart.
> He was as a bird flying into a snare, not knowing
> the fate awaiting it there.
>
> Listen to me, young men, and not only listen but
> obey; don't let your desires get out of hand; don't
> let yourself think about her. Don't go near her; stay
> away from where she walks, lest she tempt you and
> seduce you. For she has been the ruin of
> multitudes—a vast host of men have been her vic-
> tims. If you want to find the road to hell, look for
> her house (Proverbs 7:6-27 TLB).

Although it appears that Solomon was just

warning *men* not to be immoral, that is not true. The laws of God apply equally to men and women, and they are designed for our benefit. The Lord has not given us meaningless restrictions in order to interfere with our fun and happiness. Rather, He has warned us against certain behaviors that will be harmful to ourselves and to the people living around us. Just today I read this verse from the 19th Psalm:

> God's laws are perfect. They protect us, make us wise, and give us joy and light. . . . They warn us away from harm and give success to those who obey them (Psalm 19:7, 8, 11 TLB).

Don't believe those ungodly people who tell you that the "old rules" are out of date. God's instructions will *never* be out of date, and we would be wise to heed them in every aspect of our lives.

Let me share one more Scripture with you which lists those timeless instructions from the Lord:

> Away then with sinful, earthly things; deaden the evil desires lurking within you; have nothing to do with sexual sin, impurity, lust and shameful desires; don't worship the good things of life, for that is idolatry. God's terrible anger is upon those who do such things. You used to do them when your life was still part of this world; but now is the time to cast off and throw away all these rotten garments of anger, hatred, cursing, and dirty language.
>
> Don't tell lies to each other; it was your old life with all its wickedness that did that sort of thing; now it is dead and gone. You are living a brand new kind of life that is continually learning more and more of what is right, and trying constantly to be

more and more like Christ, who created this new life within you. In this new life one's nationality or race or education or social position is unimportant; such things mean nothing. Whether a person has Christ is what matters, and he is equally available to all.

Since you have been chosen by God who has given you this new kind of life, and because of his deep love and concern for you, you should practice tenderhearted mercy and kindness to others. Don't worry about making a good impression on them but be ready to suffer quietly and patiently. Be gentle and ready to forgive; never hold grudges. Remember, the Lord forgave you, so you must forgive others.

Most of all, let love guide your life, for then the whole church will stay together in perfect harmony (Colossians 3:5-14 TLB).

Love Forever?

Question Number 8: "I believe that if a couple is genuinely in love, that condition is permanent and will last a lifetime."

I answered this question within Item 5, and it is also "false." I told you that love has to be maintained or it can die. This is probably the most important of the ten items for those who are already married. Even your parents should be aware that their love can die if they don't work to keep it alive. They should take time to be together, to talk to each other and to pray together. They should not permit anything to damage or weaken their relationship. Love must be supported and fed and protected, just like a little infant that is growing up at home. I hope you will remember this point when (and if) you have a marriage of your own.

Short Courtships?

Question Number 9: "I believe that short courtships, six months or less, are best."

This issue was discussed within the response to the second question, but we'll repeat the message briefly. To the surprise of no one by this point, the correct answer again is false. You must give yourself time to know your own feelings, to let them rise and fall naturally, before they can be interpreted properly. And as I've stated, it is extremely dangerous to lock yourself into a permanent relationship before you even have a chance to become acquainted with your mind or to determine what you want out of life. I've seen many short courtships that produced equally short marriages, and I hope yours will not be one of them.

Young and Old Lovers

Question Number 10: "I believe that teenagers are more capable of genuine love than are older people."

The answer to this final item is also "false," because genuine love requires a certain measure of maturity. You see, dedicated love is only possible for

114

those who have the ability to give of themselves. Love is not grabbing, or self-centered, or selfish. Real love is being able to contribute to the happiness of another person without expecting to get anything in return. And that unselfishness demands considerable maturity, which rarely occurs during the tumultuous years of adolescence. That's why teenage marriages often begin to collapse shortly after the honeymoon.

The Frying Pan and the Fire

Let me offer one further word of advice about early marriages. By all means don't make the mistake of using marriage as a way of getting away from your parents or your present circumstances. Some seventeen- or eighteen-year-old men and women become tired of their homes, like the girl who told me the only time she gets homesick is when she is at home. They don't communicate with their parents, and they fight with their brothers and sisters. Then at a moment of great unhappiness, along comes a chance to set up housekeeping with someone else who is equally miserable at home. Getting married may seem like an easy solution to two major problems, but it rarely works that way. That's just like jumping from the frying pan into the fire. Such a union can be (and usually is) a disastrous relationship. Of all the reasons for entering into marriage, the desire to escape from mom or dad is one of the worst.

In summary, I'll repeat the suggestion offered

115

earlier: choose your mate very carefully *after your twentieth birthday*. That free advice could prevent a lifetime of grief for you and another person.

The Real Meaning of Love

Now that you've read the answers to the ten items on the test, you know that they are all false statements. The reason I chose them is because they represent the ten most common misconceptions about the meaning of love. These are the ten mistaken ideas that I hear most often when counseling with young people.

Let me summarize the message of this chapter by giving a very personal illustration. When my wife, Shirley, was seven years old, she had a very sad home situation involving an alcoholic father. That caused her to think about the person she would marry someday. More than anything else in the world, she wanted to grow up and have a happy home with a Christian husband. God saw this inconspicuous little girl go into her bedroom and shut the door. He saw her get on her knees and begin to pray in her childlike manner that God would bless her future home and give her a husband who would love and care for her. God answered that prayer. Shirley and I now have a beautiful marriage and have been blessed with two children who mean everything to us.

I met Shirley when we were in college (during September, of course) and *gradually* came to love her. Notice that I didn't say that I "fell in love" with

116

her. That phrase is misleading, making young people believe that falling in love is like tumbling into a ditch. That is not the way it happens. I didn't fall in love with Shirley . . . I *grew* into a close relationship with her. After the first surge of emotion was over, I began to develop a deep appreciation for this young lady. I enjoyed her sense of humor and her pleasant personality. I saw how she loved God and the better things of life. And little by little, I developed a desire to make her happy, meet her needs, provide a home for her, and live my life in her company.

But you should know that I don't always *feel* intensely romantic and loving toward Shirley. There are times when we are close and times when we are distant. We sometimes get tired and harrassed by the cares of life, and that affects our emotions. *However, even when the feeling of closeness disappears, the love remains!* Why? Because our relationship is not dependent on a temporary feeling; it's based on an unshakable commitment of the *will*. In other words, I have made up my mind to devote myself to Shirley's best interests, even when I feel nothing. I know the emotion of closeness will return when we have time to be together . . . when we're on vacation . . . when exciting events happen . . . when we're doing romantic things together. Sooner or later the feeling will return, and it will last for days. But when I get busy . . . when my mind is on other things . . . when there has been sickness or hardship in the family . . . it is likely that my emotions will become cool again.

Your emotions will fluctuate too. That's why

you must understand that love is more than a feeling—it also involves a commitment of the will. You need an iron-fisted determination to make your marriage succeed, which will act like the engine of a train. It will keep you moving down the right track. On the other hand, the feeling of love is like a caboose, being pulled by the powerful engine at the other end.

A Final Word

If I had to put the message of this entire chapter in one sentence, I would say that real love is caring for another person almost as much as you do for yourself. That is exactly how the Bible describes marital love—it is becoming "one flesh" with another individual. The two of you actually become one person. It's much more than marrying an individual who will do something good for *me*. Rather, it is learning to love someone as much as I do my own flesh, and by marrying, we become united. That is the real meaning of love. If you have that kind of appreciation for another person, you are on your way to a happy home.

A Notion Called Emotion

We have discussed the canyon of inferiority, the dangers of conformity, the physical changes of puberty, and the meaning of love. Now it's time to get a better understanding of the emotions (or feelings) that often occur during the teen years. This topic is especially important because the changes that are about to occur in your mind will be almost as dramatic as those which will soon affect your body. Even now you are in the final flickering moments of childhood, and once you leave it, there can be no return.

Perhaps the best way to begin acquainting you with the emotions of adolescence is to relate a personal story about the saddest day of my own childhood. It began at eleven o'clock one morning when I was in the seventh grade. I was sitting in my school classroom when a boy near me motioned toward the door. I looked in that direction and saw my father beckoning me to come outside. He said we were going home and that I would not be returning to school that day. He didn't explain why.

As we walked to the car, I knew that my dad must have something awful to tell me. I could see the tension in his eyes, but I was afraid to ask him what had happened. Finally he turned to me and said, "Jim, I have some bad news for you and I want you to take it like a man."

I said, "Is it my mom?"

He replied, "No."

I said, "Then it's my dog, isn't it?"

My father nodded and then began to tell me the details. He said that my mother had been driving home in our car a few minutes earlier. My little dog (whose name was Pippy) saw her coming and ran in the street to greet her. He jumped on the side of the car as it passed, but apparently lost his footing and fell under the rear wheel. Mother then felt the sickening thud as the dog was struck and run over. Pippy screamed in pain, eventually lying motionless at the edge of the road.

Mother stopped the car immediately and ran back to where my dog lay. She bent over him and talked softly to the pup. He could not respond because his back was broken, but he could roll his little brown eyes to see who she was. When he recognized her, Pippy wagged his stubby tail in appreciation. He was still wagging that little tail when his eyes grew glassy in death.

Loss of a Friend

Now it may not seem so terrible to lose a dog, but Pippy's death was like the end of the world for me. I simply cannot describe how important he was to me when I was thirteen years old. He was my very special friend whom I loved more than anyone can imagine. I could talk to him about things that no one else seemed to understand. He met me on the edge of the sidewalk after school each day and wagged his tail to greet me (which no one else ever did for me). I would take him out in the backyard and we would play and run together. He was always in a good mood, even when I was not. Yes, Pippy and I had something going between us that only dog lovers can comprehend.

When my father told me this story of Pippy's death, I thought *I* was going to die. I couldn't swallow and I found it very difficult to breathe. I wanted to run away ... to scream ... to cry. Instead, I sat quietly in the car with a great lump in my throat and a pounding sensation in my head.

I don't remember exactly how I spent that afternoon at home, although I do recall crying most of the day. I soon composed a poem in honor of my dog, entitled "To Pippy." It was not the greatest literary masterpiece of all time, but it expressed my feelings pretty well. The last four lines of the poem read:

My mother, she hit him, and oh how I cried
And softly and gently, a puppy dog died
And if there's a dog heaven, I know he'll be there
He's my poor little Pippy, with hair white and fair.

Later in the afternoon our family conducted a funeral service for the dearly departed dog. I dug a small hole behind the grapevine at the back part of our property, and as the sun was going down we put his stiff little body in the grave. Just before we covered him over, I reached in my pocket and retrieved a copper penny. I placed it on the bloody fur of his chest. Today I'm not sure why I did that. I guess it was merely my childish way of telling my pup that I loved him. And my father, who had told me to take the loss like a man, bawled like a baby on that day behind the grapevine. It was without question the saddest day of my childhood.

It is important to understand that there have been many more *significant* moments in my life since that day of Pippy's death. There have been more meaningful days, and certainly there have been greater losses than the one I experienced on that cloudy morning. However, there have been few sadder days even to this moment. Why? Because I was thirteen years old when Pippy died. That made it all seem so much worse.

The Strongest Feelings

You see, *everything* is felt more strongly during childhood, and especially during adolescence. Do you remember the first chocolate-covered cherry that you ate as a child? Can you recall how good it tasted, how the sweet flavor filled your mouth? I was given my first piece of this delicious candy in a doctor's office when I was six years old. I had fallen and split open my lip, which had to be stitched back together. I was such a "brave little boy" while being sewed up that the doctor gave me a chocolate-covered cherry as a reward. I had never tasted anything like that. I can still remember it today. For weeks afterward, the taste of that candy lingered in my mouth, and I longed for another one. I even considered splitting open my lip again just so I could be rewarded for additional bravery! Now obviously, candy is not that important to me today because my desires are not as strong in adulthood as they were in childhood.

Do you remember your first ferris-wheel ride? Do you remember your first trip to the dentist? (Who could forget that experience?) My point is that when you're young, the good things seem more astounding and the bad things are more intolerable. That's why the death of Pippy nearly killed me too.

Why have I told you this? What does it mean for your future? It means that your own feelings will probably become even more intense during the next few years. That's just the way adolescence is. Little things that won't bother you later in life will bug you as a teenager. Your fears will be more frightening, your pleasures will be more exciting, your irritations will be more distressing, and your frustrations will be more intolerable. Every experience will appear king-sized during early adolescence. That's why teenagers are often so explosive, why they sometimes do things without thinking and then regret their behavior later. You'll soon learn that feelings run deep and powerful during the adolescent years.

There are six other characteristics of emotions during adolescence that I would like to discuss with you briefly. We'll begin with a look at the "human yo-yo."

1. THE CYCLICAL EMOTIONS

It will help you to know that feelings tend to go from high to low to high to low. "Big deal," you say, "what does that mean?" It means that when you're depressed and unhappy and blue, when nothing is going right and life doesn't seem to be worth living, just hang tough for a few days. You won't remain depressed very long. Your circumstances will change and the sun will come up again. Sooner or later you'll wake up one morning and be glad you're alive. You'll bounce out of bed and whistle at the birds and wave at the flowers and sing "Zippity Doo Dah" all day long.

But I must warn you that this positive feeling won't continue either. You see, few people stay extremely happy or unusually depressed for very long. The usual pattern of all emotions is to move up and down, year in and year out. In fact, all of us are "yo-yo's" in that way. Therefore, when you're emotionally high, expect to come down; when you're rock bottom, expect to come up. That way you won't be surprised or depressed when sudden change occurs. Another way to describe these unstable feelings is to say that human emotions are *cyclical.* They occur in regular patterns and are influenced by the amount of sleep you've had, what kind of health you're in, and how things are going in your life. To tell the truth, the world is not the way it looks to you or me; our emotions distort or change the true picture somewhat. Now isn't that a heavy thought?

2. THE UNRELIABLE IMPRESSIONS

The second aspect of emotions that you should understand relates to the danger of impressions. An impression is an inner thought that you believe comes from God or somewhere unknown. For example, I know a young man who was driving down the street in his car, and he received the strong feeling that he would soon die. He seemed to "hear" this message deep within his mind: "Your life is almost over." He thought God was telling him to prepare for death. The sweat began to form on his forehead, and his mouth became dry. His hands got sweaty and his heart began to race. This fellow actually thought he might be enjoying the very last minutes of his life. In his distress, he nearly drove his car into a telephone pole (which would have proved the impression to be true, I suppose). But I can assure you that this young man is still alive today and is doing fine.

You may have impressions of many kinds, and if you believe them to be true, they can cause you to make wrong decisions. Some impressions might lead you to get married suddenly, or move to another town, or quit school, or join the Army. When these strong thoughts and feelings come, just remember that God rarely makes demands that require instant change. Give yourself a few days or weeks to look at all sides of the issue. And the more important the decision, the more carefully you should review the facts.

How to Know God's Will

I've said that impressions are not dependable as a basis for making quick decisions. How then can a young person know the will of God in a particular situation? How can he tell the difference between a spooky feeling and the genuine leadings of the Lord? Let me make five quick suggestions that will help with this task.

First, talk to another person about the decision to be made; discuss it with someone in whom you have confidence and with whom you can share your ideas.

Second, read the Bible for direction. God will talk to you through His Scriptures, and He will never ask you to do anything that contradicts His Word.

Third, watch to see which doors open and those that slam shut. If God is leading you in a particular direction, He'll work through what we call "providential circumstances." He will create opportunities for you to do what He wants. You won't have to "hammer down" the obstacles if God is involved.

Fourth, give yourself plenty of time to think. Don't make any big decisions while you're in a state of confusion. That's a good principle to follow throughout your life. When you're not sure what to do, avoid the final choice for as long as possible. You might have much greater confidence a few days later.

Fifth, pray for God's guidance and blessing and leading.

These are just a few suggestions to help you handle the impressions that will come during the next few years of your life. It's best to realize that these impulses are part of being a teenager. Don't let them lead you into anything that will damage the rest of your life. In other words, *be cautious!*

3. THE DECLARATION OF INDEPENDENCE

Now let's talk heart-to-heart about another emotional problem that usually arises during adolescence; we call it "the conflict between generations." This phrase refers to the irritation and harsh feelings that are likely to occur between you and your parents during the teenage years.

How can I predict that your mother and father may become upset with you, and you with them in the years to come? The reason I know is because of the stressful changes that will soon occur in your relationship. When you were born, you were totally dependent on your parents for everything. Your very life was in their hands—you could do nothing for yourself: you couldn't roll over, you couldn't scratch your head, you couldn't even ask for food except by using that ear-shattering scream which God gave you.

But as you grew and learned and developed, you began getting free from that dependence. Soon you could hold your own bottle, and a little later you were able to sleep through the night without being fed. Then you learned to crawl, and soon you were walking. Each time you learned a new behavior, you were granted additional independence from your parents. Instead of having to be washed behind your ears, you became old enough to do the job yourself. Instead of picking up your blocks and making your bed and giving you every cent you needed, your parents allowed you to carry these new responsibilities. Later you learned to complete more difficult assignments and to think for yourself. With each step in the growth process you became more independent of your parents and they gained new freedom from their task of serving you. In a few years that process will be completed. You will be totally independent of your mom and dad, and they will be totally free of their obligation to serve you.

Completely Free

You had better prepare yourself for it: you will soon be your own boss. You will decide when to go out and when to come in, with whom to spend your time, when to go to bed, what to eat, and exactly what you're going to do with your life. You'll decide whether you're going to worship God or ignore

Him. Your parents won't be able to require any-thing of you because you will no longer be a child. In fact, your relationship with your parents should become more like a friendship, instead of their being your supervisors and disciplinarians. What I'm saying is that childhood begins with great dependence at birth and moves toward total in-dependence at the far end of adolescence. During the same time, your parents are changing from ser-vants to free people again. That's what childhood and adolescence and parenthood are all about.

What does this have to do with the conflict that I have predicted? Well, when a young person becomes fourteen, fifteen, or sixteen years of age, he sometimes gets a taste of independence and begins to demand his total freedom immediately. He wants to make his own decisions. He wants to run his own life. He begins to resent the control of his parents and sets out to prove that he is no longer a child. Mom and dad, however, know that their son or daughter is not ready for complete freedom (inde-pendence). He still needs their leadership in certain areas, and they are determined to give it to him. The result can be a painful struggle that may last for three or four years.

There is another dimension to this conflict. While the teenager is demanding complete inde-pendence from parental authority, he also insists on being very *dependent* in other areas. For example, he wants hot meals on the table three times a day and expects his shirts to be ironed and his doctor bills to be paid and his socks to be washed. In other words, he wants freedom without responsibility. That combination will not work. If a person is not yet ready to accept all the responsibilities of living, then he is not ready to handle unrestricted freedom either.

I'm saying that a million other families have fought over these issues of dependence-independence, and yours will probably have some trouble at the same point. If conflict occurs between you and your parents, I hope you'll remember that this tension is part of growing up. It doesn't mean that you don't love your mom and dad or that they don't love you. It's a natural struggle that occurs when you begin to demand more freedom than your parents know is healthy at the time. The best thing for you to do is talk to them openly about these matters. If you feel they are not giving you the independence *that is consistent with your age*, quietly say so. Tell them you feel you are old enough to make more decisions for yourself (and take the responsibility that goes with them). However, you must be reasonable. I advise you to yield to the leadership of your parents when they feel strongly about an issue. They do, after all, have your best interest at heart.

My Message

Let me conclude this point by telling you what I have said to my son and daughter with regard to this matter of independence. Perhaps your parents will adopt the same attitudes which are expressed in the message below:

First, I want you to know how much I love you. One of the greatest privileges of my life has been the opportunity to raise you . . . to be your father and watch you grow. However, you're now entering a new phase of life known as adolescence, which sometimes puts a strain on a loving relationship like ours. There may be times during the next few years when you will want me to give you more freedom than I feel you can handle. You may want to be your own boss and make all of your own decisions before I feel you are ready for that independence. This situation may create some friction between us, although I don't expect the conflict to be major.

If it occurs, however, I want you to know that I'm going to compromise as much as I can on each issue. I'll listen to your point of view and then try to understand your feelings and attitudes. I will not be a "dictator" who doesn't care about the needs or desires of the other person. In other words, my love for you will lead me to try to make you happy, if possible.

On the other hand, you can expect me to say "no" when my better judgment requires it. The easiest thing in the world would be to say, "Go ahead and do what you want. I don't care what friends you're with or what kind of grades you make in school. I'll stay off your back and you can do whatever you please." That would be a simple way to avoid all conflict and bad feelings between us.

But love demands that I do what is right, even if it is unpleasant. You'll soon learn that I have the courage to make those decisions when I must. Therefore, a moment of tension may occur in the coming years. But when it happens, I want you to remember that I love you and you love me, and we're going to remain friends through these difficult times. The world can be a cold and lonely place without the support of loving family members; that's why we're going to continue to care for one another in this home. And I think when you've reached your twenties and look back on these small conflicts, you'll appreciate the fact that I loved you enough to set you free gradually and as you were ready for additional responsibility.

If you are wise and mature, you'll accept this message from your parents during the years between childhood and adulthood. In other words, you will not issue your "declaration of independence" too early.

4. NO LONGER MOMMIE'S BABY

The desire for independence creates a strange sensitivity among adolescents about being seen in the presence of mom and dad. How odd it seems that a teenager should be embarrassed to sit in a restaurant or attend a basketball game with the parents who have raised him since birth! Nevertheless, *you* may feel the same way in the near future. It's not that you will suddenly dislike your mother and father, or that you are too good for them. The problem is that you want your friends to think you are grown up, and being seen with your folks seems like a babyish thing to do. This is especially true on Friday night, which is the traditional "date night."

How do I know about this embarrassing feeling? Because I *hated* to be seen with my parents when I was in junior high school. In fact, one of my most unpleasant experiences occurred the day I graduated from the eighth grade. My dad did what any proud father would have done—he brought his movie camera and took my picture in front of the school with my friends standing around. I remember that I resented his being there that day. I felt ridiculous with that camera pointed toward me. I didn't want to be a little kid anymore, who was being filmed by his daddy. That was what he would have done if I were three years old and had been given a new tricycle. When I see that movie today, I recognize the look of embarrassment on my face as a self-conscious eighth-grader.

These are some of the feelings you're also likely to have in the next few years. Of course, not everybody is the same. That's the fantastic thing about being a human being—we all differ somewhat, and you may never experience that feeling I described. But you're likely to be embarrassed when your folks are around your friends. It's not because you don't love them; you shouldn't feel guilty about that. It's because you want to grow up and you're worried about peer pressure. It's all a normal part of the adolescent experience.

Classroom Capers

Before leaving that thought, let me tell you something funny. My mother used this social pressure to make me shape up and behave properly in school. It began during the ninth grade, when I decided that it was more fun to be a goof-off than to work and study and learn. I had a couple of teachers who didn't know how to control their students very well, and my friends and I enjoyed disrupting their classes every day. I was having a great time laughing and joking, but my grades began to drop, as you would expect. I knew this wasn't right, but I was enjoying myself. My mother somehow knew I was playing games, even before the grades were distributed. I don't know how she found out, but she always seemed to know what I was thinking.

One day she sat me down for a little chat. She said, "I know what you're doing in school. Not only could you be making better grades, but I'm sure you're being disruptive in the classroom, too. I've been thinking about what I should do in response. I could punish you or take away your privileges, or I could visit your principal. But I've decided to do none of those things. In fact, I'm not going to do anything about your behavior. *However,* if your teacher or principal ever calls me to complain about the way you're acting, then the very next day I plan to go to school with you and sit by you in all your classes. I'll hold your hand as you walk down the hall and I'll be two feet behind you as you stand with your friends. I'll have my arm draped around your neck through the entire day at school. You won't be able to get away from me for a minute!"

Believe me, that threat scared me to death! I would much rather have had my mother beat me than go to school with me. Just the thought of that awful possibility straightened me out in a hurry. I couldn't run the risk of having my mama following me around at school! That would have been social suicide. My friends would have laughed at me for the rest of the year. I'm sure my teachers wondered why I suddenly became so cooperative during the latter half of ninth grade! Think about it. This tragedy could happen to you, too!

5. THE AGE OF CONFUSION

Now let's turn our attention to a fifth aspect of adolescent emotions that you ought to anticipate. If you are like most teenagers, you'll soon experience a time of confusion over what you believe. As a little child, you were told what was true, what the world was like, what values to keep, what to respect, and what to distrust. You accepted all these teachings without doubt or suspicion. When your parents said, "Santa Claus will come down the chimney at midnight," you full expected the jolly fat man to be there.

As you progress through adolescence, however, it will be natural to examine each of the beliefs you have been taught. There will probably come a time when you will say, "Hey! Wait a minute. Do I really accept what my parents have said? Can I trust them to tell me the truth? Let's think this over before jumping to conclusions!"

This time of questioning is a very important event in your life as a young Christian. It can be the moment when you develop your *own* relationship with God instead of riding on the religion of your parents. On the other hand, it can be a distressing time because of the confusion it brings. That's why I mention it to you now, so that you won't be too upset during those days when nothing seems certain anymore. If you can keep searching for answers to the major questions of life, you'll eventually get satisfactory answers and solutions. And the chances are great that you'll discover that your parents were right in the first place.

6. THE SEARCH FOR IDENTITY

Closely related to this time of confusion will be another major event of adolescence, called the *search for identity*. This phrase refers to the need of each young person to know who he is. Let me ask how well *you* are personally acquainted with yourself. Do you know who you are? Do you know what you want in life? Do you know your own strengths and weaknesses? Do you know what you believe about God? Do you like the "image" your friends have of you? All of these questions relate to the search for identity.

Perhaps I can illustrate the importance of a well-defined identity by describing an individual who is poorly acquainted with himself. Marvin, as we'll call him, is one of four children, but he is neither the oldest nor the youngest in his family. His parents are extremely busy people and rarely have time to read to their children, or take walks, or play games, or build model airplanes. They do little except work day and night. Marvin thinks he is loved by his parents, but he doesn't feel very highly *respected* by them (or anyone else).

At five years of age, Marvin toddles off to kindergarten, where he spends most of his time riding the tricycles. A year later, he has some trouble learning to read. He has no idea why. The other students are also learning math much faster than he. Marvin rarely gets "happy faces" on his school papers. His teacher doesn't say "Nice work, Marv" in front of his classmates. And he knows his parents aren't too happy about his school performance either. He feels very dumb.

Junior high finally rolls around, and Marvin has no idea who in the world he is. He is not good at basketball or tennis or golf. He can't play a trumpet or a trombone or the drums. He doesn't draw or paint or create artistic projects. In fact, he has never done anything in his entire life that was worth mentioning or bragging about. He doesn't know what he wants to be after he grows up. In fact, he's not even sure he wants to grow up. What I'm saying is that a boy like Marvin has *no* sense of identity. If an English teacher asked him to write a one-page theme entitled "Who Am I," he couldn't compose the first line.

Marvin's problem is extreme, and it may not apply to you. However, most teenagers lack a sense of identity to some degree. If you find yourself in that situation, I urge you to shop around for who you are in the years that follow. Go out for various sports or try to learn to play a musical instrument or ask your mother to teach you to sew. You might also go to the counseling office of your school and ask to be given some interest tests and vocational inventories that will identify your likes, dislikes, and skills. Joining the Scouts can also introduce you to many new dimensions of your personality. By all means, don't let these years slip by without exploring the many possibilities that lie within you.

Becoming Men and Women

One more comment needs to be made in regard to your search for identity, and it has to do with finding the proper masculine or feminine role. You see, until now you've been a little girl or a little boy, but soon you're going to be a grown man or woman. Girls will begin taking on the behavior that is appropriate for women, and boys will adopt the very different style of men. But before these changes occur, you have to know what is masculine and what is feminine. Those differences are not as clear today as they were when your parents were children, and many young people have a very hazy sexual identity.

I heard a story the other day of a little boy and girl who had just been introduced. They were trying to decide what games to play, and the little boy said, "I have an idea—let's play baseball."

But the little girl said, "Oh, no, I wouldn't want to do that; baseball is a boy's game. It's not feminine to run around on a dusty vacant lot. No, I wouldn't want to play baseball."

So the boy replied, "Okay, then, let's play football."

She answered, "Oh, no, I wouldn't play football. That's even less feminine. I might fall and get dirty. No, that's not a girl's game."

He said, "Okay, I've got an idea. I'll race you to the corner."

She replied, "No, girls play quiet games; we don't run and get all sweaty. Girls should never race with boys."

The boy then scratched his head, trying to think of what she might want to do, and finally he said, "Okay, then, let's play house."

She said, "Good! I'll be the daddy!"

I think this young lady was a little confused on what her role as a girl was supposed to be. She will probably have some important questions to answer in the years ahead!

Maybe you too will have to answer some questions about your sexual identity between now and adulthood. If so, the easiest way to learn how to play the role of your particular sex, whether it be man or woman, is to watch an adult whom you respect. Try to be like him or her. This is called *identifying* with another person. If it's your mother or your teacher or another adult of your sex, watch and learn how he or she acts. Quietly observe how he walks and talks, and gradually you will find that it will become natural for you to be something like your model, even though you're a unique individual. This process comes under the heading of the search for identity, and it is an important part of growing up.

It is fitting that we summarize this chapter with a discussion of identity. As you may have noticed, this *entire* book has been designed to acquaint you with yourself . . . to give you a better grasp of who you are and where you appear to be going. As I said in the first chapter, I hope you will use this book as a kind of springboard to gain even more information on this important topic. After you get to know yourself, you might discover that you are a rather nice person after all.

6
This Is How It Was With Me

The final chapter of this book is very different from the five which you have just read. In fact, it may be different from anything you have *ever* read. But I think you'll find this section very helpful and interesting.

You may be surprised to learn that I didn't write the remainder of this book, nor did any other author. The following text was actually taken from the recorded comments of four teenagers whom you will soon meet. You see, I invited two boys and two girls (all fifteen or sixteen years old) to come to my house for the purpose of discussing the topics in this book. They sat in our family room and shared their experiences, while a team of technicians recorded their comments on tape. Then we made copies of their remarks and edited them slightly to make the discussion more clear. The result is an eyewitness account of what it feels like to grow up . . . from the viewpoint of four young people who have recently had that experience.

It may take you a few minutes to get accustomed to reading a person's name before knowing what he or she said, but you'll soon adjust. It's almost like reading a stage play, although here the people are not merely acting. They are real flesh-and-blood teenagers, just like you are (or soon will be). Now let's meet these new friends.

Dr. Dobson: Hello, everyone, and welcome to my home. I've invited each of you here, as you know, to participate in a rap session . . . a free and easy sharing of ideas and experiences. I've been telling young people what it feels like to become an adolescent. I've described the fears and tears and jeers that often accompany this time of life, as well as the many exciting aspects of growing up. But *you* can do the job better than I can. You are closer to that experience, and we want each of you to share your feelings with us.

Let's begin with an introduction of my guests, starting with the young lady on my left.

Gaylene: Well, my name is Gaylene, and I live in Arcadia, California.

Dr. Dobson: How old are you, Gaylene?

Gaylene: I'm fifteen, but I'll be sixteen in June.

142

Dr. Dobson: You've told us your name and how old you are, but *who* are you, Gaylene? What kind of person are you? What things do you like?

Gaylene: Drama is my big thing. I'm in Junior Jesters right now, which is a drama group at our high school.

Dr. Dobson: How many plays have you been in?

Gaylene: We've done two plays this year, and I'm working on another scene right now.

Dr. Dobson: If you sat down to write a paper called "Who Am I?" would you say that your interest in drama is the most important thing we should know about you?

Gaylene: I think so, but even this interest is just a front, because the real me is hiding beneath it, somewhere.

Dr. Dobson: That's a very interesting point . . . we'll get back to it in a moment. Darrell, introduce us to yourself now.

Darrell: My name is Darrell, and I'm a junior at John Muir High School in Pasadena. I've just been elected Youth President at my church, which I think I'll have a lot of fun doing. And I'm sixteen years old.

Dr. Dobson: Do I understand that you've also been on the debate team at your school?

Darrell: Yes, and I love it. Ever since I was small I've liked literature and speech more than I did science and math. I guess I was just brought up that way.

143

Dr. Dobson: All right, let's move around the circle to the next person.

Ceslie: I'm Ceslie and I go to Pasadena High School. I've been thinking a lot about what I want to do when I grow up, and I think the most important thing to me will be getting married and having a family.

Dr. Dobson: How do you feel, Ceslie, about the people who say that having a family and being a housewife is not worthy of a woman's time? Have you ever thought about that?

Ceslie: I don't agree with them, but that's just for me, because I'm that kind of a person. I like doing housework and I like cooking and things like that.

Dr. Dobson: And how old are you?

Ceslie: I'm sixteen, going on seventeen.

Dr. Dobson: "Going to be"—each of you has pushed your age up a little bit. (Laughter.) Let me tell you something: in about fifteen years you'll be trying to hold it down, I can guarantee that! (Laughter.) Okay, Page, tell us about yourself.

Page: Well, I've lived here in Pasadena for about five years. I was raised in upper New York before my dad was offered a job out here. And I'm sixteen years old.

Dr. Dobson: And what are your interests?

Page: I enjoy most sports. That's my greatest love.

Dr. Dobson: I can verify that Page is a very good basketball player. As a matter of fact, Page and I played basketball together last Tuesday night, and I was very impressed by his jump shot from about twenty feet.

All right, we've now introduced each of your names and let people know something about your interests. I'm pleased to see that all four of you are acquainted with your own minds in that way. I meet many young people who have no keen interests in life; they don't play the piano, or get involved in debating or home-making or basketball or drama or anything else. They have no goals, no purpose, and no reason for living. That can be a very sad situation, and it leads us to the first subject I would like to hear you discuss.

Earlier in this book I've tried to describe what feelings of inferiority can be like during the teen years. By that I'm referring to the belief by a young person that he isn't liked by anyone . . . that he's a "loser" . . . that other people are laughing behind his back . . . that he is dumb or ugly or poor . . . that he doesn't do things as well as other people . . . that he is uncoordinated and clumsy . . . that all-in-all his life is one big disaster.

Those awful feelings of inferiority and inadequacy are very widespread among young people today. It affects adults too. I recently read a book written by comedian Woody Allen in which he said that his only regret in life was that he wasn't somebody else. He is not alone in those thoughts. Many teenagers would like nothing better than to crawl out of their skin and get into someone else's body.

The four of you sitting here with me this evening look like you've got it all together. You appear poised and relaxed and confident. But have you experienced those same feelings of inferiority? Have you ever been disappointed with the person you've become? Did any of you identify with the feelings I just described?

Gaylene: I sure did. They hit me during my first year of junior high school.

Dr. Dobson: Tell us about those difficult days.

Gaylene: Well, my dad died during the summer following my fifth grade in school. This death happened at a time when I was going through many physical and emotional changes, and I didn't handle it very well. So I entered junior high school without knowing who I was. I wasn't involved in anything and I had nothing to look forward to. It was a very difficult time for me.

Dr. Dobson: How did you overcome those problems?

Gaylene: My mother encouraged me to reach out, to get involved in as many activities as I could. Also, we got interested in Christianity during those years. Neither my mother nor my brother knew which way to turn, but my grandparents were very religious people. We moved in with them, and that's when I got involved in a Sunday school program, which helped a lot.

Dr. Dobson: Gaylene, you said this difficult experience occurred during your first year of junior high school. That doesn't surprise me, because the seventh and eighth grades are often the most upsetting period of a person's life. Feelings of inferiority frequently become the strongest during those two years, for some reason. I know hundreds of thirteen-year-olds who have concluded, "I'm worthless!"

Has anyone else fallen into this same "canyon of inferiority?"

Darrell: I did, although my situation was different from Gaylene's. I was editor of the school newspaper when I was in junior high school, which gave me some satisfaction and status. But my problems during that time came from church. I was "different" from my friends because I enjoyed schoolwork and speech and subjects like that, which more or less isolated me. I was not involved in the junior high activities at church. I remember one disastrous beach trip in particular. I had looked forward to going, but I came home and I just bawled. I really did. I felt so rotten because I was teased by people throughout the trip. I didn't know why everybody was picking on me.

147

Dr. Dobson: I'm interested in the attitude of your friends at church. Did they not respect you because you liked to study?

Darrell: Yes, that was a problem. In my group you were supposed to hate school. I was expected to say, "Forget it, teachers are a drag, school is lousy, and anybody who gets interested in schoolwork is a freak." Even now, most of my friends are bored with school, and they work only to get good grades. They say, "I'm not going to study this because it won't be on a test." And that's no good. So when I was in junior high, I was interested in my studies and tried to share my experiences and be open about them, but nobody else wanted to do that. They wouldn't open themselves like I did, and it caused problems for me. From that moment I didn't want to open myself either. It has taken about two years for me to get over these feelings and to start talking again in Sunday school and wanting to be free.

Dr. Dobson: How beautifully you stated it, Darrell. Young people get laughed at . . . teased . . . ridiculed for being open with each other. Their feelings are deeply hurt, and they come home and cry, as you did. Then they begin to "close down." The next day they will be more cautious . . . more reserved . . . more phony in their social contacts.

Have you ever wondered, Darrell, why your friends were not as open as you? It's likely that they had been burned in the same way you were, only earlier. They had already learned the dangers of being free and spontaneous. The result was a very uneasy, tense society where everyone knew he could be laughed out of school if he made one social mistake. What a tough way to live!

Darrell: The pressures are great. For example, everyone is supposed to be "cool" now. I mean, you're not expected to show your feelings or reveal your true self. If you do, someone will laugh at the tenderness, the softness, inside. Well, some people recognize that it is not worth it to be so cautious. I've even seen posters at our school that say, "It's not cool to be cool anymore." That's a quick way to rip yourself apart . . . to do more harm to yourself than others can do to you.

Dr. Dobson: A mother told me a few weeks ago that her seventh-grade daughter wakes up every morning at 5:30 and spends an hour thinking, "How can I get through this day without making a mistake that will cause people to laugh at me?" Isn't that unfortunate? Ceslie, I'll bet you've had some of those feelings, haven't you?

Ceslie: I remember the third week of my first year in junior high—it was a brand-new school for me. I knew a few people there, but I wasn't familiar with everything. I was really little. I was about four feet, nine inches tall, and that's very short. I knew this one girl at our school named "Big Bertha," and she was about five feet eight. Bertha was the meanest girl in school, and everybody would run away when she came around. I thought that was really awful . . . that people shouldn't run away from her. But one day we were going up the stairs and Bertha kicked me. I didn't like that, and I turned around and said something to her, and she kicked me harder. So I went home and didn't say anything to anybody, but I was so upset that I started crying. When I told my parents why I was crying they thought it was very unkind for a person to do something like that. So they called the principal and told him the story. Then they told me to treat Bertha just like I would treat anyone else, because the reason she was kicking me was because she was so embarrassed about being too large. It wasn't because she was really that mean; she just felt bad about herself.

Dr. Dobson: That was very good advice, Ceslie. You see, there are several ways people act when they feel inferior. Darrell mentioned one approach, which is to pull into a shell and be very cautious with your associates. Another way is to become very angry and resentful. Bertha took this second alternative. Can't you imagine how she felt, first by being called Big Bertha, and then by having everyone run away from her? Those two experiences would probably make *me* want to kick people too. Bertha had been hurt deeply, and that caused her to hurt you. How did you deal with Bertha the next day at school?

Ceslie: Well, she had a little group of friends; there were three of them that stayed together. Every time I saw them in the halls, I just smiled at them. I think it kind of made them mad at me, but I just kept smiling and they never did anything to me after that.

Dr. Dobson: Did you gradually come to accept yourself?

Ceslie: I think I'm still—

Dr. Dobson: You're still working on that?

Ceslie: Yes.

Dr. Dobson: You'll probably work on that the rest of your life.

Ceslie: I know.

Dr. Dobson: Most of us are working on the same project. Page, you started to say something.

Page: You're talking about people who get hurt by their friends. Well, when I was younger, I had an accident which crippled me for a summer. I had to wear these crazy-looking shoes to school. I had broken my leg and I had to wear elevated shoes. I didn't want to. I used to sneak my other shoes from my house and put them on later so people wouldn't laugh at me. This went on for a couple of years. People used to call me "Cripple," you know, and I really wasn't, but it hurt me to be teased. Even now I sometimes feel like, "Oh, I wish I could be like a certain person because he's so great, and boy, you know, all the people would really like me because I'd be such a great athlete." That's what I always wanted to be—somebody that would stand out and not be someone that people laugh at.

Dr. Dobson: Isn't it interesting that you all have had the *same* feelings? That is precisely my point. If we selected a thousand teenagers and asked each one the question I've asked you, nearly every person would tell us a story like those we've just heard—about being laughed at, about being different, about not being accepted by others. It's something everybody goes through today.

Now tell me why—why is it that we have to endure these difficult moments? Is there any way to avoid them?

Gaylene: I tried to solve my problems in the wrong way—by becoming friends with the "in" crowd. Like there were two different groups in my high school. There was this group that was into partying all night and then coming home late and lying to their parents; then there was the other group that tried to be more responsible. They believed that being wild wasn't going to fulfill their lives. But it wasn't easy for me to choose between these friends. I barged into the tenth grade and met people from the different groups and I didn't know exactly where to turn. There were more people in the rebellious group than in the responsible group, and that's just the way it is, and I didn't want to be laughed at and I didn't want to be rejected, and I didn't want everybody to think I was weird. So I just stood there, at a crossroads in my life, not knowing where to turn.

Dr. Dobson: Did you feel tremendous pressure to do things that you knew were wrong?

Gaylene: Yes! I was just a sophomore this year, and that's when you get most of the pressure; you get a tremendous amount.

Dr. Dobson: And that pressure can cause you to behave in ways that you know are harmful. I believe, for example, that most of the drug abuse in our country occurs because of the enormous pressure that Gaylene described. It's not the "high" that attracts kids—the problem is that they lack the courage to choose the right group. Did the rest of you have a similar choice to make?

Darrell: I had to decide whether or not I was going to follow the "rules" of my peers at school. I knew that if I didn't go along I would be "out."

Dr. Dobson: Give us an example of what you mean, Darrell. What kind of rules were you expected to follow?

Darrell: Well, like the "being cool" rule. You must not show your feelings because people might

153

find something to laugh at. But there were other rules in almost every area.

Dr. Dobson: What about your clothes—did the group tell you what to wear?

Darrell: Yeah.

Dr. Dobson: How to talk?

Darrell: Yeah.

Dr. Dobson: And what slang to use?

Darrell: Yes. You sort of convince yourself after a while that it's what you really wanted anyway. I mean, you like to think that you're not conforming, that you just happen to like the same kind of Levis and shoes and sweaters that everyone else is wearing. But as styles change, you realize there must be some other force that is working on your attitudes. That other force is group pressure.

Dr. Dobson: How about the matter of drugs? Have any of you ever had anybody offer narcotics to you?

Gaylene: I have, in junior high. We had this bulletin board, and the librarian put up a poster about the dangers of taking drugs. While I was reading it, somebody came up to me and said, "Look nice, don't they?" Right there, they were offering the stuff to me! At the time (this was back in seventh grade), I didn't know much about medicines or anything, and when I told my mom about it, she was completely horrified. She said, "They never did that back in my day." She's always saying things like that.

Dr. Dobson: Don't you think it's tougher to be a teenager now than it was in the past?

Gaylene: Yes.

Dr. Dobson: There have always been pressures on young people, but now the drug problem and other dangers seem to be worse.

Have you ever been offered drugs, Ceslie, or have you ever seen them being used?

Ceslie: No, I've never hung around the wild group. I was always in the group that was quiet and—

Page: Gaylene said her mother couldn't believe drugs were actually available at school. Well, my parents have a hard time believing it too. But, you know, our society has changed. A new trend will come along and everybody wants to be part of the craze. But I worry about what will happen when we're older and we have our kids. How are we going to face this situation with our kids, if we've taken drugs and done wrong things? What answers can we give to our children?

Dr. Dobson: Those are good questions, Page, because that day will come very quickly. You'll find yourself trying to keep your own children from making the mistakes which worry your folks today.

Ceslie: I think many of our problems occur because we don't talk to our parents enough; we keep everything inside and we never talk to anybody who could help us. We talk to our friends who are having the same problems, but they don't have the answers and they don't know what to tell us. For example, Gaylene talked to her mom. That was probably the best thing she could have done. I would never have said anything to my parents, because they would have just blown up, you know, and gotten mad at the school. But I think that's very important—to have a relationship with your parents where you can talk openly to them, and not have to worry about how they'll respond. Then they can give you the answers that will be helpful to you.

Dr. Dobson: Two of you have now mentioned this matter of talking to your parents. How about the other two? Darrell, have you been able to talk to your mom and dad?

Darrell: I haven't had that much opportunity to talk to them because drugs have never been a problem with me. But I agree that adults can help us handle our difficulties if they're "tuned in." But sometimes they don't know what's going on. For example, I had one teacher in ninth grade who was out of touch. We were sitting in class one day and here comes this sweet, sickly smell of marijuana down the hall, as clear as could be. It drifted into the classroom and everybody knew what it was except the teacher (Laughter.) We were sitting there reading and looking at each other and just, you know, trying to hide our laughter, but the teacher was grading papers when all of a sudden she looked up and said, "My! What's that marvelous smell?" (Laughter.) She had no idea why we broke up. It would have blown her mind, you know? She was the kind of teacher who would never give a thought to that kind of thing. But they're doing better at our school now. They have big drug-prevention programs, but even that's not going to be enough.

Dr. Dobson: How about talking to your parents generally about other things that bother you, Darrell. Can you express your feelings to them? Let's go back to that painful night when you went to the beach. (I had a night very similar to that, by the way). Did you come home and talk to your mom and dad about it?

Darrell: Yeah, I talked to my dad. Both of my parents were brought up in a very strict Christian environment, and my mom is still—well, I'm not saying she's narrow-minded, but because my dad has had more experiences, he's more flexible. He is a minister and so he knows how to counsel people with problems. He told me not to pay too much attention to all this laughter, and helped me understand it. But you know something? I discovered that I brought some of that scorn on myself. I'd worn this real

157

goofy-looking thing—it wasn't funny, but it was goofy. (Laughter.) There's a difference between the two. You can cause people to make fun of you, and that is what I had done. Well, I got rid of that clothing the next day, you know?

Dr. Dobson: A person gradually learns to keep his peers from laughing at him. After he's been stung a couple of times, he finds out what's "dangerous" and what is not. Page?

Page: Sometimes I feel like I can talk to my father better than I can talk with my mother. Mainly, I guess, because he was a boy himself and he understands some of the situations that I'm going through. He always encourages me to choose the right kind of friends.

Dr. Dobson: Did you have to choose which group you'd join, just as the others mentioned?

Page: Yeah, and that is a very important choice. Some of my church friends began running with the wrong crowd, and they soon drifted away from God and began living the wrong kind of life. I'm thankful that I'm in a good group and that these things haven't happened to me.

Dr. Dobson: Well, Page, your comment raises an extremely important point. All of us are influenced by people around us. Even adults are swayed by social pressure. For this reason, the most critical decision you must make will involve the friends you choose. If you select the wrong group, they *will* have a bad influence on you. It is a certainty. Very few people have the self-confidence to withstand criticism by their closest friends.

Gaylene: I'd like to say that some of the nicest people are those who are not so popular with the "in" group. I'm dating a boy now who's in a wheelchair. He's extremely nice and has a fantastic personality. Some people look down on me for going with him. They say, "Well, why do you go with *him* when you could go out with someone who's normal?" I think that's unfair.

Page: I do too! But I feel the same pressure when I decide to ask a girl for a date. I know some of my friends are going to think she's not pretty enough for me, or something. And then I feel kind of low, you know?

Ceslie: Just recently, I've been realizing how important the personality of a person is. In my mind I'm always thinking, "What if I would marry that person; what would his reaction be to problems that we face? It's not going to matter what that fellow will look like at that time. Besides, he's going to get old anyhow. (Laughter.)

Dr. Dobson: That's not a very encouraging prospect, although I guess it's true! But you're right, Ceslie. I've seen a girl marry the best basketball player in school because he was such a great athletic hero. Ten years later, however, nobody could remember how the crowds cheered him. All they knew was that the guy couldn't earn a living and he couldn't make decisions and he beat the kids and screamed at his wife. Like you said, Ceslie, you need to look into the future and try to predict what your life will be like with a particular person.

Darrell: I'm in an interesting situation now. Junior high isn't that far behind me, but my little sister is already in junior high, and just last night she was really upset about the possibility that she might have to go to a different school next year. She talked to me about her worries, and I found myself saying the kind of things we've been saying tonight. As I was talking to her I said to myself, "What am I doing? This is an echo from about three years ago. I am my father and she is me." (Laughter.) You know, it's like my father's words were bouncing off the wall and coming back to her now. I could see that her problems weren't serious at all because I had been through them, and I kept saying, "Why can't she see? I'm giving her the clearest answers in the world." But yet when I was in that situation I had no idea at first what my father was talking about.

Dr. Dobson: You have to experience it before it makes sense, don't you? And, in that way, this tape recording may be a mystery to that listener who is between ten and twelve years of age who hasn't gone through the experiences we're

160

describing. You may not fully understand what we're talking about, but when it happens to you, then it will be like turning on a light bulb in your head. You will remember this tape and our conversation about feelings of inadequacy and inferiority. When that happens to you, remember this very moment when I said that you *do* have great worth as a human being.

Gaylene: There's one inferiority complex that I had when I started seventh grade—my freckles! They show, despite the fact that I used to do everything that I could think of to hide them. My mom kept telling me, you know, don't hide them, they're beautiful. And like Darrell, I found myself telling another little girl the same thing a couple of weeks ago. She has freckles and they *are* beautiful, you know? I was telling her that people are going to tease her, but yet, she shouldn't be upset about it. In fact, freckles are valuable, because if you get pimples on your face, people can't tell the difference. (Laughter.)

Darrell: I don't have a bad acne problem. But it becomes worse at some times than others.

Dr. Dobson: Explain what acne is, for the benefit of those who don't know.

Darrell: It's well—it's completely physical. All these old wives tales are silly, like the one that says, "It's the wicked coming out in you." (Laughter.) It's a completely physical problem because you have more oil flowing through your system.

Dr. Dobson: Be more specific, Darrell. Tell us what it looks like.

Darrell: You get red pimples on your face and around your neck sometimes. They make you feel real ugly when the people you see on television, like Donny and Marie, seem to have an absolutely perfect complexion. You couldn't even find a speck of dust on the lens of the camera, you know? And when acne does flare up, it can be devastating—it really can knock you out. And, even though you tell yourself, "I know where my priorities are and I know that beauty isn't the most important thing," it still affects your self-confidence.

Dr. Dobson: You become sensitive, don't you?

Darrell: I heard this on Hollywood Squares— "What's the biggest problem that teens have to face up to?" The guy was just joking, and he said, "acne" because of the pun between "acne" and something being faced up to. Then the moderator says "Right!" And the audience laughed. But really, pimples affect your self-confidence. You have to go out into the world and say, "Here I am, friends, with these red bumps on my face." And it really can hurt. It's easy to say to yourself, "Okay, physical beauty isn't important." But it's not so easy to convince yourself of that when your face is covered with blemishes.

Dr. Dobson: I saw a study of hundreds of teenagers who were asked what they most disliked about themselves, and skin problems ranked at the top of the list. That is one reason I am so strongly opposed to Barbie dolls. I suppose every girl plays with Barbie dolls when she is young, and most people don't give a second thought to them. But what bothers me about Barbie is that she is physically perfect; there are no pimples on Barbie. Her skin is air-brushed; her hair has "body" (whatever that means); there is not an ounce of fat on her anyplace. In fact, the only flaw on Barbie's pink body is a little statement on her bottom that says she was made in Hong Kong! (Laughter.) And, you see, these dolls give a little girl an image of what she's supposed to look like when she becomes a teenager. Fat chance! That's not realistic.

Ceslie: It seems like you always get pimples right before a really special event at school. It never fails. You could look great two weeks before and don't have a single blemish, but then on the big date, it's measles time.

Dr. Dobson: It seems like there's a little gremlin somewhere who plants them on you at night.

Page: What we're saying is that people just have to learn to accept themselves, as they are. That's hard to do, and it's been hard for me. People are going to mock you and it's going to hurt, and sometimes you wish, just like I said before,

163

"Why can't I be like that person who's perfectly clean and all the girls love him? Why can't I be like that? Nobody likes me." I think this is the most difficult problem junior high kids have to overcome—the acceptance of their bodies.

Ceslie: My mom once told me that beauty is something that grows inside of you, and that some people who are pretty on the outside don't take the time to work on their personality and character. Later on, those who were less attractive may even become happier because their inner beauty increases as they grow older.

Dr. Dobson: I wish everyone knew that, Ceslie. I saw another study that tended to prove what you said. The researchers identified the girls in college who were the most beautiful and those who were less attractive. Then they studied them for 25 years to see what happened in their marriages and later lives. Believe it or not, those who were less attractive tended to be more happily married 25 years later. So it's really wrong for everybody to feel like they have to be physically perfect.

Let me say, in summary, that *everybody* has something they don't like about themselves. For Page it was his shoes. He felt bad about having to wear those elevated heels. For Gaylene it was her freckles. For Ceslie it was being too short. For Darrell it was being studious instead of being athletic. If people were honest, they would all admit being embarrassed about some flaw that becomes a burden to carry throughout life. But it is unnecessary to worry! We all have great human worth, regardless of how we look. And that's the beautiful thing about Christianity. Jesus loves me, not because I am fantastically intelligent or handsome; He loves me simply because I *am*! What a comforting message! I don't have to do anything to earn His love. It is available to everyone as a free gift. For the person who has been damaged by feelings of inferiority that's quite a message.

— Break occurred at this point.—

Dr. Dobson: We have been joined by a new member of our group that I want you to get acquainted with now. Greg, tell us a little bit about yourself.

Greg: My name is Greg Nourse, and I work for One Way Library, a Christian cassette company. I came here tonight to help do the recording, but I thought it would be neat if I could join the group to discuss drugs from the point of view of a former abuser. I have been through the drug scene, so I thought it might be helpful to add a few of my comments.

Dr. Dobson: I agree, Greg. We can learn from your experience. As a place to begin, tell us how people get started taking drugs in the first place.

Greg: That's a very common question. Well, I

started taking drugs because I was inquisitive, and bored, and because it was an easy way of being entertained. But once you start taking drugs, then it's not fun to feel normal anymore. I know about that feeling because I was loaded every day.

Dr. Dobson: What kind of drugs did you take?

Greg: I started with marijuana.

Dr. Dobson: Did that lead you to take other narcotics?

Greg: Not really. At least, there was no "addiction" which led me to take harder stuff. However, when you begin with marijuana, you are around drugs and around the people who use them. That's what led me to get in deeper.

Dr. Dobson: When did you begin experimenting with pills?

Greg: Well, I started getting loaded in grade school. I think I began with "reds," and then I took cocaine and about every psychedelic substance.

Dr. Dobson: All right, Greg, let's go back to the very first experience. Can you remember what happened?

Greg: Uh huh. My friend's big sister was a big "loader," and she used to make us roll up lids for her, and so we just—

Dr. Dobson: Excuse me. You have to explain your terms.

Greg: I'm sorry, a "lid" is a certain amount of marijuana, and you get it in a baggie or something, and then you have to roll it into cigarettes. The cigarette is called a "joint." Well, this girl used to make us sit there and roll up her "lids," which takes hours to finish. Sometimes she'd bring home a "brick," which is more than a lid. One day we were rolling joints when we decided to try one ourselves. We stole a couple of joints, and that's the first time I was loaded.

Dr. Dobson: Was it your idea or were you with somebody else who said, "Why don't we do it?"

Greg: It was my idea.

Dr. Dobson: You were the one who put the other guys under pressure, weren't you?

Greg: That's right.

Dr. Dobson: And you were soon taking other substances?

Greg: Yes. That went on all through high school.

Dr. Dobson: Tell us how you felt after you had taken a drug and then started to come down.

Greg: Coming down is horrible, especially when you've taken speed, which is an amphetamine. I always became really sick. Let me tell you that getting "strung out" on a drug is an awful thing, because you wake up in the morning and you know that you have to take that drug by the end of your day or you'll be sick. If you get the stuff, you make it through the day, but then your routine starts over again the next morning.

Dr. Dobson: What if you don't have money and you can't afford to buy what you need?

Greg: Well, it depends on what drug you're hooked on. If it's "speed" or heroin, you get terribly sick. With heroin you go through "withdrawals," which are awful. "Speed" is even more dangerous because it destroys your brain cells, it interferes with your circulation, causes your hair to fall out, and changes your entire personality. You become moody and sentimental; you'll cry over anything, because you get extremely depressed, especially when you're coming down. The same thing happens with "acid" (LSD). You become exhausted the day after taking it, and your head is kind of numb. The more you take LSD, the more it deteriorates you as a person. You become more introverted and less productive. The body was simply not made for these chemical influences.

Dr. Dobson: We hear people say that the psychedelic drugs make a person more creative and more knowledgeable of himself. Did you find that to be true?

Greg: Certainly not. You see things when you're on these drugs that you can't even remember. The experience seems neat at the time, but there are no benefits after you come down.

Dr. Dobson: I described a situation earlier where a

young person was in a car with four of his friends who start passing around some reds. When he refuses to take them, everyone says, "Come on, Chicken, what are you, a baby? Are you afraid? Are you a coward? Everybody else is doing it. What's the matter with you?" What is he going to do at a moment like that? What suggestions can you offer to a young person who might someday be in that situation? He already feels inferior; he already feels that he doesn't like his freckles or the shoes he wears, or something else about himself. How is he going to handle that moment when it comes?

Greg: I'll admit that this guy is in a very difficult situation, especially if he's with people he respects and wants to be friends with. But he must make a decision in that moment that will be one of the most important choices he'll ever face. Once he starts taking drugs, after he says that first "yes," then he is in for years of trouble. So I suggest that he hang tough and refuse to go along. He should also start looking for some new friends, because the ones he has will probably be getting loaded more and more often. He can't stay in their group without also getting involved sooner or later.

Dr. Dobson: Greg, I would like you to comment on the role which inferiority plays in drug abuse, which we were discussing earlier. As you know, it is my belief that the person who feels inferior—the person who doesn't like himself—sometimes uses drugs to escape. In other words, if he takes a pill, then he can get away from himself for a few minutes or an hour or two. Do you agree with this viewpoint? Did feelings of inferiority play a role in your own experience?

Greg: Absolutely. Inferiority played the most significant role in my case. People will always say that they're not taking drugs to escape, but that's what it boils down to. Drugs offer a quick way to get away from those awful feelings of inadequacy. However, those feelings are still there, waiting for you when you get back.

Dr. Dobson: When did you begin to overcome your self-doubts?

Greg: Believe it or not, they got worse when I graduated from high school. You see, most people strive to be popular all through school, and I did the same thing. But after your senior year, it just kind of backfires. There's no one to be popular for anymore. That's when feelings of inferiority can become unbearable.

Dr. Dobson: Well, Greg, how did you get your life back together? You were obviously in a mess, and yet you sit here tonight, "clothed and in your right mind."

Greg: Jesus Christ came into my life and made the difference.

Dr. Dobson: Tell us how you found the Lord.

Greg: Well, I wasn't searching for God. I didn't feel

170

that I was searching for anything, but my friends were talking to me about the Lord. Finally, it wasn't anything they said—it was just kind of a revelation from God, I knew I needed Him. I asked, with what little faith I had, for Him to come into my life, and He did. And I knew immediately that He had.

Dr. Dobson: When you came to Jesus, did you get rid of your drug problem once and for all?

Greg: Uh huh. I did. When a person comes to the Lord, he feels clean inside and like a new person. Jesus said, "Peace I leave with you, my peace I give unto you; not as the world giveth, give I unto you. Let not your heart be troubled, neither let it be afraid."

Dr. Dobson: Greg, I appreciate your sharing your experience with us and giving us this personal testimony. I'm sure many young people will be helped by it.

Greg: Thanks for letting me tell my story. Now I'll get back to the recording.

Dr. Dobson: I would like the four of us to discuss another extremely important aspect of adolescence, and I'm referring to the physical changes that occur during the early teen years. It's not uncommon for kids to be frightened by what is happening to their bodies. Did any of you experience those fears during early adolescence?

Gaylene: I did. I began changing very early, in the

171

fourth and fifth grades. This scared me because my mom hadn't told me what to expect.

Dr. Dobson: She hadn't prepared you for these changes?

Gaylene: No, because she figured it wouldn't happen until the sixth or seventh grade. When it happened early I didn't know what was going on. And I hit the panic button!

Dr. Dobson: What kind of fears did you have, Gaylene? Did you wonder if you were abnormal in some way, or if you had a terrible disease?

Gaylene: I thought I was going to die. I really did. I was in school and ran to the nurse's office in tears. That's how scared I was. And she didn't know what was wrong because I was too hysterical to explain it to her.

Dr. Dobson: Your honesty is very helpful, Gaylene, because it will encourage others who are listening not to be afraid when their own physical changes begin to occur. They should know that the growing-up process is controlled by the pituitary gland in the brain. At a certain time and at a certain age, it sends out chemical messengers called hormones which produce these sudden changes that can be so terrifying.

Gaylene: Well, you know, when you said that we shouldn't be scared, that's easy to say, but how can a person help being scared? For example, when I found out I was allergic to bees, my mom said, "Just don't be frightened of them." But I can't help it. When they come near me, I run the opposite direction. I'm deathly afraid of them. It didn't help me get over my fear when my mother told me not to worry.

Dr. Dobson: There is a difference, though, Gaylene. You really *do* have something to fear from bees because you are allergic to their sting. However, the thing I want to convey to those who are preteenagers is that they *don't* have anything to fear from the physical changes that are occuring. It's a natural process that happens in all healthy people. Darrell?

Darrell: I was very small in junior high. Well, I guess most of the guys are shorter than the girls in junior high anyway.

Dr. Dobson: That's right.

Darrell: I'm beginning to catch up with the others now, but for awhile I was sensitive about my height. But I wasn't the only one who was uncomfortable, because the physical changes of adolescence coincided with physical education as a special class in junior high. In other words, at the time when you were most conscious of your body, you had to take showers and expose yourself to everyone in the locker room.

Dr. Dobson: Absolutely!

Darrell: I know I worried more about going to P.E. than any other class, even though it was the easiest class of the day. I enjoyed playing

173

basketball and other sports, but I was sensitive about my body, and letting others see it. Everyone felt the same way. That's why P.E. caused a lot of problems.

Dr. Dobson: Darrell, you've shown great insight by your comment. P.E. classes *do* cause many worries for junior highers. Those who haven't matured are very sensitive about their babyish bodies, especially when they notice that everybody else looks more like an adult. This causes *tremendous* anxiety, especially for the kid who is teased by his friends. I've had students say to me, "Kick me out of school, flunk me, send me to Siberia, put me in jail, do *anything*, but I'm not going to take a shower after P.E. again!" And I understand their feelings.

Gaylene: When I was told that I would have to dress-out for P.E. and then take a shower, I became very tense and worried. I didn't even want to go to school that day. I pulled every trick in the book on my mother. I got sick during the evening beforehand. I tried everything. But she made me go to school anyway. All the girls felt the same way I did, and it was funny, because the towels they gave us weren't big enough to cover us. (Laughter.) We were really supposed to dry on the towels, but everybody wrapped them around themselves, and then tried to dress and undress with the towel still in place. We didn't want anybody to see what we looked like. And oh! It was terrible!

Dr. Dobson: And everybody was going through the same thing.

Gaylene: Everybody was embarrassed and self-conscious! (Laughter.)

Dr. Dobson: Have the others of you had the same kinds of feelings and fears?

Ceslie: I used to dress in the showers! (Laughter.)

Dr. Dobson: You see, you're all in the same boat. Page, the same problem?

Page: Yes, it happened to me too.

Dr. Dobson: These experiences are more painful, of course, for those who have those old feelings of inferiority. That one problem seems to pop up everywhere.

Page: Another thing that makes boys uncomfortable is not being very strong. A lot of guys are into the "Mr. Muscleman" thing, you know, and if you're skinny they laugh at you and make fun of you. I'm not the strongest kid in the world, you know, so I always wanted to work out; I wanted to build up my muscles, so I could be like the group. I think this is why I felt inferior.

Dr. Dobson: And you see, before puberty occurs—before you grow up—your muscles are like a child's muscles. They become more powerful and more like a man's muscles shortly after the growth spurt occurs. Therefore, the boy who is late in maturing is likely to be weaker. That makes it difficult for him, because his friends are playing football and doing things that take strength. Power is very important to junior highers, and those who haven't developed feel powerless for awhile. That can bring on the feelings Page just described.

Gaylene: There's something else that embarrasses me. Boys and girls have a separate P.E. class, of course, but sometimes we all get on the same courts at the same time. Then you're really scared, because the boys are over there and they're dressed up for P.E. and you're dressed out over here. We may be playing basketball and they're playing volleyball. And the tension is terrible! You're trying to do your best, but I'm no basketball player—I'm short, sometimes I even feel crippled (laughter)—and you sure don't want to be laughed at. All the girls are trying to impress the boys and the boys are trying to impress the girls. It's a tense time.

Darrell: When the guys and girls are on the same tennis courts or something like that, that's when the bullies (the guys who want to build themselves up), take advantage of those times. When I was in junior high they would sneak up behind a guy and just go like this (demonstrates a downward pull)—just yank down his trunks. (Laughter.) Of course, the poor guy would grab them and pull them right back up. But, really, I lived in terrible fear of that happening to me. I would never show my face ever again anywhere if that ever happened, so I spent half my time playing tennis and the other half looking over my shoulder. As a result I'm not too good of a tennis player! You have to be careful, you have to watch out, not to put yourself in a vulnerable position. You can't do too much to avoid being humiliated, but you can help a little.

Page: Being with a girl is a prime time for some guys to get revenge on you, to say something about you or your family. It can hurt really bad.

Dr. Dobson: What I hear you saying is that you are most cautious when you are around the opposite sex. When the girls are around the guys and the guys around the girls, that's when you are most vulnerable. And that's easy to understand.

I'm inviting Mr. John Styll to join us now. He's also a technician who's here to run the recorders. However, this discussion we're having is so fantastically stimulating that the technicians keep wanting to jump in and offer their two bits. So why not? John, welcome to the group.

John: Thank you.

Dr. Dobson: You've been ten feet away for the past hour, and I know you have some thoughts on the subject of inferiority.

John: I just wanted to say that many of us become supersensitive about the way we look, you know, like "I'm too fat," or "I'm too skinny." I had the same problem because I never thought I was very handsome. Then I'd see people who were very attractive and I'd want to be like them. I always wanted to have black hair, for example, and I was never satisfied with the way I actually looked. Since then, I've learned that God made everybody the way they are for a reason, and He doesn't make mistakes. I've met a few people who understood that principle and refused to let their imperfections bother them. I know a girl, for example, who has to wear crutch-type braces to walk. She has some kind of crippling disease—I don't know what it's called—but her legs are very thin and she can't walk on them. Nevertheless, that girl is one of the most beautiful people I know. She is such a glory to God, because *she* knows that she's supposed to be like that. Consequently, she builds people up and makes them feel happy. That makes her feel happy in turn. It's really a wonderful thing. But people often get so concerned with the way they look that they fail to understand that God can use them just the way they are. God has a purpose for each one of us, and it's our duty to find out what His purposes are and then to fulfill them.

Dr. Dobson: That's the secret of self-confidence, John. However, a person's tiny flaws can cause him to withdraw in a corner, sit with his mouth shut, and never use the talent God has given him.

John: That can certainly happen. It's funny. I never thought of myself as being anything special, as a leader-type person. But in high school I emerged that way. You know, somebody asked me to get involved and I said "yes." So I was the editor of the high school newspaper and became involved in many other activities. But I had to be willing to take that first step.

Dr. Dobson: And as your confidence grew, your ability grew. This is a principle that I would like all our readers to understand. You may think you have no ability or skills, but your real problem is that you merely lack *confidence*. Let me tell you about the low point in my life. I was asked to share my Christian testimony at a camp when I was in high school. I only intended to talk five minutes, so I memorized a frozen little speech. But the young person who spoke before me talked for about thirty minutes without taking a breath. His words were perfect, and the more he talked, the more frightened I became. I knew I didn't have that much to say. When I finally walked out on that stage and looked at all those people my same age, my mind checked out for lunch. I stood there completely blank with nothing to say. All of those students sat in icy silence and stared at my red face. It was one of the most frightening and discouraging moments in my entire life, as I fished for something to say. Today, I speak all over the United States and receive thousands of invitations which I don't have time to accept. The difference between that first disaster and today's success is a matter of *confidence*.

John: That first experience probably made you want to succeed even more, didn't it?

Dr. Dobson: It did, but it took me five years to get over it. I can't describe how painful that failure was at the time, but as you said, John, the Lord made use of that terrible moment. It gave me a desire to learn how to handle a speaking opportunity.

Gaylene: Talking about confidence, the same thing was true for me in drama. I didn't think I was capable of acting. I thought I had to be some spectacular TV star. I signed up for a drama class, and every day the teacher kept hounding me and two other girls to get up on the stage and act. But I didn't have any confidence and I just kept hiding around the corner and being very shy. Finally I gave it a try. It was very hard the first time, but gradually I began to believe in myself. Now it's become easy for me.

John: Everybody's basically the same. In my work I meet people who are well-known and important, but they're just ordinary people, just the same as we are.

Dr. Dobson: All right, suppose you lack self-confidence. Where do you start to build it? Any suggestions?

John: Everybody, I don't care who they are, has

something that they can do. You may be able to make a bigger mudhole in your backyard than anybody. (I'm not suggesting that you do anything negative or destructive). But everyone has some undeveloped abilities, and you should identify them and cultivate them. My sister felt she could draw fairly well, so she just practiced over and over, and now art is her thing, you know? I don't think she was born an artist, but she developed her skill. My other sister is bananas over gymnastics. She's not as good as that little Russian girl—

Dr. Dobson: Olga?

John: Yeah, Olga Korbut, yeah.

Dr. Dobson: The principle that you are giving us here is one that I really believe in and tried to describe earlier. If you feel inferior and inadequate and think you don't have anything to offer, start shopping around for your hidden abilities and skills. Try to identify your own strengths and the interests that you can cultivate and then pour all of your resources into them. You'll soon be feeling better about yourself.

Page: Well, what if you try something that is really new and then you fail at it? That causes people to put you down. Aren't you worse off than before?

John: Not necessarily, because it doesn't really matter what other people think. The fact that you had the courage to try something that you didn't understand shows a lot about you, about the kind of person you are.

Page: Yeah, but sometimes your parents encourage you to plunge into something unfamiliar, and then you do lousy, you know? Then you feel low and discouraged. They shouldn't push you into doing something that you feel is not right for you.

Dr. Dobson: You're right, Page, but look at it this way. A little child who is taking his first step has to fall down before he can learn to walk, right? He would never learn to walk if he weren't willing to fall down in the beginning. And with us, the fear of falling can keep us from trying anything new. It can keep you bottled up because you're afraid to run a few of those risks. With a little confidence you can achieve something that will make you proud of yourself. That's what your parents are hoping for. Ceslie, I want to hear from you.

Ceslie: One of the things that is just terribly hard for me to do is to get up in front of a group of people and sing or talk or do anything. A year ago, I tried out for drill team at our school. (The drill team performs at football games and other school activities.) This is a big deal, and everybody tries out for it, but many don't make it. You have to be good to be chosen. The first time I tried out I was so scared that I thought I was just going to flub the whole thing. But if you practice something often enough and you've worked hard to learn it, then it becomes easier, like Gaylene said. That's what happened to me, and I was chosen for drill team. Last night was my final performance for drill team, and I wasn't even scared to go on the field. However, one year ago I thought I was going to pass out in the middle of the performance. It was just practice that pulled me through.

Dr. Dobson: It increased your confidence, didn't it?

Ceslie: Right.

Dr. Dobson: Will this success make it easier for you to try something new the next time?

Ceslie: Yes, I think so.

Dr. Dobson: Because you faced fear, didn't you?

Ceslie: Uh huh.

Dr. Dobson: If you had done what you really felt like doing, you would have run away?

Ceslie: Right.

Dr. Dobson: I know a great track star—as a matter of fact, he won three gold medals in the Olympics. He said that before every track meet he wants to run out of the stadium. Also, I'm told that Wilt Chamberlain would go into the bathroom and throw up before every basketball game in college. That tremendous tension, that fear, can keep you sitting at home in a chair, crying perhaps, instead of using those skills that God has given you.

Darrell, I don't want to put you on the spot, but

I wonder if you'd tell us in closing what Jesus Christ means to you.

Darrell: Well, we sometimes sing a song in Christian Minstrels which includes this idea: no matter what a person does for himself, he is certain to fail unless there is teamwork between him and God. That's the way I feel. Jesus Christ is always there to help me . . . to give me confidence . . . to be my friend. Of course, He expects me to do my part of the teamwork also, to develop the talents He's given me and take the opportunities that He sends my way. This relates to what we've been discussing tonight. It is our responsibility to apply these principles that have been suggested, but even if we make all the right moves, we still can't make it on our own. Speaking for myself, I depend on the partnership with God. He is always there to support me, especially during times of struggle. Not only do I have other people and friends to help me, but Christ is also working within me. That's what He means to me.

Dr. Dobson: That is beautifully said, and there is a Scripture verse that expresses the same thought. It says, "Except the Lord build the house, they labor in vain which build it." That means that you can create your own empire and become the world's greatest authority on a given subject and earn a fortune, but unless God is in it, you have wasted your time. God wants us to say to Him, "I don't have much, but my life is yours. Please take it and bless it."

Ceslie: This has helped me so much through the years. I know the Lord accepts me the way I am because He is the One who made me the way I am. I don't have to worry about the way I look or the way I talk in front of people. The Lord knows me and has my life in His hands.

Dr. Dobson: Isn't that neat? God's acceptance is *unconditional!* Even if I'm not the most admired person in the world; even if I'm not the most beautiful or intelligent person; even if I don't own a fortune; even if I haven't set any athletic records; even if I have fallen short of what I expected to accomplish, and even if I disappointed other people . . . nevertheless, I am just as worthy in the sight of God. Page, do you believe this is true? Is Jesus Christ real to you?

Page: Yes, He is. But there have been times when I've drifted away from the church and from the Lord, and I can tell you right now, without Christ in me, I am totally different in every way. But when Christ is in control, it is just like having a friend with you who helps all the time.

Dr. Dobson: Gaylene, in conclusion, would you say that it has been fun growing up, or has it been difficult and painful?

Gaylene: Both. It's been fun, but at the time I thought, "Oh, I'm not going to live through it." But now that I look back on all the experiences, I wish I were twelve again so I could do it all over. I can tell you there would be a lot of things I would want to do different.

Dr. Dobson: That's probably a pretty good place to end our conversation. I want to thank all of you for being here with us this evening and for being so honest and for sharing some of your private feelings with us. I hope these discussions have been useful to those who are listening. Perhaps they will help each person avoid the familiar pitfalls and enjoy some of the blessings that life has in store for you. Thank you again, and goodbye.

The Final Message

Well, I think we've covered the subjects that you should know about the approaching adolescent experience. We've talked about inferiority, conformity, puberty, romantic love, and emotion. All that remains is to offer one or two final suggestions that may help you cope with the pressures we've been discussing.

Today Is Not Forever

First, there is a tendency during the adolescent years to feel that "today is forever"—that present circumstances will never change—that the problems you face at this moment will continue for the rest of your life. For example, many teenagers who feel inferior and unpopular in school usually believe that they will always be unloved and rejected. They cannot imagine a situation different from what they experience in school each day. In truth, however, the teen years will pass quickly, and will soon be nothing more than a dim memory. Those friends (and enemies) who share your classes will graduate in a few months and will move across the country. Once that has occurred, no power on earth could bring them back together as things are today. The mini-society at your junior high or high school will shatter like humpty-dumpty, never to be re-assembled again.

So if you find yourself unhappy for one reason or another during adolescence, just hang tough—things will change. That fact is one of life's certainties, and understanding it can help you cope with an uncomfortable circumstance. *Tomorrow will be different.*

Normality Will Return

Let me offer another encouraging message about the adolescent years which can be summarized in three words: *normality will return.* By that I mean that you're about to go into a hectic, topsy-turvy world which will make new demands and will confront you with many new challenges. (Remember that I said you may even feel once in a while like you're hanging by your heels?) When these stressful moments arrive . . . when you ask a girl for a date and she turns you down, when you don't get invited to the party being given for the popular people, when your parents seem to hassle you over everything you do, when pimples and blackheads attack your forehead like an army of insects, when you wonder if God is really there and if He genuinely cares . . . in those moments when you're tempted to give up, please remember my words: "normality will return."

Just as I was able to predict many of the adolescent experiences which came your way, I can also predict with certainty that this stressful time of life will pass. In some ways, adolescence is like a tunnel that has a known beginning and end. As long as you stay on the road and keep your car moving forward, you can expect to emerge at the other end. Likewise, the anxieties and struggles you have experienced will soon disappear, and a new set of adult pressures will take their place. That's life, as they say.

Your Very Best Friend

The final (but most important) advice I can give you is to remain friends with Jesus Christ during the years ahead. He loves you and understands all of your needs and desires. He will be there to share your brightest days and your darkest nights. When you face the important issues of life (choosing a mate, selecting an occupation, etc.), He will guide your footsteps. He gave us that assurance in Proverbs 3:6, which says, "In all thy ways acknowledge Him, and He will direct thy paths." What a comforting promise!

I want to thank you for taking this ride through adolescence with me. Even though you and I have never been introduced, I feel that this book has permitted us to become good friends. In fact, I wish that you would write and tell me about your own teen experiences. Unfortunately, I receive more mail than I can possibly answer, but I read every letter that comes.

I trust that God will bless your life, and I hope to meet you someday.

Dr. James Dobson

NOTE FROM THE PUBLISHER: If you have enjoyed this book, you might want to hear the six cassette tapes from which this manuscript was taken. That album, also entitled *Preparing For Adolescence*, is described on the following page and can be obtained from your Christian bookstore or ordered from the address provided.

Other Materials
by Dr. James Dobson

BOOKS:
Dare to Discipline, Tyndale, 1970.
Hide or Seek: How to Build Self-Esteem in Your Child, Revell, 1974.
What Wives Wish Their Husbands Knew About Women, Tyndale, 1975.
The Strong-Willed Child, Tyndale, 1978.
Straight Talk to Men and Their Wives, Word, 1980.

CASSETTE TAPES:
Focus on the Family, Word, 12 cassettes.
30 Critical Problems Facing Today's Family, Word, 12 cassettes.

These other items are available in local bookstores or may be ordered by writing Focus on the Family, P.O. Box 500, Arcadia, CA 91006. Dr. Dobson also may be contacted through that address, although he regrets that he is unable to respond to requests for personal consultation.

FREE *from*
DR. JAMES DOBSON
Questions
Parents
Ask About
Discipline

FOCUS ON THE FAMILY
Box 500
Arcadia, CA 91006